LANDSCAPE CONTRACTORS GUIDE TO BUSINESS, LAW AND PROJECT MANAGEMENT

*North Carolina
Landscape Contractors' Licensing Board
1st Edition*

Supplemental forms and links are available at NASCLAforms.org
using access code NCL129354.

**National Association of State
Contractors Licensing Agencies
(NASCLA)**
23309 N. 17th Drive
Building 1, Unit 110
Phoenix, Arizona 85027
(623) 587-9354
(623) 587-9625 fax
Visit our web site:
www.nascla.org

Landscape Contractors Guide to Business, Law and Project Management

North Carolina Landscape Contractors' Licensing Board, 1st Edition

Copyright © 2015 by

National Association of State Contractors Licensing Agencies (NASCLA)

23309 N. 17th Drive, Building 1, Unit 110

Phoenix, Arizona 85027

ISBN-10 1-934-234-88-5

ISBN-13 978-1-934234-88-4

The information contained in this directory is being provided as a service to the landscape construction industry. Although the information contained herein is believed to be correct at the time of printing, changes in laws and regulations occur regularly. It is the contractor's responsibility to review their activities with an attorney, accountant, and tax professional. The publishers do not assume, and hereby disclaim, any liability to any party for loss or damage caused by any errors or omissions in this publication.

This publication is designed to provide authoritative information in a highly summarized manner with regard to the subject matter covered. It is sold with the understanding that the publishers are not engaged in rendering legal, technical or other professional advice or service. If legal, financial, technical or other expert assistance is required, the services of competent professionals should be sought.

INTRODUCTION

The landscape construction industry is one of the strongest industries in North Carolina. To keep the landscape construction industry thriving and to be a successful landscape contractor, you must be knowledgeable in both your trade and managing a business.

Thorough business planning and good management skills are key to success in today's market. A solid business plan lays the foundation for your financial, marketing, and management strategies and helps you maximize your potential. Competition can be fierce in the landscape construction industry. In developing a business plan, you analyze your market and competition and understand where you can gain an edge.

Good management skills entail applying knowledge from all aspects of the business to create a successful operation. Effective managers know how to win customers, satisfy employees, meet all legal obligations, and increase the bottom line. If this is where you want to take your business, this book can help you get there.

About This Book

This book is organized into three sections. Part 1 focuses on planning and starting your business. This section will help you formulate a business plan, choose a business structure, understand licensing and insurance requirements and gain basic management and marketing skills.

Part 2 covers fundamentals you will need to know in order to operate a successful landscape construction business. This section covers estimating, contract management, scheduling, project management, safety and environmental responsibilities, and building good relationships with employees, subcontractors, and customers.

Part 3 provides valuable information to assist you in running the administrative functions of your business. Financial management, tax basics, and lien laws are covered. Effective management of these areas of business is vital and can cause you serious problems if you do not give them proper attention.

Part 1: Getting Your Business Off the Ground

- ✓ Chapter 1 covers tips for writing a business plan and discusses key characteristics of entrepreneurship. A sample business plan is provided in Appendix B and on the NASCLAforms.org website using access code NCL129354.
- ✓ Chapter 2 describes each type of business entity and summarizes of their advantages and disadvantages.
- ✓ Chapter 3 reviews the licensing process and the requirements for getting a license.
- ✓ Chapter 4 discusses insurance and bonding options to protect your business against unmitigated risk.
- ✓ Chapter 5 is your business toolbox with tips on time management, delegation, business ethics, and technology. It also provides information on resources available to assist small businesses.
- ✓ Chapter 6 helps you execute your marketing plan through promotional materials, public relations and effective selling skills.

✓ Chapter 7 discusses the potential legal implications of a landscape construction project and identifies sources of information on landscape construction restrictions.

Part 2: Fundamentals for the Field

✓ Chapter 8 shows you how to formulate estimates and evaluate bid opportunities.

✓ Chapter 9 takes you through the key elements of contracts and what is needed to make them enforceable.

✓ Chapter 10 covers scheduling techniques and the fundamental skills needed to effectively manage landscape construction projects.

✓ Chapter 11 explains the importance of understanding customer expectations and handling change orders effectively. The basics of successful negotiation are also addressed.

✓ Chapter 12 is your resource for employment law, hiring and retaining of good employees, and discipline and termination of employees if unfortunate employment circumstances arise.

✓ Chapter 13 gives you the fundamentals for understanding OSHA laws and setting up a safety program for your company. Environmental considerations and possible permitting situations are covered in the event that you are creating or working with environmental hazards.

✓ Chapter 14 covers the basics of finding and hiring good subcontractors and establishing good working relationships with them.

Part 3: Office Administration

✓ Chapter 15 takes you through the accounting cycle, the preparation and analysis of financial statements and payroll procedures.

✓ Chapter 16 gives you federal and state tax basics and helps you understand the forms you need to file.

✓ Chapter 17 covers lien law regulations and the process for filing a lien.

Supplemental forms and links are available at **NASCLAforms.org** using access code **NCL129354.**

Whether you are studying for the landscape contractors' licensing exam or need an ongoing reference manual for managing your business, the *NASCLA Contractors Guide to Business, Law and Project Management* will serve as a valuable resource. We hope you find this reference useful in your daily operations and that the concepts discussed give you the tools for running a successful business.

TABLE OF CONTENTS

PART I
Getting Your Business Off the Ground

CHAPTER 7: LEGAL REQUIREMENTS

PART II
Fundamentals for the Field

CHAPTER 13: JOBSITE SAFETY AND ENVIRONMENTAL FACTORS

CHAPTER 14: WORKING WITH SUBCONTRACTORS

PART III
Office Administration

PART 1

Getting Your Business Off the Ground

Chapter 1
THE PLAN

Just as you need trade tools to successfully complete contracting jobs, you need organization tools to successfully manage your business. As a business owner you go from being an expert in your trade to requiring expertise in project management, marketing, employee management, financial management, contract management and much more.

Success Factors: It takes an organized, consistent approach to achieve success in today's market. Businesses fail every day. The top reasons businesses fail are

- ✓ poor sales,
- ✓ competitive weakness,
- ✓ high operating expenses,
- ✓ difficulty collecting on invoices,
- ✓ inventory problems,
- ✓ too many fixed assets,
- ✓ poor location, and
- ✓ fraud.

To Sum It Up...
Poor planning and inadequate management are overriding factors in business failure.

From this point forward, we will build your business management expertise so you can identify and understand these obstacles, thereby, increasing your chances of building and operating a successful business.

Being an Entrepreneur

Understanding Entrepreneurship: As a business owner, you may be referred to as an entrepreneur. There are many definitions of "entrepreneur." For our purposes, an entrepreneur is a person engaged in strategic activities that involve the initiation and development of a new business, created to build long-term value and steady cash flow streams.

Risk Taking: Entrepreneurs are often regarded as risk takers. There is risk associated with any venture, but entrepreneurs understand the importance of taking calculated risks. A calculated risk is a risk that is well-thought through where all outcomes are considered. This chapter will introduce the business planning process and help you understand the risks and opportunities associated with business ownership and how to manage them.

Something to Consider...
Entrepreneurship has its rewards as well as its drawbacks. Before embarking on any business venture, an entrepreneur must weigh all of these factors carefully.

Rewards and Challenges: Rewards of owning your own business include

- ✓ being your own boss;
- ✓ having flexibility of time;
- ✓ having more freedom and independence;
- ✓ making your own decisions; and
- ✓ receiving personal satisfaction from completing a job.

Entrepreneurship also has many frustrations and challenges, including

- ✓ long working hours;
- ✓ managing cash flow and payroll;

✓ high potential for overwhelming responsibility;

✓ finding and keeping qualified employees;

✓ paying taxes; and

✓ knowing and following government regulations.

- -
*Entrepreneurs need to decide if the rewards of
entrepreneurship outweigh the challenges.*
- -

The Benefits of a Business Plan

Preparing a business plan that outlines strategies and goals for your business is useful for a newly-formed or early-stage business. It can also be a helpful tool for a company that is making major strategic changes (i.e., providing additional product or service offerings). A business plan should be a living document that changes as your business and the market change.

Think of the business plan as a blueprint for your business. Just as you would not perform your trade without a blueprint or plan from the customer, you should not operate your company without a business plan.

Key Functions: A business plan serves three key functions:

✓ **Planning Tool:** Your business plan is a road map for the growth of the business. Putting together the plan helps you think through all possible scenarios for growth in the market.

✓ **Loan or Investor Document:** If you are planning to seek loan financing or approach an investor, you will need a business plan. Investors or loan officers will review this document to evaluate the qualifications of your management team, your projected growth, and your competitive advantage.

✓ **Benchmarking Tool:** Your business plan should also serve as a base against which to measure and monitor the company's performance. If your company exceeds or falls short of your projections, you can investigate the reasons for the difference.

A business plan will allow you to think through all aspects of your business, thus providing you with a competitive edge.

Elements of a Business Plan

The following are the typical elements found in a business plan:

✓ **Cover Page:** Contact information and a confidentiality statement are stated on the cover page.

✓ **Executive Summary:** Placed after the cover page at the beginning of the business plan, the executive summary includes highlights of the plan and captures the interest of the reader. It is usually written last.

✓ **Company Summary:** The company vision and mission, legal structure, management personnel, business location, and facilities are outlined in the company summary section.

✓ **Products and Services:** Your specific products and services, primary subcontractors and suppliers, the effect of technology on your business, and expansion opportunities are all covered in the products and services section.

✓ **Market Analysis:** Your target market, market trends, and major competitors are defined under market analysis.

✓ **Marketing Strategy:** The uniqueness of your product or service as well as your pricing, advertising, and promotional strategies are outlined in the marketing strategy.

✓ **Financial Plan:** If you already have financial statements, you should include a balance sheet, an income statement, and a cash flow statement as part of your business plan. New and existing businesses can put together financial projections as additional documentation.

A business plan template that can be customized for your company is located in Appendix B. The template provides specific guidance for completing each section.

Samples: The websites listed below offer sample business plans:

✓ www.allbusiness.com

✓ www.bplans.com

✓ www.inc.com

✓ www.sba.gov

✓ www.americanexpress.com/us/small-business/openforum

✓ www.bizmove.com/small-business/business-plan.htm

Business planning software packages that provide a step-by-step guide to creating a business plan are also available for purchase.

. . . .
Your business plan is the blueprint for your business.
. . . .

Business Plan Pitfalls

As you start creating your business plan, there are guidelines you should follow to make sure you are giving investors an accurate and honest picture of your business.

✓ Make sure your assumptions are realistic.

✓ Keep the language simple. Don't use technical terminology or jargon.

✓ Cover the risks as well as the opportunities.

✓ Analyze your competition thoroughly.

By applying these simple guidelines, your business plan will have a solid foundation.

- -

Final Inspection...

Being an Entrepreneur: Entrepreneurs should take calculated risks and weigh all factors when making business decisions.

The Benefits of a Business Plan: A business plan is sometimes required by bank loan officers or by investors. It can also be used as a planning and benchmarking tool.

Elements of a Business Plan: A business plan typically contains a cover page, an executive summary, a company summary, a listing of products and/or services, a market analysis, an explanation of the marketing strategy, and a financial plan.

Business Plan Pitfalls: It is important to portray an accurate picture of your business when formulating your business plan.

Supplemental Forms

Supplemental forms and links are available at **NASCLAforms.org** using access code **NCL129354**.

Business Plan Template	This template gives an outline for the business plan, including questions that help create detailed assumptions for each section of the plan.
Profit and Loss Pro Forma	This spreadsheet automatically calculates totals when you enter profit and loss numbers. You can adjust the numbers to determine your revenue and expense break-even point.

Chapter 2
CHOOSING YOUR BUSINESS STRUCTURE

Chapter Survey...

⇨ *Sole Proprietorships*

⇨ *Partnerships*

⇨ *C Corporations*

⇨ *S Corporations*

⇨ *Limited Liability Company (LLC)*

⇨ *Summary of Business Legal Structures*

⇨ *Joint Ventures*

⇨ *Naming Your Business*

⇨ *Registering Your Name in North Carolina*

When starting a business, one of the first things you need to decide is the legal structure your business will take. Each form of business has its advantages and disadvantages. The right choice depends on the nature of your business, plus various tax and liability issues. To ensure you are making the appropriate choice, it is best to consult with an attorney and an accountant.

Sole Proprietorships

Getting Started: Many businesses begin as sole proprietorships because it is the simplest ownership form to set up. In a sole proprietorship, you are the sole owner of the company. If the sole proprietorship does business under a name different than your own, typically, a fictitious name certificate needs to be filed at a local or state government office.

If you are doing significant business, a sole proprietorship may be a risky legal business structure, because it exposes you to unlimited liability for the business' debt.

Key Characteristics of Sole Proprietorships:

✓ *Existence:* You own the assets of the company. If you decide to sell your sole proprietorship business, you are actually selling the assets of the business. You would have to close out your business license and the new buyer would have to obtain all appropriate licenses and accounts in his or her name. A sole proprietorship is terminated upon the owner's death.

✓ *Financial Management:* Business and personal expenses must be separated and careful records must be kept, because the IRS may question the handling of these funds and you may be asked to provide supporting documentation.

✓ *Liability:* You bear personal liability for all actions undertaken in the name of the business.

✓ *Taxes:* Your net income from the business is reported as ordinary income. Sole proprietors do not pay corporate income taxes.

Advantages of a Sole Proprietorship:

✓ Minimal legal restrictions

✓ Simple ownership form

✓ Low startup costs

✓ Sole ownership of profits

✓ Freedom in decision-making process

Disadvantages of a Sole Proprietorship:

✓ Unlimited personal liability

✓ Less available capital

✓ Possible difficulty obtaining long-term financing

✓ Dissolution of the business in the event of the owner's death

Sole proprietorships are easy to form but are risky because the owner has unlimited personal liability.

Partnerships

Partnering Up: A partnership is a relationship between two or more persons who join to carry on a trade or business. Each person contributes money, property, labor, or skill, and each partner expects to share in the profits and losses of the business.

A partnership may be considered when neither partner can operate the business alone. Each partner should bring specific advantages to the business. There are two types of partnerships—general and limited. The differences are outlined in the following key characteristics.

Key Characteristics of Partnerships:

✓ *Existence:* A general partnership can be formed through an oral agreement, but it is recommended that a written partnership agreement be made. General partners own the assets of the company, just as an individual owns assets in a sole proprietorship. A limited partnership consists of one or more general partners and one or more limited partners. Limited partners have limited liability in the company. A partnership exists as long as the partners agree it will and as long as all of the general partners remain in the partnership. If a general partner leaves the partnership or dies, the partnership dissolves and the assets of the partnership must be sold or distributed to first pay the creditors and then the partners.

✓ *Financial Management:* The partnership should keep separate bank accounts and financial records for the business so that partners know whether there are profits and losses and the distribution of these amounts. The use of an outside accountant for record-keeping is recommended to prevent suspicion or doubt among partners.

✓ *Liability:* All owners in a general partnership have personal and unlimited liability for all actions undertaken in the name of the business, including all debts. Each partner is responsible for the acts of other partners when they act in the name of the business. Limited partners have no personal liability for the business of the partnership. Limited partners are liable only for the previously agreed-upon contribution to or investment in the business.

✓ *Taxes:* Business, income, and sales taxes are the responsibility of every partner. For federal income taxes, partners must file returns on IRS Form 1065.

Advantages of a General Partnership:

✓ Ease of formation
✓ Direct profit rewards
✓ Larger management base than that of a sole proprietorship

Disadvantages of a General Partnership:

✓ Unlimited personal liability of general partners
✓ Multiple decision makers
✓ Limited life of the business
✓ Changes of partners or partnership agreement may be difficult
✓ Partnership dissolves in the event of the death of a general partner

Use Caution: Partnerships should be entered into carefully. Potential partners should discuss their expectations of the business before deciding to go into business together.

Questions to ask include these:

✓ Do the partners want to grow and operate a company long-term?
✓ Do the partners want to grow a short-term company to sell?
✓ How will profits be distributed: 100 percent to partners, or a part to the business, the rest to partners? What are the profit distribution percentages?
✓ Do the partners agree on the nature of the business, including the types of jobs the business will accept?

Also, be sure to define each partner's individual responsibilities as well as the group responsibilities.

✓ Who can sign debt instruments, such as notes, bonds, and leases, for the partnership?
✓ Who determines the amount and frequency of compensation, salaries, draws, or profit-sharing for the partners?
✓ Who will handle record-keeping?
✓ If required, who oversees recruitment of additional partners or dissolution of the partnership?
✓ Who can make amendments to the partnership agreement?

Partnership Registration in North Carolina: Limited partnerships and limited liability partnerships must register through the North Carolina Secretary of State, Corporations Division. The application for registration and other partnership forms are available online at www.sosnc.com.

North Carolina Partnerships: North Carolina-based partnerships must submit domestic forms for registration.

Foreign Partnerships: Out-of-state partnerships and partnerships from other countries (both are called foreign partnerships) must submit foreign forms for registration.

. . . .

Carefully examine business expectations and responsibilities before entering into a partnership.

. . . .

C Corporations

Your Corporate Identity: If you decide to do business under a corporate identity, you will have to comply with the requirements of state law to create the corporation. A business assumes a corporate identity in North Carolina when it files with the North Carolina Secretary of State.

Key Characteristics of Corporations:

✓ *Existence:* Incorporation gives your business a legal existence. That is, the business can own assets and conduct business in its own name. A corporation lasts as long as the stockholders determine it should. A corporation continues to exist even if one or more of the shareholders die.

✓ *Financial Management:* The corporation needs separate bank accounts and separate business records. The corporation, not the shareholders, owns the money that the shareholders pay to buy the corporation's stock, all the assets, and the money earned by the corporation.

✓ *Liability:* The owners of the corporation, known as stockholders, are not personally liable for the losses of the business. Generally speaking, the corporate entity is responsible for business debts.

✓ *Taxes:* The corporation must file income tax returns and pay taxes on the profits. Dividends paid to shareholders by the corporation are also taxed to each shareholder individually. That is why there is said to be a "double tax" on corporations.

Other requirements for a corporation include

✓ a board of directors and corporate officers;

✓ stockholders as owners of the company;

✓ periodic board meetings, maintenance of board minutes, and approval of corporate resolutions; and

✓ a board empowered to authorize certain actions such as borrowing money, entering into contracts, and allocating corporate resources beyond routine business transactions.

Advantages of a C Corporation:

✓ Separate legal entity

✓ Limited liability for stockholders

✓ Unlimited life of the business

✓ Availability of capital resources

✓ Transfer of ownership through sale of stock

Disadvantages of a C Corporation:

✓ Complex and expensive organization

✓ Limitations on corporate activities and decisions by the corporate charter

✓ Extensive regulation and record-keeping requirements

✓ Double taxation (one on corporate profits and again on dividends)

Filing for Incorporation in North Carolina: To begin the filing process, contact the Secretary of State, Corporations Division to obtain the proper forms to complete.

North Carolina Secretary of State
Corporations Division
2 South Salisbury Street
Raleigh, North Carolina 27601-2903

Telephone: (919) 807-2225

Fax: (919) 807-2039

Website: www.sosnc.com

Forms are also available on the Secretary of State website.

Your corporation's name must include the following words or abbreviations: Company, Corporation, Incorporated, Limited, Co., Corp., Inc., or Ltd.

Complete the forms with appropriate signatures and turn them in with the appropriate fees.

North Carolina Corporations: North Carolina-based corporations must submit the domestic Articles of Incorporation form.

Foreign Corporations: Out-of-state corporations and corporations from other countries (both are called foreign corporations) must use foreign forms. Foreign corporations file an Application for Certificate of Authority with the Secretary of State, Corporations Division to conduct business in North Carolina.

Fee Schedule: Filing fees are as follows:

✓ North Carolina (domestic) Profit Corporation: $125

✓ Foreign Profit Corporation: $250

Any significant changes to the Articles of Incorporation or Certificate of Authority in the form of amendments, mergers, consolidations, dissolutions, or withdrawals are also filed with the division. All filings are public record and available for inspection.

Annual Filing: Corporations are required to file an annual report. Annual reports delivered to the Secretary of Revenue are due by the due date for filing the corporation's income and franchise tax returns. Electronically filed annual reports with the Secretary of State are due by the fifteenth day of the fourth month following the close of the corporation's fiscal year.

Corporations are more complex to form and operate but reduce personal liability of the owners.

S Corporations

If your business is an eligible domestic corporation, you can avoid double federal taxation (corporate and shareholder taxes on the same earnings as in a C corporation) by electing to be treated as an S corporation under the rules of Subchapter S of the Internal Revenue Code. In this way, the S corporation passes its items of income, loss, deduction, and credits through to its shareholders to be included on their separate returns.

Requirements for an S Corporation:

✓ Domestic corporation with one class of stock

✓ No more than 75 shareholders who are citizens or legal residents of the U.S.

✓ All shareholders must consent to S corporation status

✓ Use of a permitted tax year

✓ Filing of IRS Form 2553

S corporations have special tax considerations. Consult with the appropriate financial and legal professionals to find out if this option is right for you.

Limited Liability Company (LLC)

A Hybrid Structure: This legal arrangement shares characteristics of both sole proprietorships and corporate identities. LLCs must consist  of at least one member. The ownership in your LLC is invested in memberships rather than shares of stock.

Limited liability companies offer some protection from liability for actions taken by your company or by other members of your company. It does not protect from liability for personal actions. In this way, it resembles a sole proprietorship rather than a corporation.

Like an S corporation, federal income taxes are paid only on income distributed to members as ordinary income. A limited liability company can be expensive to organize and requires more administrative work. This form of organization is useful to professionals and general partnerships.

Advantages of a Limited Liability Company:

✓ Limited disclosure of owners

✓ Limited documentation

✓ No advance IRS filings

✓ No public disclosure of finances

✓ Limited liability for managers and members

✓ Ability to delegate management to a non-member

Tax Implications: LLCs are not taxed at an entity level. Depending on the number of business owners, the LLC is taxed differently.

✓ An LLC with one owner is taxed as a sole proprietorship.

✓ An LLC with more than one owner may elect to be taxed as a partnership or as a corporate entity.

Filing Articles of Organization in North Carolina: Limited liability companies (LLCs) are created by filing Articles of Organization with the Secretary of State, Corporations Division. LLCs offer protection from personal liability for the manager or members for the debts and obligations of the company. LLCs enjoy the benefit of financial and management flexibility with less paperwork than required for corporations.

North Carolina Limited Liability Companies: North Carolina-based limited liability companies must use the domestic Articles of Organization forms.

Foreign Limited Liability Companies: Foreign (formed outside of North Carolina) limited liability companies must file an Application for Certificate of Authority with the Secretary of State, Corporations Division to conduct business in North Carolina.

Fee Schedule: Filing fees are as follows:

✓ North Carolina (domestic) Limited Liability Company: $125

✓ Foreign Limited Liability Company: $250

Any significant changes to the Articles of Organization or Certificate of Authority for limited liability companies in the form of amendments, mergers, consolidations, dissolutions, or withdrawals are also filed with the division. All filings are public record and available for inspection.

Annual Filing: Limited liability companies are required to file an annual report. The first annual report is due on April 15th of the year following the creation year and every year thereafter on or before April 15th. Annual reports can be filed electronically or as a prepopulated annual report available for download on the North Carolina Secretary of State website.

Summary of Business Legal Structures

	Ownership	Liability	Formation Documents	Taxation	Management
Sole Proprietorship	One Owner	Unlimited personal liability	Doing Business As (DBA) Filing	Entity not taxed; profits and losses claimed on personal taxes	Owner
General Partnership	Unlimited number of general partners	Unlimited personal liability	General Partnership Agreement	Entity not taxed; profits and losses claimed on personal taxes of general partners	General partners
Limited Partnership	Unlimited number of general and limited partners	Unlimited personal liability of the general partners; limited partners generally have no personal liability	Limited Partnership Certificate Limited Partnership Agreement	Entity not taxed; profits and losses claimed on personal taxes of general and limited partners	General partners
Limited Liability Company (LLC)	Unlimited number of members	Generally no personal liability of the members for obligations of the business	Articles of Organization Operating Agreement	Entity not taxed (unless chosen to be taxed); profits and losses are passed through to the members	Manager or members designated in Operating Agreement
C Corporation	Unlimited number of shareholders	Generally no personal liability of the shareholders	Articles of Incorporation Bylaws Organizational Board Resolutions Stock Certificates Stock Ledger	Corporation taxed on its earnings at the corporate level and the shareholders may have a further tax on any dividends distributed ("double taxation")	Board of Directors
S Corporation	Up to 75 shareholders allowed	Generally no personal liability of the shareholders	Articles of Incorporation Bylaws Organizational Board Resolutions Stock Certificates Stock Ledger IRS and State S Corporation Election	Entity generally not taxed, as profits and losses are passed through to the shareholders ("pass-through" taxation)	Board of Directors

Joint Ventures

Complement Your Strengths: A joint venture is a special business arrangement that exists when two or more companies join to undertake a specific project. The management of a joint venture is often assigned to one individual or company. This arrangement brings  together companies with complementary resources and strengths. When forming this type of venture, it is important to consult an attorney to ensure that all aspects of risk are covered.

Individual state contractor licensing agencies may have specific laws regarding joint ventures. Obtain proper licensing prior to beginning applicable contracting work.

Naming Your Business

Choose Wisely: Selecting a name is an important part of forming your business. The name you choose affects your customers' impression of your company. The individuality of the name affects future trademarks and service marks. It is important to select a name that is distinctive.

Do your homework before you decide on a business name for your company. A search can be conducted using the following sources:

- ✓ U.S. Patent and Trademark Office (800) 786-9199 or at www.uspto.gov
- ✓ Secretary of State Office in the state where you intend to do business
- ✓ Internet search engines such as www.yahoo.com or www.google.com

A business may choose to file for a trademark or service mark. A trademark can be a word, name, symbol, sound, or color used to represent and distinguish a company's products or services. A service mark can be a word, name, symbol, sound, or color used to represent and distinguish a company's services. A trademark or service mark is not the same as a trade name. Trademarks can be filed on the state and federal level. State information is available through the North Carolina Secretary of State. Federal information is available through the U.S. Patent and Trademark Office.

Registering Your Name in North Carolina

The North Carolina Secretary of State, Corporations Division is the agency to contact in order to file Articles of Incorporation and Organization, to determine name availability for corporate and limited liability companies (LLCs), to file applications by foreign corporations seeking authority to transact business in North Carolina, and to file annual reports. The Corporations Division is responsible for the examination, custody, and maintenance of the legal documents filed by more than 400,000 corporations, limited partnerships, and limited liability companies. The duty of the Secretary of State is to ensure uniform compliance with the statutes governing the creation of these entities, record the information required to be kept as a public record, and provide that information to the public. The Corporations Division acts in an administrative capacity only and cannot give legal advice.

> *North Carolina Secretary of State*
> *Corporations Division*
> *2 South Salisbury Street*
> *Raleigh, North Carolina 27601-2903*
>
> *Telephone: (919) 807-2225*
>
> *Fax: (919) 807-2039*
>
> *Website: www.sosnc.com*

Reserving a Corporate Name: A corporate name may be reserved 120 days prior to incorporation by completing the name reservation application and paying a $30.00 fee.

The name you choose for your corporation must be clearly distinguishable from the names of all other corporations, limited liability companies, and limited partnerships already on file with the Corporations Division. You can check the corporate name you have chosen by calling (919) 807-2225. Any clearance you receive from the Corporations Division by phone for a corporate name is preliminary. There is no guarantee that the name you choose during your preliminary check will still be available when you file your registration paperwork unless you file a formal application to reserve a name.

Formally reserve the name or wait for confirmation of your filing prior to obtaining stationery, business cards, phone listings, bank accounts, etc.

Assumed Name Filing: Most companies, including sole proprietorships, select a business name other than the owner's name and often design a logo to be used on advertising, stationery, and other materials. An assumed name certificate (commonly referred to as a "doing business as" or "DBA" filing) is filed at the Registrar of Deeds in any county where you want to do business. There is no statewide name registration for sole proprietorships or general partnerships.

- -

Final Inspection...

Sole Proprietorships: This business structure offers easy formation and operation. However, unlimited personal liability is a concern because the business and owner are considered the same legal entity.

Partnerships: Partnerships can bring together two or more people with strengths and resources in different areas but also allow for unlimited personal liability of general partners. To reduce conflicts among partners, responsibilities and business goals must be clearly outlined at the beginning of the business arrangement.

C Corporations: C corporations offer liability protection to the owners and easy ownership transfer through stock sales. This business structure is more complex to operate and shareholders may be "double-taxed" on their earnings.

S Corporations: S corporations are similar to C corporations but offer special tax considerations. S corporation status can be filed with the IRS, if companies meet the specified criteria.

Limited Liability Company (LLC): LLCs have characteristics of both sole proprietorships and corporations.

Summary of Business Legal Structures: Each type of business entity has unique ownership, liability, taxation, and management characteristics. Required formation documents differ for each business structure.

Joint Ventures: Joint ventures are generally formed on a project basis in order to integrate positive attributes and resources of two or more companies.

Naming Your Business: An appropriate business name is important and defines how your customers perceive you.

Registering Your Name in North Carolina: A corporate name may be reserved 120 days prior to incorporation. The name must be distinguishable from other names on file with the Secretary of State.

Supplemental Forms

Supplemental forms and links are available at NASCLAforms.org using access code **NCL129354.**

Summary of Business Legal Structures	Table showing the primary features of each type of business entity (featured earlier in the chapter).
IRS Form 2553	IRS form to elect S corporation status

Chapter 3
BECOMING A LICENSED LANDSCAPE CONTRACTOR

Chapter Survey...

⇨ *Purpose of Licensing*

⇨ *North Carolina Landscape Contractors' Licensing Board*

⇨ *When is a Contractor License Needed for Landscape Contracting?*

⇨ *License Classification*

⇨ *License Application*

⇨ *Other Important Licenses for the Landscape Contractor*

⇨ *License Renewals*

⇨ *Disciplinary Action*

Purpose of Licensing

A major purpose of contractor licensing is to protect the health, safety, and welfare of the public. Licensing also defines the work that a contractor is allowed to do under a particular license.

Licensing establishes entrance requirements, standards of practice, and disciplinary authority to protect the public from unqualified, incompetent, and unethical contractors.

✓ *Entrance Requirements:* Licensing ensures that those practicing a trade or occupation have met a minimum set of qualifications, such as experience, training, and required examination.

✓ *Standards of Practice:* Contractors are required to adhere to standards of practice established by law. The workmanship standards ensure an appropriate level of quality is given to the public. Continuing education is required for landscape contractors.

✓ *Disciplinary Authority:* Statutes and Regulations define illegal and prohibited activities. The law provides licensing authorities with procedures to conduct investigations and to administer disciplinary actions to licensed contractors and unlicensed individuals found in violation of the law. Violations can result in penalties, fines and loss of license.

North Carolina Landscape Contractors' Licensing Board

The Landscape Contractors' Licensing Board is the state agency responsible for the administration and regulation of landscape contracting within the State of North Carolina. The Board reviews applications, administers examinations, certifies qualified individuals, issues licenses, and regulates persons engaging in landscape contracting within the State.

The Board is composed of nine members who serve staggered three-year terms and no more than two consecutive terms. The members consist of one member appointed by the Governor of North Carolina to represent the public at large; two by the Commissioner of Agriculture; two practicing nurserymen operating a nursery certified by the North Carolina Department of Agriculture and Consumer Services Plant Pest Inspection Program appointed by the Board of Directors of the North Carolina Association of Nurserymen, Inc.; two registered landscape contractors in the business of landscape contracting appointed by the Board of Directors of the North Carolina Landscape Contractors' Association, Inc.; and one registered landscape architect appointed by the Board of Directors of the North Carolina Chapter of the American Society of Landscape Architects.

North Carolina Landscape Contractors' Licensing Board
3901 Barrett Drive, Suite 202
Raleigh, NC 27609

Telephone: (919) 266-8070
Email: info@nclclb.com

Website: www.nclclb.com

When is a Contractor License Needed for Landscape Contracting?

Current laws in North Carolina define landscape contractors as any person who, for compensation or other consideration, does the following:

1. Engages in the business requiring the art, experience, ability, knowledge, science, and skill to prepare contracts and bid for the performance of landscape services, including installing, planting, repairing, and managing gardens, lawns, shrubs, vines, trees, or other decorative vegetation, including the finish grading and preparation of plots and areas of land for decorative utilitarian treatment and arrangement.

2. Practices the act of horticulture consultation or planting design for employment purposes.

3. Constructs, installs, or maintains landscape drainage systems and cisterns; provided the landscaping contractor makes no connection to pipes, fixtures, apparatus, or appurtenances installed upon the premises, or in a building, to supply water thereto or convey sewage or other waste therefrom as defined in G.S. 87-21.

4. Designs, installs, or maintains low-voltage landscape lighting systems, provided (i) the work does not exceed the scope of the exception set forth in G.S. 87-43.1(7) and (ii) the low-voltage lighting systems do not exceed 50 volts and constitute a Class II or Class III cord and plug connected power system.

5. Engages in the construction of garden pools, retaining walls, walks, patios, or other decorative landscape features.

A license is required to perform landscape contracting in the State of North Carolina for work over the amount of $30,000. The license should indicate the names of all listed qualified individuals employed by the applicant. In each separate place of business operated by a landscape contractor, all work shall be performed under an individual who is readily available to exercise supervision over the landscape construction and contracting work and who is licensed by the Board.

Exceptions: The following are not subject to obtaining a license:

✓ Any federal, State, or local governmental agency performing landscaping on public property.

✓ The North Carolina Department of Transportation (NCDOT). However, for landscape installations or establishment periods for any project that exceeds the current contract amount requiring performance and payment bonds according to State law, NCDOT shall require a licensed landscape contractor to perform the work. NCDOT, at its discretion, may require a licensed landscape contractor for landscape projects of any cost.

✓ Any property owner performing landscape work on his or her own property.

✓ Any person or business owning or operating a golf course.

✓ Any landscaping work where the price of all contracts for labor, material, and other items for a given job site during any consecutive 12-month period is less than thirty thousand dollars ($30,000). A local governmental unit shall not enact a local ordinance or regulation requiring licensure for landscaping work performed pursuant to this subdivision.

✓ A general contractor licensed under Article 1 of Chapter 87 of the General Statutes who possesses a classification under G.S. 87-10(b) as a building contractor, a residential contractor, or a public utilities contractor.

✓ Any person or business licensed as an electrical contractor under Article 4 of Chapter 87 of the General Statutes who is designing, installing, or maintaining any landscaping work, wiring, devices, appliances, or equipment.

✓ Any person or business licensed as a plumbing contractor under Article 2 of Chapter 87 of the General Statutes who is installing pipes, fixtures, apparatus, or appurtenances to supply water thereto or convey sewage or other waste therefrom, including the installation, repair, or maintenance of water mains, water taps, services lines, water meters, or backflow prevention assemblies supplying water for irrigation systems or repairs to an irrigation system.

✓ A professional engineer licensed pursuant to Chapter 89C of the General Statutes.

✓ A professional landscape architect licensed under Chapter 89A of the General Statutes.

✓ An individual or a business engaged in any of the following activities while performing that activity:

1. Clearing and grading plots and areas of land.

2. Erosion control.

3. Arboriculture, including consultations on pruning and removal of trees.

4. The installation of sod, seed, or plugs by sod producers certified by the Plant Industry Division of the North Carolina Department of Agriculture and Consumer Services.

5. Landscape construction performed by utilities contractors for the purpose of grading and erosion control.

6. Lawn mowing, turf edging, and debris removal services.

7. Turf management or lawn care services only, including fertilization, aeration, weed control, or other turf management or lawn care practices other than mowing or edging.

8. Design, installation, and maintenance of on-site wastewater disposal or reuse systems within the on-site wastewater permit specifications.

✓ Any person performing landscaping work on a farm for use in agriculture production, farming, or ranching.

Penalties: The Board may:

✓ Deny, restrict, suspend, revoke or refuse to renew or issue a license

✓ Assess costs, including reasonable attorney's fees and investigatory costs

✓ Assess civil penalty up to $2,000 for any and each violation of the law or rule

✓ Seek injunctive relief in superior court against an unlicensed individual for violations of the law or Board adopted rules.

License Classification

The primary license classification is as follows:

Type of License	License Description
Individual or Corporate	Residential, commercial, and industrial landscape work above $30,000. Includes anyone who engages in the business requiring the art, experience, ability, knowledge, science and skill to: install; plant; prepare estimates and contracts; repair and maintain gardens, lawns, shrubs, vines, trees or other decorative vegetation; grading and preparation of plots and areas of land for decorative treatment and arrangement; practices the act of horticulture consultation or planting design for employment purposes; constructs, installs, or maintains landscape drainage systems or stream bed restoration; engages in the incidental construction of garden pools, fountains, pavilions, retaining walls, fences or walks, arbors, patios, driveways, green roof systems, rain water harvesting systems or cisterns.

Bonding: A statement of bonding ability is required to activate a license. The required bond amount is $10,000.00 (ten thousand) annually.

Bonding ability forms are available for download from the North Carolina Landscape Contractors' Licensing Board website at www.nclclb.com.

Grandfathering: Any person, who on or before August 1, 2015, meets at least one of the following criteria shall be issued a landscape contractor's license by the North Carolina Landscape Contractors' Licensing Board, without the requirement of examination, upon submission of a completed application and payment of the application fee on or before August 1, 2015:

✓ Is registered as a landscape contractor.

✓ Is licensed as an irrigation contractor.

✓ Is certified as a turf grass professional.

✓ Has 10 years of documented experience in the person's own business as a landscape contractor or 10 years of documented experience as an employee in a landscape contracting business, meets all other requirements and qualifications for licensure as a landscape contractor, and has one of the following:

1. One year of credit for a two year degree in related educational training.

2. Two years of credit for a four year degree in related educational training.

3. Up to two years of credit for education or business experience in general business management.

Landscape contractors currently registered under Chapter 89D of the General Statutes shall not be required to renew the registration for the 2015 calendar year to qualify for the landscape contractor's license, as enacted by Section 1 of this act.

Licensing Application

1. Submit Application for Examination to the Board and include a $75 fee.

   Application forms are available through the Board office or online at www.nclclb.com.

   The Board has a Study Guide available which includes:

   ✓ Application forms and instructions

   ✓ Information for all exams

   ✓ Examination procedures

   ✓ Sample exam questions

   ✓ Copy of the Laws and Regulations Applicable to Landscape Contracting in the State of North Carolina

2. Board reviews application to determine eligibility for examination. The Board sends a Notice of Approval to notify candidates who are approved.

3. Register for examination through the North Carolina Landscape Contractors' Licensing Board (NCLCLB).

   NCLCLB
   Phone: (919) 266-8070
   Website: www.nclclb.com

4. The Plant I.D. will be part of the license exam administered via computer images or an applicant can take the NCNLA Certified Plantsman Exam which includes a plant I.D. exam and that will count as the plant I.D. for the landscape license exam. The plant list will be the same for both exams.

   NCNLA
   (919) 816-9119
   Website: www.ncnla.com

   After passing the Plant ID exam, send verification to the NCLCLB office by sending a copy of your congratulatory letter or certificate to:

   NCLCLB
   3901 Barrett Drive, Suite 202
   Raleigh, NC 27609

5. Take examination as scheduled through NCLCLB. You receive your score immediately after taking the test. If you fail the examination, you must resubmit a new Application for Examination.

6. Review of examination scores by the Board.

7. Pay nonrefundable license fee. Fees are as follows:

Individual	$60.00
Corporate	$60.00

8. Issuance of license by the Board for the appropriate classification.

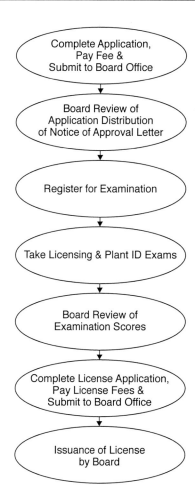

Display of License: Display of a current certificate of license is required at the landscape contractor's principal place of business and in each branch location.

Change of Address: License applicants and license holders must notify the Board in writing of a change in address within 30 days from the date of the change.

Change of Qualified Individual: License holders must notify the Board in writing of an addition/removal of a qualified individual on the license by completing a Request to Add/Remove a Qualified Individual form. The current license certificate is submitted with the form. The Board issues a new certificate once the request is processed.

Other Important Licenses for the Landscape Contractor

Landscape Architects

By law, landscape architects are defined as the performers of services in connection with the development of land areas where, and to the extent that the dominant purpose of the services is the preservation, enhancement or determination of proper land uses, natural land features, ground cover and planting, naturalistic and aesthetic values, the settings, approaches or environment for structures or other improvements, natural drainage and the consideration and determination of inherent problems of the land relating to the erosion, wear and tear, blight or other hazards. This practice shall include the preparation of plans and specifications and supervising the execution of projects involving the arranging of land and the elements set forth in this subsection used in connection with the land for public and private use and enjoyment, embracing the following, all in accordance with the accepted professional standards of public health, safety and welfare:

(a) The location and orientation of buildings and other similar site elements.

(b) The location, routing and design of public and private streets, residential and commercial subdivision roads, or roads in and providing access to private or public developments. This does not include the preparation of construction plans for proposed roads classified as major thoroughfares or a higher classification.

(c) The location, routing and design of private and public pathways and other travelways.

(d) The preparation of planting plans.

(e) The design of surface or incidental subsurface drainage systems, soil conservation and erosion control measures necessary to an overall landscape plan and site design.

This law restricts what landscape design work may be performed by NC Licensed Landscape Contractors and others not licensed as landscape architects:

(a) a single family residential project of any size;

(b) a non-single family project under one acre in total area;

(c) a residential, industrial, institutional, or commercial project over one acre in total area that involves only planting and mulching; and

(d) any other project not prohibited by, or specifically exempted from, the provisions of Chapter 89A, Chapter 83A or Chapter 89C of the General Statutes.

The North Carolina Board of Landscape Architects was established by legislation in 1969 to register professional landscape architects. The purpose of registration is the protection of public health, safety, and welfare. The NCBOLA oversees the license application, examinations, and certifications. For more information of the requirements and licensing for landscape architects, see **Appendix G** or contact the NCBOLA:

> *North Carolina Board of Landscape Architects*
> *P.O. Box 41225*
> *Raleigh, NC 27629*
>
> *Phone: (919) 850-9088*
>
> *Fax: (919) 872-1598*
>
> *Email: contact@ncbola.org*
>
> *www.ncbola.org*

Irrigation Contractors

According to law, no person shall engage in the practice of irrigation construction or contracting, use the designation 'irrigation contractor', or advertise using any title or description that implies licensure as an irrigation contractor unless the person is licensed as an irrigation contractor. No work, with by individual or group, can be undone without having the supervision of a licensed contractor. The purpose of licensure is, specifically, to protect the public health, safety, and welfare and to promote the efficient use of water. To oversee and unify the work pertaining to water irrigation, the North Carolina Irrigation Contractors' Licensing Board was established by legislation on January 1, 2009.

To learn more about the laws, rules, and licensure process, see **Appendix H: Irrigation Contractor Law** and **Appendix I: Irrigation Contractor Exemptions.** You can also contact the NCICLB:

> *North Carolina Irrigation Contractors' Licensing Board*
> *P.O. Box 41421*
> *Raleigh, NC 27629-1421*

> *Phone: (919) 872-2229*
>
> *Fax: (919) 872-1598*
>
> *Email: info@nciclb.org*
>
> *www.nciclb.org*

Pesticide Applicators

Whether you're a landscape professional, a commercial or private farmer, a pest control professional, or a pesticide dealer, the use of pesticides requires an appropriate license in the state of North Carolina. The North Carolina Department of Agriculture and Consumer Services oversees all license applications, exams, licensures, and certifications with regard to pesticides.

For more about the laws and rules regarding the handling of pesticides, see **Appendix L: Pesticide Application Law.** You may also contact the NCDA&CS:

> *The North Carolina Department of Agriculture and Consumer Services*
> *Structural Pest Control & Pesticide Division*
>
> *Mailing Address:*
> *1090 Mail Service Center, Raleigh, NC 27699-1090*
>
> *Physical Address:*
> *2109 Blue Ridge Rd., Raleigh, NC 27607*
>
> *Phone: (919) 733-3556*
>
> *Fax: (919) 733-9796*
>
> *www.ncagr.gov*

Licensing Renewals

All licenses issued by the Board will expire one year after the date of issuance.

Renewal applications are automatically emailed or mailed approximately 60 days prior to the license expiration date. If you have not received an application 30 days prior to your license expiration date, you should notify the Board office at (919) 266-8070.

Renewal applications and fees are due 30 days prior to the license expiration date. An administrative fee of $25.00 shall be imposed on all applications received after the expiration date. Applications filed with the Board by mail shall be considered filed on the postmarked date.

Disciplinary Action

The NCLCLB may discipline any licensed landscape contractor for violations that include dishonest practice, unprofessional conduct, and acts of incompetence.

The following shall be deemed to constitute "dishonest practice":

1. To make any false or deliberately misleading statements in an application for examination or in any statements or representations to this Board, to a client, or to another landscape contractor.

2. To violate the laws of North Carolina or of any other state relating to the practice of landscape contracting, or to violate any rule of this Board.

3. To use or attempt to use the title or seal under a certificate that has been suspended or revoked or which has not been renewed.

4. To use or to permit the name or the professional seal of the landscape contractor to be used on the plans or specifications or other professional documents not personally prepared, or prepared under the immediate supervision of such landscape contractor.

The following acts shall be deemed to constitute "unprofessional conduct":

1. To use any gift or donation as a device for obtaining competitive advantage over another landscape contractor;

2. To do any act that would falsely or maliciously injure the professional reputation, prospects, practice or employment position of another landscape contractor;

3. To attempt to supplant another landscape contractor after definite steps have been taken by a client towards the latter's employment; or to undertake a commission for which he knows another landscape contractor has been employed, unless and until he has been notified by either the client or the other landscape contractor that the original employment has been terminated;

4. To allow his name to be associated with an undertaking in any professional capacity unless he has served specifically in that capacity;

5. To offer payment directly or indirectly to others in order to obtain work.

The following acts or omissions shall be deemed to constitute "acts of incompetence":

1. To fail to use diligence in planning, supervising, performing, or inspecting landscape work directly resulting in improper and unprofessional practices and results;

2. To be guilty of such acts or omissions as to demonstrate to the satisfaction of the Board that the holder of the certificate is mentally incompetent or habitually addicted to alcohol or drugs so as to render the registrant unfit to practice landscape contracting.

Penalties: Performing a prohibited action may result in one or more of the following penalties.

✓ Reprimand

✓ Suspension from practice for a period not to exceed 12 months

✓ Revocation of the right to serve as a listed qualified individual on any license issued by the Board

✓ Revocation of license

✓ Probationary revocation of license or the right to serve as a listed qualified individual on any license issued by the Board, upon conditions set by the Board as the case warrants, and revocation upon failure to comply with the conditions

✓ Revocation of certification

✓ Refusal to certify an applicant or a qualified individual

✓ Refusal to issue a license to an applicant

✓ Refusal to renew a license

Final Inspection...

Purpose of Licensing: A major purpose of licensing is to protect the health, safety, and welfare of the public.

North Carolina Landscape Contractors' Licensing Board: The North Carolina Landscape Contractors' Licensing Board regulates landscape contracting activities through examination, licensure and disciplinary action.

When is a Contractor License Needed for Landscape Contracting? A license is required for anyone engaging in landscape contracting on individual projects exceeding $30,000 within a year; with a few exceptions defined by law.

License Classification: The Board issues 2 different types of license classifications—individual and corporate.

Licensing Application: You must complete the licensing process in order to obtain a landscape contractor license. The license certificate must be displayed at the licensee's place of business.

Licensing Renewals: Licenses expire one year after the date of issuance.

Disciplinary Action: Penalties for prohibited activities include being fined and refusal to issue a license or revocation of license.

Chapter 4
MANAGING RISK

Chapter Survey...

Managing risk can be one of the biggest challenges you'll face in the landscape construction industry. The weather, site conditions, customer changes, and employees can be just a few of the unpredictable factors in a job. Some of the risks are preventable and others can be minimized.

Risk assessment is one of the most important steps in the risk management process. You must determine the probability of loss occurring and the consequences if the loss occurs. Your approach to a risk with the potential for a large loss and a low probability of occurring is handled differently from a risk with a potential for minimum loss but a high likelihood of occurring.

Potential risk must be examined on both a project and overall business basis. Future chapters will focus on the skills you need to assess, manage, and ultimately protect yourself against risks for certain situations, such as environmental and safety risks.

Risk Management Benefits

Unmanaged risk can harm your business, resulting in financial loss, lower profit margins, and unnecessary liabilities. Risk management involves assessing all areas of your business from operations to administrative functions. Good risk management provides several benefits that can affect your reputation and bottom line:

✓ Lower business and liability insurance premiums

✓ Reduce chances of being sued

✓ Improve chances of prevailing in a lawsuit

Risk is managed in several ways. There may be provisions added to a contract to reduce your risk (discussed in Chapter 9) or safety programs or operating procedures can be put in place.

Other risks can be minimized through insurance coverage and bonding, which will be discussed in this chapter.

Insurance

While some risks can be minimized, others are uncontrollable. Insurance is a way to supplement your risk management program to protect your business against unforeseen events, such as accidents and theft. Without it, you could lose your business in a lawsuit as a result of one bad accident. The less coverage your business has, the more risk you assume. As you increase coverage, you reduce your risk.

Insurance Defined: Insurance is a protective measure in which coverage is obtained for a specific risk (or set of risks) through a contract. In this contract or policy, one party indemnifies another against specified loss in return for premiums paid. Indemnity is a way to transfer risk and exemption from loss incurred by any course of action. Sometimes an insurance payout is called an indemnity.

An insurance policy outlines the specifics of the contract between your business and the insurance company. At a minimum, the policy lists the policy term, coverage, premiums, and deductibles.

Finding the Right Insurance Company and Agent: Large companies often employ full-time risk managers. Most small business owners do not have this benefit, and this makes finding the right insurance company and agent important to the risk management process. There are two types of agents: those who work with only one insurance company and independent agents who can shop around for policies with competing companies. Regardless of which type of agent you choose, it is important to find a professional you can trust. Your agent will provide you with a wealth of knowledge on insurance and risk management topics and help you assess your insurance needs.

Required Coverage: The law may require you to carry a certain level of coverage, such as workers' compensation, unemployment, and vehicle insurance.

Many landscape construction contracts require a contractor to maintain certain types of insurance and coverage levels. The following chart gives an example of how insurance coverage requirements might be outlined in a contract.

Type of Insurance	Minimum Insurance Coverage (Combined Single Limit Per Occurrence/Aggregate)

Commercial General Liability including
 	
   Premises - Operations
 	
   Products / Completed Operations
 	
   Contractual Insurance
 	
   Property Damage
 	
   Independent Contractors
 	
   Bodily Injury
	$3,000,000 / $3,000,000

Automobile Liability Owned, Non-owned, or Rented	$3,000,000 / $3,000,000
Workers' Compensation and Occupational Diseases	As Required by Applicable Laws
Employer's Liability	$3,000,000

It is important to conduct a site survey to assess any special conditions that may cause added risk to a project. You should also consider the nature of each project to be sure you have adequate coverage for the work you are performing. You may want to talk this over with your insurance agent and add supplemental coverage when necessary.

In this chapter, we will focus on policies that apply to the landscape construction industry, but you should consult with your insurance carrier for a plan that is right for you and provides your business with the best protection.

Property Insurance

Property insurance typically covers your business and personal property when damage, theft, or loss occurs. You can buy property insurance to cover specific risks such as fire or theft or you can purchase a broad-based policy to cover a variety of risks (including fire, theft, vandalism, and "acts of God" such as lightning strikes). In considering property insurance, evaluate your physical location and the region in which you do business to determine which risks are likely to occur, such as hurricanes or floods.

Types of Property You May Want to Cover:

- ✓ Buildings and other structures (owned or leased)
- ✓ Furniture, equipment, and supplies
- ✓ Inventory
- ✓ Machinery
- ✓ Computers
- ✓ Intellectual property, (i.e., books and documents)
- ✓ Automobiles, trucks, and construction equipment
- ✓ Intangible property (i.e., good will, trademarks, etc.)
- ✓ Leased equipment

All-Risk Builders' Risk Insurance

All-risk builders' risk insurance is a form of property insurance that covers property owners and builders for buildings under construction. This type of insurance typically covers machinery, equipment, materials, supplies, and fixtures that are part of the structure or will become part of the structure. Additional coverage can be added for items, such as temporary structures and scaffolding, used during construction. In general, major construction defects such as poor workmanship and faulty design are not covered. Your tools also may not be covered under this type of policy. You should talk to your insurance agent about getting separate coverage for these items.

All-risk coverage provides for direct loss by those perils that are not specifically excluded by the policy. It generally provides coverage for almost all risks, including theft, vandalism, accidental losses, and damage or destruction. Construction must be in progress for coverage to exist.

The American Institute of Architects (AIA) and the Associated General Contractors of America (AGC) publish contract documents useful for owners and contractors (for AIA documents, check the AIA website at www.aia.org/docs_default; for AGC documents, see the organization's website at www.agc.org). These standard documents require the purchase of all-risk coverage. An owner has the option of giving the responsibility of purchasing all-risk coverage to the general contractor. If this is the case, the owner is required to notify the general contractor in writing. General contractors may prefer to purchase the insurance because they have a deeper understanding of the project and the potential risk. The cost of the insurance is then passed on to the owner.

The standard AIA and AGC documents require replacement cost coverage for losses that occur. Replacement cost coverage replaces damaged property without any allowances or deductions, such as depreciation.

If you use documents other than the AIA and AGC standard forms, carefully examine the insurance obligations for both you and the owner and discuss any concerns with your insurance agent.

A subrogation clause is generally included in the builders' risk insurance policy. Subrogation typically occurs when the insurance company pays the insured for damage or loss and then sues the negligent third party to pay for the loss. This can lead to a situation where the contractor is sued by the owner's insurance company for a loss that occurred.

To avoid this situation between the owner, contractor, and subcontractors, the contract may contain a clause waiving the parties' right to sue one another.

Named Peril Builders' Risk Insurance

Named peril builders' risk insurance policies have narrower coverage than all-risk insurance and specify what perils are covered. Typical named peril policies are written for fire and lightning but can also include events such as wind damage, explosion, water damage, terrorism, or earthquake.

Inland Marine/Equipment Theft Insurance

Inland marine insurance is a type of property insurance that you can purchase for your tools and equipment. It provides coverage for goods in transit and projects under construction. The cost of the insurance may be more than the cost of putting preventive measures in place to deter theft. It is important to secure your equipment by using proper locks, creating limited access through fencing and locked storage areas, and removing keys from the ignition of all vehicles. Equipment theft increases the cost of insurance premiums, and if it happens often, you might find it difficult to obtain coverage.

Equipment Floater Policy

An equipment floater policy is a type of inland marine insurance. Coverage for equipment is available on an all-risk or specified-peril basis. The coverage provided is for direct physical loss to the equipment and is designed to cover mobile equipment while it is stored on premises, in transit, or at temporary locations or jobsites. An endorsement can be added for rented or leased equipment. Normal wear and tear is generally not covered by the equipment floater policy.

Transportation Floater and Motor Truck Cargo Insurance

Both transportation floater and motor truck cargo insurance are types of inland marine insurance. A transportation floater policy protects the transporter against damage that occurs to freight during transport. Motor truck cargo insurance protects the transporter in the event of damaged or lost freight. This protection also applies to contractors who transport equipment or materials to and from the jobsite.

Liability Insurance

Liability insurance is designed to protect against third-party claims that arise from alleged negligence resulting in bodily injury or property damage. Payment is not typically made to the insured but rather to someone suffering loss who is not a party to the insurance contract.

Commercial General Liability (CGL)

Commercial general liability (CGL) insurance offers basic liability coverage. CGL covers four types of injuries, including

✓ bodily injury that results in actual physical damage or loss for individuals who are not employees;

✓ damage or loss to property not belonging to the business;

✓ personal injury, including slander or damage to reputation; and

✓ advertising injury, including charges of negligence that result from promotion of goods or services.

Most businesses in the landscape construction industry will need to supplement their CGL policy with other types of insurance, such as a vehicle insurance policy.

Umbrella Liability Insurance

An umbrella liability insurance policy can supplement your CGL policy. The umbrella policy provides additional coverage in the areas that are not covered in the CGL policy. This type of insurance takes effect once a certain deductible or self-insured retention level is met. Umbrella insurance coverage can be customized to meet the needs of your business.

Director's and Officer's Liability Insurance (D and O)

Director's and officer's liability insurance protects directors and officers from liability due to actions connected with their corporate positions. These actions include such things as misstatement of financial reports, misuse of company funds, and failure to honor an employment contract. This insurance does not cover intentional or illegal acts.

Other Types of Liability Insurance

Other types of liability insurance may be purchased in order to cover exclusions that exist in your CGL policy. Examples of additional liability coverage include:

✓ **Contractual liability insurance** provides contractors with protection for damages that result from their negligence while under written contract.

✓ Completed operations liability insurance provides coverage for loss arising out of completed projects.

✓ **Contractor's protective public and property damage liability insurance** protects contractors who supervise and subsequently are held liable for actions of subcontractors from claims for personal injury and property damage.

✓ Professional liability insurance (sometimes called errors and omissions insurance) protects contractors from negligence resulting from errors or omissions of designers and architects.

✓ **Construction wrap-up liability insurance** bundles liability and workers' compensation insurance for general contractors and subcontractors on large construction projects. This type of insurance helps eliminate gaps in coverage. To qualify for this type of insurance, certain contract cost requirements must be met. These requirements vary by state.

Business Owner's Policies (BOPs)

Business owner's policies (BOPs) bundle property and liability coverage together. This type of coverage can eliminate gaps or overlaps between separate property and liability policies. Small and mid-sized companies usually qualify for this type of policy. A business selects the amount of liability coverage it needs based on its assets. Additional coverage can be purchased depending on the particular risks of the company.

Automobile Insurance

If you have a company vehicle or a fleet of vehicles, auto insurance provides coverage for liability and physical damage associated with vehicles owned by your company. All states require vehicle owners to carry some level of liability insurance covering bodily injury and property damage incurred in a vehicle accident. Physical damage coverage pays for the damage to the insured vehicle. Different types of automobile insurance are available. Various options include coverage for only vehicles owned; vehicles owned, leased or hired; and for all automobiles, including those not owned, leased, or hired.

Burglary and Theft Insurance

Burglary and theft insurance covers loss or damage by burglary, theft, larceny, robbery, forgery, fraud, and vandalism. However, this type of insurance generally does not cover employee acts.

A fidelity bond or employee theft insurance is used to cover criminal acts of burglary and theft by employees.

Key Man Life Insurance

This type of coverage is beneficial if your company depends on specific individuals for continuing success of your business. For example, if your legal structure is a partnership, the success or ongoing existence of the company would not continue if one of the partners died or became incapacitated. Key man insurance is available as life insurance, disability insurance, or both.

Coverage Gaps and Overlaps

It is important to understand the coverage that each of your policies provides. You must be aware of gaps and overlaps that may exist between policies. Differences in coverage can cause difficulties in claim settlement, particularly when a claim falls in the gray area between coverages. For example, if a claim involves both an automobile and property, there may be a conflict between which policy covers the damage. To minimize these conflicts, you may want one insurer for all policies. If you have overlapping coverage, make sure that each policy has fairly equal reimbursement levels. This will ensure that you receive equal coverage if more than one policy covers a claim.

Carefully evaluate your risk management program and supplement it with the appropriate insurance coverage.

Employment-Related Insurance

Workers' Compensation Insurance

Workers' compensation insurance provides coverage for employees who are injured on the job. The insurance is purchased by the employer; no part of

it should be paid for by employees or deducted from their pay.

North Carolina Coverage Requirements: If you are a sole proprietorship, partnership, or LLC, you are required by law to carry workers' compensation coverage if you have three or more employees. Employees can be full-time, part-time, regular, seasonal, or family members. Sole proprietors, partners, and managers and members of the LLC are not included in the headcount.

All forms of corporations with a total of three or more people are required by law to carry workers' compensation coverage. Everyone is included in the headcount, including corporate officers.

If one or more employees are employed in activities which involve the use or presence of radiation, workers' compensation is required.

Subcontractor Coverage: Any contractor who sublets any part of a contract must first obtain documentation that the subcontractor is in compliance with the North Carolina Workers' Compensation Act. Subcontractors must provide compliance documentation regardless of whether the subcontractor employs fewer than three employees. If proper documentation is not obtained, the party subletting the contract is liable for payment of compensation and other benefits if any of the subcontractor's employees are injured or die from an accident associated with the work covered by the subcontract.

As part of your operating policies, you may require subcontractors to carry workers' compensation coverage even if the subcontractor has less than three employees.

Information on North Carolina's program is available through the Industrial Commission.

> *North Carolina Industrial Commission*
> *4340 Mail Service Center*
> *Raleigh, North Carolina 27699-4340*

Physical Address:

> *430 N. Salisbury Street*
> *Raleigh, North Carolina 27603*
>
> *Telephone (919) 807-2501*
>
> *Fax: (919) 715-0280*
>
> *Website: www.ic.nc.gov*

Chapter 12, Employee Management, covers workers' compensation insurance in more detail.

Employer's liability insurance can be purchased to supplement your workers' compensation insurance in the event you are sued for negligence as a result of an employee injury or death.

Unemployment Insurance

Unemployment insurance (UI) programs provide unemployment benefits to eligible workers who become unemployed through no fault of their own and meet certain other eligibility requirements. This program is jointly financed through federal and state employer payroll taxes (federal/state UI tax).

Generally, employers must pay both state and federal unemployment taxes if

✓ they pay wages to employees totaling $1,500 or more in any quarter of a calendar year; or

✓ they had at least one employee during any day of a week during 20 weeks in a calendar year, regardless of whether or not the weeks were consecutive.

North Carolina Program: The North Carolina Employment Security Law establishes guidelines for state unemployment tax. Business entities are subject to an unemployment payroll tax if they have one or more employees for 20 weeks during a calendar year or pay $1,500 in wages in any calendar quarter during a calendar year in North Carolina.

The tax is payable quarterly. Tax wage base and tax rate may vary from year to year. For the most current information, refer to the North Carolina Division of Employment Security (DES). Current tax rates are available online at www.ncesc.com. New business entities in North Carolina are subject to a new business tax rate for the first two years. The rate may be changed after the entity comes under an experience rating.

Additional information regarding the North Carolina state unemployment tax is available at:

State of North Carolina
Division of Employment Security (DES)
P.O. Box 25903
Raleigh, North Carolina 27611-6504

Tax Telephone: (919) 733-7395

Claims Telephone: (919) 733-7883

Website: www.ncesc.com

Chapter 12, Employee Management, covers unemployment insurance in more detail.

SUTA Dumping: SUTA dumping is a transfer of employees between businesses for the purpose of obtaining a lower unemployment compensation tax rate. SUTA dumping is prohibited and subject to criminal and/or civil penalties according to state law. The state agency responsible for the state unemployment program investigates suspicious activity in the transfer or acquisition of a business or shifting of employees to identify SUTA dumping.

Social Security Insurance

The Social Security Administration (SSA) is a federal agency responsible for paying retirement, disability, and survivors benefits to workers and their families. The SSA is also responsible for administering the Supplemental Security Income program. The SSA issues Social Security numbers, which are required for employees to legally work in the United States. Chapter 16, Tax Basics, explains how to submit Social Security tax for employees.

Insurance Coverage for Subcontractors

When hiring subcontractors, you should verify their insurance coverage to ensure it is adequate enough to cover any liability arising from their work.

There are a few simple questions you can ask to assess proper coverage.

✓ **Does the subcontractor carry the appropriate insurance?** Determine what type of insurance is needed. For example, you may require the subcontractor to carry commercial general liability (CGL) insurance.

✓ **Is the coverage adequate for the type of work being performed?** You can be held responsible for damages not covered by the subcontractor's insurance. Make sure their coverage limits are large enough to cover your project.

✓ **Is the insurance coverage current?** You can check with the insurance company listed on the insurance certificate to verify that the subcontractor's insurance coverage is current and that it will cover your project.

If insurance coverage is required, it is prudent to write the requirements into the contract. Chapter 9, Contract Management, talks about indemnification clauses as a contract provision to limit risk. This provision can also be included in your contract with the subcontractor. Indemnification absolves your company or holds your company free from liability from any losses or damages incurred by the subcontractor.

What is a Bond?

A surety bond is a risk transfer mechanism between a surety bonding company, the contractor, and the project owner. The agreement binds the contractor to comply with the terms and conditions of a contract. If the contractor cannot perform the contract, the surety bonding company assumes the contractor's responsibilities and ensures that the project is completed.

Statutory and Common-Law Bonds: The federal government uses surety bonds on construction projects as a way to pre-qualify prospective construction firms. A surety bond is often required by law for public projects. It is referred to as a statutory bond. The owner of a private construction project may also opt to require a bond as an added guarantee that a project will be completed on-time, on budget, and within specified requirements. These private construction bonds are sometimes referred to as common-law bonds.

Surety Bonding Companies: When selecting a surety bonding company, check with the U.S. Department of the Treasury or similar state agency (i.e., Department of Insurance) to ensure that the company is licensed for bonding. The surety company is the primary risk-taker in a bonding agreement, so it is important that it complies with all applicable laws and regulations.

Bond Language

Bonds generally contain four basic requirements:

✓ **Total dollar amount required for the bond**
The bond amount is generally set as a percentage of the estimated cost. This number can vary and can be up to 100 percent of the estimated cost of construction. Maintenance bonds often use a figure of 10 percent of construction cost as the required amount.

✓ **Length of the bond**
Bond lengths are typically required for a fixed rate of time following a project milestone, after which the bond is released. For construction performance bonds, this is usually after completion and final approval of the project.

✓ **Requirements for notice of defect or lack of maintenance**
A period for completion of corrections is generally outlined after a notice of defect. The bond also establishes a time period for response from the bonding company, if the contractor fails to meet the obligations of the contract.

✓ **Bond enforcement**
If the contractor does not successfully complete all required work or violates any requirement of the bond, enforcement measures are outlined to ensure project completion and proper maintenance.

Types of Bonds

A **bid bond** guarantees that the contractor, if awarded the job, will do work at the submitted bid price, enter into a contract with the owner, and furnish the required performance and payment bonds. Bid bonds serve as a deterrent against frivolous or unqualified bidders. If the contractor defaults on the bid agreement, the bid bond can be used to make up the pricing difference with the next lowest bidder.

A **performance bond** guarantees that the contractor will complete a contract within its time frame and conditions.

A **payment bond** guarantees subcontractors and suppliers that they will be paid for work if they perform properly under the contract.

A **maintenance bond** guarantees that for a stated period, typically for one year, no defective workmanship or material will appear in the completed project.

A **completion bond** provides assurance to the financial backers of a construction project that it will be completed on time.

A **fidelity bond** covers business owners for losses due to dishonest acts by their employees.

A **lien bond** guarantees that liens cannot be placed against the owner's property by contractors for payment of services. This type of bond allows someone to "bond around" a labor or materialmen's lien.

Just as the owner may require the general contractor to obtain a performance bond, a payment bond, or both, the general contractor may require the same of the subcontractor. The **subcontractor's bond** protects the general contractor in the event that the subcontractor does not fully perform the contract and/or pay for labor and materials.

A **bank letter of credit** is not a bond but is a cash guarantee to the owner. It is not a guarantee of performance but can be converted to a payment to the owner by a bank or lending institution. The letter of credit typically does not cover 100 percent of the contract but customarily 5 percent to 10 percent of the contract.

. . . .

Various types of bonds are issued as a protective measure in the event that contractual obligations are not met.

. . . .

Qualifying for a Bond

Before issuing a bond, a surety company will examine your business thoroughly to make sure it is established, profitable, and well-managed. Some of the items the surety company will evaluate to make this determination include

- ✓ good references;
- ✓ ability to meet current and future obligations;
- ✓ experience matching contract requirements;
- ✓ necessary equipment to complete the work;
- ✓ financial stability;
- ✓ good credit; and
- ✓ established bank relationship and line of credit.

A surety's underwriting process consists of an extensive prequalification process in order to guarantee to the project owner that the contractor will fulfill the terms of the contract.

Bonds are priced on the basis of a percentage of the contract amount. Market conditions and prevailing industry practices set the percentage. Bond premiums vary among surety companies, but typically range from a half percent to two percent of the contract amount.

Bond Claims

Filing Process: Construction law and contractual relationships govern the bond claims process. The filing process is outlined in the bond language for common-law bonds. Government statutes outline the filing process for statutory bonds.

Project Changes: Unless specifically outlined in the bond agreement, the surety company will not cover changes to the original contract. In most cases, a request for additional coverage must be made and the bonding company must be notified of the contract changes.

Payment in the Event of Default: In the event of contractor default, the surety has several options. The surety may

- ✓ provide additional financing for the contractor to finish the project;
- ✓ arrange for a new contractor or hire subcontractors to complete the work; or
- ✓ pay out the amount of the bond.

Laws Governing Bonding of Federal Construction Projects

Miller Act: As a result of the high failure rate for completion of public construction projects, the Heard Act was enacted in 1894, allowing the use of surety bonds for federally funded projects. In 1935, the Miller Act replaced the Heard Act. The Miller Act is the current law requiring performance and payment bonds on all federal construction projects valued at greater than $100,000.

The surety amounts are defined as follows:

- ✓ A performance bond is required in an amount that the contracting officer regards as adequate. The bond is normally 100 percent of the contracted price.
- ✓ A separate payment bond is required for the protection of the suppliers of labor and materials.

The sum of the payment bond varies, based on the size of the contract. These amounts include:

- Fifty percent of the contract amount for projects less than $1 million
- Forty percent of the contract amount for projects between $1 million and $5 million
- $2.5 million payment bond for contracts in excess of $5 million

Little Miller Acts: Most states and local governments also have similar surety laws on public works projects that are referred to as "Little Miller Acts."

Construction Industry Payment Protection Act of 1999: The Construction Industry Payment Protection Act of 1999 makes several amendments to the Miller Act of 1935. Its purpose is to improve payment bond protections for persons who furnish labor or material for use on federal construction projects. This law was passed because the bonding amounts specified in the Miller Act may not provide subcontractors with adequate protection.

The Construction Industry Payment Protection Act of 1999 outlines three specific requirements:

- ✓ The general contractor of a project generally must obtain a payment bond in an amount that is equal to the total value of the federal contract, unless a lesser amount is specified by the contracting officer. The payment bond cannot be less than the performance bond.

- ✓ Subcontractors are permitted to notify contractors of intent to sue by any means which provides written, third-party verification of delivery.

- ✓ Waivers of Miller Act payment bond protections are void before the work begins. Any waiver of a subcontractor's right to sue on a payment bond must be in writing, signed, and executed after the subcontractor has first furnished labor or materials for use in the project.

Laws Governing Bonding of North Carolina State Public Construction Projects

State public projects meeting the following criteria require the contractor to obtain a performance and payment bond.

- ✓ The total amount of contracts awarded exceeds $300,000.

- ✓ The contractor or construction manager's contract exceeds $50,000 on the project.

- ✓ State departments, state agencies, and the University of North Carolina and its constituent institutions require a performance and payment bond if the total amount of construction contracts awarded for any one project exceeds five hundred thousand dollars ($500,000).

The performance and payment bond must each be in the amount of 100 percent of the construction contract. The bond must be executed by one or more surety companies approved to do business in the State of North Carolina.

- -

Final Inspection...

Risk Management Benefits: Managing risk is challenging but is important to your reputation and bottom line.

Insurance: Insurance should supplement your risk management program. It provides protection against unforeseen events and is sometimes required by law. Several different types of insurance coverage are available to fit the needs of your business.

Property Insurance: Property insurance typically covers your business and personal property when damage, theft, or loss occurs. All-risk builders' risk, named peril builders' risk, inland marine/equipment theft, equipment floater, transportation floater, and motor truck cargo policies are types of property insurance that may benefit your business.

Liability Insurance: Liability insurance is designed to protect against third-party claims that arise from alleged negligence resulting in bodily injury or property damage. Several types of liability insurance policies are available, such as commercial general, umbrella, and director's and officer's liability insurance.

Business Owner's Policies (BOPs): Property and liability coverage are bundled under business owner's policies.

Automobile Insurance: Liability and physical damage associated with vehicles owned or leased by your company are covered under automobile insurance. Several types of coverage are available.

Burglary and Theft Insurance: Loss or damage by burglary, theft, larceny, robbery, forgery, fraud, and vandalism is covered under burglary and theft insurance.

Key Man Life Insurance: This type of insurance is available as life insurance or disability insurance, or both, to protect the continuing success of the business.

Coverage Gaps and Overlaps: It is important to evaluate all of your insurance coverage. Using one insurer may minimize gaps and overlaps in coverage.

Employment-Related Insurance: Workers' compensation, unemployment, and social security are employment-related insurance regulated by state and/or federal government.

Insurance Coverage for Subcontractors: When hiring subcontractors, ensure that they carry proper insurance coverage. These requirements should be outlined in the construction contract.

What is a Bond? Bonds provide protection in the event that contractual obligations are not met.

Bond Language: At a minimum, bonds should contain the total dollar amount, length of the bond, requirements for notice of defect or lack of maintenance, and bond enforcement.

Types of Bonds: Several types of bonds are available depending on the desired coverage.

Qualifying for a Bond: Before issuing a bond, the surety company will review your business to ensure it is established, profitable, and well-managed.

Bond Claims: The bond claim filing process is outlined in the bond language for common-law bonds and in government statutes for statutory bonds.

Laws Governing Bonding of Federal Construction Projects: The Miller Act and Construction Industry Payment Protection Act of 1999 outline bonding requirements for federal construction projects.

Laws Governing Bonding of North Carolina State Public Construction Projects: A payment and performance bond is required for the following types of projects: when the total amount of construction contracts for a project is $300,000 or more; the contractor or construction manager's contract exceeds $50,000; or state department, state agency, or the University of North Carolina and its constituent institutions contracts awarded for any one project exceeds five hundred thousand dollars ($500,000). The bonds must be in the amount of 100 percent of the contract price.

Chapter 5
YOUR BUSINESS TOOLBOX

Chapter Survey...

⇨ *Time Management*

⇨ *Delegation*

⇨ *Business Ethics*

⇨ *Technology*

⇨ *Small Business Assistance and Loans*

⇨ *Small Business Certifications*

Just as you need a toolbox filled with tools to accomplish jobs in your trade, you need a toolbox of resources and skills to help you run your business. This chapter will introduce a few of these tools and lay a foundation for tools covered in subsequent chapters.

Time Management

Time Is Money: This familiar phrase holds special meaning for business owners. Your ability to manage time effectively can make the difference between completing a job successfully and failing to meet customer expectations. Time is one of your most important tools. Use it wisely.

Setting Goals: Effective goal setting is a key cornerstone to time management success. Once goals are set, they should be documented. This gives you a visual reminder and ensures proper communication to the whole work team. A methodical approach should be used to move forward towards achieving your goals. Your management team and employees should understand your goals and can help put together the plan tactics.

Four Time Management Tips: These habits will help you organize and manage your time.

✓ Prioritize tasks daily

✓ Delegate effectively when possible

✓ Use checklists and calendars (find a time management system that works for you)

✓ Do not procrastinate

Advantage of Technology: Learning about new technology and using it in your operations can save you time. Research ways to automate your operations without taking away from the quality of your products and services. Putting a new technology or process in place can give you more time to focus on strategic activities.

Competitive Edge: Although multitasking is an important skill, effective time management requires that you focus on the necessary task at hand to move forward towards achievement of the set goals. It gives you a competitive edge and helps you anticipate problems before they occur. Planning your time puts you in control, gives you the ability to be proactive and helps reduce anxieties caused by "putting out fires". Your professionalism will be appreciated by your customers, subcontractors, and suppliers.

Time is money.
Use it wisely.

Delegation

You Can't Do It All: When you become a business owner, you go from a tradesperson to a manager of many jobs and a business administrator. Delegation is a key tool that will ensure that you get all tasks accomplished. You simply cannot do it all and be efficient.

Preparing to Delegate: Learning to delegate is often difficult because you are giving up control of certain tasks. You may feel that a task won't be done correctly or that it takes longer to explain a task than just doing it yourself.

Delegation is a way of developing your employees and building a solid team. Giving your employees increased responsibility builds their self-confidence, provides motivation, and makes them more productive and loyal. Delegation gives you the chance to concentrate strategically on running your business.

How to Delegate: Here are simple steps on how to delegate:

1. Identify a person for the task.

2. Explain the task clearly and make sure you are understood. You may want to ask the person to repeat their understanding of the task back to you.

3. Follow up with the person throughout the process.

4. Give positive feedback and provide guidance on how the task can be improved, if necessary.

Effective delegation increases your efficiency.

Business Ethics

Your Reputation: Good business ethics are a must if you want to safeguard your reputation in the industry. Practicing good business ethics, when dealing with customers, employees, subcontractors, and suppliers, is not only the right thing to do, it is the best way to avoid litigation.

Defining Ethics: You may ask, "What are ethics?" In general, the term as it applies to business means behaving in a trustworthy, fair, honest, and respectful manner toward everyone with whom you interact. Your core values serve as your moral compass and guide this standard.

Studies Say...

Top management has the strongest influence on employees' ethical behavior. If top managers demonstrate unethical behavior, employees are likely to do the same.

Establishing a code of conduct is the first step to ensuring that good ethics are practiced throughout your company. A code of conduct is a documented way that an organization should operate.

This document can include

✓ guidelines for employees, management, subcontractors, and suppliers;

✓ standards for doing business; and

✓ a statement of commitment to the community.

You may want to provide your customers with your code of conduct. It will reinforce your commitment to good ethics and demonstrate professionalism.

Make the right ethical choices to protect your reputation and avoid litigation.

Technology

Technology as an Essential Tool: Technology is an essential tool for communicating and keeping your business competitive. Purchasing technology is becoming increasingly cost-effective. There are many technological tools specifically designed for the landscape construction industry. These tools increase efficiency and aid in various tasks, such as

✓ estimating and bidding,

✓ accounting,

✓ job costing,

✓ scheduling, and

✓ construction management.

If you have not jumped into the technology age, here are a few basics to start with:

Computer: For a business owner, a computer has many uses which will help in streamlining administrative functions. This is the basic tool you need to operate programs for applications such as writing, accounting, scheduling, estimating, and e-mail. Some builders opt to have laptop computers to perform these functions on the jobsite.

Phone: Cell phone technology has advanced in the area of two-way radio communications (sometimes referred to as a push-to-talk feature), use of e-mail, photography, and calendar management. Regardless of the features you choose for your business cell phone, it is important that you are always accessible to your customers and employees.

Fax Machine: Although e-mail has become the prevalent means for communication, it is still important for businesses to have a fax machine so that copies of important documents can be transmitted quickly and efficiently.

Printer: A printer allows you to produce hard copies of the files you have on your computer. A printer will come in handy when creating customer correspondence and contracts. Portable printers small enough to bring to the jobsite are also available.

Scanner: Documents and small objects can be copied or scanned in a form that can be stored on a computer and then these files can be manipulated and printed for use.

Multifunction Hardware: You can purchase a single machine that works as a photocopier, fax, printer, and scanner. This type of hardware can be convenient and cost-effective if your business uses such functions frequently. However, bear in mind that if the unit breaks, you may lose several or all of the functions until it is repaired or replaced.

Digital Camera: A digital camera is a great way to store photos on the computer. It is important for you to document your work every step of the way, and digital pictures are a cost effective way to organize that information. Your pictures can be stored on a disk with project files and e-mailed as necessary.

Internet: The Internet is a powerful tool. It can be used for research, communication, or marketing your company.

Word Processing Software: Word processing can save you a lot of time because the information you need is stored in the computer. Handwritten documents need to be rewritten each time, while documents entered in the computer can be modified and reused. Many word processing programs have templates of commonly used business documents which can be used, modified, and reused at any time.

Spreadsheet Program: This type of software gives you the flexibility to create financial worksheets on the computer. You can set up the worksheet to automatically calculate figures, reducing mathematical errors.

A Warning about Software: Although software is designed to streamline your processes, you must still understand the basics. For example, if you purchase accounting software but do not understand the fundamentals of accounting, the software is useless to you. In future chapters, we will cover basic skills that will help you utilize software packages.

Once you become comfortable with technology, you may want to purchase other advanced tools and software.

- -
Using technology can increase your efficiency and keep you competitive.
- -

Small Business Assistance and Loans

Various federal, state and local resources can help you with small business services or education you might need. Many of these services are free or available at a minimal cost to business owners. Below are some of the resources available to you.

North Carolina Department of Commerce

The North Carolina Department of Commerce has resources for starting and operating your business. The website has several links to topic areas such as financing, licensing, business start up, and technology assistance.

North Carolina Department of Commerce
301 North Wilmington Street
Raleigh, North Carolina 27601-1058

Mailing Address:

4301 Mail Service Center
Raleigh, North Carolina 27699-4301

Telephone: (919) 715-2864

Toll-free: (800) 228-8443

Fax: (919) 715-2855

Website: www.nccommerce.com/business

Local Community Colleges and Universities

Business education opportunities are available through local community colleges and universities. Seminars, workshops, and courses are offered on business skills and small business management.

The Small Business Center Network offered through the North Carolina Community College System conducts training and seminars for business owners, offers business counseling, and has many resources available on their website. To find a local Small Business Center, visit the website at www.ncsbc.net.

Small Business Administration (SBA)

The Small Business Administration's mission is to counsel, assist, and protect the interests of small business. The SBA provides training and online help for small businesses.

The SBA website at www.sba.gov has several online resources to Federal, state, and local information for business owners. Resources include:

- ✓ Starting a Business
- ✓ Registrations, Licenses, and Permits
- ✓ Finance and Taxes
- ✓ Expanding Your Business
- ✓ Legal Compliance
- ✓ Industry Specifics
- ✓ State and Local Resources

A partnership program through the SBA links business owners from across the nation to create a social network and provide access to experts.

The SBA Headquarters is located in Washington, D.C., but you can check the website at www.sba.gov or call 1-800-U-ASK-SBA to find an office near you.

Small Business Administration
North Carolina District Office
6302 Fairview Road, Suite 300
Charlotte, North Carolina 28210

Telephone: (704) 344-6563

Fax: (704) 344-6769

Website: www.sba.gov/nc

Service Corps of Retired Executives (SCORE)

SCORE is a national volunteer organization of retired executives who can provide counseling and training to you if you are an entrepreneur and/or business owner. There are several SCORE offices located throughout the United States. You can find the SCORE office nearest to you on the website.

SCORE Association
409 3rd Street, SW
6th Floor
Washington, D.C. 20024

Phone: (800) 634-0245

Website: www.score.org

Appendix C contains additional references and website links on topics covered in this book.

Small Business Certifications

Federal and state governments often have opportunities for businesses to bid on contracts. These contracts are highly sought after for a number of reasons. To level the playing field, the government has established certifications for small, minority-owned, and women-owned businesses. If your company fits the criteria, you can obtain one or more certifications, which can provide additional opportunities for you to bid on government contracts.

The U.S. Small Business Administration has several different certification and assistance programs for small businesses. These programs include the following:

- ✓ Historically Underutilized Business Zone (HUBZone) Certification
- ✓ 8(a) Business Development Program
- ✓ Small Business Certification
- ✓ Women-Owned Small Business Federal Contract Program
- ✓ Veteran and Service-Disabled Veteran Owned Business Assistance Program
- ✓ Native American Owned Business Certification
- ✓ Alaskan Owned Business Assistance Program
- ✓ Native Hawaiian Owned Business Assistance Program

Information on these certifications is found on the SBA website at www.sba.gov/category/navigation-structure/contracting/working-with-government/small-business-certifications-audiences or by calling 1-800-U ASK SBA. In addition to certification information, the SBA website contains helpful links about government contracting and business development.

Certifications are also available at the state and local level.

The Minority Business Development Center is a partnership program between the North Carolina Institute of Minority Economic Development (IMED) and the U.S. Minority Business Development Agency (MBDA). The North Carolina Minority Business Development Center provides technical and financial assistance to existing and emerging minority businesses across the state.

North Carolina Minority Business Development Center
114 W. Parrish Street
Durham, North Carolina 27701

Telephone: (919) 956-8889

Fax: (919) 688-7668

Website: www.ncimed.com

- -

Final Inspection...

Time Management: Effective time management gives you a competitive edge and helps you anticipate problems before they occur.

Delegation: Effective delegation increases your efficiency and helps develop your employees.

Business Ethics: The right ethical choices help protect your reputation and avoid litigation.

Technology: Technology is an essential tool for communicating and keeping your business competitive.

Small Business Assistance and Loans: Several organizations are available to help small businesses with a variety of functions.

Small Business Certifications: Certifications for small, minority, and women-owned businesses are available through the government. If your company qualifies, certifications can provide additional opportunities for you to bid on government contracts.

Chapter 6
MARKETING AND SALES

Chapter Survey...

⇨ *Executing Your Marketing Plan*

⇨ *Logos, Stationery, and Business Cards*

⇨ *Promotional Materials*

⇨ *Public Relations*

⇨ *Effective Selling Skills*

⇨ *Organizing the Sales Process*

⇨ *Your Sales Presentation*

Start Off on the Right Foot: First impressions can tell your potential customers a lot about your business. Customers may judge your professionalism or reputation on this initial contact. Marketing, in some cases, may be the first impression of your business, and you want to make sure customers feel comfortable with you and your company from this point on.

The purpose of marketing is to bring in new customers and retain current customers. A good marketing program helps ensure a steady flow of leads and customers and, more important, a steady flow of incoming cash.

First impressions are lasting ones.
Make your company's first impression a positive one.

Executing Your Marketing Plan

Maximize Your Marketing Potential: When developing your market analysis and marketing strategy (featured in the business plan template in Appendix B), you should answer questions such as these:

✓ What is the vision for my business?

✓ Who are my customers?

✓ What is the best way to reach these customers?

✓ What is my competitive advantage?

✓ What is the best way to promote my products and services (e.g. advertising, public relations, online marketing, direct sales, etc.)?

✓ What will my marketing efforts cost?

✓ How much revenue do I expect to gain as a result of marketing efforts?

✓ Who will manage the marketing program? Will I need to hire outside help to execute the program?

✓ What growth opportunities exist in my industry?

✓ What challenges for growth exist in my industry?

Now it is time to put these thoughts into action. Developing a promotion plan will help you bring these ideas to life.

Logos, Stationery, and Business Cards

Create Your Identity: A simple start to developing your promotion plan is to create a logo. Not only will your name distinguish you in the market but a logo will set you apart from your competitors. Logos become part of your company identity and convey a professional look, which is important for that first impression.

A good logo design should be

✓ simple and easy to remember;

✓ attractive in color and black and white;

✓ limited to one or two colors;

✓ representative of your company identity; and

✓ scalable up or down and attractive in any size.

Once your logo is created, you should include it on your business cards and stationery.

Promotional Materials

You may also apply your logo to several different promotional items. These items include

- ✓ brochures,
- ✓ direct mailings,
- ✓ jobsite signs,
- ✓ truck signs,
- ✓ yellow pages, and
- ✓ websites.

Using promotional materials will give you name recognition. When potential customers have an upcoming job, they may be more likely to approach your company to put in a bid because your name is out in the market.

Business promotion through social media has become a prevalent means of marketing. You can create a business account on social media websites, such as Facebook, Twitter, and LinkedIn, to advertise your services, post updates on your business, and gain name recognition. Participation in social media can be an inexpensive way to market and increase traffic to your business website. In addition to creating a business page on social media sites for promotion, these sites have areas where you can buy advertising space.

A good marketing program is an investment that can help you gain customers and strengthen your reputation.

Public Relations

Benefits of Networking: Public relations are an inexpensive but effective marketing tool. It is important to build name recognition; good public relations constantly keeps your business in the eye of the public—your potential customers. The downside to public relations is its labor-intensive nature, but the time invested will give you great rewards. You may use this approach to not only get potential customers but as a way to get referrals to good subcontractors, suppliers, or employees.

In the Public Eye: Here are some ideas to get you started.

- ✓ *Join local trade associations*
  This is a good opportunity to meet new people in your industry. You can also volunteer to speak at meetings and conferences to showcase your knowledge and expertise.

- ✓ *Participate in a local non-profit initiative (for example, be a volunteer Habitat for Humanity worker)*
  High-profile projects will put you in a positive light in the public eye and may get some press coverage.

- ✓ *Volunteer for local leadership opportunities*
  Leadership positions in organizations such as schools or the local Chamber of Commerce may give you time with other influential people in the community who can make good referrals about you and your business.

- ✓ *Sponsor community events*
  When you sponsor community events, your business name is often featured in event brochures, signage, and media promotions such as newspapers and radio advertisements.

- ✓ *Send press releases to the local media*
  This public relations technique offers exposure to a broad audience and gives you credibility because it is communicated through a third-party. Press releases can report your involvement in the local community, new landscape construction trends, or any ideas that might be interesting to the public and will promote your company.

- ✓ *Hold an open house*
  You can hold an open house at your office or at a job where you can showcase your work. An open house gives you a chance to reinforce current business relationships and make new ones.

Effective Selling Skills

Don't Underestimate Your Selling Skills: Selling is often perceived as a salesperson pitching a product or service and the customer saying yes or no. Many people don't feel comfortable with the process of selling, because it makes them feel pushy and overbearing. Selling should be the simple process of matching your company's skills and expertise with what the customer needs.

Listen Up: Active listening is the golden rule to effective selling. Without listening, you cannot clearly understand what your customer needs. You may ask yourself, "What exactly is active listening?" Here are a few simple rules:

- ✓ Maintain good eye contact.
- ✓ Be attentive.
- ✓ Keep an open mind.
- ✓ Don't interrupt.
- ✓ Ask clarifying questions.
- ✓ Put yourself in the "shoes" of the other person.
- ✓ Pay attention to body language (i.e., facial expressions).

Using these simple guidelines, you will gain a more thorough understanding of your potential customers and be able to target your response to their needs.

A Word of Caution...

Be careful not to make unrealistic or inaccurate statements just to make a sale. You will hurt your business in the long run and potentially leave yourself open to a lawsuit. All advertising and marketing claims must be truthful and not deceptive. Individual state contractor licensing boards may have specific guidelines regarding licensed contractor advertising such as including a licensing number and specific verbiage required by law.

Organizing the Sales Process

Track and Prioritize: Selling is a process. Generally speaking, higher-value sales have a longer selling process than a lower-value sale. To manage this selling process and provide the best service possible, you must be organized. Tracking potential customers is made simple by developing a sales tracking sheet for each contact you make. Your tracking sheet should contain the contact information for the potential customer, the type of work the customer wants, a summary of communication, the source of referral for that customer, and any other information you feel is necessary.

The next step is to prioritize your sales leads. Prioritizing leads is a way to manage your time in the sales process and can give you key insights into the effectiveness of your marketing program. You want to concentrate most of your time on the strong leads.

Tracking and prioritizing leads makes the sales process most effective.

Your Sales Presentation

Present Your Best Side: Once you have determined your strongest sales leads, you should schedule time to make a sales presentation. This is your opportunity to show customers how your company can meet their needs; in the sales presentation you try to gain a commitment to perform the work.

Presentation materials are important visuals and give the customer something concrete to take away and read after the meeting. These materials can include

- ✓ a company information sheet,
- ✓ brochures,
- ✓ business cards,
- ✓ past customer testimonials,
- ✓ warranty information, and
- ✓ photographs of past projects.

To avoid awkward stumbling in the presentation, have materials prepared ahead of time. This demonstrates your professionalism and ensures that you have thought through the presentation.

Overcoming "No": Handling objections is one of the more difficult parts of the sales process. This is the time to use your active listening skills and overcome the objection.

- ✓ Repeat the objection to ensure that you completely understand the potential customer's reservation.
- ✓ No question is a stupid question. The person with the objection may just not understand the process.

✓ Give an example of a customer with the same question and how you effectively fulfilled his/her needs.

Communication Is Key: Closing the sale is a very important part of the process. Try to gain a commitment from the potential customer, whether it is hiring your company to do the work or just scheduling a follow-up appointment.

Follow up on all sales presentations. This may be as simple as making a phone call or sending a card or small gift. Consistent follow-up ensures that you are at the top of your potential customer's mind and gives you an advantage over competitors.

Clearly understanding your potential customer's needs is imperative.

Final Inspection...

Executing Your Marketing Plan: Once you develop your marketing plan, the next step is implementing it.

Logos, Stationery, and Business Cards: These simple marketing tools can help establish your company's identity.

Promotional Materials: You can extend your marketing program by using various promotional materials.

Public Relations: This is an inexpensive but effective way to market your company.

Effective Selling Skills: Effective selling involves carefully listening to your potential customer's needs.

Organizing the Sales Process: Tracking potential sales leads can help you organize the process of selling.

Your Sales Presentation: Preparation and follow-up are important when presenting to potential customers.

Chapter 7
LEGAL REQUIREMENTS

Objectives

By reading and practicing the techniques described in this chapter, the reader should be able to successfully complete the following activities:

- ✓ Develop relationships with other contractors.
- ✓ List the potential legal implications of a landscape construction project.
- ✓ Identify sources of information on construction restrictions.

Many legal controls can and often do influence landscape construction work. Few activities that the landscape contractor undertakes will be without some form of standard—either voluntary or involuntary. Although these standards influence the speed and efficiency of a landscape operation, the contractor's attitude toward controls should be tempered with the understanding that most legal requirements protect the health, safety, and welfare of the public and of the contractor.

This chapter covers typical relationships, rules, contracts, standards, and entities that govern the profession of landscape contracting in many parts of the nation. National standards, or codes, provide guidance in the form of construction standards. Local ordinances and building departments provide requirements for location, construction, and, occasionally, style of landscape improvements that can be installed. Local governments may also require that owners or contractors obtain permits and pay fees prior to construction. Contract documents, a legally binding set of instructions, guide projects by placing control over the materials and methods that may be used. In addition, insurance standards, usually expressed in limitations and restrictions incorporated into policies and contracts, also provide some level of control over landscape work.

Before beginning a landscape construction project, the contractor must verify legal requirements. Failure to do so may mean paying fines or removing parts of a project that do not comply with regulations. To verify that the locale has regulations by which the contractor must abide, look in the government section of the phone book for county and city building departments or for a zoning administrator. In some areas, planning departments and forestry departments may be the local regulatory agencies. When you describe the work being done, these officials should be able to provide direction through the appropriate process. Ignorance of legal requirements will not relieve the contractor of liability.

A Word of Caution...

Legal counsel should be obtained for the interpretation of any information described herein.

Related Information

Information provided in this chapter is supplemented by instructions provided elsewhere in this text. Since this chapter covers subjects specifically under the umbrella of legal requirements, some information is being purposely reinforced or introduced despite being covered in other chapters.

Contractor/Client Relationships

Entering the world of business requires the contractor to be aware of the many methods for obtaining work, to understand relationships with clients and related parties, and to execute contractual relationships with clients. Because space is limited in this text, this chapter provides an overview of the most common contractor/client relationships. The author suggests supplemental reading to obtain additional information regarding design and construction contracts.

Obtaining Landscape Contracting Work

Obtaining work is essential for the contractor to maintain a business. Methods to obtain, or procure, work in the contracting field range from informal marketing efforts to formal contracting with owners and developers and formal subcontracting arrangements with major builders. Several aspects of the contractor's work may influence the success in obtaining contracts. These aspects include such factors as how the contractor's rates for performing services compare with others in the market area, how efficiently the contractor works, and how quickly the contractor can provide services. Experience in performing similar types of projects and the quality of the contractor's work are also crucial selling points. Depending on the type of procurement method, one or more of these factors may be critical. Three basic methods for obtaining work in the landscape contracting field can be identified: direct procurement, competitive negotiation, and competitive bidding. These opportunities may present themselves in various forms. Oftentimes, a request for pricing a project comes in the form of an RFQ (Request for Qualifications) or RFP (Request for Proposal).

Direct Procurement

Direct procurement involves the acquisition of contracts for landscape services directly from a client. The contractor may initiate direct procurement through advertising or marketing of services, by the client through referral from another client, or by what the industry terms "walk-in" business. In any instance, the contractor sells materials and services to the client without direct competition from other parties.

Competitive Negotiation

Many customers prefer to "shop" for landscape services and receive proposals from several service providers. This form of procurement often requires the contractor to submit detailed explanations and itemization to ensure the selection of services based on similar proposals. Competitive projects may be client-originated or solicited from general contractors, also known as prime contractors (contractors who hold the prime contract for completion of a large construction project) or from design professionals (landscape architects, architects, and engineers) who have projects with private clients. General contractors or specialized contractors, those who perform specific

operations for a project, often use competitive negotiation to select subcontractors.

Although negotiation is standard practice, it is very important to understand the process and insure that all parties are negotiating the same or very similar products. This "apples per apples" approach can limit misunderstandings in the process. Slight differences between interpretations of client needs can lead to substantial differences in price and the client often ends up not knowing what they are really getting. The inconsistencies of this process underscore the importance of providing design services as a separate phase from installation services. With a set design, all bidders are pricing 'apples for apples.'

Competitive Bidding

Bidding is a formal process practiced by public clients for all but small projects and by private clients for most large projects. Competitive bidding requires that contractors offer, or bid, a sealed project cost based on a specific design. A client will open all proposals at a designated time and place. Selection of a contractor is typically based on the lowest bid submitted by a qualified contractor. A design professional or the client's agent generally determines a qualified contractor. Certain contractors may be disqualified from bidding based on sound legal reasons such as lack of experience, financial insolvency, or government sanction.

Submission of bids is typically restricted to prime contractors. In many projects, the landscape contractor will not be the entity submitting the bid. Landscape contractors may submit a bid or negotiated price to a prime contractor, who will add that total to the other subcontractor prices and submit it as part of that contractor's bid. It is not unusual for a landscape contractor to submit prices to several different prime contractors for the same project. Bidding opportunities can be obtained by reviewing public notices, contacting plan houses (such as Dodge House, a private publisher who tracks major invitations to bid), prime contractors, and design professionals. Prices prepared for bids may take different forms.

Relationships Between Contractor and Client

When work is secured, the contractor's relationship with the client is defined as either a prime contractor or a subcontractor. Whichever of these positions the contractor holds will have a significant impact on control of the project. Third parties, such as design professionals acting as owner's agents and consulting construction managers, also affect the relationship between contractor and client.

Prime Contractor Relationships

Responsible for completing all aspects of a project, a general contractor holds the prime construction contract with the client, who is typically the project owner or financier. This relationship is framed by the terms of a contract spelling out each party's rights and responsibilities. On complex projects, the prime contractor may be responsible for numerous suppliers and subcontractors, including those doing the landscape installation, as well as his or her own workforce. When subcontractors complete portions of a project, the prime contractor may or may not assume responsibility for the work. Protection from damage by others may be the responsibility of the subcontractor for that portion of work. Insure that this detail is understood and agreed to by all involved parties.

In projects that cover only landscape construction elements, the landscape contractor may serve as a prime contractor. The landscape contractor is then responsible for completion of all work, including those elements that are subcontracted to others.

Another arrangement under the contractual arrangements for a project is the concept of multiple general contractors. For reasons of timing, cost, or quality control, the client may choose to separate major work areas into separate contracts. Prime contracts will be offered for each of the work areas, with each general contractor being responsible for work within the appropriate trade. The general contractors, owner's agent, and other parties to the work must then coordinate activities among all the contracts.

Subcontractor Relationships

Subcontractors perform specialized work for a project; and although they seldom have a contractual relationship with the project owner or financier, subcontractors maintain a formal or informal relationship with the general contractor. Employing several subcontractors from many building trades for large building projects is a common practice, as is subcontracting landscape elements of a project. Specialization within the landscape contracting field has also increased the possibility of having several landscape-related subcontractors for a single project, such as those who specialize in irrigation, wall construction, plant installation, and turf establishment.

Third Parties to Contractor/Client Relationships

Communications between the prime contractor and owner will typically be referred to the owner's agent. In many projects, this will be the design professional. The owner's agent will serve as the clearinghouse for all communications with the owner, accepting and approving submissions and providing instructions to the general contractor. Whether a general contractor performs landscaping work on a small project or a subcontractor performs landscaping work on a large project, any change or deviation from the plans and specifications will require approval from the owner's agent.

Construction Managers

An alternative to completing a project using the typical contractor/subcontractor relationship is to employ a project management firm. The project management firm bridges between design and construction by contracting with the project owner to advise on design and construction and by maintaining the integrity of the project by managing its installation.

The construction management model has three variations. First is the design-build firm, which project owners employ to complete both the design and implementation of a project. Another variation is the agency construction manager who, in exchange for a fee, assists the owner in employing both designers and contractors. Either of these two methods provides advantages to owners. For example, some owners may have too many projects or very complex projects and may need assistance to manage them. Other owners may be novices in the implementation of construction projects and may need an experienced manager. Additional advantages in the form of cost savings are often derived from integrating design and construction. Construction management reduces the adversarial roles often found between designers and contractors and maintains tighter control over the scheduling of activities. Yet a third form of construction management is the at-risk model, in which the manager acts as designer and general contractor for a project, providing the owner a guaranteed maximum price.

Forms of Contracts

A written contract should guide the execution of work in any form. Whether simple or extensive, the contract forms a basis for a relationship between parties and provides a mechanism whereby disputes can be resolved. As mentioned earlier, seek the advice of appropriate legal counsel before preparing and entering into any contract.

Required Conditions of a Contract

Certain conditions must be written into or contained within contracts. They must contain lawful subject matter, must include an offer and exchange (a fee for services rendered), must be negotiated between competent parties, and must not be signed under duress. Contracts must also include agreement and be in proper form for the jurisdiction in which the work will be performed. In addition, the following items should be included in a contract for landscape services[1]:

- ✓ Names and addresses of the parties involved
- ✓ Date of contract preparation
- ✓ Description of the work to be accomplished (also called the scope of services) and the materials or services to be provided, including the location where it is to be accomplished
- ✓ The terms of completion, including inspection, the completion date, and the penalty for not completing on time
- ✓ The terms of payment
- ✓ The signatures of both parties or their legal representatives
- ✓ The date of signing

Contract Documents

The documents used to bid and construct large projects are collectively referred to as contract documents or construction drawings. Included in a full set of contract documents for a large project would be instructions for bidding, contracts for construction, general instructions, and specific technical instructions. These preceding elements are collectively referred to as specifications. Also included within the contract document definition would be the set of plans used to guide construction, provisions for change orders if construction is altered, and payment and completion documents to be used during construction. All elements of this project documentation are part of a legally binding contract, whether work is performed as a general contractor or as a subcontractor.

Subcontractor/Contractor Agreements

The relationship between a subcontractor and general contractor may be in the form of a contract, an informal letter agreement, or, inadvisably, through oral agreement. Formal and informal agreements should address issues such as recognition of the prime contract, work to be performed by the subcontractor, payments to the subcontractor, timing of the work, insurance and bonding required of the subcontractor, special conditions required by the project, and agreement by the parties.

Two-Party Contracts

Smaller projects may proceed without the benefit of an expansive set of contract documents. Contractors may work from written proposals or landscape drawings that have been presented to, and agreed upon by, the client. Although it varies according to where the contract is prepared and how the proposal is worded, most written proposals are legally binding if both parties sign the document. Proposals lack the type of specific instructions for every element of the project that contract documents provide. Hence, a great deal of communication and understanding by the parties is required to avoid disputes.

Building Codes

Codes are typically prepared by national institutes or organizations that have an interest in advancing the safe application of their trade. Two of the most prominent types of building codes are structure building codes and the National Electrical Code (NEC).

Structure Building Codes

When landscape projects involve the construction of decorative landscape features, the guidelines of the standardized building codes typically come into play. Building codes provide a wealth of information regarding the safe planning of structures. Information regarding material standards, connectors, area planning, dimensions, and other details of building construction are included in these codes. Building codes are adopted on a locality-by-locality basis, so check with the city or county zoning administrator or building office to determine if the codes apply to work being performed.

Ordinances and Deed Restrictions

Local control over construction projects is typically expressed through the use of ordinances that control zoning and building. These regulations place stipulations on the use of land and the construction of improvements on property that lies within a legal jurisdiction. In large communities, these regulations can be extensive and complex; in small communities, they may not exist at all. In absence of an ordinance and permit system, a governmental unit may require adherence to one or more of the codes mentioned in the previous section. Some local government controls are listed in the following section. Contact local building officials, zoning administrators, city foresters, or homeowner association officials to determine if any regulations apply to the work being done.

Zoning Ordinance

Zoning ordinances control how land within a government's jurisdiction may be used. This control may restrict the type of structure one may place on a property, the dimensions of that structure, and the uses of the structure. Also common in a zoning ordinance are requirements for setbacks, or distances between improvements and property lines. Elements of a zoning ordinance that may influence landscape construction include provisions that control fence requirements (such as around a swimming pool) and location, fence height and materials, deck location, deck materials and construction, and railing requirements.

Sign Ordinance

Signage controls may be located within a zoning ordinance, but some locales place regulations on signage in a separate ordinance. Controls on sign use, materials, location, lighting, and size are common in developed areas.

Parking Ordinance

Quantity and location of parking spaces, as well as control of access drives, can sometimes be found in an ordinance separate from the zoning ordinance.

Landscape Ordinances

Many municipalities and counties have landscape ordinances that prescribe planting requirements for certain conditions and uses. These requirements often include plant sizes at planting time, quantities required and the species of plants that may or may not be used. These ordinances can cover a broad range of situations, including street tree plantings, parking lot plantings, screening, and protection of existing plants and their critical root zones. These rules may be organized in one section of the ordinance or may be spread throughout different portions of the ordinance.

Plant Pruning and Removal Regulations

In communities where plant material is protected from development, permission may be required before trees and shrubs are pruned or removed. In selected communities, trees that are of select species or of a certain age or size may be declared heritage or historic trees. Such a designation is intended to protect the plant from damage, particularly from maintenance and construction operations. In addition, the removal of smaller plants or pruning to allow construction may be regulated. Discuss any plans that require major plant pruning or removal of plants with the city forester, parks department, or zoning administrator.

Floodplain and Restricted Area Regulations

Protection of waterways and natural areas has proven beneficial to reducing pollution, enhancing wildlife, and improving overall environmental quality. Many waterways, water bodies, and natural areas are protected from construction activities by entities such as city ordinances, water quality boards, water districts, and the Army Corps of Engineers.

Conducting construction operations within these areas may be prohibited, or at least restricted, and may require special permits. Typical restrictions include requirement of permits, limits on the amount and location of earthmoving, limits on plant material, design control over outfall and discharge structures, and requirement of installation of erosion control protection.

If contractors are not sure of, or are not notified of, work conducted in restricted areas, they should communicate with city or county officials. Indications that restricted areas may exist are the presence of standing or moving water bodies within 100 feet of the construction site or the existence of wetland plants (cattails, rushes, sedges) within your work area.

Disposal of Site Drainage

When construction plans require water to be collected and diverted away from improvements, verify that the planned outlet location is acceptable for dumping. Pollution or flooding regulations may restrict the emptying of drainage into storm sewers, streams, and other waterways. Changing the drainage of runoff in a manner that damages neighboring property could be considered trespassing (see "Tort Issues" later in this chapter). The local water district or city engineer should be able to provide information regarding legal outlets for tiles and drainage swales.

Deed Restrictions

Planned communities, condominium housing complexes, historic districts, and other communities may have restrictions that control what type of exterior improvements can be planned and built. These restrictions are intended to develop uniformity of development or to protect historical authenticity. Review plans with authorities in these situations to verify if construction work must follow established guidelines.

Historic Districts

Neighborhoods with unique and older homes could be designated as historic districts and the homes as historic properties. If the property is on the National Historic Register or within a National Historic District, work on the exterior of a site could be restricted. Even if there is no national historic designation, many jurisdictions have state and local equivalent

designations to protect the site. Limitations often include the type and number of changes that can be made to building exteriors, dictation of specific materials, and possibly controls over a wide range of design materials. To verify if the site has such restrictions, contact city or county zoning officials, or check with a state historical society.

In addition to structures on them, sites may also have protection according to their archeological, Native American, or ancient graveyards status. Although the designer is often asked to verify if such restrictions apply, contractors should also be aware of the protected status of the site and be prepared to ask what conditions might apply to their work. During construction, contractors should be observant of any antiquity or artifact unearthed during their work and be prepared to suspend activity until the authorities can clear the site.

Building Permits and Site Plan Reviews

To verify compliance with ordinances, counties and communities often require that a building permit be obtained prior to beginning construction. The process of obtaining a permit may simply involve an official who reviews ideas, or it may require a series of committee meetings in a process called a site plan review. Either method will most likely require preparation of a plan that contains descriptions of the work, along with elevations and dimensions. Building and zoning officials typically supervise the issuance of building permits and submissions for a site plan review.

Insurance, Bonding, and Licensure

Insurance, bonding, and licensure are means in which contractors can protect themselves and the business being operated.

Insurance

Considering the risks involved in construction, contractors are advised to obtain necessary insurance to cover the perils faced when building landscapes. Risk in the landscaping industry comes primarily in the form of comprehensive liability from accidental destruction of property, employee accidents, and vehicular accidents. Natural peril coverage and errors in workmanship are also risk areas for which protection may be sought. Other activities that may require insurance protection might include umbrella liability policies, equipment and materials coverage, and crime policies.

Contracted projects typically require that contractors have insurance coverage before work begins, and contractors should not begin any work without securing basic coverage. An insurance agent can best advise about the extent or amount of coverage needed for a particular job.

Bonding

Bonding is a surety tool in which a bonding agency guarantees payment in the event a contractor fails to complete a legal obligation. Common for large projects, bonding is required for licensing in North Carolina. Bonding protects the project owner from losses, damages, liens, and unpaid bills on the contractor's part. Common bonds used in construction are described in the following section. Bonding agents are typically contacted to obtain proper construction bonding.

Bid Bond

The bid bond protects the owner if a contractor withdraws a bid after opening. Most formal bids require that a bond in the amount of 5–10 percent of the total bid be included with the bid. If the low bidder on a project withdraws, the owner may apply the bond against the expense of rebidding the project.

Performance and Payment Bonds

Successful bidders are often required to submit performance and payment bond(s) prior to beginning construction. Performance bonds provide protection to the owner in the event that the contractor fails to complete the conditions of the construction contract. Payment bonds (also known as labor and material payment bonds) guarantee payment of labor and material bills that the contractor incurs in the construction of the contracted project.

Performance and payment bonds that combine these two sureties are available, but many projects require submission of dual bonds—one covering each risk. Typically, bonding for performance and payment is 100 percent of the contract value. If either of these conditions for which the contractor is bonded occurs,

the bonding company may be contacted for assistance in completing the project and/or payments.

Business Licensing

Several states, counties, and cities require that anyone providing products and services to the public obtain a business license to operate in their jurisdiction. The process for obtaining a license may be as simple as filling out an application and paying a fee, or it could include bonding and proof of insurance. The issuing agency may stipulate additional licensure requirements. In some cases, the contractor may be required to obtain a license for every jurisdiction in which the firm works. Contact state departments of commerce, county clerks, and city clerks for information regarding business licenses.

Contractor Licensing

North Carolina requires that landscape and irrigation contractors be licensed to practice their trade. By licensing the professions, states can provide some level of protection for the public's health, safety, and welfare by screening out unqualified practitioners. Licensure procedures vary from state to state and may include completing legal documents, taking exams, or providing evidence of capability to perform work. To determine whether a business will require licensure, contact the North Carolina Landscape Contractors' Licensing Board. Bonding and verification of insurance may be additional requirements.

If your company is planning to engage in design/ build operations, verify licensure requirements for contracting and designing. North Carolina requires the licensure of landscape architects and restricts the level of design work that can be performed by others. Landscape architecture licensure laws are either title or practice laws. Title laws prohibit an unlicensed design professional from using the title *Landscape Architect* in any form, whereas practice laws limit the scope of work that an unlicensed professional may design. In some areas, work on public and commercial projects may legally require the design skills of a licensed landscape architect, rather than the landscape designer or contractor. In North Carolina, landscape design by unlicensed individuals is limited to residential properties, sites under one acre and sites where only planting and mulching is designed.

Tort Issues

A contractor will be required to perform activities within the boundaries of the law. Although specific legal requirements vary from region to region, several general requirements are similar without regard to locality. Failure to abide by legal requirements resulting in damage to another's property is considered a tort and could result in payment of damages to the offended party. It is to the contractor's benefit to discuss common legal requirements with industry officials, association members, and insurance and legal advisors before beginning work in the landscaping field. The next section discusses common issues that could lead to legal action.

Trespass

Trespass is an offense committed against another's property. A charge of trespass requires physical entry without permission and the commission of damage. Trespassing is not limited to humans physically entering a site and committing damages. It involves anything under the contractor's control, including equipment, debris, drainage, or other entities, that enters someone else's property and causes damage.

Nuisance

A disruption that causes discomfort to another is considered a nuisance. Working in an unsafe manner or at odd hours may be considered a nuisance. If they meet the legal tests, excessive noise and dust or even disruption caused by construction activities may also be construed as a nuisance.

Negligence

Failure of a professional to act in a reasonable and prudent manner to safeguard the well-being of others leads to negligence. For example, failing to mark construction areas or performing overhead work without any safeguards could lead to legal action if a contractor does not engage in actions or protective measures that would be reasonably expected to protect the public.

Riparian Rights

Subject to state and federal laws, landowners have rights regarding access to and use of waterways that run through or abut their properties. Changing the conditions of that waterway, possibly through irrigation or damming, may create a legal violation of those laws.

Lateral and Subjacent Rights

Construction activities that affect the lateral support of neighboring properties may lead to legal action. Landowners are entitled to maintenance of the grade at their property line. For example, if excavation for a parking lot collapses the neighboring grade, lateral support has been denied. Grade change activities must be completed within the boundaries of a project, not outside those boundaries unless neighboring property owners have given prior approval.

Note

1. Jack Ingels, *Landscaping Principles and Practices*, 7th ed. (Clifton Park, NY: Delmar Cengage Learning, 2009).

PART 2

Fundamentals for the Field

Chapter 8
BIDDING AND ESTIMATING

Accurate estimating is important to the profitability of a landscape construction company. If a job is estimated correctly, the contractor has a good chance at getting the job and making money. If the job is poorly estimated, the contractor may lose the bid or win the bid and lose money on the project.

The estimator must ask these questions when assessing whether to bid on a project.

✓ **Company Resources and Type of Work:** Does our company have the resources to perform this work? Is this project consistent with the type of work we do?

✓ **Site Considerations:** Are there any special site considerations that we need to consider? Do the site conditions create any additional costs for our company?

✓ **Location and Cost Effectiveness:** How can we do the work efficiently and in the most cost effective manner? Does the location present special considerations and added cost through travel time and limited accessibility?

✓ **Risk Assessment:** What are the risks and how will we manage them?

✓ **Profitability of Project:** What is our profit margin on this work?

If you know you cannot complete the job on time or there is a chance you could lose money on the project, we recommend that you *not bid the job.* The jobs you choose should contribute to your long-term goals and the reputation you want your company to have in the market.

Bid Documents

In a competitive bid situation, a bid package is often put together that includes

✓ **an invitation to bid** that gives a brief overview of the project, deadlines, and general requirements;

✓ **bid instructions** that contain specifics of how the bid should be completed and submitted;

✓ **bid forms**, including but not limited to items such as a bid sheet, bid schedule, bidder's questionnaire on experience, financial responsibility and capability, and a copy of the contract; and

✓ **supplements**, including items important to the overall bid process such as a property survey and soil analysis.

It is important to follow all the instructions in the bid package carefully and submit all documents according to the required specifications. The bidder can be found unresponsive if information is incorrectly submitted or omitted altogether.

Pre-bid meetings may also be scheduled, especially for larger projects. In a pre-bid meeting, the project specifications and any changes to the bid package are discussed.

If changes are made to a bid package before it is due, an **addendum** is issued. The addendum becomes part of the bid documents and, ultimately, part of the contract when awarded. It is important to carefully review all addenda to evaluate the impact on your bid.

Changes in plans and specifications may affect your bid pricing or even your decision to bid at all.

Carefully evaluate whether bidding on a project is the right decision for your company.

Ethics in Bidding

Good ethical conduct is necessary to maintain the integrity of the bidding process. The situations listed below are not only a poor way to do business, but some state statutes forbid these practices on public projects.

✓ **Bid Shopping**
Bid shopping occurs when the general contractor approaches subcontractors other than those who have submitted bids to seek a lower offer than what was quoted in original bids. In this situation, the general contractor reveals the original bids submitted and tries to reduce the price.

✓ **Bid Peddling**
Bid peddling occurs when the subcontractor approaches the general contractor after the project was awarded with the intent of lowering the original price submitted on bid day.

✓ **Bid Rigging**
Bid rigging is a form of collusion where contractors coordinate their bids to fix the award outcome of a project.

Estimate Planning

Once you have determined that you want to submit a bid, you must prepare your estimate. An estimate is the sum of the costs to complete the project, plus your added overhead and profit margin. Before you start putting numbers down on paper, you should understand all the factors that impact the cost of the job. A good estimate will fall within 1 percent to 2 percent of actual construction costs.

Project Documents

A complete set of project documents is required to prepare an accurate cost estimate. These documents include the following:

✓ **Construction or architectural drawings** that show a schematic diagram of the job.

The drawings may illustrate many different views or elevations of the job.

✓ **Specifications** are details that determine the type of materials or methods to be used in construction. If there is a conflict between the specifications and applicable codes, you must follow the stricter of the two. The codes are the minimum requirements by law. You must always meet or exceed the applicable codes.

✓ **The contract** is the agreement between you and your customer to complete the specified work. The conditions outlining the obligations of each party, such as the owner and contractor, are included in the contract. If your bid is accepted, the construction drawings and specifications become part of the contract package. Contracts are covered in more detail in Chapters 7 and 10.

✓ **Bonds** may be required as part of the bid submittal (discussed in Chapters 5 and 7). Bonds commonly required are bid and performance bonds.

You should carefully review these documents to understand the project and the expectations of the customer.

Site Visit

There may be specifics about the site that influence the cost estimate. These details cannot always be determined from the construction documents. It is important that you go to the actual site and look at any factors that may impact the project. Soil type, grading, vehicle access, and availability to electricity and water are some of the variables that could affect the cost of the project. You want to anticipate as many of these problems as you can before beginning work.

During this time, you should consider the environmental aspects of the project. If you need to obtain environmental permits, this process will affect your estimated costs. Your project may also require special equipment and processes that should be factored into your estimate. Chapter 14, Safety and Environmental Considerations, discusses environmental impacts in more depth.

Estimating Framework

Estimating should be a systematic process. Approaching the estimate in an organized way will help you avoid errors or omissions. Taking the extra time to construct a framework for the estimate will increase your accuracy.

Your estimating framework essentially lists the process for completing the job. This can be accomplished by

✓ defining the phases of the project; and

✓ listing each task and materials needed for each phase.

Once your framework is established, you can enter the time and cost for each task. If you are awarded the job, you can easily convert your estimating framework into your job schedule.

Define the Phases

The first thing you need to consider when you build your estimate is the phases of the project that you are working on. For example, you might list the phases as preconstruction, construction, and post-construction. The order of tasks will drive your scheduling process.

List Each Task and Materials Needed

Once you list the phases of the project, you need to develop a list of tasks and materials for each phase. Be very specific in this step. If you omit an item or add an unnecessary item, your estimate will be inaccurate. The task and material list should also include labor time needed and material amounts. By identifying these items early in the process, you may determine the need for items such as overtime to meet certain project deadlines and temporary storage. All of these items play a part in the cost estimate.

Estimating Checklist

The Construction Specifications Institute publishes a classification system called MasterFormat. This system includes numbers and job tasks grouped by major construction activities. This is a helpful tool when setting up your estimating framework to ensure that you have accounted for all aspects of materials and labor. After you become familiar with the estimating process, you may develop your own estimating checklist customized for your needs.

Determining Estimated Costs

Quantity Take-off Method

One accurate method of estimating is the quantity take-off method. Using this method, you individually estimate units of materials and labor for each task you listed in your estimating framework.

After estimating materials and labor, the following items are added:

✓ subcontractor fees,

✓ labor burden,

✓ project overhead costs,

✓ project equipment,

✓ contingencies,

✓ allowances,

✓ company overhead, and

✓ profit.

By going through the items individually, you can adjust your estimate to accommodate the unique aspects of the project you may have uncovered when reviewing the construction documents or during your site survey.

STEP 1 ## Determine Labor Cost for Each Task

Using your estimating framework, you can begin to enter your labor cost. Information from previous jobs can help you determine accurate job costs. There are also published costs available through books such as the RSMeans cost data series, but this is no substitute for your knowledge of the industry. Your experience with your local labor market and wages should be factored into your estimated costs.

For each labor item on your estimating framework list, use the following formula to determine the labor cost.

Required Labor Hours per Task x Labor Rate = Labor Cost per Task

The required labor hours can vary based on several different factors, such as employee skill level, size of crew, and weather conditions. These factors must be taken into account when determining the required labor hours. Hours spent planning and scheduling must also be figured into the labor cost equation.

Another helpful tool when determining labor cost is your historical cost data. Determining your final labor cost from past projects will help you put together more accurate estimates for future jobs. Developing a cost-tracking system is discussed later in this chapter.

Add Labor Burden

STEP 2

As an employer, you incur costs such as employment taxes and insurance. These obligations add approximately 30 percent to your labor cost. This additional amount is referred to as labor burden.

Labor burden includes items such as

✓ Medicare and social security (discussed in Chapter 16),

✓ federal unemployment insurance (discussed in Chapter 16),

✓ workers' compensation,

✓ liability insurance,

✓ state unemployment insurance, and

✓ company benefits (such as health insurance, vacations, etc.).

Labor burden must be factored into your total labor cost.

Determine Materials Cost

STEP 3

Just as you plugged labor cost into your estimating framework, you can do the same with materials cost. For each material item listed on your estimating framework, you need to obtain a cost.

Your suppliers can provide you with the materials price per unit or a lump sum. The cost of materials can fluctuate according to the availability of raw materials and demand, so it is important to keep current cost data. In addition to tracking wage, earnings, employment, and benefit statistics, the Bureau of Labor Statistics (www.bls.gov) tracks the prices of major groups of construction materials as part of its Producer Price Index (PPI) program. Periodically reviewing this resource can help you understand potential increases and decreases in materials cost.

You may receive the materials cost as a unit cost. If necessary, use the following formula to determine the total material cost per unit for each of the materials categories on your take-off sheet.

Price per Unit x Number of Units Needed =
Total Material Unit Cost

To make sure you are receiving the best price, obtain at least three bids from suppliers. You should also add a small contingency for waste. Depending on the type of material and the job specifications, your waste contingency will vary.

Determine Project Equipment Cost

STEP 4

Equipment needed to complete the job is figured as a direct cost of the project and added to your estimate.

For example, if you need a crane to set an air handling unit on top of a building as part of a HVAC project, it is considered a direct cost.

Small tools and pickup trucks are considered an indirect cost and not part of project equipment. These indirect costs are figured into project overhead.

Figuring the direct cost of equipment differs depending if you rent or own the equipment.

Owned Equipment: To estimate owned equipment, you must arrive at a unit cost for the equipment. To calculate unit cost, consider the following factors:

✓ actual value of equipment factoring in its age and amount of depreciation from the original purchase price;

✓ maintenance and operating costs;

✓ taxes and fees;

✓ labor to operate equipment, including any training or licensing costs; and

✓ insurance.

Unit cost is calculated by estimating the number of hours you will use the equipment per year and dividing this number by the total yearly cost of the equipment calculated by considering the operational factors.

For example, if you figure the total cost of the equipment for the year is $30,000 and you plan to use the equipment for a total of 1,000 hours, your unit cost to operate the equipment is $30 an hour.

If you estimate using the equipment for 40 hours on a project, your estimated project equipment cost for that project is $1,200.

Rental Equipment: The following items are considered when figuring the cost of rental equipment:

✓ equipment rental rate;

✓ labor cost to pick up and return equipment or delivery fees;

✓ labor cost to operate equipment; and

✓ other costs associated with operating the equipment (e.g., cost of fuel).

Subcontracting: You may decide that neither option is cost effective or feasible and subcontract the work. In this case, this line item would appear under subcontractor fees.

Rent, Lease, or Buy? Construction equipment is vital to the completion of construction projects. Equipment can range from cranes to computers. The decision to rent, lease, or purchase this equipment is a challenging one, and there are many considerations to each option.

Leasing is a long-term rental agreement that provides the benefits of using the equipment without purchasing. Lease payments are made to the owner of the equipment in exchange for the use of the equipment. At the end of the lease term, the owner takes possession of the equipment.

Leasing equipment has many advantages. One of the biggest is the ability to use the equipment with a limited capital expenditure. Other advantages compared to purchasing include

✓ no down payment;

✓ duration of payments over a longer period making them lower;

✓ lease payments (as defined by the IRS) deductible as operating expenses; and

✓ obsolete equipment is returned to the owner at end of the lease.

Equipment ownership allows you to take advantage of certain tax benefits and in the long run usually costs less than leasing. Leases are long-term contractual agreements that generally cannot be cancelled. If you no longer need the equipment, you must still make payments for the full term of the lease.

Purchasing equipment is advantageous when the equipment has a long and useful life and will not become obsolete in the short-term. You gain ownership of the equipment after the purchase is made but you should consider how the equipment will hold value over a long-term period. For this reason, salvage value is a benefit to purchasing equipment.

Renting equipment may be an alternative to purchasing or leasing. Although renting equipment

is usually the costliest, it is the best option in certain circumstances. These include

✓ short-term, specialized projects;

✓ replacement for equipment being repaired;

✓ equipment with high maintenance costs; and

✓ jobs that require transportation and storage to distant locations.

The decision to rent, purchase, or lease is one that should be analyzed carefully to provide the most cost-effective solution for your company.

 ### Add Subcontractor Fees

STEP 5 Subcontractors will be a consideration if you need to outsource work that your company does not have the resources to complete. Chapters 7 and 14 cover hiring and working with subcontractors. You should get at least three bids from subcontractors, so you have a good measure of comparison. Carefully evaluate subcontractors to determine that they have the proper qualifications, licensure, and insurance coverage. Subcontractor fees must be added to the estimate that you give your customer.

 ### Add Allowances

STEP 6 There may be items that are not specified in the project plans, such as finish materials (carpeting, fixtures, lighting, etc.). For these items, you can specify an allowance in your estimate. This is the owner's budget for these items. If the owner's choices exceed or fall short of the allowance amount, the contract should clearly address who is responsible for the difference. Typically, a change order is created stating the amount under or over what is stated in the contract. Change orders are discussed in Chapter 10.

 ### Add Contingencies

STEP 7 A contingency percentage is sometimes added to an estimate to protect the contractor if an unanticipated problem or condition arises during the course of the project. Contingency markups are generally based on the risk level of the project.

For example, a low risk project might have a 2 percent contingency markup, but a project that has more unknown factors would have a higher markup.

 ### Add Project Overhead

STEP 8 Project overhead costs are items that are necessary to complete the project but are not

directly associated with labor and materials. These costs typically account for 5 percent to 10 percent of the total bid, but these costs should be itemized as much as possible to achieve the most accurate result.

Examples of project overhead costs include

✓ bonds,

✓ temporary storage,

✓ temporary office,

✓ security guard,

✓ utilities,

✓ dumpsters, and

✓ portable toilets.

Project overhead differs from company overhead. Company overhead cannot be directly linked with a project.

 STEP 9
Add Company Overhead

Company overhead is the cost of doing business. These expenses are necessary to keeping the operation running. Examples of these expenses are

✓ office rent,

✓ accounting fees,

✓ taxes,

✓ telephone,

✓ legal fees, and

✓ administrative labor.

Calculating an Overhead Percentage

Using historical information from the past year is the best way to predict overhead for the following year. Overhead percentages generally average between 5 percent and 20 percent, so it is best to calculate the overhead rates specific to your company.

Company Overhead: To arrive at a company overhead percentage, you can make the following calculations.

✓ Add up all of your overhead costs from the previous year. These numbers may be found on your income statement as part of your administrative expenses.

✓ Divide your overhead costs by your revenues (also found on your income statement) to arrive at your overhead percentage.

Project Overhead: Project overhead is a similar calculation.

✓ Add up all of your project overhead costs from the previous year.

✓ Divide your project overhead costs by your revenues (found on your income statement) to arrive at your overhead percentage.

Adding Overhead to the Bid: You must add these overhead percentages to your estimate to cover overhead costs.

For example, let's say you calculated the direct costs for your bid at $100,000, your project overhead at 9 percent, and company overhead percentage at 11 percent. Your direct costs are then 80 percent of your total bid price. Since overhead is a percentage of revenue, you should divide the direct costs of your bid by 80 percent (.80).

Here is what the calculation should look like:

$$\$100,000 \div .80 = \$125,000$$

After adding in overhead, the bid price with direct costs and overhead is $125,000.

STEP 10
Add Markup and Determine Profit Margin

Considerations for properly pricing a job include

✓ cost estimate,

✓ customer needs and expectations,

✓ local market and competition, and

✓ expected profit margin.

Determining the right pricing based on these factors is important to maximizing your profit and satisfying your customers.

Cost-based pricing is one of the most common ways to price a bid. Essentially, the cost of the project is determined through the cost estimate and an overhead percentage, plus a markup percentage. The markup percentage is divided into the direct costs of the project, just like the overhead costs in the previous example. If you estimated correctly, you will achieve your internal profit margin goals.

The standard industry markup is 15 percent, but you should consider the market and competition. You must be careful to keep your estimate in line with your competition and understand how much your customers are willing to pay for your work.

In your estimate, markup is applied to the direct costs of the project, such as labor, material, project equipment, project overhead, and subcontractors.

If your markup is too low, you may not cover your project costs, causing you to break even, or lose money on the job. To get the work, you may decide to bid low by lowering your profit markup and make it up on future projects, but this should not be a common practice. You will eventually go out of business if an insufficient amount of profit is achieved over time.

On the flip side, if your markup is too high, you may bid yourself out of jobs. Typically, the higher the markup, the fewer jobs you receive. The lower the markup, the more jobs you receive. You must estimate and choose your markup carefully to ensure a steady flow of jobs and profits for your company.

Attention to detail is important to preparing an accurate estimate.

Other Methods of Estimating

Quantity take-off is generally the most accurate way to estimate, but there are other estimating methods you can use.

✓ A **conceptual estimate** is generally prepared by the architect using cost models from previous projects. The contractor may arrive at a much different cost because of the project's unique characteristics.

✓ Using the **square-foot method** of estimating, the project cost is a calculation of the square footage of the project multiplied by a unit cost. This is a quick way to arrive at an estimated cost, but this method does not account for project specifics that affect cost. Another variation of this method is putting together an estimate using cubic feet of the project multiplied by a unit cost.

✓ The **unit price method** of estimating bundles all cost factors such as labor, materials, equipment, and subcontractors to come up with a unit price for the entire task. For example, let's say you are placing and finishing a 2,000-square-foot concrete slab and you determined that your unit price is $2.00 per square foot for this task. The total unit price is $4,000.

Estimating Pitfalls

Accurate estimating is a vital function for landscape construction businesses and can make the difference between getting the right jobs and making a profit on a job. There are pitfalls that are detrimental to the estimating function that you want to avoid.

Preliminary Estimates

Your customers may be eager to determine what their project will cost and will ask for an estimate on the spot. Quoting a price before you have a chance to make accurate calculations is a risky practice. If you quote a price too high, it is possible that you could lose the bid. If you quote a price too low, the potential customer may be disappointed and feel you were dishonest in your initial contact.

Inaccurate Estimates

Inaccuracies occur when you make errors and omissions in your estimate. To avoid inaccuracies, you should always check your estimates. Errors to look for:

✓ **Mathematical errors:** Always check your work and if possible, have someone else check the mathematical accuracy of the estimate.

✓ **Omissions in labor or materials:** Be as thorough as possible when setting up the framework for your estimate. The use of a standard format, such as MasterFormat, will help you avoid this mistake.

✓ **Non-standard abbreviations:** Non-standard abbreviations may be interpreted as a different measurement or material. Spell out the actual word rather than inventing an abbreviation that is unclear or vague.

✓ **Units of measure:** Define linear, square, and cubic measure accurately. The difference between these measures can make a drastic difference in cost.

The more accurately you prepare your estimates, the better chance you have to make your projected profit.

Accurate estimates help you get the right jobs and make a profit.

Using an Estimator

Estimators develop the cost information business owners or managers need to bid for a contract. Small business owners or managers may perform this function without the use of a professional estimator. Large companies or a large project may need to use an estimator.

Estimators follow the same estimating process: performing the quantity take-off, analyzing subcontractor bids, determining equipment needs and sequence of operations, analyzing physical constraints at the site and contingencies, and determining allowances and overhead costs. The estimator may also have a say in setting the profit for the project and the terms and conditions of the contract. The estimator's job is solely to perform the estimating function and, if used, the estimator is an important member of the project team.

Submitting Your Bid

Once your estimate is complete and you are ready to submit your bid, you must make sure to follow all of the instructions in the bid package. These instructions include submitting all of the required documents and the exact information requested by the bid submission deadline. Even though you may have a template put together for the estimating process, you may need to customize your bid so as to respond to the bid specifications. Once your bid is submitted, it is reviewed by the owner. Bid review is generally a 30 to 90-day process. You are notified of the acceptance or rejection of your bid after this review process is complete.

Job Cost Recording System

A job cost recording system provides many benefits to the estimating and project management process.

✓ Current projects are monitored more closely with a cost tracking system. Cost overruns are identified and corrective action is taken sooner.

✓ Information from a job cost recording system helps with future estimates by creating more accurate unit costs.

✓ Many analytical reports can be generated from cost data to review performance by project, activity, year, etc. Using this data can help you make more strategic decisions.

There are many ways to set up a job cost recording system, but to ensure accuracy, it must remain consistent for all projects.

The first step is to develop a cost code system. A cost code system includes the following components.

✓ **Project Number:** A project numbering system could be as simple as starting with the number one (1) and consecutively numbering subsequent projects. A more complex project numbering system might also include a code for the type of project and the year it was started. For example, let's say you are working on a remodel project (R) that started in 2006 (06) and was the first (01) project of the year. Your project number could be R-06-01.

✓ **Activity Classification Code:** You may want to develop your own system or use a classification system such as the CSI MasterFormat. For example, for a finish carpentry job you could use MasterFormat number 06200. If you use the same classifications on your estimate, it will be easier to compare estimated to actual costs.

✓ **Distribution Code:** These are items such as material, labor, equipment, and project overhead. For example, coding might be as simple as one-letter abbreviations:

Material = M
Labor = L
Equipment = E
Project Overhead = P

This code can be placed behind the activity classification code. For example, the labor for finish carpentry could be classified as 06200L and materials as 06200M.

Once your system is set up, you can begin entering the cost data. Materials, equipment, and project overhead costs can be gathered from purchase orders, receipts, and invoices. Labor costs can be taken from timecards. It is important that employees fill out timecards completely and with enough detail so you can accurately record labor costs. A sample time card is located in Chapter 16.

Technology Tools for Estimating

Many computer tools are available to help streamline the estimating process. This technology provides many benefits:

- ✓ shorter time to prepare the estimate;
- ✓ improved accuracy; and
- ✓ professional presentation to the customer.

Estimating software ranges from a basic spreadsheet format to complex databases. However, the programs share some common features:

- ✓ databases for unit cost items, such as material and labor;
- ✓ multiple estimate report formats to present to the customer (hard copy and electronic);
- ✓ tracking method for historical information;
- ✓ ability to recall and modify past projects; and
- ✓ job costing capabilities.

As with any software, you must understand the fundamentals. If you do not know how to estimate, the software available will provide limited benefits to the process.

- -

Final Inspection...

Bid Documents: All bid documents should be completed according to the specific requirements of the bid.

Ethics in Bidding: Good ethical practices are important to maintaining the integrity of the bid process.

Estimate Planning: Careful review of construction documents and a site visit are important first steps to creating an accurate estimate.

Estimating Framework: An estimating framework includes the project phases and the labor and materials needed for each phase.

Determining Estimated Costs: The quantity take-off method is one of the more accurate estimating methods. All direct and indirect costs must be added to ensure the estimate is complete.

Other Methods of Estimating: Estimates can be prepared using different methods with varying degrees of accuracy.

Estimating Pitfalls: It is important to be accurate and detailed when estimating a job. You may not make your expected profit if you make mistakes in your estimate.

Using an Estimator: An estimator is used to perform the estimating function on a project. The estimator may also make recommendations on the project profit margin and terms of the contract.

Submitting Your Bid: All instructions in a bid package must be followed or the bid may be rejected. There is typically a 30- to 90-day bid review process.

Job Cost Recording System: Monitoring current projects, creating more accurate future estimates, and providing reports for analysis are benefits of implementing a job cost recording system.

Technology Tools for Estimating: There are several computer tools to help you create your estimate, but it is still important to fully understand the process.

Chapter 9
CONTRACT MANAGEMENT

Chapter Survey...

Legally Speaking: Contracts are legally binding agreements between two or more parties. The main purpose of contracts is to prevent disputes between parties entering into an agreement. Many times, agreements are made verbally, but it is best to get a contract in writing.

Contracts serve many purposes including:

✓ defining the obligations of the agreement;

✓ outlining payment terms; and

✓ limiting the liability of the parties involved.

Contracts need to be worded carefully to protect your company. It is recommended you consult with an attorney experienced in construction law to ensure you have a legally enforceable contract.

Required Contract Elements

Make it Binding: You may have reached an agreement to do work for a customer, but that does not mean that you have a contract. There are four key elements that must be in effect to make a contract binding.

✓ Offer and Acceptance

✓ Consideration

✓ Competent Parties

✓ Legal Purpose

Offer and Acceptance

The Offer is on the Table: An offer specifically outlines the obligations of the contract, including the work to be done and compensation for this work. When you submit an estimate or bid for work, this is considered an offer. All parties must be clear on the essential details and obligations 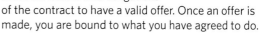 of the contract to have a valid offer. Once an offer is made, you are bound to what you have agreed to do.

An offer generally has a specific amount of time in which an acceptance needs to be made. This time frame is typically 30 days, but it should be stated in the offer. If a deadline for acceptance is not outlined in the offer, it expires in a "reasonable time." Reasonable time is up to court interpretation and is considered on an individual case basis.

Negotiation: Negotiation is the process where the owner and contractor come to an agreement on the price and terms of the contract. Both Chapters 7 and 11 discuss techniques that help guide you through the negotiation process. An offer is usually the outcome of a negotiation, but parties are not bound to the contract terms until an offer is made and acceptance is achieved. It is important to be clear when a communication is for negotiation purposes so it is not misconstrued as an offer.

Acceptance: The next step of the process is acceptance. Acceptance is agreeing to the offer made and generally is done by signing the offer. In some cases, a counteroffer is made. A counteroffer is not considered acceptance. It is only when both parties agree to the contract terms that you obtain acceptance.

Offer Checklist: Your offer should contain certain components because, if accepted, you are contractually bound to it:

✓ Date of offer
✓ Names and contact information of contracting parties
✓ Name and location of project
✓ Description of the work to be performed
✓ Contract time or start and completion date
✓ Payment terms, including progress payment schedule and final payment
✓ Conditions for schedule delays
✓ List of contract documents, including general conditions, drawings, and specifications
✓ Contract sum, including contract type such as lump sum, unit price, or cost plus (discussed later in this chapter)
✓ Expiration date of offer

Once accepted, this agreement becomes part of the contract's Standard Form of Agreement.

Consideration

An Exchange: Both parties must give up something of value to have consideration. Most likely this will be money, but it could be anything of value. Payment terms should be clearly outlined in the contract. Typically, the contractor provides services and in exchange, the owner provides monetary compensation.

Competent Parties

Legal Capacity: The parties in agreement should have the legal capacity to enter into a contract. Simply put, the parties must both be of sound mind in order for the contract to be valid. A situation where parties may not have legal capacity might be if you contracted with someone who is heavily under the influence of drugs or alcohol. The courts may rule someone incompetent if they are mentally disabled. Minors are prohibited from entering into contracts without parental consent.

Legal Purpose

Contracts must be possible to perform, not intended to harm anyone, and cannot require any illegal activity. For example, a contract that requires the contractor to build a house that does not comply with building codes does not have a legal purpose and is invalid.

Consult with an attorney to ensure your contracts are legally enforceable.

Contract Provisions

Make it Clear: Contracts should be clear and concise. It is important that both parties understand the terms of the contract. There are provisions that you need to include in your contracts to ensure that all details are clearly outlined. Provisions are simply clauses that outline the stipulations of the contract.

Key Contract Provisions: Contracts are full of provisions, but a few key ones you will want to include:

✓ Contract Price and Payment Terms
✓ Obligation of the Parties
✓ Supplemental Conditions
✓ Breach of Contract

Contract Price and Payment Terms

Getting Paid: The contract should specify how the contract price is calculated. Whether you choose to use a lump-sum, unit-price or cost-plus method, include all fees the customer is expected to pay.

Payment terms should be very specific and include

✓ who is issuing payment,
✓ amount of the payment,
✓ form of payment, and
✓ when the payment will be issued.

Progress Payments: Progress payments are partial payments made after specified phases of construction are complete. Payments are generally calculated by taking the difference between the completed work and materials delivered and a predetermined schedule of unit costs.

Requirements for the schedule of progress payments should be clearly outlined in the construction contract including

✓ number of payments,
✓ amount of each payment,

✓ stage of progress between payments, and

✓ date or stage when each one is due.

It is important to monitor the progress payment schedule to ensure timeliness. You may be required to submit a partial payment estimate to the project architect or engineer prior to the payment due date. The partial payment estimate outlines the work performed and proof of materials and equipment delivery required for the next stage of construction. The architect or engineer certifies each progress payment by confirming the information in the partial payment estimate.

Progress payments have two functions: one, to protect the owner by holding the contractor responsible for following the planned schedule and two, to allow the contractor to pay for labor and material expenditures as they occur. This method of payment also protects both parties in the event of a contract breach on either side.

Retainage: Retainage is used by the owner to ensure completion of the construction project and provide protection against liens, claims, and defaults. It is calculated as a percentage (generally 10 percent) withheld from each progress payment. The retainage amount may be reduced further after substantial completion of the project (for example, retainage amounts may drop to 5 percent after 75 percent completion of the project). Retainage amounts must be clearly stated in the construction contract. Prime contractors generally hold the same percentage of retainage for their subcontractors.

The architect or engineer certifies when the project is complete and the work meets the conditions of the contract documents.

The retained amounts are generally due to the contractor upon completion and acceptance of the work.

Final Payment: Once the structure can be used for its intended purpose, the architect issues a certificate of substantial completion. A certificate of occupancy, issued by a building inspector, deems the structure meets all applicable codes and is safe for occupancy.

Final payment is generally due when all punch list items are complete as agreed between the owner and contractor, proper approvals are obtained, and all paperwork is complete.

To receive a final payment, the following documentation should be prepared and delivered to the owner upon completion of the project:

✓ Completion certificates issued by the architect

✓ Inspection certificates

✓ Guaranties and warranties

✓ Affidavits that all subcontractors and project bills have been paid

✓ Equipment operation manuals

✓ Final lien waivers for those who submitted preliminary notices

✓ Final project drawings

✓ Any other documents as required by contract

It is important to organize paperwork throughout the construction process. A delay in putting the final paperwork together can consequently delay the final payment.

Obligations of the Parties

Contract Conditions: The obligations of the parties should be specifically outlined in the contract and include both the contractor's obligations and the owner's obligations. The obligations of the parties are the contract conditions.

Contractor's obligations include but are not limited to

✓ having proper licensure;

✓ securing building permits;

✓ ordering all materials and supplies and arranging for site delivery;

✓ furnishing all labor, including obtaining required subcontractors to complete the job;

✓ completing all work in compliance with all applicable codes and scheduling inspections on a timely basis;

✓ completing all work according to plans and specifications; and

✓ keeping the construction site clean and removing all debris during and upon completion of construction.

Owner's obligations include but are not limited to

✓ ensuring prompt approval of all plans and specifications;

✓ ensuring project meets zoning specifications;

✓ issuing payments according to the specified progress payment schedule;

✓ paying for all required permits, assessments, and charges required by public agencies and utilities;

✓ furnishing all surveys and recording plats and a legal description of the property; and

✓ providing access to the construction site in a timely manner.

Each list of obligations must be customized according to the agreement reached and the individual job being performed. Most contracts require agreement by both parties if obligations are assigned to another party.

Supplemental Conditions

The supplemental conditions modify the general conditions of the contract and are often prepared in a separate document. Supplemental conditions are tailored specifically to each project. They may outline items such as specific insurance requirements, project procedures, and local law requirements.

Be very specific when outlining the obligations of both parties.

Breach of Contract

A breach of contract occurs when one of the parties involved fails to perform in accordance with any of the terms and conditions of the contract.

A breach may occur when a party

✓ refuses to perform the contract;

✓ performs an act prohibited by the contract; or

✓ prevents the other party from performing its obligations.

There are two types of breaches: **material** and **immaterial**.

A **material breach** is a serious violation of the contract. For example, if a contractor refuses to perform or complete a job or if an owner refuses to pay for completed or partial jobs, this is considered a breach of contract. This type of breach may void the contract and will most likely end up in litigation.

The injured party can seek monetary damages for the loss suffered as a result of the breach. Sometimes the damages are written into the contract. These are called **liquidated or stated damages**.

Breach of contract can occur if contracts are not completed within the time frame specified in the contract. If a time is not specified in the contract, the project must be completed in a "reasonable time." If the project has an unexcused delay, the owner may be entitled to liquidated damages for the "loss of use." Some contracts specify a per-day rate for liquidated damages. For example, if a contract specifies a $400 per day assessment and the contractor finishes 30 days late, $12,000 in liquidated damages is assessed to the contractor. An owner who sues for liquidated damages cannot sue for actual damages.

If you sue for breach of contract, you must do so within the statute of limitations. Statutes of limitations are laws that set a maximum period of time within which a lawsuit or claim may be filed. The deadlines vary depending on the circumstances of the case and the type of claim. If a claim is not filed before the statutory deadline, you may lose the right to file a claim.

An **immaterial or partial breach** is a less serious violation and usually does not result in termination of the contract. The injured party may only sue for the value of the damages.

Boilerplate Provisions

Standard Language: The term "boilerplate" refers to standard language or clauses used in a legal contract. Sometimes they are referred to as "miscellaneous" clauses. They generally appear at the end of the contract and their purpose is to protect the business in the event of a lawsuit. Attorney's fees, arbitration, and consent to jurisdiction (meaning where the disputes will be settled) are a few examples of boilerplate provisions. When dealing with contracts, make sure to draft and read the boilerplate provisions carefully. These provisions affect your legal rights just as much as the other parts of the contract.

Provisions to Limit Risk

Allocating Risk: As mentioned at the beginning of the chapter, one of the purposes of a contract is to limit the liabilities of the parties involved. Your contract should address the allocation of risk among parties. Examples of risk allocation provisions are listed below:

✓ **Force majeure** addresses "acts of God" and other external events such as war or labor strikes. This provision is written to either absolve the owner or contractor of costs associated with these occurrences.

✓ **Indemnification** absolves the indemnified party from any payment for losses and damages incurred by a third party. Simply put, it is a way to shift payment or liability for any loss or damage that has occurred. Indemnification clauses must be examined carefully to ensure the proper liability is distributed between the contractor and owner.

✓ **Differing site conditions** provision allocates the responsibility for extra costs due to unexpected site conditions. As discussed in Chapter 8, the site conditions must be investigated and taken into consideration when putting together the bid. The owner is responsible for disclosing all site information during the bid process. If errors or omissions occur, the owner may be responsible for incurring the extra construction cost.

✓ **Warranties or guarantees** define the contractor's responsibility for the repair of defects to the construction project after the completion of work. Warranties are often set forth for a defined time period.

✓ **Delays and extensions of time** provide a contingency in case the completion deadline is not met. Delays at no fault of the contractor, such as changes by the owner or architect and environmental or severe weather delays, are generally not considered breach of contract. These types of delays are considered excusable and are granted time extensions. This contingency needs to be clearly outlined in the contract.

✓ **Schedule acceleration** provides assignment of costs incurred to complete a project ahead of schedule. In general, if the owner requires the contractor to accelerate the schedule, the owner is responsible for all associated costs. If the owner requests the schedule be accelerated due to project delays caused by the contractor, the contractor is generally liable for additional costs incurred.

✓ **Artistic changes** clause addresses changes made by the architect or design professional during the course of the project for artistic or creative purposes. The drawings and specifications outline the technical aspects of the project, but may not show the artistic objectives of the project. Including an artistic changes clause will put a limit on the number of changes that can occur as a result of artistic decisions.

Standard legal language must be used when specifying risk assignments to make the contract enforceable. Since legal language is often difficult to understand, it is recommended that you consult with legal counsel when drafting and/or interpreting these provisions.

What Are Recitals?

Background Information: Recitals are language at the beginning of the contract that provide background to the contract, such as the parties entering into the contract, the contract contents, and reasons for the parties' entering into the contract. Recitals cannot always be enforced by law, so it is important to provide specific terms throughout the contract.

Types of Construction Contracts

The differences in the types of contracts are primarily

✓ who takes the risk that the work will be performed for the estimated cost;

✓ who pays for cost overruns; and

✓ who keeps the cost savings if the project performed is less than the estimate.

Contracts between the owner and primary contractor may differ from contracts between the primary contractor and subcontractors.

Lump-Sum Contract

In a lump-sum contract, the contractor agrees to complete the project for a predetermined, specified price. The contractor essentially assumes all of the risk under this contract agreement because the contractor is responsible for additional costs associated with unforeseen circumstances. For example, if extra cost is incurred due to inclement weather, the contractor must absorb these costs. Conversely, the contractor gets to keep any cost savings achieved.

If you use this type of contract, you may be required to formally submit a specific schedule and your quality assurance program so your customer knows you are completing the project to the highest standards. You should avoid this type of contract unless plans and specifications are detailed enough that a final cost can be determined in advance.

Unit-Price Contract

A unit-price contract may be used for jobs where the extent of work cannot be fully determined, or the actual quantities of required items cannot be accurately calculated in advance. A price per unit is calculated for each item and the contractor is paid according to the actual quantities used.

Cost-Plus Contract

Using the cost-plus contract method, the contractor is reimbursed for the actual cost of labor and materials and is paid a markup fee for overhead and profit. The cost-plus contract can be calculated different ways. The owner may pay the actual costs, plus a percentage markup or a fixed fee markup.

Contracting Methods

Single Prime

The single prime method is the traditional form of contracting. The project owner typically hires an architectural firm to design the project. The contractor then performs the work according to the specifications of the project and is responsible for the costs of all materials and labor to obtain project completion.

Design/Build

Using the design/build method of construction, the owner contracts with one company to complete the process from start to finish. The company awarded the design/build contract puts together a team of construction professionals, which may include designers, architects, engineers, and contractors that take a project from design through completed construction. The team works closely to satisfy the owner's needs within a predetermined budget.

Construction Management

Under the construction management method, the project owner contracts with a professional construction manager to coordinate and manage the project. The construction manager generally receives a fee to manage, coordinate, and supervise the construction process from the conceptual development stage through final construction. Work must be performed in a timely manner and on an economical basis.

Turnkey

Turnkey construction is similar to the design/build construction model. In addition to managing the construction and design team, the contractor also obtains financing and land. Under the turnkey model, the construction firm is obligated to complete a project according to pre-specified criteria but with expanded responsibilities and liability. A price is generally fixed at the time the contract is signed.

Fast-Track Construction

Under fast-track construction management, the construction process begins before completion of the contract documents. Fast-track construction involves a phased approach to the project. A contract may be drawn up for each phase. Generally, the cost is not fixed until after construction documents are complete and some construction commitments have already been made.

Multiple Prime Contracts

Large construction projects may involve multiple prime contracts. The owner may contract with two or more prime contractors to complete the same project. This contracting method may integrate elements of the construction management and fast-track construction models. The owner takes on a more active role in managing the different prime contractors. Contractor and owner obligations must be clearly defined in the contract.

Partnering

Partnering starts with setting common objectives and goals for a construction project. All parties involved, such as the owner, design professionals, engineers, and contractors, work together to achieve these objectives and goals. Several meetings are held throughout the bid and construction process to evaluate the decisions made by all parties and adjustments occur when necessary. Partnering increases communication and trust, consequently reducing potential litigation and claims.

Sources of Contracts

Standard forms for contracts are readily available through many sources. There are numerous books available that provide sample contracts and forms. Associations such as the American Institute of Architects (AIA) or the Associated General Contractors (AGC) also have standard forms for contracts.

In situations where the form of the contract is not written by you, it is important to

✓ read the contract very carefully;
✓ highlight anything that is vaguely worded for further clarification;

- ✓ make necessary additions;
- ✓ review changes with the other party;
- ✓ make sure any requested changes have been added prior to signing; and
- ✓ review the contract again, prior to signing.

Always make sure you keep a signed copy of every contract you sign, in case you need to refer to it in the future.

Making Changes to the Contract

A **change order** is a written agreement between the owner and contractor to change the contract. Change orders add to, delete from, or otherwise alter the work set forth in the construction documents. Change orders are standard in the construction industry as a legal means for making changes to the contract.

Common reasons for generating a change order include

- ✓ change in scope (for example, owner requests a design change or owner exceeds allowance amount);
- ✓ unforeseen conditions when site conditions differ from the expected; and
- ✓ errors or omissions in construction plans or specifications.

The AIA and AGC have standardized forms that you can use to execute change orders. Change orders are legally binding and it is important that all of the provisions are clear to both parties. Change orders should include

- ✓ date of change order;
- ✓ description of the change in work;
- ✓ reason for change;
- ✓ change in contract price;
- ✓ change, if any, in contracted time; and
- ✓ signatures from both parties.

Chapters 7 and 11 further discuss how to handle change orders from a customer relations perspective.

Changes prior to the contract award are called addenda. Changes made after the contract is signed and executed are called **modifications**.

Resolving Claims

The claims resolution process provides a way for the owner and contractor to resolve disputes about additional amounts owed as a result of contract changes. As discussed in the previous section, the purpose of written change orders is to avoid disputes. If a change is made to the contract without a change order, claims may arise.

Claims Procedure: The contract may stipulate specific procedures for handling claims. Many times, the contract defers to the architect to initially resolve claims. If claims cannot be resolved by the architect, the contractor and owner may proceed to mediation. If mediation fails, the next step is arbitration. The contract should specify the time allowed to request arbitration. A typical deadline for an arbitration request is 30 days from the time the architect makes a decision on the claim.

Project Schedule: During the claims resolution process, the project cannot be delayed. All schedules and deadlines must be followed. The only exception is disputes involving safety. Work must cease on disputed activities until all safety issues are resolved.

Alternative Dispute Resolution

Alternative dispute resolution (ADR) involves settling legal disputes by avoiding the often costly and time intensive process of a government judicial trial. The most common forms of ADR are: negotiation, mediation, collaborative law, and arbitration.

Negotiation: Negotiation is a dialogue entered into for the purpose of resolving disputes or producing an agreed upon course or courses of action. Negotiation is inexpensive and generally the first step in ADR. Negotiation allows for an unstructured discussion between both parties and generally does not involve anyone other than the affected parties. If an agreement is not reached, more formal methods of dispute resolution are required.

Mediation: In mediation, the parties themselves set forth the conditions of any agreement with dialogue facilitated by an independent, third party mediator. The mediator is not a judge or arbitrator who sets forth the terms of an agreement, rather a mediator is a trained professional in negotiations and the process of mediation. The goal of mediation is to find areas of agreement between the parties involved by using strategies and techniques designed to allow the parties to work towards a mutual and fair agreement. If a settlement is not reached, the dispute may go through mediation again or sent to litigation arbitration. The option to take legal disputes to mediation is desirable from a cost perspective because it is generally less expensive and allows for a quicker resolution than going to trial.

Collaborative Law: Collaborative law is a facilitative process wherein all parties agree at the onset to work to identify a solution that is beneficial to all parties involved. In collaborative law, the parties use their advocates, most often their lawyers, to facilitate a mutually beneficial result through the process of negotiation. There is no neutral mediator or arbitrator involved and the parties are expected to reach a settlement without using further methods of ADR or litigation.

Arbitration: Arbitration uses a third-party arbitrator or arbitrators to act as a judge or judges to render a decision by which all parties are legally bound. Arbitration is held in a format less formal than a trial. The arbitrator(s), unlike a mediator, is not involved in the negotiation discussion towards a settlement. Arbitrators may be attorneys or retired judges who serve individually or as a panel. They are either chosen by the parties involved in the dispute or appointed by the court according to the terms of the contract. Arbitrators with industry-specific experience (such as construction litigation experience) may be appointed to certain types of disputes. The decision or arbitral award made by the arbitrator(s) is legally binding unlike in mediation. Many times, contracts call for disputes to be resolved through arbitration over taking matters to a costly trial. Arbitration may be required by law for certain types of disputes. Nearly all states have adopted the federal Uniform Arbitration Act making arbitral awards binding by both state and federal law.

Making Substitutions

When bidding on a project, many contractors bid from their normal manufacturers and suppliers and not the manufacturer that appears on the plans. When bidding, you need to make sure you can pay for the cost of all items and products as specified. Failure to do so could cost you a lot of money.

Substitution Approval Process: The best way to ensure a specific substitution is by the "prior approval" process. A "prior approval" occurs during the bid stage only. If a particular product or item is desired other than the specified item, you must submit a request while the project is being bid. If approved, all bidders will be allowed to use that item or product in their bids. That is why the "prior approval" is done in the bidding stage. It keeps the playing field level for all competitors.

Substitutions After the Bid Process: A substitution may be made after the bid has been accepted. Nevertheless, any substitution must meet certain criteria to even be considered. The specifications should describe the conditions for such substitutions. Usually there are only four reasons that a substitution would be entertained:

✓ the specific item or product is no longer available;
✓ a cost savings;
✓ a time savings; or
✓ combination of cost and time savings.

Discontinued Products: A product no longer available is generally the only event that will not require a change order reducing cost and/or time, unless it was approved under the "prior approval" process. Do not forget to note those reductions in the substitution request. The reason a reduction of cost and/or time is required is due to the fact that it is understood that the bid was based on the specific item or product. To make a change, the result must benefit the owner; otherwise, there is no reason to make the substitution.

Substitution Specifications: If there is a basis for the substitution, the next requirement is that the item or product must be equal to that which was specified. Just as the reference of a 2 x 4 to contractors is not measured as 2" x 4", its nomenclature is referred to as "nominal." Many other products are referred to as "nominal" sizing. HVAC systems are especially that way. Just because one manufacturer references a unit as five-tons, it does not mean that it produces the same capacity as a five-ton unit from another manufacturer under the same conditions.

The specifications must be analyzed carefully before submitting the substitution request. Be sure to cover the cost of the specified item, as a substitution may not be granted, not even in the "prior approval" process.

Contract Documents and Project Manual

The project manual is a central location for bid documents, contract provisions, technical specifications, and addenda. This bound manual is a useful tool easily referenced on the jobsite. It can be reproduced and distributed to contractors, subcontractors, and suppliers. The following is a detailed summary of the documents contained in a typical project manual.

Bid Documents:

✓ Invitation to bid
✓ Bid instructions
✓ Bid forms
✓ Supplements
✓ Addenda

Contract Provisions:

✓ Form of agreement
✓ General conditions or obligation of parties
✓ Supplemental conditions
✓ Change orders
✓ Index of drawings

Supplemental Forms:

✓ Required bonds
✓ Certificate of insurance

Technical Specifications are generally organized by a classification system, such as the CSI MasterFormat.

The **construction drawings** are also part of the contract documents. For larger projects, the drawings are divided by design discipline and trades. Drawings may include but are not limited to:

✓ architectural,
✓ structural,
✓ plumbing,
✓ electrical,
✓ mechanical,
✓ landscape, and
✓ civil.

The drawings are kept separate but can be indexed in the project manual.

Are Oral Agreements Legally Binding?

Under most circumstances, oral agreements are just as binding as written agreements with a few exceptions. Exceptions include contracts which have a high risk of fraud such as the sale or purchase of land. Oral agreements present a challenge because it is difficult to prove what terms were agreed upon if a dispute arises. Needless to say, it is a risky way to do business and it is best to get everything in writing.

Sometimes parties enter into agreements that are partially oral and partially written. For example, you may have carefully put together a written contract to do work. The customer then verbally gives you a change order. Now you are in a situation where you have an oral agreement for the change. To protect yourself, it is best to follow up with a written change order. In a legal judgment, written agreements always take precedence over oral agreements.

Oral agreements are not a good way to do business. Get it in writing!

Legal Interpretation

Clarity of language and meaning is one of the most important aspects of interpreting contracts and avoiding disputes. It is strongly recommended that you use an attorney when drafting contracts to ensure that the contract will stand up in a dispute. There are also necessary provisions that should be included in a contract. A contract lawyer can advise you on this matter.

The use of plain language is important when establishing intent in a contract. If a dispute arises, the contract will be interpreted using the plain meaning of the words in the contract. If your contract goes to litigation, the judge may not have a background in the construction industry. This is why it is important to clearly state the terms in the contract using plain language.

Technical terminology in contracts between parties who understand their technical meaning may be used. However, many customers may not understand technical jargon so you may want to use caution putting these terms in a contract. Rather, you should express your intentions in layman terms. Disputes may arise when parties do not understand undefined technical language and contract interpretation may not end up in your favor.

If the provision being disputed is vague, the actions of the parties will be examined first. If the parties conducted themselves consistently with what they thought the provision meant at that time, the provision would likely take that meaning. If the contract cannot be clarified based on this method, the interpretation will go against the party who wrote it.

Subcontracting

Subcontractors contract with the general contractor or other subcontractors to complete a portion of a larger project. The same principles that apply to owner/contractor contracts also apply to subcontracts.

Subcontracts should include similar content as owner/contractor contracts, such as

- ✓ Date
- ✓ Names and contact information of contracting parties
- ✓ Name and location of project
- ✓ Description of the work to be performed
- ✓ Subcontract time or start and completion date
- ✓ Payment terms, including progress payment schedule and final payment
- ✓ Conditions for schedule delays
- ✓ Drawings and specifications
- ✓ Contract sum
- ✓ Any general and supplemental conditions that apply
- ✓ Signatures from both parties

Depending on the stipulations in the owner/contractor agreement, the owner may need to approve subcontractors.

It is also important to get subcontracts in writing to avoid disputes. In providing a written contract, both parties have a clear understanding of the agreement. Oral contracts can lead to ambiguity and one party may interpret the agreement differently than the other.

Clarity is very important to an enforceable contract.

Final Inspection...

Required Contract Elements: Required contract elements include offer and acceptance, consideration, competent parties, and legal purpose.

Contract Provisions: Your contract should contain provisions that clearly outline the terms of the contract. A few key provisions you want to include are contract price and payment terms, obligation of the parties, and breach of contract.

Breach of Contract: A breach of contract occurs when one of the parties involved fails to perform in accordance with any of the terms and conditions of the contract.

Boilerplate Provisions: These provisions contain standard language designed to protect you in the event of a lawsuit.

Provisions to Limit Risk: These provisions limit the liability of the contracting parties by addressing allocation of risk.

What Are Recitals? This language appears at the beginning of the contract and is intended to give background information.

Types of Construction Contracts: Different types of contracts address who is responsible for cost savings and overruns for estimated work.

Contracting Methods: Depending on the level of involvement in a construction project, different types of contracting methods are used.

Sources of Contracts: Contracts are available through several different sources, including associations such as the American Institute of Architects (AIA) or the Associated General Contractors (AGC).

Making Changes to the Contract: To change the contract, a change order is written and agreed to by the owner and contractor.

Resolving Claims: The claims resolution process provides a way for the owner and contractor to resolve disputes about additional amounts owed as a result of contract changes.

Alternative Dispute Resolution (ADR): This process involves settling legal disputes by avoiding the process of a government judicial trial. The most common forms of ADR are: negotiation, mediation, collaborative law, and arbitration.

Making Substitutions: Specifications must be analyzed carefully before submitting the substitution request. Substitutions may be granted if products are discontinued or to provide a cost or time savings.

Contract Documents and Project Manual: The project manual is a central location for bid documents, contract provisions, technical specifications, and addenda.

Are Oral Agreements Legally Binding? Oral agreements can be binding, but it makes good business sense to get a contract in writing.

Legal Interpretation: Clarity of language and meaning in contracts is important to avoid disputes and ensure proper legal interpretation in the event of a lawsuit.

Subcontracting: The same principles that apply to owner/contractor contracts also apply to subcontracts. Similar language is used to ensure that each party is clear on terms and conditions of the contract.

Chapter 10
SCHEDULING AND PROJECT MANAGEMENT

Many landscape construction jobs are performed every day without using a formal scheduling method. Knowing how to schedule and organize tasks helps you complete projects on time, which increases customer satisfaction and ultimately your competitive edge.

Using the quantity take-off method, as explained in Chapter 8, you developed the basis for your project schedule. Each task was assigned the number of labor hours for completion to determine labor cost. Scheduling takes the list of tasks and labor hours and assigns an order of completion.

Scheduling Process

Planning is a key element to formulating an accurate schedule and effectively managing the project. Planning allows you to visualize the project and anticipate potential conflicts and challenges. The project start and completion dates are outlined in the contract. It is the job of the scheduler to fit in all necessary tasks within this time frame in the most efficient manner.

Sequence of Tasks: Understanding the correct sequence of tasks is critical to completing your project on time. As you created your estimate (discussed in Chapter 8), you probably listed your tasks in the order of completion. This determination is particularly important when scheduling subcontractors. Be sure to review the tasks outlined in the estimate and make any necessary corrections to the sequence of tasks.

Some tasks may be completed at the same time while other tasks must come before starting the next task. For example, interior and exterior paint may be applied at the same time but drywall must be completed before paint is applied.

Activity Duration: When creating your estimate, you determined the number of labor hours it takes to complete each task on the project. Using this estimate, you need to determine the duration of the task. The duration of each task depends on a few factors:

✓ size of the project;

✓ labor hours estimated; and

✓ length of time dedicated to the task each day. For example, if a task is estimated at four hours but your crew only has two hours per day to work on the task, the activity duration is two working days.

When determining activity duration, it is important to get input from your subcontractors and the experienced members of your crew.

Once the duration is determined for each activity, you can compare the total time against the project completion time outlined in the contract. If the total time exceeds the project completion time, adjustments must be made. Consideration must be given to increasing labor resources, requiring overtime, or extending the project completion date. These options must be weighed carefully due to added costs and possible timeline conflicts with the owner.

Contingency Time: Contingency time is used as a buffer between tasks to protect against unforeseen task delays. To determine contingency time, the task is analyzed to determine the likelihood of a delay occurring. A few general rules apply to determining contingency time.

✓ Tasks subject to weather delays require more contingency time.

✓ Standard work requires less contingency time than custom work.

✓ Tasks performed in areas with limited access require more contingency time.

With contingency time in place, the likelihood of a delayed task impacting the entire schedule is reduced.

Task Time Ranges: After completing the sequence of tasks, activity duration, and contingency time, the earliest and latest start date and earliest and latest end date are calculated. If the task completion falls outside these dates during the construction process, the project manager has an accurate calculation of the amount of time the project is ahead or behind.

Float Time: Float time is the remaining time after a task is complete and before the next task begins.

✓ The amount of time an activity can be delayed without impacting the early start of the next activity is called free float time.

✓ Total float time refers to the amount of leeway allowed in starting or completing an activity without delaying the project completion date.

✓ Activities with "zero float" are considered critical activities.

Scheduling Methods

A schedule is your blueprint to finishing the project on time. There are three main types of scheduling methods used in the construction industry:

✓ Calendar Scheduling

✓ Bar Chart Scheduling

✓ Critical Path Method

The type of schedule you use depends on factors such as project size, complexity, and location.

Calendar Scheduling

Calendar scheduling is a simple method and can be done on a regular desk calendar. The primary advantage to this method is that you can link project tasks to specific dates, such as

✓ dates of other projects,

✓ delivery dates of materials,

✓ payment schedules, and

✓ employee vacations and holidays.

To create a calendar schedule, you need to know the sequence of tasks and activity duration. After these factors are determined, you can plug the activities into the calendar.

The following is a sample calendar schedule. Calendar scheduling works for smaller, less complex projects but is not recommended for large ones.

Calendar Schedule

Project _____   Start _____   Finish _____

Sunday	Monday	Tuesday	Wednesday	Thursday	Friday	Saturday
1	2	3	4	5	6	7
	Pre const meeting	Erosion Control	Erosion Control	Erosion Control	Erosion Control	OFF
8	9	10	11	12	13	14
OFF	Rough Grading	Rough Grading	Drainage	Drainage	Drainage Ret. Walls	OFF
15	16	17	18	19	Erosion	21
OFF	Retaining Walls	Retaining Walls	Retaining Walls	Terrace Paving	Terrace Paving	OFF
22	23	24	25	26	27	28
OFF	Sidewalk Paving	Fine Grading	Irrigation Lighting	Irrigation Lighting	Planting	OFF
29	31	31				
OFF	Planting	Planting				
			APRIL			
			1	2	3	4
OFF			Set heads Set fixtures	Sod	Remove EC Cleanup	Owner Site Review

Bar Chart Scheduling

Similar to the calendar scheduling method, the bar chart schedule shows the activity duration and sequence of tasks to be completed. It is an easy-to-read visual showing a graphical depiction of the schedule in its entirety.

One of the main weaknesses of the bar chart and calendar scheduling methods is that they do not show the interdependencies of activities.

For example, if there is a delay in a task, the bar chart does not show the impact it has on other tasks. The following is a sample bar chart schedule.

Schedule Bar Chart

Description of Tasks	MARCH				APRIL				MAY			
	W1	W2	W3	W4	W1	W2	W3	W4	W1	W2	W3	W4
Contract Award	■											
Field Survey		■										
Permits		■										
Pre Construction Meeting			■									
Order Plant Material			■									
Erosion Control				■								
Demolition					■							
Rough Grading						■						
Drainage						■						
Retaining Walls							■					
Terrace Paving								■				
Sidewalk Paving								■				
Fine Grade									■			
Irrigation Rough In									■			
Soil Preparation										■		
Plant Material Delivery										■		
Planting/Mulching											■	
Lighting											■	
Set Irrigation Heads/Drip											■	
Sod											■	
Cleanup/Remove Er. Control												■
Site Review with Owner												■
Project Closeout												■

Critical Path Method

The critical path method (CPM) of scheduling illustrates the interdependent relationship of tasks. To develop a CPM schedule, you start by determining the sequence of tasks and activity duration as you would with bar chart or calendar scheduling. In addition, you need to outline the following:

✓ Relationship between tasks

✓ Simultaneous events

✓ Critical path

Relationship Between Tasks: Most construction tasks are interrelated. For example, you can't start framing until you pour the foundation. A CPM schedule graphically shows which tasks are related and which ones are not. When you create your CPM schedule, you need to determine how each task impacts another.

Simultaneous Events: If you know which tasks can be performed simultaneously, you can shorten project completion time. When creating the CPM schedule, you must show when simultaneous tasks are possible.

Critical Path: The critical path is the sequence of tasks that determines the duration of the project. If a task on the critical path is delayed by one week, the project is delayed by one week. You must know which subsequent tasks cannot begin until a critical path item is completed.

The following diagram illustrates a simple critical path example.

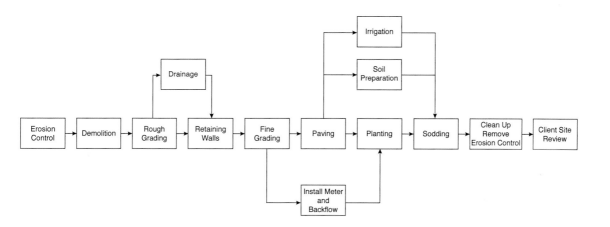

Adding Activity Duration to the CPM Schedule: The CPM schedule can be placed against a timeline. An example of this is illustrated in the bar chart schedule earlier in the chapter. Another alternative is to place the activity duration with each task. You can also put a code with the activity to correlate it to your estimate. If you use your estimating format, you could use the CSI MasterFormat to code the tasks in your schedule. For example, let's say the task of painting the interior has a three-day duration and you use MasterFormat code 09900. Your task might look like this on the CPM chart.

Paint Interior	
09900	3

Many different types of software are available to help you create schedules. You want to choose a program that is right for your needs whether it is simple or more complex. Some programs allow you to adjust the timelines if, for example, you experience a delay in the project. Scheduling software also facilitates the tracking function of a project schedule, which is a key project management tool.

Scheduling and Cash Management

It is important to track incoming cash and expenditures during the landscape construction project to ensure you have enough working capital to complete the job. "Working capital" refers to the amount of cash available after the liabilities or debts are paid. Balancing incoming progress payments and outgoing expenditures is important to manage the project effectively and should be a consideration when preparing your schedule.

If you have more expenditures than incoming cash in any stage of construction, you may not have enough money to proceed to the next stage of construction or pay your debts.

A preliminary cash flow budget, outlining stages of construction with anticipated revenues and expenditures, should be completed during the scheduling phase to anticipate any cash shortages. Cash flow should be tracked through the duration of the project.

What is Project Management?

Effective project management is a challenging task on a landscape construction project. It requires a carefully balanced combination of management skills with an understanding of the design and construction process. Project managers may manage several projects at the same time with projects at different stages of the process. A project manager not only has to manage time through the scheduling process but must also consider many other factors:

✓ Budget constraints
✓ Quality standards
✓ Project plans and specifications
✓ Resource management such as labor, materials, etc.

Project management has applications that are unique in nearly every industry, including landscape construction.

The ability to effectively manage significantly contributes to the success or failure of the project.

Who is the Project Manager?

Construction project managers plan and coordinate construction projects to meet the overall goals of the project and serve as the main contact with the owner. Responsibilities generally include but are not limited to

✓ preparing budgets;
✓ reviewing shop drawings to determine appropriate construction methods;
✓ determining labor requirements and preparing schedules;
✓ monitoring overall progress of the project and preparing job records;
✓ monitoring compliance with building and safety codes;
✓ ensuring proper handling of change orders; and
✓ regularly meeting with owners, trade contractors, architects, and other design professionals on project progress.

Construction project managers work closely with the project superintendent who manages daily site operations.

Construction managers may be owners or salaried employees of a construction management or contracting firm, or they may work under contract or as a salaried employee of the owner, developer, contractor, or management firm overseeing the construction project. They may plan and direct a whole project or just a part of a larger project.

What Qualities Does a Good Manager Need?

A good manager must possess several qualities to effectively lead a team.

✓ Good communication skills
✓ Honesty and integrity
✓ Positive attitude
✓ Effective delegation skills
✓ Team and morale building skills

Project Supervisory Team

While the project manager has a high level understanding of the project, supervisors coordinate and monitor the daily aspects of the project. Depending on the size of the project, the number of supervisory team members may vary.

Superintendent: The superintendent is the onsite supervisor responsible for daily operations. Depending on the size of the project and amount of responsibility the project manager wants to delegate, the superintendent's duties may include

✓ coordinating project activities and serving as a liaison with subcontractors, architects, utilities, and others;
✓ participating in project construction development and planning;
✓ processing utility requests for construction projects;
✓ representing the company regarding onsite construction quality control reviews;
✓ making recommendations and processing change order requests;
✓ reviewing punch lists;
✓ assuring construction specifications are met;
✓ tracking deviations from project schedules and costs; and
✓ maintaining project records and reports.

Communication between the project manager and superintendent is important to keeping the project on-time and within budget and providing a quality product.

Foreman: The foreman assists the superintendent with daily project operations. The superintendent generally oversees all of the daily operations, but the foreman usually supervises specific areas by trade. For example, a carpentry foreman may supervise rough and finish carpentry while the masonry foreman supervises formwork and concrete installation.

The foreman assists the supervisor by

✓ reviewing project plans and blueprints;
✓ providing input on estimated time, material, equipment and supplies needed;
✓ developing schedules and crew assignments;
✓ inspecting work areas;
✓ evaluating employee and subcontractor performance;
✓ completing time sheets, accident reports, and work orders; and
✓ training employees.

Materials Expediter: Timely delivery of materials is important to keeping a project schedule on track.

A materials expediter supervises the materials procurement process to ensure accurate and timely delivery of materials.

Later in the chapter, we will discuss the importance of effective materials management.

Architect and Owner's Representative: The owner will sometimes defer to an appointed representative to oversee a project. In this case, the owner's representative and/or architect will deal with the project manager. The owner's representative and architect usually do not have supervisory authority over the employees and subcontractors but they may communicate with the project manager in order to express any concerns with the project work.

In general, the owner's representative and architect have access to the jobsite and work records and can contribute to quality control on the project. The architect (or sometimes the engineer) must certify each progress payment, so it is in the best interest of the project manager to work closely with the architect and owner's representative.

Project Life Cycle

Each project has a start point, project life cycle, and end point. Through each phase of the project life cycle, you must manage each aspect of the project such as customer relations, materials, budget, and subcontractors. Using the customer relations category as an example, the following illustrates various management aspects in the project life cycle.

Contract Award

After you are successfully offered the job, you should get a contract signed as soon as possible. A few weeks before the job starts, schedule a pre-construction meeting with your customer and any other relevant parties (i.e., architect, subcontractors, etc.).

Pre-Construction Phase

During the pre-construction meeting, you should go over customer expectations. Chapter 11 discusses creating realistic expectations for your customer to avoid disappointment. At this time, you should have a preliminary schedule prepared, so potential scheduling conflicts can be discussed. Be sure to follow up with written meeting notes and distribute to those in attendance as well as those who could not attend.

Construction Phase

As the project progresses, you should carefully monitor the budget, schedule, and project quality. Regularly meet with your customer to discuss the progress of the project and any issues or questions that arise. If you are billing in progress payments, make sure you are invoicing regularly and collecting payments within the defined terms.

Job Completion and Closeout

After the job is complete, you must do a walkthrough and develop a punch list of follow-up items. Discuss any warranties contained in your contract and how the customer can request warranty repairs. Send a customer satisfaction survey to gather feedback for future improvements.

> *Key Elements for a Successful Project Outcome*
>
> Many elements go into a successful project outcome:
>
> ✓ Project manager who understands the total project as a big picture
>
> ✓ Early preparation and planning
>
> ✓ Good management and front-line supervision
>
> ✓ Effective responses to problems and changes
>
> ✓ Active customer involvement
>
> ✓ Good communication skills

Tracking the Progress of the Project

Daily Reports

Many contractors find that keeping a daily log is a useful project tool. You can use a log to track the progress of a project and as legal backup in case any disputes arise.

The daily log can list:

✓ Project name and location

✓ Date

✓ Weather conditions

✓ Personnel on the job

✓ Description of work

✓ Hours worked on each task

✓ Change orders

✓ Progress of the job

✓ Other relevant information

Personal comments should not be made in the daily report. It should contain only factual information.

There are specific guidelines you should follow to increase the credibility of the daily report, if a legal dispute arises.

✓ The report should be completed daily. If there was no work completed, note that fact and the reason for it.

✓ Writing should be in ink and not altered.

✓ Pages should be in consecutive order and in a bound book.

Photos are a good way to document the progress of a project and can serve as a supplement to the daily log. Photos should be taken of the site prior to starting work and at critical points during the project to document any problem areas. Digital cameras make photo-taking easy with instant results. You also have the flexibility to store photos on your computer and send them through e-mail.

Status Reports

Status reports summarize project highlights, addressing items completed, in progress, and outstanding. This report is a helpful tool to communicate with the customer, managers, subcontractors, and suppliers periodically throughout the project.

To support your status reports, you should have work records easily accessible for review. These work records include

✓ daily reports,
✓ project photographs,
✓ previous status reports,
✓ safety and accident reports,
✓ change orders,
✓ shop drawings,
✓ purchase orders,
✓ receiving documentation, and
✓ relevant written correspondence.

You should solicit feedback on any anticipated problems or concerns and encourage two-way communication throughout the project. Status reports are a good way to initiate this communication.

Tracking the Schedule

A good project manager makes sure that deadlines are met on time. As discussed earlier, the first step is to develop the schedule. Next, you want to make sure you communicate the schedule to anyone who is impacted by it, such as your crew, subcontractors, and suppliers. You need to make sure they understand the deadlines and their assignments. You may want to present the schedule in a graphical format so team members can get a visual snapshot of the timeline.

Budget and Cost Controls

Project management involves working with budget constraints. A good project manager will control costs and make sure that the project comes in on budget.

If the budget is not monitored carefully, a job that was estimated correctly can turn into a loss for the company.

Materials

Just-In-Time (JIT): Just-in-time deliveries will keep your inventory cost low. This process allows you to time deliveries to arrive as you need the materials in the construction process. Using your schedule, you can closely predict when you need materials according to the work being completed and then coordinate timing with your suppliers. Less inventory onsite will also cut down on the risk of theft or vandalism.

Purchase Orders: Using a purchase order system can help you organize and document your materials purchases. If you prepare your purchase orders in advance, you can review these with your customers. This process can potentially reduce change orders by allowing customers to make decisions and sign off on them in advance. Your purchase orders can also serve as delivery date documentation so you can organize just-in-time deliveries.

Receiving: You can control material costs through proper receiving. When materials are delivered, someone should check the materials against the purchase order to confirm the correct quantity and items ordered were received. If there are discrepancies, follow up with the supplier as soon as possible to ensure you receive the proper credits or replacements.

To the best of your ability, you want to estimate and order the correct amount of materials. If you have excess materials, check with your supplier for a return policy. Excess materials should be stored correctly to preserve their condition. Some suppliers charge a restocking fee, but it is generally nominal and worth your time to receive a materials credit.

Budget Tracking

The easiest way to track your budget is to use the cost estimate and a job cost system to determine if you have any cost overruns.

Cost overruns occur when you exceed budgeted amounts in your estimate. These overruns can happen in many areas of the project such as exceeding the amount of labor through improper scheduling and excessive materials waste. Chapters 7 and 9 summarize types of contracts that address who is responsible for cost overruns.

It is important to track costs as the project progresses because cost overruns can indicate a possible problem. The sooner these problems are identified, the easier it will be to take corrective action.

Cost overruns may occur because you have a bad estimate. Tracking your budget will help you or your estimator prepare more accurate estimates in the future.

Cost overruns reduce the amount of profit you make on the job. If you are not making a profit or you are losing money on your projects, you will eventually go out of business.

Quality Assurance

Ensuring the customer receives a quality built product is one of the most important aspects of project management. You may find ways to cut corners, but neglecting quality can cost you in the long run. You may also run into ethical considerations when neglecting quality. Concealing defective work and design flaws can leave you open to a lawsuit and ruin your reputation.

Accurate and Detailed Specifications and Plans

Accurate and detailed specifications and plans are important to setting the quality standards of the project. These items will help you put together a more accurate estimate and should be part of the contract documents. If details are vague, your decisions on material quality and construction methods may differ from the owner's. This misunderstanding can cause conflict and disappoint your customer. It is best to set expectations and obtain agreement from the customer early in the project.

Detailed Shop Drawings

In addition to specifications and plans, shop drawings are often required to detail specific aspects of a project. Shop drawings outline specific details, materials, dimensions, and installation for specific items. Product data and samples may accompany shop drawings to provide additional information. Shop drawings are produced by the material supplier, contractor, subcontractor, or manufacturer. As part of the quality control process, the architect and contractor must review and approve shop drawings.

Quality Assurance Program

Setting up a quality assurance program is a good way to let your employees and customers know the importance of producing a high quality product. Internal inspections should take place at different stages of the construction process to review the completed work and confirm that it meets your quality standards.

Your company philosophy should stress quality. You want your employees to take pride in their work. As an employer, you can create a positive work atmosphere and provide the tools employees need to be successful. Providing ongoing training for employees so they can expand their knowledge base helps improve the quality of their work. Employees should know the standards they are expected to follow. Documenting work standards and conducting regular performance reviews are good ways to create a mutual understanding of the level of quality you expect.

Customer Satisfaction Surveys

Customer satisfaction surveys are also a good tool to receive feedback about the quality of your work. Customer surveys are good for asking about the professionalism of your employees, quality of work, and overall service. Potential customers may be interested that you have a continuous improvement program. Positive feedback from your current or former customers can serve as a good marketing tool to gain new business.

Value Engineering

Value engineering is a project management approach. The objective is to understand the owner's cost, quality, and time priorities to deliver a product of the highest value. Many owners will provide incentives to contractors to meet these objectives. For example, an owner may provide a bonus for a contractor who can cut costs without sacrificing quality while meeting all deadlines. If value engineering bonuses exist, it is important that they are included in the construction contract.

The Society of American Value Engineering International (SAVE) publishes a methodology for the construction industry. The purpose of this methodology is to reduce costs, improve productivity, and develop innovative ways to solve problems.

- -

Final Inspection...

Scheduling Process: During the project scheduling process, the sequence of tasks, activity duration, contingency time, task time ranges, and float time are determined.

Scheduling Methods: The three main types of scheduling are calendar scheduling, bar chart scheduling, and critical path method (CPM).

Scheduling and Cash Management: Effective cash management helps ensure you have enough working capital to complete your project.

What is Project Management? Project management involves managing several different factors including budgets, quality controls, project plans and specifications, and resource management.

Who is the Project Manager? Construction project managers plan and coordinate construction projects to meet the overall goals of the project and serve as the main contact with the owner. The ability to manage effectively contributes significantly to the success or failure of a project.

Project Supervisory Team: Depending on the size of the project, the supervisory team may consist of a superintendent, foreman, materials expediter, architect, and owner's representative.

Project Life Cycle: Through each phase of the project life cycle, you must manage each aspect of the project such as customer relations, materials, budget, and subcontractors.

Tracking the Progress of the Project: A good project manager makes sure that deadlines are met on time. Daily reports and status reports are tools you can use to track your progress.

Budget and Cost Controls: A good project manager will control costs and make sure the project comes in on budget.

Quality Assurance: Ensuring that the customer receives a quality built product is one of the most important aspects of project management.

Value Engineering: Balancing the owner's cost, quality, and time priorities while delivering the highest value product are objectives of the value engineering approach.

Chapter 11
CUSTOMER RELATIONS

Chapter Survey...

⇨ *Communication with Customers*

⇨ *Handling Customer Change Orders*

⇨ *Negotiation Basics*

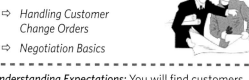

Understanding Expectations: You will find customers have specific expectations of the outcome of your work. If those expectations are not satisfied, your customers will be disappointed, which will reflect poorly on your company. Instead of promising your customers an unrealistic outcome, it is easier to be honest and bring expectations to a realistic level. If customers have a realistic picture of the project, you can avoid disappointing them. The best way to accomplish this is through consistent and effective communication with your customers.

Communication with Customers

It is important for customers to understand the status of their project and have all the information needed to make informed decisions. This communication will not only keep the customer's expectations realistic but also build a trusting relationship with you and your company.

Communication Opportunities: You have several opportunities to communicate with your customers and keep their expectations at a realistic level, including

✓ contract negotiations,

✓ contract acceptance,

✓ weekly meetings,

✓ punch list and final walkthrough, and

✓ post-job follow-up.

Establishing communication at these times will ensure that your customer is aware of your progress and of issues that arise during any step of the process.

Communication Basics: Now that we have established when to communicate with customers, let's go over a few basics on how to communicate.

✓ Understand that your customer may not have the same level of technical knowledge as you. Avoid using technical terminology and clarify when necessary.

✓ Give your customer a chance to ask questions and express any concerns. Use active listening skills, and remember that all questions are important to the customer.

✓ When dealing with difficult customers, always remain professional.

✓ Use e-mail or written communication as a follow-up to verbal conversations to document key items discussed and any changes agreed to.

✓ Don't forget the personal touch. E-mail and fax are great tools, but schedule time to talk to the customer in person.

✓ Return phone calls promptly.

Good communication can build customer trust and help you understand customer expectations.

Handling Customer Change Orders

Proper handling of customer change orders is very important. This is a critical point in the customer-contractor relationship that can result in a positive or negative outcome. If you do not follow through with the change order as the customer expects, it will result in disappointment and mistrust. If you follow through to the customer's specifications, you will reinforce that you are responsive and understand the importance of customer service.

You should always apply a few general rules when change orders arise:

- ✓ Always obtain a signed change order for significant amounts of change work.
- ✓ Small changes done with verbal approval should be followed up with a written and signed change order.
- ✓ Invoice for change order work promptly.
- ✓ Include any complementary work done without charge on the invoice.
- ✓ Show labor and quantity details when pricing change orders as you would when creating your initial estimate.

Negotiation Basics

Good negotiation skills can benefit you personally and in all areas of your business. When a successful negotiation occurs, both parties are satisfied with the outcome.

Preparing to Negotiate: Negotiation is a process and it is important to prepare ahead of time to get the most out of the negotiation. Considering these questions will help:

- ✓ What are you negotiating (i.e., money, time, conditions, etc.)?
- ✓ What is the ideal outcome?
- ✓ How much are you willing to compromise?
- ✓ What is the other person trying to achieve?

A negotiation may not always involve price. Consider what is valuable to your business. For example, if time is a critical factor to completing your current projects, you may want to negotiate on project timelines. It is important not to compromise your reputation in a negotiation. You don't want to lose your best customer or future referrals.

Confident Negotiations: Now that you are prepared, you can come to the negotiation confident in knowing what you want. Aim high in your negotiation and you will get more. If you ask for more than you want, people will tend to meet you in the middle. It is important to be flexible during the negotiation. Even though you have prepared ahead of time, the other party may change the direction of the negotiation to different terms. For example, you may have prepared to negotiate on price, but your counterpart may want to deal on the timeline of the work.

When possible, it is important to get the final outcome of your negotiation in writing. Once it is in writing, both parties can sign off on what they agreed to, which will help avoid any disappointment or confusion.

- -

Final Inspection...

Communication with Customers: Good communication helps you build trust and understand customer expectations.

Handling Customer Change Orders: Change orders should be handled carefully and accurately documented.

Negotiation Basics: Come to a negotiation prepared, and, when possible, make sure you get any agreement in writing.

Chapter 12
EMPLOYEE MANAGEMENT

Chapter Survey...

Finding good, hardworking employees can sometimes mean the difference between success and failure in business. It is easier to delegate to good employees and produce high-quality work from employees who care about their job. Poor employees can cost a company wasted time and ultimately money. The first step to finding good employees is taking the extra time to hire the right people for the job.

Employees should start off with a few fundamental qualities. They should be

✓ qualified for the position;

✓ motivated to do the job and show initiative;

✓ responsible for their work and actions;

✓ dependable to show up on time and keep work commitments; and

✓ open to learning new skills.

These basic qualities will result in an employee who is capable of performing their present job responsibilities and taking on more tasks in the future.

Interviewing and Hiring Employees

Asking Questions: Asking the right interview questions is key to finding the right employee. The wrong interview questions can get you into trouble. You must convey that you are a fair and non-discriminatory employer. If you ask questions implying otherwise, you will open yourself to a lawsuit. Some questions could lead to legal action and are strictly off-limits, especially the following:

✓ How old are you?

✓ Do you have any disabilities?

✓ Are you pregnant?

✓ Are you married?

✓ Do you have children?

✓ What is your religious affiliation?

✓ What is your sexual orientation?

✓ What ethnic background are you?

Now that you know what questions not to ask, here are some areas to cover during the job interview that will be helpful in determining if an employee is the right fit for your company.

Questions should be asked to elicit information about the candidate's

✓ ability to work with other members of a construction team;

✓ ability to handle conflict;

✓ expectations of the job (e.g. salary, benefits, working hours, etc.);

✓ past work history and reasons for leaving previous jobs;

✓ level of skill or expertise;

✓ training and education;

✓ safety record;

✓ ability to solve problems;

✓ knowledge of your company; and

✓ questions about the job.

Appendix C contains links to websites that provide sample job interview questions for the construction industry that you can customize for your business.

Hiring the right people for the job is the first step to finding good employees.

New Hire Reporting

Reporting Requirements: You are required to report all new employees to the North Carolina New Hire Reporting Program no later than 20 days from the date of hire, rehire or recall. Employers who submit reports magnetically or electronically must submit the reports in two monthly transmissions not more than sixteen days apart.

You can use one of several reporting methods.

✓ *Internet:* Use the online data entry form or secure file upload at www.ncnewhires.com.

✓ *Electronic New Hire Reports:* Format new hire information to specifications outlined by the North Carolina New Hire Reporting Program. You can submit this form electronically through the new hire website or via file transfer protocol (FTP).

✓ *New Hire Data Entry Software:* Download the new hire software from the website. Using the software, you can complete the employee information and send it electronically.

✓ *Diskette or CD-R:* Download the new hire information onto a diskette or CD-R and mail it to

North Carolina State Directory of New Hires
P.O. Box 90369
East Point, Georgia 30364-0369

Telephone: (888) 514-4568

✓ *Mail:* Mail W-4 forms, state reporting forms, or other approved paper report to the above address.

✓ *Fax:* Fax W-4 forms, state reporting forms, or other approved paper report to (866) 257-7005.

✓ *Payroll Service:* If you use a payroll service, inquire if it can report new hires for you.

Failure to comply with the New Hire Law could result in a $25 fine per incident for failure to report or, if conspiracy to avoid reporting is determined, a fine of up to $500.

Required Information: The following data must be included for each new hire:

✓ Employer name (use corporate name)

✓ Employer mailing address

✓ Employer federal identification number (If you have more than one FEIN, use the same FEIN you use to report your quarterly wage information when reporting new hires.)

✓ Employer state identification number (This is the state employer number used on the NCUI101 Employer Quarterly Tax and Wage Report.)

✓ Employee name

✓ Employee address

✓ Employee social security number

✓ Employee date of birth (if available)

✓ Employee date of hire (if available)

Purpose of New Hire Reporting: The purpose of new hire reporting is to aid in child support enforcement. The National Directory of New Hires compiles new hire information from all states to track child support obligations on a national basis. It is also a good tool in preventing fraudulent unemployment and welfare benefit payments.

Hiring Minors for Landscape Construction Work

The State of North Carolina and the U.S. Department of Labor have strict rules for the hiring of minors. State law requires employers to obtain an employment certificate for minors under the age of 18. The purpose of the employment certificate is to provide conclusive evidence of the minor's age and educational standing. In addition, it confirms that the minor is not employed in a prohibited profession or during prohibited hours.

Working Hours:

✓ When school is in session, a minor 14 or 15 years of age may not begin work before 7 a.m., work later than 7 p.m. (9 p.m. between June 1 and Labor Day), or more than three hours a day, or more than 18 hours a week. Work is prohibited during school hours.

✓ A minor 14 or 15 years of age may not begin work before 7 a.m., work past 7 p.m. (9 p.m. between June 1 and Labor Day), or more than eight hours a day, or more than 40 hours a week when school is not in session.

✓ Federal restrictions on working hours or number of hours do not exist for minors 16 or 17 years of age.

Prohibited Tasks: Minors ages 14 or 15 years of age may work in office, clerical, and sales jobs. They are prohibited from performing certain job tasks, including the use of scaffolding, operation, cleaning, or adjusting of any power-driven machinery with the exception of office machines, construction, and manufacturing, mechanical, and processing occupations including workrooms, workplaces, or storage areas where goods are manufactured or processed.

All minors are prohibited from employment in occupations considered hazardous. Specific tasks outlined as hazardous or detrimental that apply to the construction industry (with the exception of apprentices as defined by law) include but are not limited to

✓ operating power-driven woodworking machines or power-driven circular saws, band saws, or guillotine shears;

✓ operating elevators or any other power-driven hoisting apparatus;

✓ operating power-driven metal-forming punching and shearing machines;

✓ driving any motor vehicle and being an outside helper;

✓ exposure to radioactive substances and to ionizing radiations;

✓ manufacturing brick, tile, and related products;

✓ roofing operations; and

✓ excavation operations.

Investigations: Federal investigators may conduct investigations at any time, tour the business establishment or worksite, review employment records, and interview employees.

Penalties: Employers that violate child labor laws are subject to a civil penalty of up to $11,000 per worker for each violation. If the violation causes death or

serious injury, employers are subject to a civil penalty of up to $50,000 per worker for each violation. If willful or repeated violations result in death or serious injury, the penalty may be doubled totaling up to $100,000 per worker for each violation. Violators are also subject to a criminal fine of up to $10,000 upon conviction for a willful violation. For a second conviction of a willful violation, violators are subject to a fine of not more than $10,000 and imprisonment for up to six months, or both.

Further Information: For further information on Youth Labor Laws, contact:

> *U.S. Department of Labor*
> *Frances Perkins Building*
> *200 Constitution Avenue N.W.*
> *Washington, D.C. 20210*
>
> *Phone: 1-866-4-USA-DOL (1-866-487-2365)*
> *TTY: 1-877-889-5627*
>
> *Website: www.dol.gov*

Employee Documentation

Once you hire an employee, you should make sure you set up an employee file.

These items should be included in your employee files:

✓ Form I-9: The United States Customs and Immigration Service requires this form. It shows that the worker has legal immigration status in the United States. (For more information on I-9s, see the following section on the Immigration and Nationality Act.)

✓ IRS Form W-4: This form is required to determine the appropriate level of federal tax withholding. Employees can change the amount of federal tax withholding at anytime by completing a new W-4 form.

✓ IRS Form W-5: To receive earned income credit (EIC) in advance, employees can complete a W-5 form. Advance EIC is a special tax benefit for working people who earn low or moderate incomes. If the employee wants to continue to receive advance EIC, he or she must complete a new W-5 form each year.

✓ State Tax Form: This form is required to determine the appropriate level of state tax withholding, if applicable. Employees must complete the NC-4

Employee's Withholding Allowance Certificate to designate the amount of state tax withholding.

✓ Employment Application: All employees should complete an application before being hired. It should contain basic information such as the employee's name, address, and phone number. The application should also be signed, giving your company authorization to check references on the employment history section.

✓ Policy Signoffs: If you have written policies or an employee handbook, have your employees sign a receipt that the employee has received and reviewed it.

✓ Emergency Notification Form: It is important that you know who to contact in the event of an emergency. Make sure to update this information periodically.

The employee file should be maintained throughout employment and other relevant documentation can be added, such as disciplinary action forms or insurance enrollment forms.

* *

Setting up employee files will help keep you organized.

* *

Key Employment Laws

There are several key laws governing equal employment opportunities and prohibiting discrimination in employment. It is important to understand and abide by these laws, not only to protect your company from a lawsuit but also to safeguard your reputation as a good employer.

Fair Labor Standards Act (FLSA)

The Fair Labor Standards Act, which prescribes standards for the basic minimum wage and overtime pay, affects most private and public employment. It applies to employers who have one or more employees. Individual states may also have additional minimum wage requirements.

✓ Effective July 24, 2009, federal minimum wage increased to $7.25 per hour. Many states have individual minimum wage laws. If the state minimum wage rate differs from the federal rate, the employer must pay the higher of the two

rates. Minors under 20 years of age may be paid a minimum wage of not less than $4.25 per hour during the first 90 consecutive calendar days of employment. Employers may not displace any employee to hire someone at the youth minimum wage.

✓ Employers must pay overtime compensation of one-and-one-half-times the regular rate after 40 hours of work in a workweek.

✓ Wages must be paid on the regular payday for the pay period covered.

✓ The act restricts the hours that children under age 16 can work and forbids the employment of children under age 18 in certain jobs deemed too dangerous.

FLSA is administered by the Employment Standards Administration's Wage and Hour Division within the U.S. Department of Labor.

Determining Exemption Status: Some employees are exempt from the overtime pay provisions or both the minimum wage and overtime pay provisions as defined under the Fair Labor Standards Act (FLSA). This rule would apply to the following examples of employees who might be employed in the construction industry:

✓ Executives

✓ Administrative personnel

✓ Professional employees

✓ Outside sales employees

✓ Employees in certain computer-related occupations as defined in the Department of Labor regulations

Workweek Defined under FLSA: A workweek is a period of 168 hours during seven consecutive 24-hour periods. It may begin on any day of the week and at any hour of the day established by the employer. Generally, for purposes of minimum wage and overtime payment, each workweek stands alone; you may not average two or more workweeks. Employee coverage, compliance with wage payment requirements, and the application of most exemptions are determined on a workweek basis.

Work Hours Defined Under FLSA: Work hours ordinarily include all time during which an employee is required to be on the employer's premises, on duty, or at a prescribed work place.

Bona fide meal periods (typically 30 minutes or more) generally need not be compensated as work time. The employee must be completely relieved from duty for the purpose of eating regular meals. The employee is not relieved if he or she is required to perform any duties, whether active or inactive, while eating.

Employment Practices Not Covered: While FLSA does set basic minimum wage and overtime pay standards and regulates the employment of minors, there are a number of employment practices that FLSA does not regulate.

FLSA does not require

- ✓ vacation, holiday, severance, or sick pay;
- ✓ meal or rest periods, holidays off, or vacations;
- ✓ premium pay for weekend or holiday work;
- ✓ pay raises or fringe benefits; or
- ✓ reason for discharge, immediate payment of final wages to a terminated employee, or discharge notices.

For employees at least 16 years old, FLSA does not limit the number of hours in a day or days in a week an employee may be required or scheduled to work, including overtime hours.

Matters not covered by FLSA are left for agreement between the employer and the employees or their authorized representatives. Individual state labor departments may have specific regulations separate from FLSA regarding these requirements.

For more information, contact:

> *State of North Carolina*
> *Department of Labor*
> *1001 Mail Service Center*
> *Raleigh, North Carolina 27699-1101*
>
> *Phone: (800) NC LABOR or (800) 625-2267*
>
> *Website: www.nclabor.com*

Recordkeeping under the FLSA

The FLSA requires employers to keep records on wages, hours, and other items as specified in Department of Labor recordkeeping regulations. Most of this information is maintained by employers in ordinary business practice and in compliance with other laws and regulations. The records do not have to be kept in any particular form, and time clocks need not be used.

Required Information: For employees subject to the minimum wage provisions or both the minimum wage and overtime pay provisions, the following records must be kept:

- ✓ personal information, including employee's name, home address, occupation, sex, and birth date (if under 19 years of age);
- ✓ basis on which employee wages are paid;
- ✓ hour and day when workweek begins;
- ✓ total hours worked each workday and each workweek;
- ✓ total daily or weekly straight-time earnings;
- ✓ regular hourly pay rate;
- ✓ weekly overtime earnings;
- ✓ total overtime pay for the workweek;
- ✓ deductions from or additions to wages;
- ✓ total wages paid each pay period; and
- ✓ date of payment and pay period covered.

Special information is required for home workers, for employees working under uncommon pay arrangements, for employees to whom lodging or other facilities are furnished, and for employees receiving remedial education.

Chapter 15, Financial Management, covers the basics of payroll accounting and how to process the listed information.

Penalties

Enforcement of FLSA is carried out by investigators stationed across the U.S. They conduct investigations and gather data on wages, hours, and other employment conditions or practices in order to determine compliance with the law. Where violations are found, they may recommend changes in employment practices to bring an employer into compliance.

Retaliation against an employee for filing a complaint or for participating in a legal proceeding under FLSA is against the law.

Willful violations of employment under FLSA may be prosecuted criminally, and the violator fined up to $10,000. A second conviction may result in imprisonment.

Employers who willfully or repeatedly violate the minimum wage or overtime pay requirements are subject to a civil money penalty of up to $1,100 for each violation.

Immigration and Nationality Act

The employment eligibility provisions of the Immigration and Nationality Act require employers to verify the employment eligibility of all individuals hired. Immigration and Naturalization Service forms (I-9) must be kept on file for at least three years after the date of hire or for one year after the date employment ends, whichever is later.

I-9 forms must be completed with required documentation within three days of hire. A sample I-9 form is located at the end of this chapter.

The law does not require businesses to obtain I-9 documentation for independent contractors and their employees.

Unlawful Discrimination: Discrimination based on national origin or citizenship status is prohibited. If an Office of Special Counsel for Unfair Employment-Related Discrimination (OSC) or Equal Employment Opportunity Commission (EEOC) investigation reveals employment discrimination covered by the Immigration and Nationality Act, the employer will be ordered to cease the prohibited practice and may be ordered to take one or more of the following steps:

✓ hire or reinstate, with or without back pay, individuals directly injured by the discrimination;

✓ lift any restrictions on an employee's assignments, work shifts, or movements;

✓ post notices to employees about their rights and about employers' obligations;

✓ educate all personnel involved in hiring and in complying with employer sanctions and anti-discrimination laws; and

✓ remove a false performance review or false warning from an employee's personnel file.

Employers may also be ordered to pay civil monetary penalties of $375 to $3,200 per individual discriminated against for the first offense, $3,200 to $6,500 per individual discriminated against for the second offense, and $4,300 to $16,000 per individual discriminated against for subsequent offenses.

Completing the I-9 Form for New Hires

Form I-9 is available for download on the U.S. Citizenship and Immigration Services website at www.uscis.gov or by calling (800) 870-3676. The National Customer Service Center at (800) 375-5283

can answer questions on USCIS forms and information on immigration laws, regulations and procedures.

The following gives step-by-step instructions on how to complete the form properly.

Section One

The employee completes section one of the I-9 form at the start of employment. The employee's name, address, date of birth, and social security number (optional unless the employer participates in the USCIS E-Verify Program), certification of legal status, and expiration date for temporary work authorization are required. Permanent aliens and authorized aliens must fill in either their alien number or authorization number. The employee must sign and date the form. If a preparer or translator is used, the appropriate signature block must be completed.

Section Two

An authorized employee representative completes section two by examining one document from list A or by examining one document from list B and one document from list C (a summary of approved documents is listed in the following section and a complete list is on the back of the I-9 form). The representative must view original documentation and keep copies of the front and back of this documentation on file.

Acceptable Documentation: The purpose of providing documentation is to establish identity and employment eligibility. Listed below are common forms of identification used when completing the I-9 form. A complete list is included on the back of the I-9 form located at the end of this chapter. If employers participate in the USCIS E-Verify Program, only documents from List B on the I-9 form that bear a photograph are acceptable. I-9 forms must be updated when identity and employment eligibility documents are changed or renewed.

Employees can provide one of the following documents that establishes both identity and employment eligibility:

✓ U.S. passport

✓ Certificate of U.S. citizenship

✓ Certificate of naturalization

✓ Unexpired foreign passport with I-551 stamp or attached I-94 form indicating current employment authorization

✓ Permanent resident card or alien registration receipt with photograph

Employees also have the option of providing two documents—one to establish identity and the other to establish employment eligibility.

Documents that establish identity include

✓ state-issued driver's license with photo;

✓ ID card with photo issued by federal, state or local government agencies;

✓ voter's registration card; and

✓ U.S. military card.

Documents that establish employment eligibility include

✓ U.S. Social Security card issued by the Social Security Administration;

✓ original or certified birth certificate;

✓ U.S. citizen ID card (form I-197);

✓ resident ID card; and

✓ Native American tribal document.

Certification

The date to be used in the certification section must correspond with the current employment date. The authorized employee representative must sign and date this section.

Additional Information: U.S. Citizen and Immigration Services publishes a Handbook for Employers which is a helpful resource for completing the I-9 form. This publication is available online at www.uscis.gov/files/form/m-274.pdf.

Americans with Disabilities Act (ADA)

This law prohibits discrimination against persons with disabilities and applies to employers with 15 or more employees. In general, the employment provisions of the ADA require

✓ equal opportunity in selecting, testing, and hiring qualified applicants with disabilities;

✓ job accommodation for applicants and workers with disabilities when such accommodations would not impose "undue hardship;" and

✓ equal opportunity in promotion and benefits.

Employment Discrimination: ADA prohibits discrimination in all employment practices, including job application procedures, hiring, firing, advancement, compensation, training, and other terms, conditions, and privileges of employment. It applies to recruitment, advertising, tenure, layoff, leave, fringe benefits, and all other employment-related activities.

Qualified Individuals with Disabilities: Employment discrimination is prohibited against "qualified individuals with disabilities" including applicants for employment and employees. An individual is considered to have a "disability" if that individual has a physical or mental impairment that substantially limits one or more major life activities or has a record of such an impairment, or is regarded as having such an impairment.

Conditions Covered: The ADA applies to persons who have impairments that substantially limit major life activities such as seeing, hearing, speaking, walking, breathing, performing manual tasks, learning, caring for oneself, and working.

Examples include an individual with

✓ epilepsy,

✓ paralysis,

✓ HIV infection,

✓ AIDS,

✓ substantial hearing or visual impairment,

✓ mental retardation, or

✓ specific learning disability.

An individual with a minor, non-chronic condition of short duration, such as a sprain, broken limb, or the flu, generally would not be covered by the ADA.

Reasonable Accommodations: An employer is required to accommodate a "known" disability of a qualified applicant or employee unless it imposes an "undue hardship" on the operation of the employer's business. A reasonable accommodation is any modification or adjustment to a job or the work environment that will enable a qualified applicant or employee with a disability to participate in the application process or to perform essential job functions. Reasonable accommodations also include adjustments to assure that a qualified individual with a disability has rights and privileges in employment equal to those of employees without disabilities.

Additional Resources: The Equal Employment Opportunity Commission has developed several resources to help employers and people with disabilities understand and comply with the employment provisions of the ADA. Resources include

✓ a technical assistance manual that provides "how-to" guidance on the employment provisions of the ADA as well as a resource directory to help individuals find specific information; and

✓ a variety of brochures, booklets, and fact sheets.

For more information about the ADA, contact:

U.S. Equal Employment Opportunity Commission
131 M Street, NE
Fourth Floor, Suite 4NWO2F
Washington, D.C. 20507

Phone: (202) 669-4000
TTY: (202) 669-6820
Website: www.eeoc.gov

Other Labor Laws

Many other labor laws protect the rights of employees.

✓ The **Davis-Bacon Act** requires payment of prevailing wage rates and fringe benefits on federally-financed or assisted construction.

✓ The **Walsh-Healey Public Contracts Act** requires payment of minimum wage rates and overtime pay on contracts that provide goods to the federal government.

✓ The **Service Contract Act** requires payment of prevailing wage rates and fringe benefits on contracts to provide services to the federal government.

✓ The **Contract Work Hours and Safety Standards Act** sets overtime standards for service and construction contracts on federal projects.

✓ The **Wage Garnishment Law** limits the amount of an individual's income that may be legally garnished and prohibits firing an employee whose pay is garnished for payment of a single debt.

✓ The **Employee Polygraph Protection Act** prohibits most private employers from using any type of lie detector test, either for pre-employment screening of job applicants or for testing current employees during the course of employment.

✓ The **Family and Medical Leave Act** entitles eligible employees of covered employers to take up to 12 weeks of unpaid job-protected leave each year, with the maintenance of group health insurance, for the birth and care of a child, for the placement of a child for adoption or foster care, for the care of a child, spouse, or parent with a serious health condition, or for the employee's serious health condition.

✓ **Title VII of the Civil Rights Act of 1964** prohibits discrimination on the basis of race, color, religion, national origin, and sex. Sexual harassment is considered a form of sex discrimination and is a violation of Title VII. An amendment to Title VII provides protection against sex discrimination on the basis of pregnancy, childbirth, and related medical conditions.

✓ **The Equal Pay Act of 1963** prohibits employers from paying different wages to men and women who perform essentially the same work under similar working conditions.

✓ **The Age Discrimination in Employment Act (ADEA)** prohibits discrimination against individuals who are age 40 or older. It applies to employers with 20 or more employees.

✓ **The Worker Adjustment and Retraining Notification Act (WARN)** offers protection to workers, their families, and communities by requiring employers to provide notice 60 days in advance of covered plant closings and covered mass layoffs.

✓ **Title III of the Consumer Credit Protection Act (CCPA)** protects employees from being discharged by their employers because their wages have been garnished for any one debt and limits the amount of employees' earnings that may be garnished in any one week.

✓ **The Uniformed Services Employment and Reemployment Rights Act (USERRA)** protects service members' reemployment rights when returning from a period of service in the uniformed services, including those called up from the reserves or National Guard, and prohibits employer discrimination based on military service or obligation.

✓ Numerous labor organizing, collective bargaining and dispute resolution acts give employees the right to organize, join labor unions, bargain collectively, and strike.

✓ **Right-to-work** laws secure the right of employees to decide for themselves whether or not to join or financially support a union.

North Carolina Wage and Hour Laws

The North Carolina Department of Labor is the regulating agency for the state wage and hour laws.

Listed below is a summary of the rules that may apply to your business.

✓ *Wage Payment:* Wages are due on the regular payday. If requested, final paychecks must be mailed.

✓ *Payment on Termination:* The employer must pay an employee who is voluntarily or involuntarily terminated within 48 hours or the next regular payday, not to exceed 30 days after termination.

✓ *Withholding of Wages:* No employer may withhold or divert any portion of an employee's wages unless required or empowered by state or federal law or unless the employer has written authorization from the employee.

✓ *Employer to Furnish Certain Information:* Employees must be notified of paydays, pay rates, policies on vacation and sick leave, commissions, bonuses, and other pay matters. Employers must notify employees in writing or through a posted notice maintained in a place accessible to employees, of any reduction in the amount of promised wages at least 24 hours before the change.

✓ *Wage Disputes:* When the amount of wages is in dispute, the employer's payment of the undisputed portion cannot restrict the right of the employee to continue his or her claim for the rest of the wages. The Department of Labor will, upon complaint, investigate wage complaints to determine if any violations have occurred.

✓ *Overtime:* Time and a half must be paid after 40 hours of work in any one workweek. The state overtime provision does not apply to some employers or to employees who are exempt.

Be aware of the labor laws that apply to your business.

Required Postings

Some of the statutes and regulations enforced by agencies within the U.S. Department of Labor require that posters or notices be posted in the workplace. A complete list of postings can be found at www.dol.gov. A summary of postings that may apply to you as listed on U.S. Department of Labor website is as follows:

Poster	Description of Employers Required to Post Notice
Safety and Health Protection on the Job	Employers located in states with OSHA-approved state plans should obtain and post the state's equivalent poster.
Equal Opportunity is the Law	Businesses holding federal contracts or subcontracts or federally assisted construction contracts of $10,000 or more.
Employee Rights for Workers with Disabilities/Special Minimum Wage Poster	All employers having workers employed under special minimum wage certificates must post this notice.
National Labor Relations Act (NLRA) Poster (effective January 31, 2012)	All private-sector employers (excluding agricultural, railroad and airline employers) must post this notice.
Your Rights Under the Family and Medical Leave Act	Public agencies (including state, local, and federal employers), public and private elementary and secondary schools, as well as private sector employers who employ 50 or more employees in 20 or more work weeks and who are engaged in commerce or in any industry or activity affecting commerce, including joint employers and successors of covered employers
Fair Labor Standards Act (FLSA): Minimum Wage Poster	All private, federal, state and local government employers subject to the FLSA
Uniformed Services Employment and Reemployment Rights Act	The full text of the notice must be provided by each employer to persons entitled to rights and benefits under USERRA.

Poster	Description of Employers Required to Post Notice
Notice to All Employees Working on Federal or Federally Financed Construction Projects	Any contractor/subcontractor engaged in contracts in excess of $2,000 for the actual construction, alteration/repair of a public building or public work or building or work financed in whole or in part from federal funds, federal guarantee, or federal pledge
Notice to Employees Working on Government Contracts	Every contractor or subcontractor engaged in a contract with the United States or the District of Columbia in excess of $2,500 the principal purpose of which is to furnish services in the U.S. through the use of service employees.
Notice: Employee Polygraph Protection Act	Any employer engaged in or affecting commerce or in the production of goods for commerce. Does not apply to federal, state and local governments, or to circumstances covered by the national defense and security exemption.
Notification of Employee Rights Under Federal Labor Laws	Federal contractors and subcontractors are required to post the prescribed employee notice conspicuously in plants and offices where employees covered by the National Labor Relations Act (NLRA) perform contract-related activity, including all places where notices to employees are customarily posted both physically and electronically.

Additional postings may be required for federal contractors.

North Carolina state law requires posting the following notices:

✓ Safety and Health (OSHA)—N.C. Department of Labor Responsibilities, Employer Rights and Responsibilities, Employee Rights and Responsibilities, and Other OSHA Information

✓ Wage and Hour Act—Minimum Wage, Overtime, Youth Employment, Wage Payment, Complaints, and Right to Work Laws

✓ Unemployment Insurance—Certificate of Coverage and Notice to Workers as to Benefit Rights (Form NCESC 524)

✓ Workers' Compensation Notice Posters (NCIC Form No. 17)

Required state postings are available for download on the Department of Labor website at www.nclabor.com. Other state agencies may also require display of specific documents in the workplace. Contact the appropriate agencies directly to verify any poster display requirements.

Posters are periodically updated. Ensure you post the most current version, if required.

Employee Handbook and Policies

Having clear and well-documented policies helps employees understand the rules of the workplace and protects you if a disgruntled employee files a lawsuit or complaint against you.

Enforcing Policies and Procedures: An employee handbook is a document you put together that lists company policies and employee benefits and rights. It is important for employees to sign a receipt that they have read and understand the contents of the handbook. This documentation is helpful in enforcing the policies and procedures of your company.

Changing Your Handbook: An employee handbook is not a static document. You can add items to the handbook but make sure you distribute these amendments to employees and have them sign off on the changes.

Writing Your Employee Handbook

It may be difficult to determine where to start when writing your employee handbook and policies. Consider the following sections when putting your handbook together:

✓ Company history
✓ Compensation guidelines (i.e., introductory period, full-time status requirements, etc.)
✓ Payroll distribution dates and times
✓ Benefits
✓ Normal working hours
✓ Overtime pay
✓ Vacation time
✓ Sick days
✓ Policy on sexual harassment
✓ Policy on the use of illegal drugs or alcohol

✓ Non-discrimination policy
✓ Rules of conduct (i.e., disciplinary action for insubordination, fighting, etc.)
✓ Safety policies
✓ Equipment and tool policies
✓ Disciplinary action procedures

You may want to have an attorney review your employee handbook. In many states, the employee handbook is considered an employment contract. There may be certain wording and disclaimers that should be contained in your employee handbook to protect you against legal action.

Employee Satisfaction

Benefits of Employee Satisfaction: Keeping employees happy and motivated can have a tremendous effect on the performance of your work teams. Your company can benefit from satisfied employees in several ways:

✓ Stronger company loyalty and corporate culture
✓ Higher quality work and customer satisfaction
✓ Lower employee turnover
✓ Increased productivity

Maintaining employee satisfaction is not as easy as it sounds. Even though employers may have good intentions, when faced with tight deadlines and day-to-day operations, employee satisfaction sometimes drops to the bottom of the priority list.

Motivating Employees: The following checklist includes simple ways you can motivate your employees and give them a feeling of achievement:

✓ Provide informal and formal training opportunities for employees to learn new skills.
✓ Empower employees to make decisions and give positive and constructive feedback.
✓ Provide clear expectations for your employees.
✓ Conduct performance reviews on a regular basis.
✓ Mentor your employees and tell them about advancement opportunities in your company and the industry.
✓ Recognize and reward employees for good work.

The Value of Job Descriptions

Job descriptions give employees a guideline for the responsibilities of their job. Job descriptions benefit employees because they understand your expectation for their performance. It also makes it easier for you to monitor their performance, conduct reviews, and take disciplinary action if necessary.

Job descriptions should contain a few basic elements:

✓ Job title
✓ Job description, including who the position reports to and summary of job purpose
✓ Key responsibilities
✓ Required licenses and/or certifications
✓ Skills and knowledge needed

Sample Job Description: Listed below is a sample job description for a construction superintendent position using the above categories. All job descriptions must be carefully reviewed and modified to fit the individual company's requirements.

Job Title: Construction Superintendent

Description: Under general direction of the company owner, the construction superintendent serves as a member of the construction management team with broad authority over assigned projects, participating in all phases of construction from project planning to completion. Emphasis is on quality control, evaluation of change order requests, and timely completion of construction schedules.

Key Responsibilities: The duties listed below are intended only as illustrations of the various types of work that may be performed by the construction superintendent:

✓ Coordinates activities associated with the company's construction projects.
✓ Serves as liaison with subcontractors, architects, utilities, and others.
✓ Participates in project construction development and planning.
✓ Processes utility requests for construction projects.
✓ Represents the company regarding onsite construction quality control reviews.
✓ Makes recommendations and processes change order requests.
✓ Reviews punch lists.
✓ Assures construction specifications are met.
✓ Notes deviations from project schedules and costs.
✓ Maintains records and prepares reports.

The omission of specific statements of duties does not exclude them from the position if the work is similar, related, or a logical assignment to this class.

Required Licenses or Certifications: Requires a valid driver's license.

Skills and Knowledge Needed:

✓ Principles and practices of construction management, building operation and maintenance, quality assurance programs and systems, budget administration, construction specifications, and bidding processes.

✓ Ability to plan, organize, and manage time to track progress and elements of assigned construction projects effectively.

✓ Establish and maintain effective working relationships with coworkers, employees of subcontractors, and outside entities.

✓ Prepare or participate in the development of construction and other budgets and monitor performance against the approved budget.

✓ Communicate effectively, both orally and in writing.

✓ Ability to lift up to 50 pounds.

Providing Benefits

Offering benefit plans can be an effective means of attracting and retaining good employees, keeping up with the competition, and boosting employee morale. Traditional employee plans include

✓ health insurance,
✓ dental insurance,
✓ vision insurance,
✓ long-term disability,
✓ life insurance, and
✓ 401(k) or other retirement plan.

Some employers also opt to offer more creative benefit options, such as tuition reimbursement, gym subsidies, and child care referral services.

However you decide to package your benefits plan, a few key laws are important.

Workers' Compensation Laws provide monetary compensation to employees who are injured or disabled on the job. These laws also provide benefits for dependents of those workers who are killed because of work-related accidents or illnesses. Some laws protect employers by limiting the amount an injured employee can recover from an employer and by eliminating the liability of coworkers in most accidents.

Workers' compensation laws and programs are established at the state level for most employment.

Workers' compensation fraud is committed when an individual willfully intends to provide false or inaccurate information to receive workers' compensation benefits. Examples of fraud include

✓ reporting an injury as work-related when it was not;

✓ continuing to work and receive benefits at the same time; and

✓ misrepresenting an injury.

Employers are in the best position to identify workers' compensation fraud. Workers' compensation fraud is illegal. Your workers' compensation administrator should be notified if you suspect fraud.

Workers' compensation insurance is purchased by the employer; no part of it should be paid for by employees or deducted from their pay.

North Carolina Program: If you are a sole proprietorship, partnership, or LLC, you are required by law to carry workers' compensation coverage if you have three or more employees. Employees can be full-time, part-time, regular, seasonal, or family members. Sole proprietors, partners, and managers and members of the LLC are not included in the headcount.

All forms of corporations with a total of three or more people are required by law to carry workers' compensation coverage. Everyone is included in the headcount, including corporate officers.

If one or more employees are employed in activities which involve the use or presence of radiation, workers' compensation is required.

Coverage is provided through the following ways.

✓ *Self-Insurance:* You may qualify to become self-insured. To receive information on this process, contact the Department of Insurance at (919) 733-5631.

✓ *Self-Insured Fund:* Your business may be placed in a self-insured fund. To receive a list of the self-insured funds in North Carolina, contact the Department of Insurance at (919) 733-5631.

✓ *Coverage through Private Carrier:* You may find coverage in the conventional and open market. To do so, contact an independent insurance agent and request assistance in providing your business with coverage.

✓ *Assigned Risk Pool:* You may be placed in the assigned risk pool, which is administered by the North Carolina Rate Bureau. You may contact them directly for information at (919) 582-1056, or you may ask your insurance agent for information.

Any contractor who sublets any part of a contract must first obtain documentation that the subcontractor is in compliance with the North Carolina Workers' Compensation Act. Subcontractors must provide compliance documentation regardless of whether the subcontractor employs fewer than three employees. If proper documentation is not obtained, the party subletting the contract is liable for payment of compensation and other benefits if any of the subcontractor's employees are injured or die from an accident associated with the work covered by the subcontract. As part of your operating policies, you may require subcontractors to carry workers' compensation coverage even if the subcontractor has fewer than three employees.

N.C. Gen. Stat. §97-94(b) outlines penalties for noncompliance of workers' compensation laws. Employers are subject to penalties of $50.00 to $100.00 for each day of noncompliance until proper coverage is obtained.

Contractors cannot obtain a building permit until proof of proper workers' compensation coverage is provided to the building official issuing the permit.

Information on North Carolina's program is available through the Industrial Commission.

> *North Carolina Industrial Commission*
> *4340 Mail Service Center*
> *Raleigh, North Carolina 27699-4340*

Physical Address:

> *430 N. Salisbury Street*
> *Raleigh, North Carolina 27603*
>
> *Telephone (919) 807-2501*
>
> *Fax: (919) 715-0282*

Unemployment Compensation programs provide unemployment benefits to eligible workers who become unemployed through no fault of their own and meet certain other eligibility requirements. This program is jointly financed through federal and state employer payroll taxes through the federal/state unemployment insurance tax.

Generally, employers must pay both state and federal unemployment taxes if

✓ they pay wages to employees totaling $1,500 or more in any quarter of a calendar year; or

✓ they had at least one employee during any day of a week during 20 weeks in a calendar year, regardless of whether or not the weeks were consecutive.

North Carolina Program: The North Carolina Employment Security Law establishes guidelines for state unemployment tax. Business entities are subject to an unemployment payroll tax if they have one or more employees for 20 weeks during a calendar year or pay $1,500 in wages in any calendar quarter during a calendar year in North Carolina.

The tax is payable quarterly. Tax wage base and tax rate may vary from year to year. For the most current information, refer to the North Carolina Division of Employment Security. Current tax rates are available online at www.ncesc.com. New business entities in North Carolina are assigned a new business tax rate for the first two years. The rate may be changed after the entity comes under an experience rating.

Employers liable to one or more states for unemployment insurance tax receive a federal unemployment tax (FUTA) credit for timely tax payments made to the state(s). The FUTA tax base and tax rate is calculated at the current prevailing rate. The current federal tax information is available online at www.irs.gov.

The state taxable wage base differs from the federal taxable wage base and is recomputed each year. Employers are notified of the taxable wage base applicable for the coming calendar year on their tax rate notification. The taxable wage base is also printed on the Employer's Quarterly Tax and Wage Report.

Employers must pay 100 percent of federal and state unemployment tax due. Deductions cannot be made from employee payroll for the purpose of paying this tax.

All employers doing business in North Carolina are required to complete and file form NCUI 604, Status Report to determine their liability for unemployment insurance.

To report unemployment taxes, you must file form NCUI 101, Employer's Quarterly Tax and Wage Report. Payment of state unemployment tax is made quarterly by the end of the month following the end of each calendar quarter. State unemployment tax reports are due by January 31 (for the fourth quarter of the previous calendar year), April 30, July 31, and October 31.

All employers must maintain records for each person they employ (including corporate officers). These records must show

✓ the employee's name and social security number;

✓ the beginning and ending dates worked;

✓ the amount of wages paid; and

✓ all other payments made to the employee including vacation pay, tips, reasonable value of board and lodging, and other compensation for services.

Records must be maintained for at least five years and be available for inspection by authorized personnel of the Division of Employment Security.

SUTA Dumping: SUTA dumping is a transfer of employees between businesses for the purpose of obtaining a lower unemployment compensation tax rate. SUTA dumping is prohibited and subject to criminal and/or civil penalties according to state law. The Division of Employment Security investigates suspicious activity in the transfer or acquisition of a business or shifting of employees to identify SUTA dumping.

Contact Information: Additional information regarding the North Carolina state unemployment tax is available at:

State of North Carolina
Division of Employment Security (DES)
P.O. Box 25903
Raleigh, North Carolina 27611-6504

Tax Telephone: (919) 733-7395
Claims Telephone: (919) 733-7883

Website: www.ncesc.com

The **Consolidated Omnibus Budget Act of 1985 (COBRA)** includes provisions for continuing health care coverage. These provisions apply to group health plans of employers with 20 or more employees on 50 percent of the typical working days in the previous calendar year. COBRA gives "qualified beneficiaries" (a covered employee's spouse and dependent children) the right to maintain, at their own expense, coverage under their health plan that would be lost due to a "qualifying event," such as termination of

employment, at a cost comparable to what it would be if they were still members of the employer's group.

Health Insurance Portability and Accountability Act of 1996 (HIPAA) provides for improved portability and continuity of health insurance coverage connected with employment. These provisions include rules relating to exclusions for preexisting conditions, special enrollment rights, and prohibition of discrimination against individuals based on health status-related factors. HIPAA also addresses an employee's right to privacy concerning their health information. As an employer, you need to be aware of this act and keep records concerning any employee's medical conditions in a confidential file.

Disciplining Employees

Corrective action may be necessary from time to time for employees who are not following employment policies and procedures properly. Employers need to administer discipline fairly to promote a respectful work environment and to avoid trouble later.

Progressive Discipline: Progressive discipline is a method of corrective action where the consequences of the improper behavior become more significant if it continues. Progressive discipline gives the employee a chance to take corrective action to prevent future disciplinary action. There are certain offenses that may be cause for immediate termination (i.e., theft, endangering the safety of others, etc.) and are not appropriate for progressive discipline.

The employee manual is a good place to have written disciplinary policies and a comprehensive list of offenses that lead to immediate dismissal.

Terminating Employees

At one time or another, most employers encounter circumstances where they need to terminate employees. It is not a fun or rewarding task but sometimes a necessary one. When terminating an employee, you want to make sure that you have followed the proper procedures to minimize your risk of a wrongful termination lawsuit.

Employment relationships are either contractual or at-will; the definition of the relationship influences the procedures for termination.

Contractual Employees

Union employees and some executives have employment contracts. When terminating a contractual employee, it is important to comply with the terms of the contract. If the contract is breached, you may be subject to a lawsuit.

At-Will Employees

"At-will employment" means that either the employer or the employee may terminate employment at any time without notice or cause. It is not exactly that easy, and there are restrictions that you should be aware of as an employer. These restrictions include:

✓ An employer may not terminate an employee for discriminatory reasons (i.e., race, gender, etc.).

✓ An employer cannot terminate an employee for taking time off to serve on a jury.

✓ Reporting health and safety violations and abuses of power cannot lead to termination. There are "whistle-blower laws" that protect employees if this circumstance does occur.

✓ All employers should use good faith and fair dealing throughout employment. This is why documenting poor performance is strongly recommended. Without documentation, the termination may be perceived as a breach of good faith.

These are general guidelines, and it is recommended you consult with an expert in Human Resources or an attorney regarding specific situations.

. . . .

Proper documentation is important when disciplining and terminating employees.

. . . .

Final Inspection...

Interviewing and Hiring Employees: Your interviews should focus on skills, experience, and qualities. There are certain questions you should avoid because they are not legal to ask.

New Hire Reporting: North Carolina has mandatory requirements for reporting new hires.

Hiring Minors for Landscape Construction Work: The U.S. Department of Labor has strict rules for hiring minors, including limited working hours and prohibited tasks.

Employee Documentation: Employee files with relevant documents, such as tax forms and disciplinary forms, should be maintained throughout employment.

Key Employment Laws: There are several employment laws that you must comply with, such as the Fair Labor Standards Act (FLSA), Immigration and Nationality Act, and the Americans with Disabilities Act (ADA).

Fair Labor Standards Act (FLSA): Standards for basic minimum wage and overtime pay are outlined in the Fair Labor Standards Act. The Act applies to most private and public employers who have one or more employees.

Immigration and Nationality Act: Employers are required to verify the employment eligibility of all individuals hired through I-9 forms. These forms must be kept on file for at least three years after the date of hire or for one year after the date employment ends, whichever is later. U.S. Citizen and Immigration Services publishes a *Handbook for Employers* which is a helpful resource for completing the I-9 form. This publication is available online at www.uscis.gov/files/nativedocuments/m-274_3apr09.pdf.

Americans with Disabilities Act (ADA): This law prohibits discrimination against persons with disabilities. It applies to employers with 15 or more employees.

Other Labor Laws: Several other labor laws protect the rights of employees. Specific laws exist that set guidelines for federal contractors, wage garnishment, and an employee's right to join a union. Other laws provide protection against discriminatory actions of employers.

North Carolina Wage and Hour Laws: The North Carolina Department of Labor regulates specific laws pertaining to employment, such as payment of wages, overtime, payment on termination, withholding of wages, wage disputes, and an employer's obligation to furnish certain information.

Required Postings: Employers must post certain notices for employees under federal and state law. Posters are periodically updated. Ensure you post the most current version, if required.

Employee Handbook and Policies: An employee handbook is a useful document for communicating your policies and procedures.

Employee Satisfaction: Your company can benefit in several ways from putting employee satisfaction programs in place.

Providing Benefits: There are some mandatory benefits you must provide employees. Other benefits, such as health insurance, may also be offered to attract and retain employees.

Disciplining Employees: Discipline should be administered in a fair manner and documented appropriately.

Terminating Employees: Using proper termination procedures will help minimize your risk of a wrongful termination lawsuit.

Supplemental Forms

Supplemental forms and links are available at **NASCLAforms.org** using access code **NCL129354**.

IRS Form W-4	IRS form to determine federal income tax withholding
IRS Form W-5	IRS form for employees to elect advance earned income credit
Form I-9	Required form to confirm legal immigration status
Fair Labor Standards Act (FLSA)	Copy of the FLSA law from the U.S. Department of Labor
Americans with Disabilities Act (ADA)	ADA guide for small businesses published by the U.S. Department of Justice
Job Description Template	Form featured earlier in the chapter that shows a sample job description
Employer's Tax Guide (Circular E)	Publication used to determine federal income tax withholding for employees

Instructions for Employment Eligibility Verification

Department of Homeland Security
U.S. Citizenship and Immigration Services

USCIS
Form I-9
OMB No. 1615-0047
Expires 03/31/2016

Read all instructions carefully before completing this form.

Anti-Discrimination Notice. It is illegal to discriminate against any work-authorized individual in hiring, discharge, recruitment or referral for a fee, or in the employment eligibility verification (Form I-9 and E-Verify) process based on that individual's citizenship status, immigration status or national origin. Employers **CANNOT** specify which document(s) they will accept from an employee. The refusal to hire an individual because the documentation presented has a future expiration date may also constitute illegal discrimination. For more information, call the Office of Special Counsel for Immigration-Related Unfair Employment Practices (OSC) at 1-800-255-7688 (employees), 1-800-255-8155 (employers), or 1-800-237-2515 (TDD), or visit **www.justice.gov/crt/about/osc**.

What Is the Purpose of This Form?

Employers must complete Form I-9 to document verification of the identity and employment authorization of each new employee (both citizen and noncitizen) hired after November 6, 1986, to work in the United States. In the Commonwealth of the Northern Mariana Islands (CNMI), employers must complete Form I-9 to document verification of the identity and employment authorization of each new employee (both citizen and noncitizen) hired after November 27, 2011. Employers should have used Form I-9 CNMI between November 28, 2009 and November 27, 2011.

General Instructions

Employers are responsible for completing and retaining Form I-9. For the purpose of completing this form, the term "employer" means all employers, including those recruiters and referrers for a fee who are agricultural associations, agricultural employers, or farm labor contractors.

Form I-9 is made up of three sections. Employers may be fined if the form is not complete. Employers are responsible for retaining completed forms. Do not mail completed forms to U.S. Citizenship and Immigration Services (USCIS) or Immigration and Customs Enforcement (ICE).

Section 1. Employee Information and Attestation

Newly hired employees must complete and sign Section 1 of Form I-9 **no later than the first day of employment**. Section 1 should never be completed before the employee has accepted a job offer.

Provide the following information to complete Section 1:

Name: Provide your full legal last name, first name, and middle initial. Your last name is your family name or surname. If you have two last names or a hyphenated last name, include both names in the last name field. Your first name is your given name. Your middle initial is the first letter of your second given name, or the first letter of your middle name, if any.

Other names used: Provide all other names used, if any (including maiden name). If you have had no other legal names, write "N/A."

Address: Provide the address where you currently live, including Street Number and Name, Apartment Number (if applicable), City, State, and Zip Code. Do not provide a post office box address (P.O. Box). Only border commuters from Canada or Mexico may use an international address in this field.

Date of Birth: Provide your date of birth in the mm/dd/yyyy format. For example, January 23, 1950, should be written as 01/23/1950.

U.S. Social Security Number: Provide your 9-digit Social Security number. Providing your Social Security number is voluntary. However, if your employer participates in E-Verify, you must provide your Social Security number.

E-mail Address and Telephone Number (Optional): You may provide your e-mail address and telephone number. Department of Homeland Security (DHS) may contact you if DHS learns of a potential mismatch between the information provided and the information in DHS or Social Security Administration (SSA) records. You may write "N/A" if you choose not to provide this information.

All employees must attest in Section 1, under penalty of perjury, to their citizenship or immigration status by checking one of the following four boxes provided on the form:

1. **A citizen of the United States**

2. **A noncitizen national of the United States:** Noncitizen nationals of the United States are persons born in American Samoa, certain former citizens of the former Trust Territory of the Pacific Islands, and certain children of noncitizen nationals born abroad.

3. **A lawful permanent resident:** A lawful permanent resident is any person who is not a U.S. citizen and who resides in the United States under legally recognized and lawfully recorded permanent residence as an immigrant. The term "lawful permanent resident" includes conditional residents. If you check this box, write either your Alien Registration Number (A-Number) or USCIS Number in the field next to your selection. At this time, the USCIS Number is the same as the A-Number without the "A" prefix.

4. **An alien authorized to work:** If you are not a citizen or national of the United States or a lawful permanent resident, but are authorized to work in the United States, check this box.

   If you check this box:

   a. Record the date that your employment authorization expires, if any. Aliens whose employment authorization does not expire, such as refugees, asylees, and certain citizens of the Federated States of Micronesia, the Republic of the Marshall Islands, or Palau, may write "N/A" on this line.

   b. Next, enter your Alien Registration Number (A-Number)/USCIS Number. At this time, the USCIS Number is the same as your A-Number without the "A" prefix. If you have not received an A-Number/USCIS Number, record your Admission Number. You can find your Admission Number on Form I-94, "Arrival-Departure Record," or as directed by USCIS or U.S. Customs and Border Protection (CBP).

      (1) If you obtained your admission number from CBP in connection with your arrival in the United States, then also record information about the foreign passport you used to enter the United States (number and country of issuance).

      (2) If you obtained your admission number from USCIS *within the United States*, or you entered the United States without a foreign passport, you must write "N/A" in the Foreign Passport Number and Country of Issuance fields.

Sign your name in the "Signature of Employee" block and record the date you completed and signed Section 1. By signing and dating this form, you attest that the citizenship or immigration status you selected is correct and that you are aware that you may be imprisoned and/or fined for making false statements or using false documentation when completing this form. To fully complete this form, you must present to your employer documentation that establishes your identity and employment authorization. Choose which documents to present from the Lists of Acceptable Documents, found on the last page of this form. You must present this documentation no later than the third day after beginning employment, although you may present the required documentation before this date.

Preparer and/or Translator Certification

The Preparer and/or Translator Certification must be completed if the employee requires assistance to complete Section 1 (e.g., the employee needs the instructions or responses translated, someone other than the employee fills out the information blocks, or someone with disabilities needs additional assistance). The employee must still sign Section 1.

Minors and Certain Employees with Disabilities (Special Placement)

Parents or legal guardians assisting minors (individuals under 18) and certain employees with disabilities should review the guidelines in the *Handbook for Employers: Instructions for Completing Form I-9 (M-274)* on **www.uscis.gov/ I-9Central** before completing Section 1. These individuals have special procedures for establishing identity if they cannot present an identity document for Form I-9. The special procedures include **(1)** the parent or legal guardian filling out Section 1 and writing "minor under age 18" or "special placement," whichever applies, in the employee signature block; and **(2)** the employer writing "minor under age 18" or "special placement" under List B in Section 2.

Section 2. Employer or Authorized Representative Review and Verification

Before completing Section 2, employers must ensure that Section 1 is completed properly and on time. Employers may not ask an individual to complete Section 1 before he or she has accepted a job offer.

Employers or their authorized representative must complete Section 2 by examining evidence of identity and employment authorization within 3 business days of the employee's first day of employment. For example, if an employee begins employment on Monday, the employer must complete Section 2 by Thursday of that week. However, if an employer hires an individual for less than 3 business days, Section 2 must be completed no later than the first day of employment. An employer may complete Form I-9 before the first day of employment if the employer has offered the individual a job and the individual has accepted.

Employers cannot specify which document(s) employees may present from the Lists of Acceptable Documents, found on the last page of Form I-9, to establish identity and employment authorization. Employees must present one selection from List A **OR** a combination of one selection from List B and one selection from List C. List A contains documents that show both identity and employment authorization. Some List A documents are combination documents. The employee must present combination documents together to be considered a List A document. For example, a foreign passport and a Form I-94 containing an endorsement of the alien's nonimmigrant status must be presented together to be considered a List A document. List B contains documents that show identity only, and List C contains documents that show employment authorization only. If an employee presents a List A document, he or she should **not** present a List B and List C document, and vice versa. If an employer participates in E-Verify, the List B document must include a photograph.

In the field below the Section 2 introduction, employers must enter the last name, first name and middle initial, if any, that the employee entered in Section 1. This will help to identify the pages of the form should they get separated.

Employers or their authorized representative must:

1. Physically examine each original document the employee presents to determine if it reasonably appears to be genuine and to relate to the person presenting it. The person who examines the documents must be the same person who signs Section 2. The examiner of the documents and the employee must both be physically present during the examination of the employee's documents.

2. Record the document title shown on the Lists of Acceptable Documents, issuing authority, document number and expiration date (if any) from the original document(s) the employee presents. You may write "N/A" in any unused fields.

   If the employee is a student or exchange visitor who presented a foreign passport with a Form I-94, the employer should also enter in Section 2:

   a. The student's Form I-20 or DS-2019 number (Student and Exchange Visitor Information System-SEVIS Number); **and** the program end date from Form I-20 or DS-2019.

3. Under Certification, enter the employee's first day of employment. Temporary staffing agencies may enter the first day the employee was placed in a job pool. Recruiters and recruiters for a fee do not enter the employee's first day of employment.

4. Provide the name and title of the person completing Section 2 in the Signature of Employer or Authorized Representative field.

5. Sign and date the attestation on the date Section 2 is completed.

6. Record the employer's business name and address.

7. Return the employee's documentation.

Employers may, but are not required to, photocopy the document(s) presented. If photocopies are made, they should be made for **ALL** new hires or reverifications. Photocopies must be retained and presented with Form I-9 in case of an inspection by DHS or other federal government agency. Employers must always complete Section 2 even if they photocopy an employee's document(s). Making photocopies of an employee's document(s) cannot take the place of completing Form I-9. Employers are still responsible for completing and retaining Form I-9.

Unexpired Documents

Generally, only unexpired, original documentation is acceptable. The only exception is that an employee may present a certified copy of a birth certificate. Additionally, in some instances, a document that appears to be expired may be acceptable if the expiration date shown on the face of the document has been extended, such as for individuals with temporary protected status. Refer to the *Handbook for Employers: Instructions for Completing Form I-9 (M-274)* or I-9 Central (www.uscis.gov/I-9Central) for examples.

Receipts

If an employee is unable to present a required document (or documents), the employee can present an acceptable receipt in lieu of a document from the Lists of Acceptable Documents on the last page of this form. Receipts showing that a person has applied for an initial grant of employment authorization, or for renewal of employment authorization, are not acceptable. Employers cannot accept receipts if employment will last less than 3 days. Receipts are acceptable when completing Form I-9 for a new hire or when reverification is required.

Employees must present receipts within 3 business days of their first day of employment, or in the case of reverification, by the date that reverification is required, and must present valid replacement documents within the time frames described below.

There are three types of acceptable receipts:

1. A receipt showing that the employee has applied to replace a document that was lost, stolen or damaged. The employee must present the actual document within 90 days from the date of hire.

2. The arrival portion of Form I-94/I-94A with a temporary I-551 stamp and a photograph of the individual. The employee must present the actual Permanent Resident Card (Form I-551) by the expiration date of the temporary I-551 stamp, or, if there is no expiration date, within 1 year from the date of issue.

3. The departure portion of Form I-94/I-94A with a refugee admission stamp. The employee must present an unexpired Employment Authorization Document (Form I-766) or a combination of a List B document and an unrestricted Social Security card within 90 days.

When the employee provides an acceptable receipt, the employer should:

1. Record the document title in Section 2 under the sections titled List A, List B, or List C, as applicable.

2. Write the word "receipt" and its document number in the "Document Number" field. Record the last day that the receipt is valid in the "Expiration Date" field.

By the end of the receipt validity period, the employer should:

1. Cross out the word "receipt" and any accompanying document number and expiration date.

2. Record the number and other required document information from the actual document presented.

3. Initial and date the change.

See the *Handbook for Employers: Instructions for Completing Form I-9 (M-274)* at **www.uscis.gov/I-9Central** for more information on receipts.

Section 3. Reverification and Rehires

Employers or their authorized representatives should complete Section 3 when reverifying that an employee is authorized to work. When rehiring an employee within 3 years of the date Form I-9 was originally completed, employers have the option to complete a new Form I-9 or complete Section 3. When completing Section 3 in either a reverification or rehire situation, if the employee's name has changed, record the name change in Block A.

For employees who provide an employment authorization expiration date in Section 1, employers must reverify employment authorization on or before the date provided.

Some employees may write "N/A" in the space provided for the expiration date in Section 1 if they are aliens whose employment authorization does not expire (e.g., asylees, refugees, certain citizens of the Federated States of Micronesia, the Republic of the Marshall Islands, or Palau). Reverification does not apply for such employees unless they chose to present evidence of employment authorization in Section 2 that contains an expiration date and requires reverification, such as Form I-766, Employment Authorization Document.

Reverification applies if evidence of employment authorization (List A or List C document) presented in Section 2 expires. However, employers should not reverify:

1. U.S. citizens and noncitizen nationals; or

2. Lawful permanent residents who presented a Permanent Resident Card (Form I-551) for Section 2.

Reverification does not apply to List B documents.

If both Section 1 and Section 2 indicate expiration dates triggering the reverification requirement, the employer should reverify by the earlier date.

For reverification, an employee must present unexpired documentation from either List A or List C showing he or she is still authorized to work. Employers CANNOT require the employee to present a particular document from List A or List C. The employee may choose which document to present.

To complete Section 3, employers should follow these instructions:

1. Complete Block A if an employee's name has changed at the time you complete Section 3.

2. Complete Block B with the date of rehire if you rehire an employee within 3 years of the date this form was originally completed, and the employee is still authorized to be employed on the same basis as previously indicated on this form. Also complete the "Signature of Employer or Authorized Representative" block.

3. Complete Block C if:

   a. The employment authorization or employment authorization document of a current employee is about to expire and requires reverification; or

   b. You rehire an employee within 3 years of the date this form was originally completed and his or her employment authorization or employment authorization document has expired. (Complete Block B for this employee as well.)

   To complete Block C:

   a. Examine either a List A or List C document the employee presents that shows that the employee is currently authorized to work in the United States; and

   b. Record the document title, document number, and expiration date (if any).

4. After completing block A, B or C, complete the "Signature of Employer or Authorized Representative" block, including the date.

   For reverification purposes, employers may either complete Section 3 of a new Form I-9 or Section 3 of the previously completed Form I-9. Any new pages of Form I-9 completed during reverification must be attached to the employee's original Form I-9. If you choose to complete Section 3 of a new Form I-9, you may attach just the page containing Section 3, with the employee's name entered at the top of the page, to the employee's original Form I-9. If there is a more current version of Form I-9 at the time of reverification, you must complete Section 3 of that version of the form.

What Is the Filing Fee?

There is no fee for completing Form I-9. This form is not filed with USCIS or any government agency. Form I-9 must be retained by the employer and made available for inspection by U.S. Government officials as specified in the **"USCIS Privacy Act Statement"** below.

USCIS Forms and Information

For more detailed information about completing Form I-9, employers and employees should refer to the *Handbook for Employers: Instructions for Completing Form I-9 (M-274)*.

You can also obtain information about Form I-9 from the USCIS Web site at www.uscis.gov/I-9Central, by e-mailing USCIS at **I-9Central@dhs.gov**, or by calling **1-888-464-4218**. For TDD (hearing impaired), call **1-877-875-6028**.

To obtain USCIS forms or the *Handbook for Employers*, you can download them from the USCIS Web site at www.uscis.gov/forms. You may order USCIS forms by calling our toll-free number at **1-800-870-3676**. You may also obtain forms and information by contacting the USCIS National Customer Service Center at **1-800-375-5283**. For TDD (hearing impaired), call **1-800-767-1833**.

Information about E-Verify, a free and voluntary program that allows participating employers to electronically verify the employment eligibility of their newly hired employees, can be obtained from the USCIS Web site at www.dhs.gov/E-Verify, by e-mailing USCIS at **E-Verify@dhs.gov** or by calling **1-888-464-4218**. For TDD (hearing impaired), call **1-877-875-6028**.

Employees with questions about Form I-9 and/or E-Verify can reach the USCIS employee hotline by calling **1-888-897-7781**. For TDD (hearing impaired), call **1-877-875-6028**.

Photocopying and Retaining Form I-9

A blank Form I-9 may be reproduced, provided all sides are copied. The instructions and Lists of Acceptable Documents must be available to all employees completing this form. Employers must retain each employee's completed Form I-9 for as long as the individual works for the employer. Employers are required to retain the pages of the form on which the employee and employer enter data. If copies of documentation presented by the employee are made, those copies must also be kept with the form. Once the individual's employment ends, the employer must retain this form for either 3 years after the date of hire or 1 year after the date employment ended, whichever is later.

Form I-9 may be signed and retained electronically, in compliance with Department of Homeland Security regulations at 8 CFR 274a.2.

USCIS Privacy Act Statement

AUTHORITIES: The authority for collecting this information is the Immigration Reform and Control Act of 1986, Public Law 99-603 (8 USC 1324a).

PURPOSE: This information is collected by employers to comply with the requirements of the Immigration Reform and Control Act of 1986. This law requires that employers verify the identity and employment authorization of individuals they hire for employment to preclude the unlawful hiring, or recruiting or referring for a fee, of aliens who are not authorized to work in the United States.

DISCLOSURE: Submission of the information required in this form is voluntary. However, failure of the employer to ensure proper completion of this form for each employee may result in the imposition of civil or criminal penalties. In addition, employing individuals knowing that they are unauthorized to work in the United States may subject the employer to civil and/or criminal penalties.

ROUTINE USES: This information will be used by employers as a record of their basis for determining eligibility of an employee to work in the United States. The employer will keep this form and make it available for inspection by authorized officials of the Department of Homeland Security, Department of Labor, and Office of Special Counsel for Immigration-Related Unfair Employment Practices.

Paperwork Reduction Act

An agency may not conduct or sponsor an information collection and a person is not required to respond to a collection of information unless it displays a currently valid OMB control number. The public reporting burden for this collection of information is estimated at 35 minutes per response, including the time for reviewing instructions and completing and retaining the form. Send comments regarding this burden estimate or any other aspect of this collection of information, including suggestions for reducing this burden, to: U.S. Citizenship and Immigration Services, Regulatory Coordination Division, Office of Policy and Strategy, 20 Massachusetts Avenue NW, Washington, DC 20529-2140; OMB No. 1615-0047. **Do not mail your completed Form I-9 to this address.**

Employment Eligibility Verification
Department of Homeland Security
U.S. Citizenship and Immigration Services

USCIS
Form I-9
OMB No. 1615-0047
Expires 03/31/2016

▶**START HERE. Read instructions carefully before completing this form. The instructions must be available during completion of this form.**
ANTI-DISCRIMINATION NOTICE: It is illegal to discriminate against work-authorized individuals. Employers **CANNOT** specify which document(s) they will accept from an employee. The refusal to hire an individual because the documentation presented has a future expiration date may also constitute illegal discrimination.

Section 1. Employee Information and Attestation *(Employees must complete and sign Section 1 of Form I-9 no later than the **first day of employment**, but not before accepting a job offer.)*

Last Name *(Family Name)*	First Name *(Given Name)*	Middle Initial	Other Names Used *(if any)*

Address *(Street Number and Name)*	Apt. Number	City or Town	State	Zip Code

Date of Birth *(mm/dd/yyyy)*	U.S. Social Security Number	E-mail Address	Telephone Number
	☐☐☐-☐☐-☐☐☐☐		

I am aware that federal law provides for imprisonment and/or fines for false statements or use of false documents in connection with the completion of this form.

I attest, under penalty of perjury, that I am (check one of the following):

☐ A citizen of the United States

☐ A noncitizen national of the United States *(See instructions)*

☐ A lawful permanent resident (Alien Registration Number/USCIS Number): _____

☐ An alien authorized to work until (expiration date, if applicable, mm/dd/yyyy) _____ . Some aliens may write "N/A" in this field. *(See instructions)*

For aliens authorized to work, provide your Alien Registration Number/USCIS Number **OR** *Form I-94 Admission Number:*

1. Alien Registration Number/USCIS Number: _____

OR

2. Form I-94 Admission Number: _____

If you obtained your admission number from CBP in connection with your arrival in the United States, include the following:

Foreign Passport Number: _____

Country of Issuance: _____

Some aliens may write "N/A" on the Foreign Passport Number and Country of Issuance fields. *(See instructions)*

3-D Barcode
Do Not Write in This Space

Signature of Employee:	Date *(mm/dd/yyyy)*:

Preparer and/or Translator Certification *(To be completed and signed if Section 1 is prepared by a person other than the employee.)*

I attest, under penalty of perjury, that I have assisted in the completion of this form and that to the best of my knowledge the information is true and correct.

Signature of Preparer or Translator:	Date *(mm/dd/yyyy)*:

Last Name *(Family Name)*	First Name *(Given Name)*		

Address *(Street Number and Name)*	City or Town	State	Zip Code

🛑 *Employer Completes Next Page* 🛑

Section 2. Employer or Authorized Representative Review and Verification

(Employers or their authorized representative must complete and sign Section 2 within 3 business days of the employee's first day of employment. You must physically examine one document from List A OR examine a combination of one document from List B and one document from List C as listed on the "Lists of Acceptable Documents" on the next page of this form. For each document you review, record the following information: document title, issuing authority, document number, and expiration date, if any.)

Employee Last Name, First Name and Middle Initial from Section 1:

List A Identity and Employment Authorization	OR	List B Identity	AND	List C Employment Authorization
Document Title:		Document Title:		Document Title:
Issuing Authority:		Issuing Authority:		Issuing Authority:
Document Number:		Document Number:		Document Number:
Expiration Date *(if any)(mm/dd/yyyy)*:		Expiration Date *(if any)(mm/dd/yyyy)*:		Expiration Date *(if any)(mm/dd/yyyy)*:
Document Title:				
Issuing Authority:				
Document Number:				
Expiration Date *(if any)(mm/dd/yyyy)*:				
Document Title:				3-D Barcode Do Not Write in This Space
Issuing Authority:				
Document Number:				
Expiration Date *(if any)(mm/dd/yyyy)*:				

Certification

I attest, under penalty of perjury, that (1) I have examined the document(s) presented by the above-named employee, (2) the above-listed document(s) appear to be genuine and to relate to the employee named, and (3) to the best of my knowledge the employee is authorized to work in the United States.

The employee's first day of employment *(mm/dd/yyyy)*: _____ *(See instructions for exemptions.)*

Signature of Employer or Authorized Representative	Date *(mm/dd/yyyy)*	Title of Employer or Authorized Representative		
Last Name *(Family Name)*	First Name *(Given Name)*	Employer's Business or Organization Name		
Employer's Business or Organization Address *(Street Number and Name)*	City or Town		State	Zip Code

Section 3. Reverification and Rehires *(To be completed and signed by employer or authorized representative.)*

A. New Name *(if applicable)* Last Name *(Family Name)* First Name *(Given Name)*	Middle Initial	B. Date of Rehire *(if applicable) (mm/dd/yyyy)*:

C. If employee's previous grant of employment authorization has expired, provide the information for the document from List A or List C the employee presented that establishes current employment authorization in the space provided below.

Document Title:	Document Number:	Expiration Date *(if any)(mm/dd/yyyy)*:

I attest, under penalty of perjury, that to the best of my knowledge, this employee is authorized to work in the United States, and if the employee presented document(s), the document(s) I have examined appear to be genuine and to relate to the individual.

Signature of Employer or Authorized Representative:	Date *(mm/dd/yyyy)*:	Print Name of Employer or Authorized Representative:

LISTS OF ACCEPTABLE DOCUMENTS
All documents must be UNEXPIRED

Employees may present one selection from List A
or a combination of one selection from List B and one selection from List C.

LIST A		LIST B	LIST C
Documents that Establish Both Identity and Employment Authorization	OR	Documents that Establish Identity AND	Documents that Establish Employment Authorization
1. U.S. Passport or U.S. Passport Card		1. Driver's license or ID card issued by a State or outlying possession of the United States provided it contains a photograph or information such as name, date of birth, gender, height, eye color, and address	1. A Social Security Account Number card, unless the card includes one of the following restrictions: (1) NOT VALID FOR EMPLOYMENT (2) VALID FOR WORK ONLY WITH INS AUTHORIZATION (3) VALID FOR WORK ONLY WITH DHS AUTHORIZATION
2. Permanent Resident Card or Alien Registration Receipt Card (Form I-551)			
3. Foreign passport that contains a temporary I-551 stamp or temporary I-551 printed notation on a machine-readable immigrant visa			
		2. ID card issued by federal, state or local government agencies or entities, provided it contains a photograph or information such as name, date of birth, gender, height, eye color, and address	
4. Employment Authorization Document that contains a photograph (Form I-766)			2. Certification of Birth Abroad issued by the Department of State (Form FS-545)
		3. School ID card with a photograph	
5. For a nonimmigrant alien authorized to work for a specific employer because of his or her status:		4. Voter's registration card	3. Certification of Report of Birth issued by the Department of State (Form DS-1350)
		5. U.S. Military card or draft record	
a. Foreign passport; and		6. Military dependent's ID card	4. Original or certified copy of birth certificate issued by a State, county, municipal authority, or territory of the United States bearing an official seal
b. Form I-94 or Form I-94A that has the following:		7. U.S. Coast Guard Merchant Mariner Card	
(1) The same name as the passport; and		8. Native American tribal document	5. Native American tribal document
(2) An endorsement of the alien's nonimmigrant status as long as that period of endorsement has not yet expired and the proposed employment is not in conflict with any restrictions or limitations identified on the form.		9. Driver's license issued by a Canadian government authority **For persons under age 18 who are unable to present a document listed above:**	6. U.S. Citizen ID Card (Form I-197) 7. Identification Card for Use of Resident Citizen in the United States (Form I-179)
6. Passport from the Federated States of Micronesia (FSM) or the Republic of the Marshall Islands (RMI) with Form I-94 or Form I-94A indicating nonimmigrant admission under the Compact of Free Association Between the United States and the FSM or RMI		10. School record or report card 11. Clinic, doctor, or hospital record 12. Day-care or nursery school record	8. Employment authorization document issued by the Department of Homeland Security

Illustrations of many of these documents appear in Part 8 of the Handbook for Employers (M-274).

Refer to Section 2 of the instructions, titled "Employer or Authorized Representative Review and Verification," for more information about acceptable receipts.

Chapter 13
JOBSITE SAFETY AND ENVIRONMENTAL FACTORS

Chapter Survey...

Safety First: Creating a safe working environment is not only a good way to run your business, it is the law. Effective management and implementation of workplace safety and health programs add significant value to individuals and companies by reducing the extent, severity, and consequences of work-related injury and illness. As a whole, businesses spend between $145 billion to $290 billion a year in indirect and direct costs associated with occupational injuries and illnesses.

✓ Workplace injuries and illnesses are reduced by approximately 20 to 40 percent when employers establish safety and health programs.

✓ Workers' compensation premiums, employee retraining costs, and absenteeism are decreased by reducing workplace injuries and illnesses.

✓ Increased workplace safety results in increased productivity and morale and ultimately, profits.

Safety Standards

Understanding OSHA: The Occupational Safety and Health Administration (OSHA) was established by the Occupational Safety and Health Act of 1970 (OSH Act). All employers are subject to federal OSHA requirements and some states have adopted a state plan. State standards are at least as strict as the federal plan. The first step to complying with OSHA is to learn the published standards.

The OSHA standards that apply to the construction industry are

✓ 29 CFR 1926, Safety and Health Regulations for the Construction Industry;

✓ 29 CFR 1910, Occupational Safety and Health Standards; and

✓ 29 CFR 1904, Recording and Reporting Occupational Injuries and Illnesses.

It is the employer's responsibility to understand the OSHA standards and quickly correct any violations. Putting together a safety program with these standards in mind can help maximize employee safety and prevent violations before they occur.

OSHA Poster: All employers must post the OSHA poster (or state plan equivalent) in a prominent location in the workplace. In construction, employees are generally dispersed to different sites and the

OSHA poster must be posted at the location to which employees report each day.

The OSHA poster is downloadable from the OSHA website (www.osha.gov). This website also has useful links to many safety and environmental topics including compliance assistance and laws and regulations. For more information about OSHA, contact

> *Occupational Safety and Health Administration (OSHA)*
> *Office of Small Business Assistance*
> *Directorate of Cooperative and State Programs*
> *200 Constitution Avenue, NW*
> *Washington, DC 20210*
>
> *Phone: (800) 321-6742 (OSHA)*
>
> *Website: www.osha.gov*

OSHA Construction Safety Act: The Contract Work Hours and Safety Standards Act, commonly known as the Construction Safety Act, sets safety standards for construction contracts on federal projects.

North Carolina Safety Program: North Carolina does not have a state-adopted OSHA plan and falls under federal OSHA laws. The Department of Labor, Occupational Safety & Health Division is responsible for assisting employers in complying with federal OSHA requirements and reducing work-related injuries and illnesses.

> *North Carolina Department of Labor*
> *Occupational Safety & Health Division*
> *1001 Mail Service Center*
> *Raleigh, North Carolina 27699-1101*
>
> *Telephone: (919) 807-2900*
>
> *Website: www.nclabor.com/osha/osh.htm*

The division has several services available to employers:

✓ Complaint, accident, and fatality investigations

✓ Random inspections

✓ Free safety consultation services

✓ Training classes on safety and health issues

✓ Safety awards

Safe Hiring and Training

Hire Safe: The first step to improving safety in the workplace is to hire employees who have a good safety track record. The majority of accidents are caused by unsafe actions, not unsafe conditions. It is important to do thorough applicant screening and check all employment references. If you find that an applicant had safety accidents with a previous employer, chances for additional accidents while working for you are greater.

Regular Training: Training on safety practices and policies should be conducted regularly. New employees should receive a copy of your safety policies and sign off on them. Brief 10-minute training sessions can be conducted at the jobsite with your crew daily. During these training sessions, you can review policies and receive feedback from your employees on potential hazards that occur on the jobsite.

Conduct regular safety training for your employees.

Substance Abuse Policies

Your Bottom Line: Substance abuse in the workplace can have a profound effect on your business and significantly impact your bottom line. This problem costs American businesses more than $100 billion every year. This loss occurs in

✓ workers' compensation claims,

✓ medical costs,

✓ absenteeism,

✓ lost productivity, and

✓ employee turnover.

For this reason, you should develop a substance free workplace program and make sure that all employees know that substance abuse is not permitted.

Employee Program: Develop your program together with your employees. Talk about the benefits of having a substance free workplace and your concern for them to have a safe and healthy work environment. Eliminating substance abuse increases productivity, reduces accidents, and lowers insurance claim costs. Solicit input from your employees on how to implement the program in the workplace and any other suggestions they have.

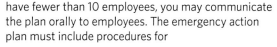

Consider this...

Ninety percent of large businesses have drug-free workplace programs in place today, while 5 percent to 10 percent of small- and medium-sized businesses have implemented similar programs. The irony here is that 75 percent of employed Americans work for small- and medium-sized businesses.

Communicate Your Policy: Once you have developed a program, distribute the policy to all employees and have them sign off on it. Your policies should expressly prohibit the illegal use of drugs and/or abuse of alcohol by any employee and spell out the consequences of policy violations. All new employees should receive your policy as part of their orientation. You should also check with your workers' compensation carrier to see if you can receive a credit for having this policy in place.

Encourage employee participation in developing company safety programs.

Safety Equipment

Prevent Injuries: Using proper safety equipment can lower the occurrence of injuries on the job. This equipment might include

- ✓ hard hats,
- ✓ safety shoes/boots,
- ✓ protective eyewear,
- ✓ gloves,
- ✓ fall protection,
- ✓ hearing protection,
- ✓ respirators,
- ✓ protective coveralls, and
- ✓ face shields.

Make sure you consult OSHA safety standards to determine what safety equipment is required by law and assess your jobsite to determine additional equipment you want your employees to have.

Emergency Action Plan

Your Plan of Action: OSHA regulations require you have an emergency action plan. If you have more than 10 employees, your plan must be in writing. If you

have fewer than 10 employees, you may communicate the plan orally to employees. The emergency action plan must include procedures for

- ✓ reporting a fire or other emergency;
- ✓ emergency evacuation;
- ✓ employees who remain for critical operations before evacuating;
- ✓ accounting for all employees after evacuation; and
- ✓ employees performing rescue or medical duties.

The plan should also include the name or job title of the plan administrator. You must review the plan with your employees, designate and train employees to assist in a safe evacuation, and have a distinctive signal that serves as an employee alarm system.

Other OSHA recommendations, although not required, for inclusion in the emergency action plan are

- ✓ a description of the employee alarm system defining each of the alarm signals and corresponding employee action;
- ✓ an alternative site for communication in the event of a fire or explosion; and
- ✓ a secure location, either onsite or offsite, where important information, such as accounting documents, legal files, and employee emergency contact numbers, can be stored.

OSHA Recordkeeping

For the Record: Every employer covered by OSHA who has more than 10 employees, except for employers in certain low-hazard industries in the retail, finance, insurance, real estate, and service sectors, must maintain three types of OSHA-specified records of job-related injuries and illnesses.

These forms are located at the end of the chapter.

- ✓ OSHA Form 300
- ✓ OSHA Form 300A
- ✓ OSHA Form 301

The **OSHA Form 300** is an injury/illness log, with a separate line entry for each recordable injury or illness. Such events include work-related deaths, injuries, and illnesses other than minor injuries that require only first aid treatment and do not involve medical treatment, loss of consciousness, restriction of work, days away from work, or transfer to another job.

Construction site operations that last for more than one year must keep a separate OSHA 300 log.

Each year, the employer must conspicuously post in the workplace a **Form 300A**, which includes a summary of the previous year's work-related injuries and illnesses. The data from Form 300 is used to complete this form. Form 300A must be posted by February 1 and kept in place until at least April 30 following the year covered by the form.

OSHA Form 301 is an individual incident report that provides added detail about each specific recordable injury or illness. An alternative form, such as an insurance or workers' compensation form that provides the same details may be substituted for OSHA Form 301.

Who Needs to Complete the Forms? Employers with 10 or fewer employees are exempt from maintaining these records. However, such employers must keep these records if they receive an annual illness and injury survey form either from the Bureau of Labor Statistics (BLS) or from OSHA. Employers selected for these surveys will be notified before the end of the prior year to begin keeping records during the year covered by the survey.

Timeframe to Retain Records: OSHA records must be kept by the employer for five years following the year to which they pertain.

Exposure Records and Medical Records: Exposure records (including employee exposure to toxic substances and harmful physical agents) must be maintained for 30 years and medical records for the duration of employment plus 30 years. Analysis using exposure or medical records must be kept for 30 years.

Toxic substances and harmful agents include

✓ any material listed in the National Institute for Occupational Safety and Health (NIOSH) Registry of Toxic Effects of Chemical Hazards (RTECHS);
✓ substances which have evidenced an acute or chronic health hazard in testing conducted by or known to the employer; and
✓ substances in a material safety data sheet kept by or known to the employer, indicating that the material may pose a health hazard.

Reporting Fatalities and Hospitalizations: When a work-related fatality or incident that requires hospitalization of three or more employees occurs,

✓ employers must orally report the fatality or incident to the nearest OSHA Area Office within eight hours; and
✓ if a death occurs within 30 days of the incident, employers must report it within eight hours.

Employers do not need to report a death occurring more than 30 days after a work-related incident.

Recordable Illnesses and Injuries: Cases that meet the general recording criteria involve a significant injury or illness diagnosed by a physician or other licensed health care professional, even if it does not result in death, days away from work, restricted work or job transfer, medical treatment beyond first aid, or loss of consciousness.

Medical Treatment Defined: Medical treatment means the management and care of a patient to combat a disease or disorder. It does not include

✓ visits to a physician or other licensed health care professional solely for observation or counseling;
✓ conduct of diagnostic procedures, such as x-rays and blood tests, including the administration of prescription medications used solely for diagnostic purposes (i.e., eye drops to dilate pupils); or
✓ first aid.

First Aid Defined: The following treatments are considered first aid according to 29 CFR 1904:

✓ Using a non-prescription medication at the non-prescription strength
✓ Administering tetanus immunizations (other immunizations, such as the Hepatitis B vaccine or rabies vaccine, are considered medical treatment)
✓ Cleaning, flushing or soaking wounds on the surface of the skin
✓ Using wound coverings such as bandages, Band-Aids™, gauze pads, etc.; or using butterfly bandages or Steri-Strips™; other wound closing devices such as sutures, staples, etc., are considered medical treatment
✓ Using hot or cold therapy
✓ Using any non-rigid means of support, such as elastic bandages, wraps, non-rigid back belts, etc.; devices with rigid stays or other systems designed to immobilize parts of the body are considered medical treatment for recordkeeping purposes

- ✓ Using temporary immobilization devices while transporting an accident victim (i.e., splints, slings, neck collars, back boards, etc.)
- ✓ Drilling of a fingernail or toenail to relieve pressure or draining fluid from a blister
- ✓ Using eye patches
- ✓ Removing foreign bodies from the eye using only irrigation or a cotton swab
- ✓ Removing splinters or foreign material from areas other than the eye by irrigation, tweezers, cotton swabs or other simple means

- ✓ Using finger guards
- ✓ Using massages; physical therapy or chiropractic treatment are considered medical treatment for recordkeeping purposes
- ✓ Drinking fluids for relief of heat stress

OSHA Injury Decision Tree

The OSHA injury decision tree shows the steps involved in making the determination for recording work-related injuries or illnesses.

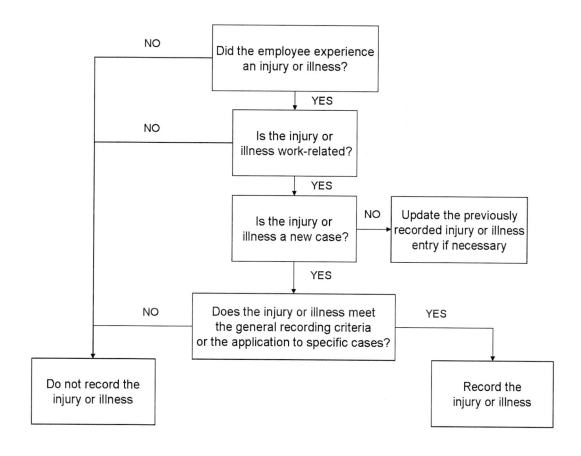

Material Safety Data Sheets (MSDS)

Chemical Safety: Material safety data sheets (MSDS) are a requirement of OSHA's Hazard Communication Standard (HCS). The purpose of the HCS is to ensure chemical safety in the workplace. Requirements of the MSDS program include:

✓ Manufacturers and importers of hazardous materials are required to conduct hazard evaluations of the products they manufacture or import.

✓ If a product is found to be hazardous under the terms of the standard, the manufacturer or importer must so indicate on containers of the material, and the first shipment of the material to a new customer must include a material safety data sheet (MSDS).

✓ Employers must use these MSDSs to train their employees to recognize and avoid the hazards presented by the materials.

Emergency Treatment: Employers must keep MSDSs on hand for all chemicals used in the workplace. The MSDS provides emergency information in case of contact with the chemical either internally or externally. The MSDS also explains the proper precautions to take when using a chemical. In the event of an OSHA inspection, the compliance officer will confirm that all MSDSs are at the worksite.

Inspection Guidelines: OSHA publishes inspection guidelines for enforcement of the Hazard Communication Standard. A summary of items that are reviewed during an inspection is included below:

✓ Is there a written hazard communication plan?

✓ Who is responsible for obtaining and maintaining MSDSs?

✓ Is there an MSDS for every chemical used?

✓ How are the MSDSs maintained (i.e., in notebooks in the work area(s), in a pickup truck at the jobsite, etc.) and do employees have proper access to them?

✓ Who is responsible for conducting training on chemicals and what are the elements of the training program?

The detailed procedure can be downloaded off the OSHA website (www.osha.gov).

Underground Utility Safety

Excavating without identifying underground utilities is a safety issue and can cost you unnecessary fines, repair costs, and utility outages. Although laws on marking underground utilities vary from state to state, contractors should identify underground utilities before digging on

✓ public and private property;

✓ public streets;

✓ alleys;

✓ utility easements; and

✓ all other rights-of-way.

In order to request a locater to come out to your site and locate underground utilities, the Common Ground Alliance (CGA) can be reached by calling 811. Your call is then routed to a local One Call Center. If you prefer to contact your local One Call Center directly, contact information for each state is located on the CGA website at www.call811.com/state-specific.aspx. For direct access to the North Carolina safe digging information, see **Appendix M** and visit www.nc811.org/safe-digging-process.html.

Overhead Power Line Safety

OSHA has several programs focused on safety for those who work around overhead power lines. Listed below are a few key points from OSHA to consider when formulating a health and safety program and worksite planning.

Considerations include the following:

✓ perform a thorough site survey prior to beginning construction work;

✓ stay at least 10 feet away from overhead power lines;

✓ assume that all power lines are energized unless confirmed by proper authorities;

✓ call the utility company if overhead lines are present to determine voltage and if the lines can be shut off or insulated during construction work;

✓ use non-conductive ladders when working around overhead power lines;

✓ keep conductive objects at least 10 feet away from overhead power lines unless otherwise trained and qualified to use insulated tools specifically designed for high voltage lines; and

✓ perform thorough research on the location and voltage of overhead power lines when using cranes and heavy equipment to determine a minimum safe distance for operation.

Additional information on overhead power line safety is available on the OSHA website at www.osha.gov.

Benefits of Providing a Safe and Healthy Workplace

Ignoring safety and health regulations in the workplace is detrimental in many ways. Employees are put at risk, company reputation is at stake, and costs are high when accidents happen which affects overall company profits.

The most frequent citations that OSHA issues to the construction industry are for violations pertaining to

✓ scaffolding;

✓ fall protection (scope, application, definitions);

✓ excavations (general requirements and requirements for protective systems);

✓ ladders;

✓ head protection;

✓ hazard communication;

✓ fall protection (training requirements);

✓ construction (general safety and health provisions); and

✓ electrical (wiring methods, design and protection).

Ensuring workers are healthy and safe provides many direct benefits to employers.

✓ lower workers' compensation insurance costs;

✓ reduced medical expenditures;

✓ smaller expenditures for return-to-work programs;

✓ fewer faulty products;

✓ lower costs for job accommodations for injured workers;

✓ less money spent for overtime benefits.

Following safety and health regulations and proper procedures has indirect benefits as well.

✓ increased productivity;

✓ higher quality products;

✓ increased morale;

✓ better labor/management relations;

✓ reduced turnover;

✓ better use of human resources.

The impact of a safety and health program extends beyond the workplace providing employees and their families the security that their incomes are protected, family life is not hindered by injury, and overall reduced stress.

Employee Rights

The OSH Act grants employees several important rights. Among them are the rights to

✓ complain to OSHA about safety and health conditions in their workplace and, to the extent permitted by law, have their identities kept confidential from their employer;

✓ contest the amount of time OSHA allows for correcting violations of standards; and

✓ participate in OSHA workplace inspections.

Retaliation is Prohibited: Private sector employees who exercise their rights under OSHA can be protected against employer reprisal. Employees must notify OSHA within 30 days of the time they learn of the alleged discriminatory action. OSHA will then investigate. If it agrees that discrimination has occurred, OSHA will ask the employer to restore any lost benefits to the affected employee. If necessary, OSHA can initiate legal action against the employer. In such cases, the worker pays no legal fees. The OSHA-approved state plans have similar employee rights provisions, including protections against employer reprisal.

Penalties

OSHA Enforcement: Every establishment covered by the OSH Act is subject to inspection by OSHA compliance safety and health officers (CSHOs). These individuals are chosen for their knowledge and experience in occupational safety and health. They are thoroughly trained in OSHA standards and in the recognition of occupational safety and health hazards. In states with their own OSHA-approved state plan, state officials conduct inspections, issue citations for violations, and propose penalties in a manner that is at least as strict as the federal program.

The following table illustrates penalty types, descriptions, and amounts assessed to the employer.

Penalty Type and Description	Penalty Amount
Other Than Serious Violation - A violation that has a direct relationship to workplace safety and health, but probably would not cause death or serious physical harm.	Discretionary penalty up to $7,000 for each violation
Serious Violation - A violation where there is substantial probability that death or serious physical harm could result and that the employer knew, or should have known, of the hazard.	Mandatory penalty up to $7,000 for each violation
Willful Violation - A violation that the employer knowingly commits or commits with plain indifference to the law. The employer either knows that what he or she is doing constitutes a violation, or is aware that a hazardous condition existed and made no reasonable effort to eliminate it.	Penalties of up to $70,000 with a minimum penalty of $5,000 for each violation. *If an employer is convicted of a willful violation of a standard that has resulted in the death of an employee, the offense is punishable by a court-imposed fine or by imprisonment for up to six months, or both. A fine of up to $250,000 for an individual, or $500,000 for a corporation, may be imposed for a criminal conviction.*
Repeated Violation - A violation of any standard, regulation, rule, or order where, upon reinspection, a substantially similar violation is found.	Penalties of up to $70,000
Failure to Abate Prior Violation - A violation given when a previous violation has not been corrected.	Civil penalty of up to $7,000 for each day the violation continues beyond the prescribed abatement date
De Minimis Violation – A violation of standards which have no direct or immediate relationship to safety or health.	Violation documented but not cited

Violations may be adjusted depending on the employer's good faith (demonstrated by efforts to comply with the act), history of previous violations, and size of business.

Additional violations for which citations and proposed penalties may be issued upon conviction include the following:

✓ Falsifying records, reports, or applications can bring a fine of $10,000 or up to six months in jail, or both.

✓ Violations of posting requirements can bring a civil penalty of up to $7,000.

✓ Assaulting a compliance officer, or otherwise resisting, opposing, intimidating, or interfering with a compliance officer while they are engaged in the performance of their duties is a criminal offense, subject to a fine of not more than $5,000 and imprisonment for not more than three years.

Citation and penalty procedures may differ somewhat in states with their own occupational safety and health programs.

Inspections: OSHA conducts two general types of inspections: **programmed** and **unprogrammed**.

✓ **Programmed inspections** are performed on establishments with high injury rates.

✓ **Unprogrammed inspections** are used in response to fatalities, catastrophes, and complaints.

Various OSHA publications and documents detail OSHA's policies and procedures for inspections and the penalties for violations.

Environmental Considerations

You need to be aware of the environmental considerations surrounding construction during all phases of the project.

✓ During the **pre-bid phase**, you must learn the regulations that pertain to the project and factor in the cost of compliance into the estimate.

✓ Obtaining the necessary permits occurs during the **pre-construction phase** and environmental responsibilities should be assigned to the construction crew.

✓ Self-audits help ensure compliance during the **construction phase**.

✓ For **post-construction**, you need to ensure that all the close-down procedures were done properly.

Going Green: Integrating eco-friendly practices in your business may help you control costs, tap into a new customer base, and enhance your socially responsible reputation. The demand for energy-efficient building design and construction is increasing. The Energy Star website at www.energystar.gov provides numerous resources on home improvement and commercial and residential construction. The EPA website at www.epa.gov/greenbuilding has information on components of green building, national, state and local funding opportunities, and publications on various environmental topics.

U.S. Environmental Protection Agency

Environmental Regulation: The U.S. Environmental Protection Agency (EPA) leads the nation's environmental science, research, education, and assessment efforts. The EPA works to develop and enforce regulations that implement environmental laws enacted by Congress. The EPA is responsible for researching and setting national standards for a variety of environmental programs and delegates to states the responsibility for issuing permits and for monitoring and enforcing compliance. If national standards are not met, the EPA can issue sanctions and take other steps to assist states in reaching the desired levels of environmental quality.

Compliance Assistance: The EPA publishes a guide called *Managing Your Responsibilities: A Planning Guide for Construction and Development*. This publication is available for download at: www.epa.gov/compliance/resources/publications/assistance/sectors/constructmyer/myerguide.pdf.

This guide provides comprehensive information for all types of environmental hazards and compliance requirements. Summarized briefly below are some of the environmental hazards impacting construction projects.

North Carolina Department of Environment and Natural Resources (NCDENR)

The North Carolina Department of Environment and Natural Resources (NCDENR) preserves and protects North Carolina's natural resources through proactive programs and enforcement of environmental regulations. Regulatory programs are designed to protect air quality, water quality, and the public's health. NCDENR also offers technical assistance to businesses and local governments. Through its natural resource divisions, NCDENR works to protect fish, wildlife, and wilderness areas.

North Carolina Department of Environment and Natural Resources
1601 Mail Service Center
Raleigh, North Carolina 27699-1601

Telephone: 1-877-623-6748

Environmental Emergency: 1-800-858-0368

Fax: (919) 715-3060

Website: www.ncdenr.gov

Before beginning a project, you should assess the jobsite and determine if you need an environmental permit. The NCDENR website has several resources available to help with the permitting process. The online Customer Service Center offers Express Permitting, One Stop Permit Coordination, and an interactive database to help businesses find the required permits.

Environmental Law

There are several environmental laws that may impact your construction activities.

✓ The **Clean Water Act** establishes the basic structure for regulating discharges of pollutants into the waters of the United States. This act gives the EPA authority to implement pollution control programs, such as setting wastewater standards for the industry and water quality standards for all contaminants in surface waters. This act is discussed in more depth later in this chapter.

✓ Through the **Clean Air Act**, the EPA sets limits on how much of a pollutant is allowed in the air anywhere in the United States.

✓ The Endangered Species Act (ESA) protects threatened or endangered species from further harm. You should consider the impact of your construction activities on these species before you start your project.

✓ The **National Environmental Policy Act (NEPA)** applies to your construction project only if it is considered a "federal action." This act ensures that federal agencies consider environmental impacts in federal planning and decision making and covers construction and post-construction activities.

✓ The **National Historic Preservation Act (NHPA)** applies to your construction project if your project might have a potential impact on a property that is eligible for or included on the National Register of Historic Places (NRHP).

A thorough environmental assessment of your construction site is recommended for all projects. This assessment allows you to understand the environmental impacts of your project early, causing fewer delays and problems.

Air Quality

Outdoor Air Quality: Air regulations for construction activities are designed to limit the generation of particulate and ozone depleting substances.

Air quality issues that may impact your business are

✓ uncontrolled open burning of debris,

✓ dust generation,

✓ vehicle emissions,

✓ combustion gases from oil-fired equipment, and

✓ releases of chlorofluorocarbons (CFCs).

Indoor Air: Indoor air quality can be just as important as outdoor air quality. For the safety of those on the construction site, you should give special consideration to materials that contain harmful chemicals including

✓ paint/primers,

✓ adhesives,

✓ floor coatings,

✓ carpet, and

✓ plywood/particle board.

Properly installed HVAC units and drain pans are important to avoid biological contaminants that breed in stagnant water. Most air permitting requirements for construction activities are at the state and local level.

Division of Air Quality: The Division of Air Quality within the North Carolina Department of Environment and Natural Resources is responsible for issuing air quality permits. North Carolina General Statute 143-215.108A specifies that the following activities require a permit:

✓ establishing or operating any air containment source;

✓ building, erecting, using, or operating any equipment that may result in the emission of an air contaminant or that is likely to cause air pollution; or

✓ altering or changing the construction or method of operation of any equipment or process from which air contaminants are or may be emitted.

The law also allows for certain activities to take place before securing a permit. These activities include

✓ clearing and grading;

✓ construction of access roads, driveways, and parking lots;

✓ building and installing underground pipework including water, sewer, electric, and telecommunications utilities; and

✓ building ancillary structures, including fences and office buildings that are not a necessary component of an air contaminant source, equipment, or associated air cleaning device as defined by law.

Air Quality Contacts:

Main Number: (919) 707-8400

Emergency Management: (800) 858-0368 or (919) 707-8425

Air Quality Regional Offices:

Asheville: (828) 296-4500

Fayetteville: (910) 433-3300

Mooresville: (704) 663-1699

Raleigh: (919) 791-4200

Washington: (252) 946-6481

Wilmington: (910) 796-7215

Winston-Salem: (336) 771-5000

. . . .
Be aware of both indoor and outdoor pollution.
. . . .

Asbestos

Before beginning any demolition or renovation activities on existing buildings, you should evaluate the potential for releasing asbestos. Exposure to asbestos can cause serious health problems and the EPA and OSHA have published rules regulating its production, use, and disposal.

Evaluation Guidelines: When evaluating whether or not asbestos may be present, you want to note possible asbestos-containing material, such as

✓ Insulation, including blown, rolled and wrapped

✓ Resilient floor coverings (tiles)

✓ Asbestos siding shingles

✓ Asbestos-cement products

✓ Asphalt roofing products

✓ Vermiculite insulation

The EPA has a comprehensive list of suspected asbestos-containing materials at: www.epa.gov/asbestos.

Inspections: If you are working with asbestos, you should have your site inspected by a certified asbestos inspector prior to construction. You must submit a written Notice of Intent 10 working days prior to starting construction activities. Written notices should

be submitted to your delegated state/local pollution control agency and your EPA Regional Office.

Permit and Notification: Removal and demolition projects containing asbestos require a permit and notification. Applications are available on the Health Hazards Control Unit website at epi.publichealth.nc.gov/asbestos/ahmp.html.

Health Hazards Control Unit
NCDHHS-Division of Public Health
1912 Mail Service Center
Raleigh, North Carolina 27699-1912

Telephone: (919) 707-5950

Fax: (919) 870-4808

Buncombe, Forsyth, and Mecklenburg counties have additional asbestos-related ordinances.

Buncombe County
WNC Regional Air Pollution Control Agency
(828) 255-5655

Forsyth County
Environmental Affairs Department
(336) 727-8064

Mecklenburg County
Land Use and Environmental Services Agency,
Air Quality
(704) 336-5430

Open burning is regulated through the Division of Air Quality.

Open Burning Line: (877) OPEN BURN or (877) 673-6287

Clean Water Act

Water pollution can negatively affect the use of water for drinking, household needs, recreation, fishing, transportation and commerce. The EPA enforces federal clean water and safe drinking water laws, provides support for municipal wastewater treatment plants, and takes part in pollution prevention efforts aimed at protecting watersheds and sources of drinking water.

The Clean Water Act establishes the basic structure for regulating discharges of pollutants into the waters of the United States. This includes

✓ giving the EPA the authority to implement pollution control programs such as setting wastewater standards for industry;

✓ continuing requirements to set water quality standards for all contaminants in surface waters; and

✓ making it unlawful for any person to discharge any pollutant from a point source into navigable waters, unless a National Pollutant Discharge Elimination System (NPDES) permit was obtained under its provisions.

Stormwater Discharges and Construction Site Runoff: Before beginning any construction project, you must consider runoff and stormwater discharges that may originate from your site. These discharges often contain sediment and pollutants such as phosphorous and nitrogen (fertilizer), pesticides, oil and grease, concrete truck washout, construction chemicals, and solid waste in quantities that could adversely affect water quality.

National Pollutant Discharge Elimination System (NPDES): The EPA has estimated that about 30 percent of known pollution to our nation's waters is attributable to stormwater runoff. In 1987, Congress directed the EPA to develop a regulatory program to address the stormwater problem. The EPA issued regulations in 1990 authorizing the creation of a NPDES permitting system for stormwater discharges from a select group, including construction activities disturbing five or more acres.

In 1999, the EPA expanded this program (called Phase II). This phase brought about two major new permittees:

✓ Construction sites that disturb one acre but less than five acres with possible exceptions allowing a waiver

✓ Small municipal separate storm sewer systems (MS4)

A "larger common plan of development or sale" is subject to stormwater permitting, even if the land is parceled off or sold, and construction occurs on plots that are less than one acre by separate, independent builders.

Assessing Stormwater Discharge: Listed below are questions that you need to consider when determining the need for a stormwater permit for your construction project:

✓ Will your construction project disturb one or more acres of land?

✓ Will your construction project disturb less than one acre of land, but is part of a larger common plan of development or sale that will disturb one or more acres?

✓ Will your construction project disturb less than one acre of land, but is designated by the NPDES (state agency or EPA) permitting authority as a regulated construction activity?

✓ Will stormwater from the construction site flow to a separate municipal storm sewer system or a body of water in the United States such as a lake, river, or wetland?

Municipal Technologies Agency: The EPA's Municipal Technologies Agency provides assistance in the area of municipal wastewater treatment technologies. Available assistance includes

✓ consultation on design, operation, and maintenance of systems;

✓ identification and solution of problems;

✓ contributions in the development of regulations; and

✓ technical information, guidance, assessments, evaluation, and cost estimates for the design, construction, and operation and maintenance of municipal wastewater treatment facilities.

Division of Water Quality: The Division of Water Quality within the North Carolina Department of Environment and Natural Resources is responsible for providing guidance and preparing several types of water permits, such as NPDES permits, stormwater general permits, wastewater general permits, and state stormwater management program permits.

This list of permits is not all-inclusive. Contact the permitting division for additional requirements.

Water Quality Regional Offices:

Asheville: (828) 296-4500

Fayetteville: (910) 433-3300

Mooresville: (704) 663-1699

Raleigh: (919) 791-4200

Washington: (252) 946-6481

Wilmington: (910) 796-7215

Winston-Salem: (336) 771-5000

Sedimentation and Erosion Control Measures

During a short period of time, construction sites can contribute more sediment to streams than can be deposited naturally during several decades. Excess sediment can quickly fill rivers and lakes, requiring dredging, and destroying aquatic habitats.

Measures can be taken to minimize erosion and sedimentation on construction sites:

✓ Sediment control measures include a silt fence or hay bales placed at the down gradient side of the construction site.

✓ Erosion control measures include placing mulch and vegetation as soon as feasible to permanently stabilize the site soil.

✓ A water misting system can control dust generated on the jobsite and loss of soil.

Erosion and sediment control minimizes pollution and contractor costs to rework eroded areas and replace lost soil. Individual states may have required sedimentation and erosion control measures.

Hazardous and Non-Hazardous Solid Waste

In general, construction sites generate more non-hazardous waste than hazardous waste. You should be aware of the regulations surrounding both.

Non-Hazardous Waste: Common non-hazardous waste generated at construction sites includes

✓ scrap wood,

✓ drywall,

✓ bricks,

✓ concrete,

✓ plumbing fixtures and piping,

✓ roof coverings,

✓ metal scraps, and

✓ electrical wiring and components.

Non-hazardous waste is regulated at the state and local level and you should identify any requirements. For more information on state requirements, refer to the Construction Industry Compliance Assistance Center at www.cicacenter.org.

Hazardous Waste: Hazardous waste is regulated at the federal level and your state may have additional requirements.

Examples of hazardous waste are

✓ lead-based paint,

✓ used oil,

✓ hydraulic fluid,

✓ gypsum drywall (due to sulfate), and

✓ mercury-containing demolition wastes such as batteries and thermostats.

Proper Notification: If you discover hazardous waste on your jobsite, you must notify state and local authorities or the National Response Center Hotline at 1-800-424-8802. Criminal charges may be filed if hazardous waste is present at the site and proper notification does not take place. If hazardous waste is produced through construction activities, the party that generated the waste is generally responsible for cleaning it up. Hazardous waste must be treated and disposed of at a facility permitted or licensed for that purpose by the state or federal government.

Hazardous Substances

Site Survey: Before beginning any construction or demolition activities at your construction site, you should evaluate the site for any hazardous substances.

Hazardous substances referred to in this section are chemicals that most likely induce serious acute reactions from short-term airborne exposure.

Notification: When you do a site survey, you should review historical records to determine previous uses of the site. A review of state and local files will help you identify past environmental concerns. If during construction you uncover hazardous substances, you must stop construction activities immediately and notify the owner and contact the National Response Center Hotline at 1-800-424-8802.

Underground Storage Tanks (UST): An underground storage tank system (UST) is defined by the EPA as "a tank and any underground piping connected to the tank that has at least 10 percent of its combined volume underground." The federal UST regulations apply only to underground tanks and piping storing either petroleum or certain hazardous substances.

Federal regulations do not apply to the following types of underground storage tanks:

✓ Farm and residential tanks of 1,100 gallons or less capacity holding motor fuel used for noncommercial purposes

✓ Tanks storing heating oil used on the premises where it is stored

✓ Tanks on or above the floor of underground areas, such as basements or tunnels

✓ Septic tanks and systems for collecting storm water and wastewater

✓ Flow-through process tanks

✓ Tanks of 110 gallons or less capacity

✓ Emergency spill and overfill tanks

Conduct a thorough site survey to anticipate any environmental hazards.

Lead

Exposure Hazards: Lead is considered a toxic and hazardous substance and can cause a serious risk of lead poisoning if overexposure occurs. OSHA regulates the amount of lead that workers can be exposed to (no more than 50 micrograms of lead per cubic meter of air averaged over an 8-hour day). Traditionally, most over-exposure occurs in trades such as plumbing, welding, and painting.

Hazard Protection: The most effective way to protect workers is through good work practices and engineering controls. Respirators are not a substitute for these practices, but should be an additional measure of safety. Employers are required to supply respirators at no cost to employees who will potentially be exposed to lead and adopt a respirator program, including a written standard operating procedure, training, and regular equipment inspection.

Engineering controls to reduce worker exposure include

✓ exhaust ventilation, such as power tools with dust collection shrouds or other attachments exhausted through a high-efficiency particulate air (HEPA) vacuum system;

✓ enclosure or encapsulation of lead particles (for example, lead-based paint can be made

inaccessible by encapsulating it with a material that bonds to the surface such as epoxy coating);

✓ substituting lead-based products or products that create lead exposure with a comparable product;

✓ replacing lead components with non-lead components;

✓ process or equipment modifications that create less lead exposure from dust; and

✓ isolating the lead exposure area so other areas are not contaminated.

Construction Assistance: OSHA has downloadable software on its website designed to help small business owners understand the Lead in Construction standard. Users should still refer to OSHA standards for specific details as it represents the most up-to-date source.

Remodeling or Renovating a Home with Lead-Based Paint

If not conducted properly, certain types of renovations can release lead from paint and dust into the air. The Lead Pre-Renovation Education Rule (Lead PRE) is a federal regulation involving those performing renovations for compensation in residential housing that may contain lead paint.

In December 2008 (with amendments in 2010 and 2011), the EPA passed the Lead-Based Paint Renovation, Repair and Painting Program Rule that imposes additional lead-based paint regulations. Under this rule, only certified contractors can perform renovation, repair and painting projects that disturb lead-based paint in homes, child care facilities, and schools built before 1978. The EPA has authorized Alabama, Georgia, Iowa, Kansas, Massachusetts, Mississippi, North Carolina, Oregon, Rhode Island, Utah, Washington, and Wisconsin to administer their own Renovation, Repair and Painting Program. Contractors working in these states must follow the regulations put forth by the state program.

Contractors can become certified renovators by submitting an application and fee to the EPA or state-based program and taking an eight-hour training course from an EPA-accredited training provider. Certified contractors must follow specific work practices to prevent lead contamination. Three simple principles are applied when working with lead which includes:

✓ containing the work area to minimize lead contamination in other work areas;

✓ minimizing dust to prevent harmful airborne particles from being inhaled; and

✓ cleaning up the work area thoroughly.

Required Notification: Under Lead PRE, federal law requires that contractors provide lead information to residents before renovating pre-1978 housing. The EPA publishes a pamphlet titled Protect Your Family from Lead in Your Home which must be distributed to the owner and occupants before starting work. Confirmation of receipt of the lead pamphlet or a certificate of mailing must be kept for 3 years. For work in common areas of multi-family housing, renovation notices must be distributed to all tenants.

For renovations to child-occupied facilities, renovators must distribute the pamphlet titled Renovate Right: Important Lead Hazard Information for Families, Child Care Providers and Schools to owners, administrators, and parents or guardians of children under the age of six that attend these facilities.

Exemptions: This rule applies to nearly all remodeling or renovation work with the exception of the following circumstances:

✓ Housing for the elderly or disabled persons unless children will reside there

✓ Zero-bedroom dwellings

✓ Emergency renovations or repairs

✓ Minor repair and maintenance that disturb two square feet or less of paint per component

✓ Housing or components declared lead-free by a certified inspector or risk assessor

Lead Abatement: Work designed to permanently eliminate lead-based paint hazards is considered lead abatement and is not subject to the guidelines under Lead PRE. This does not include renovation, remodeling, landscaping, or other activities designed to repair, restore, and redesign a given building. The EPA outlines strict regulations for this type of work as discussed in the previous section on lead.

Renovation: Renovations under Lead PRE are modifications of all or part of any existing structure that disturbs a painted surface. This includes

✓ removal/modification of painted surfaces, components or structures;

✓ surface preparation activities (sanding/scraping/ other activities that may create paint dust); and

✓ window replacement.

Penalties: Failure to comply with regulations concerning lead is a serious violation. Non-compliance carries substantial fines of up to $37,500 per day for each violation. Criminal penalties of imprisonment for up to one year also apply to willful or intentional violation of the regulation.

Assistance: You can obtain additional information by going online to the EPA website at www.epa.gov/lead or by contacting The National Lead Information Center (NLIC) at 1-800-424-LEAD.

Final Inspection...

Safety Standards: It is important to know the OSHA standards that pertain to the construction industry.

Safe Hiring and Training: Background checks can help you hire workers with good safety records. Regular training contributes to a safe working environment.

Substance Abuse Policies: Substance abuse compromises safety in the workplace. Clearly written and communicated policies are useful tools in reducing substance abuse.

Safety Equipment: Certain safety equipment may be required according to OSHA regulations, depending on the work being performed.

Emergency Action Plan: Either a written or an orally communicated emergency action plan is required by OSHA, depending on the number of employees you have.

OSHA Recordkeeping: Your company may be required to complete OSHA forms 300, 300A and 301.

OSHA Injury Decision Tree: The OSHA injury decision tree outlines the steps in making the determination for recording work-related injuries and illnesses.

Material Safety Data Sheets (MSDS): A material safety data sheet (MSDS) is required for all chemicals used.

Underground Utility Safety: Although laws on marking underground utilities vary from state to state, contractors should identify underground utilities before excavating.

Overhead Power Line Safety: Overhead power line safety should be considered when formulating a health and safety program and worksite planning. As a general rule, workers should a minimum distance of 10 feet from overhead power lines.

Benefits of Providing a Safe and Healthy Workplace: OSHA can assess citations for failing to provide a safe work environment. Ensuring workers are healthy and safe provides many direct and indirect benefits to employers.

Employee Rights: Employees are allowed to report OSHA violations without fear of retaliation.

Penalties: Penalties vary depending on the severity of OSHA violations. OSHA may conduct programmed or unprogrammed inspections.

Environmental Considerations: Environmental factors should be considered throughout all phases of construction. Obtaining proper permits is important for following environmental regulations.

U.S. Environmental Protection Agency (EPA): The EPA works to develop and enforce regulations that implement environmental laws enacted by Congress.

The North Carolina Department of Environment and Natural Resources (NCDENR): The NCDENR preserves and protects North Carolina's natural resources through programs and environmental regulations. www.ncdenr.gov

Environmental Law: Several laws exist to protect the environment. An assessment of environmental impacts should be done early on in the construction project.

Air Quality: Indoor and outdoor quality should be monitored throughout the construction project.

Asbestos: Before beginning remodeling or demolition of any project, assess whether you may encounter asbestos-releasing materials. Certain permitting and notification requirements may apply.

Clean Water Act: The Clean Water Act establishes the basic structure for regulating discharges of pollutants into the waters of the United States.

Sedimentation and Erosion Control Measures: Erosion and sediment control measures minimize pollution and contractor costs to rework eroded areas and replace lost soil.

Hazardous and Non-Hazardous Solid Waste: Most construction waste is non-hazardous. Both hazardous and non-hazardous waste must be disposed of properly.

Hazardous Substances: Early identification of hazardous substances is important and proper notification is required.

Lead: Contact with lead can cause lead poisoning and you and your employees must follow specific regulations when working with it.

Remodeling or Renovating a Home with Lead-Based Paint: The Lead Pre-Renovation Education Rule (Lead PRE) and Lead-Based Paint Renovation, Repair and Painting Program Rule are federal regulations involving those performing renovations for compensation in residential housing that may contain lead paint.

Supplemental Forms

Supplemental forms and links are available at **NASCLAforms.org** using access code **NCL129354**.

OSHA Forms for Recording Work-Related Injuries and Illnesses	OSHA forms 300, 300A and 301 with instructions
OSHA Compliance Assistance Employment Law Guide	OSHA guide summarizing employer responsibilities under the OSH Act
Managing Your Environmental Responsibilities: A Planning Guide for Construction and Development	EPA guide customized for the construction industry that outlines specific environmental responsibilities
Protect Your Family From Lead in Your Home	Mandatory brochure to distribute to the owner if you are doing renovations on pre-1978 housing

OSHA's Form 300 (Rev. 01/2004)

Log of Work-Related Injuries and Illnesses

Attention: This form contains information relating to employee health and must be used in a manner that protects the confidentiality of employees to the extent possible while the information is being used for occupational safety and health purposes.

Year 20____

U.S. Department of Labor
Occupational Safety and Health Administration

Form approved OMB no. 1218-0176

You must record information about every work-related death and about every work-related injury or illness that involves loss of consciousness, restricted work activity or job transfer, days away from work, or medical treatment beyond first aid. You must also record significant work-related injuries and illnesses that are diagnosed by a physician or licensed health care professional. You must also record work-related injuries and illnesses that meet any of the specific recording criteria listed in 29 CFR Part 1904.8 through 1904.12. Feel free to use two lines for a single case if you need to. You must complete an injury and illness Incident Report (OSHA Form 301) or equivalent form for each injury or illness recorded on this form. If you're not sure whether a case is recordable, call your local OSHA office for help.

Establishment name _____

City _____ State _____

Identify the person

(A) Case no.	(B) Employee's name	(C) Job title (e.g., Welder)	(D) Date of injury or onset of illness

Describe the case

(E) Where the event occurred (e.g., Loading dock north end)	(F) Describe injury or illness, parts of body affected, and object/substance that directly injured or made person ill (e.g., Second degree burns on right forearm from acetylene torch)

Classify the case

CHECK ONLY ONE box for each case based on the most serious outcome for that case:

(G) Death	(H) Days away from work	(I) Remained at Work — Job transfer or restriction	(J) Remained at Work — Other recordable cases

Enter the number of days the injured or ill worker was:

(K) Away from work — days	(L) On job transfer or restriction — days

Check the "Injury" column or choose one type of illness:

(M)	(1) Injury	(2) Skin disorder	(3) Respiratory condition	(4) Poisoning	(5) Hearing loss	(6) All other illnesses

month/day (repeated per row)

Page totals ▶

Be sure to transfer these totals to the Summary page (Form 300A) before you post it.

Page ____ of ____

Public reporting burden for this collection of information is estimated to average 14 minutes per response, including time to review the instructions, search and gather the data needed, and complete and review the collection of information. Persons are not required to respond to the collection of information unless it displays a currently valid OMB control number. If you have any comments about these estimates or any other aspects of this data collection, contact: US Department of Labor, OSHA Office of Statistical Analysis, Room N-3644, 200 Constitution Avenue, NW, Washington, DC 20210. Do not send the completed forms to this office.

OSHA's Form 300A (Rev. 01/2004)

Summary of Work-Related Injuries and Illnesses

Year 20___

U.S. Department of Labor
Occupational Safety and Health Administration

Form approved OMB no. 1218-0176

All establishments covered by Part 1904 must complete this Summary page, even if no work-related injuries or illnesses occurred during the year. Remember to review the Log to verify that the entries are complete and accurate before completing this summary.

Using the Log, count the individual entries you made for each category. Then write the totals below, making sure you've added the entries from every page of the Log. If you had no cases, write "0."

Employees, former employees, and their representatives have the right to review the OSHA Form 300 in its entirety. They also have limited access to the OSHA Form 301 or its equivalent. See 29 CFR Part 1904.35, in OSHA's recordkeeping rule, for further details on the access provisions for these forms.

Number of Cases

Total number of deaths	Total number of cases with days away from work	Total number of cases with job transfer or restriction	Total number of other recordable cases
_____ (G)	_____ (H)	_____ (I)	_____ (J)

Number of Days

Total number of days away from work	Total number of days of job transfer or restriction
_____ (K)	_____ (L)

Injury and Illness Types

Total number of . . .
(M)

(1) Injuries _____

(2) Skin disorders _____

(3) Respiratory conditions _____

(4) Poisonings _____

(5) Hearing loss _____

(6) All other illnesses _____

Post this Summary page from February 1 to April 30 of the year following the year covered by the form.

Public reporting burden for this collection of information is estimated to average 50 minutes per response, including time to review the instructions, search and gather the data needed, and complete and review the collection of information. Persons are not required to respond to the collection of information unless it displays a currently valid OMB control number. If you have any comments about these estimates or any other aspects of this data collection, contact: US Department of Labor, OSHA, Office of Statistical Analysis, Room N-3644, 200 Constitution Avenue, NW, Washington, DC 20210. Do not send the completed forms to this office.

Establishment information

Your establishment name _____

Street _____

City _____ State _____ ZIP _____

Industry description (e.g., Manufacture of motor truck trailers) _____

Standard Industrial Classification (SIC), if known (e.g., 3715) _____

OR

North American Industrial Classification (NAICS), if known (e.g., 336212) _____

Employment information *(If you don't have these figures, see the Worksheet on the back of this page to estimate.)*

Annual average number of employees _____

Total hours worked by all employees last year _____

Sign here

Knowingly falsifying this document may result in a fine.

I certify that I have examined this document and that to the best of my knowledge the entries are true, accurate, and complete.

_____ Company executive

_____ Title

(___) _____ Phone

___/___/___ Date

OSHA's Form 301

Injury and Illness Incident Report

U.S. Department of Labor
Occupational Safety and Health Administration

Form approved OMB no. 1218-0176

This *Injury and Illness Incident Report* is one of the first forms you must fill out when a recordable work-related injury or illness has occurred. Together with the *Log of Work-Related Injuries and Illnesses* and the accompanying *Summary*, these forms help the employer and OSHA develop a picture of the extent and severity of work-related incidents.

Within 7 calendar days after you receive information that a recordable work-related injury or illness has occurred, you must fill out this form or an equivalent form. Some state workers' compensation, insurance, or other reports may be acceptable substitutes. To be considered an equivalent form, any substitute must contain all the information asked for on this form.

According to Public Law 91-596 and 29 CFR 1904, OSHA's recordkeeping rule, you must keep this form on file for 5 years following the year to which it pertains.

If you need additional copies of this form, you may photocopy and use as many as you need.

Completed by _____

Title _____

Phone (_____) _____ Date ___/___/___

Attention: This form contains information relating to employee health and must be used in a manner that protects the confidentiality of employees to the extent possible while the information is being used for occupational safety and health purposes.

Information about the employee

1) Full name _____

2) Street _____

City _____ State _____ ZIP _____

3) Date of birth ___/___/___

4) Date hired ___/___/___

5) ☐ Male
   ☐ Female

Information about the physician or other health care professional

6) Name of physician or other health care professional _____

7) If treatment was given away from the worksite, where was it given?

Facility _____

Street _____

City _____ State _____ ZIP _____

8) Was employee treated in an emergency room?
   ☐ Yes
   ☐ No

9) Was employee hospitalized overnight as an in-patient?
   ☐ Yes
   ☐ No

Information about the case

10) Case number from the Log _____ *(Transfer the case number from the Log after you record the case.)*

11) Date of injury or illness ___/___/___

12) Time employee began work _____ AM / PM

13) Time of event _____ AM / PM ☐ Check if time cannot be determined

14) **What was the employee doing just before the incident occurred?** Describe the activity, as well as the tools, equipment, or material the employee was using. Be specific. *Examples:* "climbing a ladder while carrying roofing materials"; "spraying chlorine from hand sprayer"; "daily computer key-entry."

15) **What happened?** Tell us how the injury occurred. *Examples:* "When ladder slipped on wet floor, worker fell 20 feet"; "Worker was sprayed with chlorine when gasket broke during replacement"; "Worker developed soreness in wrist over time."

16) **What was the injury or illness?** Tell us the part of the body that was affected and how it was affected; be more specific than "hurt," "pain," or sore." *Examples:* "strained back"; "chemical burn, hand"; "carpal tunnel syndrome."

17) **What object or substance directly harmed the employee?** *Examples:* "concrete floor"; "chlorine"; "radial arm saw." *If this question does not apply to the incident, leave it blank.*

18) **If the employee died, when did death occur?** Date of death ___/___/___

Public reporting burden for this collection of information is estimated to average 22 minutes per response, including time for reviewing instructions, searching existing data sources, gathering and maintaining the data needed, and completing and reviewing the collection of information. Persons are not required to respond to the collection of information unless it displays a current valid OMB control number. If you have any comments about this estimate or any other aspects of this data collection, including suggestions for reducing this burden, contact: US Department of Labor, OSHA Office of Statistical Analysis, Room N-3644, 200 Constitution Avenue, NW, Washington, DC 20210. Do not send the completed forms to this office.

Chapter 14
WORKING WITH SUBCONTRACTORS

Chapter Survey...

⇨ *Sources for Finding the Right Subcontractor*

⇨ *Creating a Winning Partnership*

⇨ *Site Rules for Contractors*

⇨ *Employee or Independent Contractor: IRS Guidelines*

Subcontractors contract with the general contractor or other subcontractors to complete a portion of a larger project.

It is important to hire the right subcontractors because their work impacts your company's reputation. Just as you want employees who are easy to work with, the same applies to subcontractors.

There are basic criteria you can use to evaluate whether you want to hire a subcontractor:

✓ Do they sell or produce quality products?

✓ Are they reliable? Are they able to complete the project according to the schedule?

✓ Do they have good customer service skills?

✓ Are they able to effectively deal with problems?

✓ Do they give an overall impression of professionalism?

✓ Are they properly licensed and carry appropriate insurance coverage?

✓ Do they remedy situations that involve material defects or failures?

✓ How do they handle change orders?

✓ Are they competitively priced?

Now that you have established your requirements, it is time to find qualified leads.

Sources for Finding the Right Subcontractor

If you have a good reputation, the word travels fast. This also holds true for good subcontractors and suppliers. Some of your best subcontractors can come from referrals. Sources for these referrals might include:

✓ subcontractors in a different field who have worked with other subcontractors on other jobs;

✓ other contractors in your field;

✓ members of your local trade association;

✓ suppliers (for example, electrical supply firms can give referrals on electricians); and

✓ architects or engineers.

Once you come up with credible referrals, you want to make sure that you take extra steps to organize the process.

✓ Keep a list of qualified subcontractors.

✓ Allow sufficient lead time to line up subcontractors for jobs.

✓ Interview subcontractors for their qualifications, even when you are not scheduling them for a job.

✓ Check references if you have not worked with the subcontractor before.

✓ Ensure all subcontractors you work with have proper insurance coverage; request copies of insurance certificates and follow up to ensure coverage is current (as discussed in Chapter 4).

Creating a Winning Partnership

Once you have done all your homework and made your subcontractor selections, you'll want to create a relationship that will set both parties up for success.

✓ Provide an orientation on your policies and procedures.

✓ Be clear on all instructions and solicit questions.
✓ Be open to feedback and suggestions.
✓ Reward good work and provide constructive comments on improvements.
✓ Schedule trades so the job is ready for them and there are minimal barriers for them to complete their job.
✓ Visit the jobsite before the start of your portion of the project to tell other subcontractors your requirements (if it applies).
✓ Complete an IRS W-9 form prior to starting work.

Site Rules for Contractors

As part of an orientation with your subcontractors, you may want to review your site rules. Listed below are some rules to consider:

✓ Keep the jobsite clean and free of debris.
✓ All safety policies and OSHA regulations must be followed.
✓ You must provide your own tools and equipment.
✓ Work must be compliant with all applicable codes.
✓ Keep radios on the jobsite at a moderate listening level and free of offensive content.
✓ Behave professionally and do not use foul language.
✓ Salvage of items is prohibited without permission.

Site rules can be posted at the jobsite so they are visible to everyone and serve as a continual reminder.

Employee or Independent Contractor: IRS Guidelines

The IRS outlines specific guidelines regarding the difference between employees and independent contractors. Make sure you are working within an independent contractor relationship and not an employer-employee basis. If you do have an employer-employee relationship, your company is liable for payroll taxes, workers' compensation and employee benefits for that subcontractor.

To determine whether an individual is an employee or an independent contractor under common law, the relationship of the worker and your company must be examined. In any employee-independent contractor determination, all information that provides evidence of the degree of control and the degree of independence must be considered.

Evidence of the degree of control and independence falls into three categories: **behavioral control**, **financial control** and the **type of relationship of the parties**.

Behavioral Control

Facts that show whether a business has a right to direct and control how the worker does the task for which the worker is hired include the type and degree of:

✓ Instruction the business gives to the worker: An employee is generally subject to the business' instructions about when, where, and how to work. In a subcontractor relationship, the business generally gives up the right to control the details of the worker's performance.
✓ Training the business gives to the worker: An employee may be trained to perform services in a particular manner. Independent contractors ordinarily use their own methods.

Financial Control

Facts that show whether the business has a right to control the business aspects of the worker's job include:

✓ The extent to which the worker has un-reimbursed business expenses: Independent contractors are more likely to have un-reimbursed expenses than are employees. Fixed ongoing costs that are incurred regardless of whether work is currently being performed are especially important.
✓ The extent of the worker's investment: An independent contractor often has a significant investment in the facilities he or she uses in performing services for someone else. However, a significant investment is not necessary for independent contractor status.
✓ The extent to which the worker makes his or her services available to the relevant market: An employee is generally guaranteed a regular wage amount for an hourly, weekly, or other period of time for one employer. An independent contractor is usually paid a flat fee by the business with which he or she has contracted. An independent contractor is free to manage multiple contracts.
✓ The extent to which the worker can realize a profit or loss: An independent contractor can make a profit or loss.

Type of Relationship

Facts that show the parties' type of relationship include:

✓ **Written contracts** describing the relationship the parties intend to create

✓ **Whether the business provides the worker with employee-type benefits**, such as insurance, a pension plan, vacation pay, or sick pay

✓ **The permanency of the relationship:** If you engage a worker with the expectation that the relationship will continue indefinitely rather than for a specific project or period, this is generally considered an employer-employee relationship.

✓ **The extent to which services performed by the worker are a key aspect of the regular business of the company:** If a worker provides services that are a key aspect of your regular business activity, it is more likely that you will have a right to direct and control his or her activities, indicating an employer-employee relationship.

Now that you know the rules, let's look at a few practical examples to demonstrate how classifications are made.

Example 1: Milton Manning, an experienced tile setter, orally agreed with a corporation to perform full-time services at construction sites. He uses his own tools and performs services in the order designated by the corporation and according to its specifications. The corporation supplies all materials, makes frequent inspections of his work, pays him on a piecework basis, and carries workers' compensation insurance on him. He does not have a place of business or hold himself out to perform similar services for others. Either party can end the services at any time. Milton Manning is an employee of the corporation.

Example 2: Vera Elm, an electrician, submitted a job estimate to a housing complex for electrical work at $16 per hour for 400 hours. She is to receive $1,280

every two weeks for the next 10 weeks. This is not considered payment by the hour. Even if she works more or less than 400 hours to complete the work, Vera Elm will receive $6,400. She also performs additional electrical installations under contracts with other companies that she obtained through advertisements. Vera is an independent contractor.

Assistance in Determining Status: If you are unable to determine whether the working relationship is on an employer-employee or employer-independent contractor basis, the IRS can assist by reviewing the circumstances of the working relationship and officially determining the individual's status. To request this review, a Form SS-8, Determination of Worker Status for Purposes of Federal Employment Taxes and Income Tax Withholding, is submitted to the IRS. This form and other assistance are available online at www.irs.gov.

- -

Final Inspection...

Sources for Finding the Right Subcontractor: Referrals are a good way to find the right subcontractors. As you collect referrals, develop a process to organize and appropriately schedule them.

Creating a Winning Partnership: Establishing good communication and having clear policies in place set a solid foundation for positive subcontractor relationships.

Site Rules for Contractors: Subcontractors should receive an orientation on your site rules before starting work. Site rules should be posted at the jobsite so they are visible to everyone and serve as a continual reminder.

Employee or Independent Contractor: IRS Guidelines: The IRS uses behavioral control, financial control, and the type of relationship of the parties to make a determination whether someone is an employee or independent contractor.

PART 3

Office
Administration

Chapter 15
FINANCIAL MANAGEMENT

Chapter Survey...
⇨ *Bookkeeping*
⇨ *The Accounting Cycle*
⇨ *Methods of Accounting*
⇨ *Contract Accounting*
⇨ *Cash Management*
⇨ *Equipment Records and Accounting*
⇨ *Accounting Process for Materials*
⇨ *Payroll Accounting*
⇨ *Technology Solutions for Accounting*

Accounting is important to all businesses because it helps measure the financial fitness of the company. It is a process of collecting, analyzing, and reporting information to develop tools, such as financial statements, that are used to evaluate different financial aspects of the company.

Bookkeeping

The first step in the accounting process is bookkeeping. Bookkeeping involves the accurate recording of all financial transactions that occur in the business. Financial statements are derived from this information.

Here are a few tips to maintain accurate and timely bookkeeping:

✓ Open a separate business checking account and obtain a business credit card to keep business and personal finances separate.

✓ Keep track of all deductible expenses (discussed later in this chapter).

✓ Keep all receipts and identify the source of all receipts so you can separate business from personal receipts and taxable from non-taxable income.

✓ Update business records daily to have quick access to the daily financial position of your business.

✓ Accurately record all information in the checkbook ledger including date, who the check was written to, the amount, and the reason the check was written.

✓ Record expenses when they occur, so you have an accurate picture of your cash situation.

✓ Avoid paying with cash, so you have a "paper trail" of your expenditures.

✓ Balance your checking account monthly. You may want to request month-end bank statements to coordinate with other month-end records.

✓ Keep all financial records for the required amount of time as designated by the IRS.

Bookkeeping involves the clerical side of accounting and requires only minimal knowledge of the entire accounting cycle. You may want to consult with a professional accountant for the more complex financial decision-making of your business.

The Accounting Cycle

The accounting cycle is a series of events that is repeated each reporting period. The cycle begins with a transaction and ends with closing the books and preparing financial statements. Steps in the accounting cycle include

1. **Classifying and recording transactions,**
2. **Posting transactions,**
3. **Preparing a trial balance,**
4. **Preparing an adjusted trial balance,**
5. **Preparing financial statements, and**
6. **Analyzing financial statements.**

Classify and Record Transactions

The accounting cycle begins with classifying and recording daily transactions. A **transaction** is an event that either increases or decreases an account balance. A **source document** is the proof that a transaction took place. Examples of source documents include

- ✓ cash receipts,
- ✓ credit card receipts,
- ✓ customer invoices,
- ✓ purchase orders,
- ✓ materials invoices,
- ✓ deposit slips, and
- ✓ time cards.

Daily transactions are recorded in a set of books called **journals**. Typical journals that companies keep include:

- ✓ **Cash receipts and sales journal:** This journal is used when cash comes in or a sale is charged to a customer.
- ✓ **Purchases journal:** This journal tracks all purchases made by the company.
- ✓ **Cash disbursements journal:** This journal is used when cash is paid out. Transactions such as loan payments and payments on vendor invoices are recorded here.
- ✓ **Payroll journal:** This journal is used to record a summary of payroll details, such as salaries and wages, deductions, and employer contributions.
- ✓ **General journal:** This journal is used for non-cash transactions.

 STEP 2

Post Transactions

Posting is the process of transferring the transactions recorded in the journals to the appropriate accounts. An **account** is a register of value. Each account can be totaled to determine the balance. For example, cash is an asset account having a specific balance. Most companies use five basic types of accounts:

- ✓ Asset
- ✓ Liability
- ✓ Equity
- ✓ Income
- ✓ Expense

The chart of accounts is a numbering system that organizes these account types. A typical chart of accounts is listed below.

1000–1999: Assets
2000–2999: Liabilities
3000–3999: Equity
4000–4999: Revenue

5000–5999: Cost of Goods Sold
6000–6999: Expenses
7000–7999: Other Revenue (i.e., interest income)
8000–8999: Other Expenses (i.e., income taxes)

The accounts are located in the general ledger. When you post transactions, you are transferring them from the journal to the general ledger.

 STEP 3

Prepare Trial Balance

When you tally the accounts, you prepare a trial balance. The **trial balance** is a total of all the ledger accounts.

At this point in the accounting cycle, you want to make sure the debits equal the credits.

Understanding Debits and Credits: Every accounting entry in the general ledger contains both a debit and a credit which must equal each other. Depending on what type of account you are dealing with, a debit or credit will either increase or decrease the account balance. The entries that increase or decrease each type of account are listed below.

Account Type	Debit	Credit
Assets	Increases	Decreases
Liabilities	Decreases	Increases
Equity	Decreases	Increases
Income	Decreases	Increases
Expenses	Increases	Decreases

For the accounts to balance, there must be a debit in one account and a credit in another. You may hear terms such as the left side or right side of the balance sheet. Something on the left side is simply a debit and the right side is a credit.

If you have any ledger account column totals that do not balance, look for math, posting, and recording errors.

STEP 4

Prepare Adjusted Trial Balance

There are six general types of adjusting entries:

- ✓ prepaid expense,
- ✓ accrued expense,
- ✓ accrued revenue,
- ✓ unearned revenue,
- ✓ estimated items, and
- ✓ inventory adjustment.

When you make adjusting entries, include an explanation as to why the change was made. Once adjusting entries are made, you must go back and tally the account balances where changes were made.

 Prepare Financial Statements

Now that you have posted transactions to your accounts and made adjusting entries, you can prepare your financial statements.

The three basic types of financial statements companies use are

✓ balance sheet,

✓ income statement, and

✓ statement of cash flows.

Financial statements are tools that give insight into the financial health and activities of the company.

Balance Sheet

The balance sheet is one of the basic accounting financial statements. It gives the owner good insight into the growth and stability of the company at a particular point in time.

The balance sheet equation is comprised of assets, liabilities, and owners' equity:

Assets = Liabilities + Owners' Equity

Assets are items of value owned by the business. The cash in your bank account and other assets that can be converted into cash in less than one year are considered **current assets**. They are important because they are used to fund daily operations and can be liquidated easily.

Property and **equipment** (sometimes referred to as **capital** or **fixed assets**) are assets needed to carry on the business of a company and are not normally consumed in the operation of the business. Land,

buildings, equipment, and furniture would all be considered fixed assets.

Other current assets consist of prepaid expenses, such as security deposits, and other miscellaneous assets, such as long-term investments.

Your company may also own **intangible assets**. Examples of these include patents, franchises, and goodwill from the acquisition of another company. It is not as easy to value these assets. Generally, the value of intangible assets is a value both parties agree to when the assets are created.

Liabilities are all debt and obligations owed by the business. Liabilities that will mature and must be paid within one year are called current liabilities. Trade credit is usually considered a current liability because it is a short-term debt.

Long-term liabilities are debt obligations that extend beyond one year. Examples of this type of liability include bank loans and deferred taxes.

Owners' equity is made up of the initial investment in the business, plus accumulated net profits not paid out to the owners.

Working capital can also be determined by looking at the balance sheet. The following equation is used to determine working capital.

Current Assets – Current Liabilities = Working Capital

Working capital measures the liquidity of the company's assets. Liquid assets are those that are easily converted to cash. Licensing agencies may look at working capital to determine license limitations.

The balance sheet is usually requested by potential lenders to determine credit limits. The following sample illustrates how the balance sheet equation and accounts are used in the balance sheet.

Quality Construction Compay
Balance Sheet
December 31, 20XX

ASSETS

Current Assets:		
Cash	$ 1,200	
Accounts Receivable	25,200	
Total Current Assets		$ 26,400
Property and Equipment:		
Equipment	$ 53,200	
Building	120,000	
Land	75,000	
Total Property and Equipment		248,200
TOTAL ASSETS		$ 274,600

LIABILITIES AND OWNERS' EQUITY

Current Liabilities:		
Accounts Payable	$ 4,900	
Payroll Taxes Payable	$ 3,300	
Total Current Liabilities		$ 8,200
Long-term Liabilities		
Notes Payable	$ 6,700	
Mortgage Payable	$ 195,000	
Total Long-term Liabilities		201,700
Owners' Equity		64,700
TOTAL LIABILITIES AND OWNERS' EQUITY		$ 274,600

Income Statement

The income statement, sometimes called the **profit-and-loss statement**, is a summary of the company's revenues and expenses over a given period of time.

The profit equation provides the basis for the income statement and is comprised of the following:

Income – Cost of Goods Sold = Gross Profit

Gross Profit – Expenses = Net Income

Revenues are the income received from the daily operations of the business. Most companies have only a few revenue accounts, but if you have several lines of business, you may want to create an account for each.

Expenses are the monies paid out or owed for goods or services over a given period of time. Most companies have separate accounts for the different types of expenses incurred.

Direct costs are those directly linked with a particular project. On a landscape construction project, your direct costs might include materials, subcontractor fees, permit fees, and labor.

Operating expenses (sometimes called indirect expenses) are the general items that contribute to the cost of operating the business. These expenses can be put into two categories, **selling expenses** and **fixed overhead**. Selling expenses are the costs incurred to market the business. Fixed overhead expenses are those that cannot be linked to a specific project but are necessary for the operation of the business. For example, if you rent warehouse space to store your equipment year round, you would include this item in your bookkeeping under fixed overhead.

Tax provision expenses are the tax liabilities your company has for federal, state, and local taxes. Depending on your business structure, this section of the income statement will vary.

Net profit is the difference between revenues and expenses. Net profit directly contributes to the net worth of the company.

If net profit is on the positive side, those earnings are placed in a retained earnings or equity account.

If net profit is negative, it will reduce the net worth of the company.

The income statement is used by investors or lenders to determine the profitability of the company. The following sample illustrates how the income statement equation and accounts are used in the income statement.

Quality Construction Compay
Income Statement
For the Period Ended December 31, 20XX

REVENUES:		
Construction Sales	$ 545,600	
Less Direct Labor	120,500	
Less Direct Materials	257,000	
Gross Profit		$ 168,100
EXPENSES:		
Selling Expenses:		
Advertising	$ 3,400	
Salaries - Sales	49,500	
Total Selling Expense	$ 52,900	
Administrative Expenses:		
Salaries - Office	$ 34,400	
Telephone	4,800	
Insurance Expenses	29,700	
Total Administrative Expenses	$ 68,900	
Total Expenses		121,800
NET INCOME		$ 46,300

Quality Construction Compay
Statement of Owners' Equity
For the Period Ended December 31, 20XX

Beginning Owners' Equity	$ 92,400
Add Net Income	46,300
Less Distributions to Owners	74,000
Ending Owners' Equity	$ 64,700

Statement of Cash Flows

The statement of cash flows summarizes your current cash position, your cash sources, and use of these funds over a given period of time. This financial statement lists changes in cash based on operating, investing, and financing activities.

The operating activities portion of the statement shows the performance of the company to generate a positive or negative cash flow from the operations.

The investing activities section lists the cash used or provided to purchase or sell revenue-producing assets.

The financing activities section measures the flow of cash between the owners and creditors.

If you want to finance a major project, the lender will likely want to look at your statement of cash flows. This financial statement provides good insight into the company's ability to meet its obligations. The company may appear profitable on other statements, but a lack of cash flow may indicate pending financial problems.

Notes to the Financial Statements

The notes to the financial statements contain important information that is relevant but have no specific place within the financial statement.

✓ **Accounting policies and procedures** important to the company's financial condition and results are disclosed in the notes section.

✓ Detailed information about **current and deferred income taxes** is broken down by federal, state, and local categories. The primary factors that affect the company's tax rate are described.

✓ Specific information about the assets and costs of a **pension plan and other retirement programs** are explained and indicate whether the plans are over- or underfunded.

Anything that affects the financial health of the company that cannot be reflected in the financial statements should be reported in this section.

STEP 6 — Analyze Financial Statements Using Financial Ratios

By using the basic concepts of the balance sheet and income statement, you can analyze them through financial ratios. Ratios can serve as a benchmark for the company's internal performance and as a comparison against industry averages.

Liquidity Ratio

The liquidity ratio (sometimes called the current ratio) is calculated by dividing the current liabilities into the current assets.

$$\text{Current Assets} \div \text{Current Liabilities} = \text{Liquidity (or Current) Ratio}$$

The liquidity ratio determines if the company can pay its current debts. If the ratio is greater than one, the company is in a positive liquidity position. The higher the number, the better liquidity position the company has.

Quick Ratio

The quick ratio (sometimes called the acid test ratio) is similar to the liquidity ratio. It is calculated by dividing the current liabilities into the current assets minus inventory.

$$(\text{Current Assets} - \text{Inventory}) \div \text{Current Liabilities} = \text{Quick Ratio}$$

A quick ratio of one or more is generally acceptable by most creditors. A higher number indicates a stronger financial position and a lower number a weaker position.

Activity Ratio

The activity ratio measures how effectively the company manages its credit. The formula for determining the average collection period is as follows:

$$\text{Revenue} \div \text{Days in the Business Year} = \text{Sales per Day}$$

$$\text{Current Receivables} \div \text{Sales per Day} = \text{Average Collection Period}$$

The company is in a better position when the average collection period is shorter (or the number is lower). This means that the company is converting credit accounts into cash faster.

Debt Ratio

The debt ratio measures the percent of total funds provided by creditors. The formula is as follows:

$$\text{Total Debt} \div \text{Total Assets} = \text{Debt Ratio}$$

Companies want to keep their debt ratio relatively low to avoid overextending debt.

Profitability Ratio

The profitability ratio is used to calculate the profit margin of the company. The formula is as follows:

$$Net\ Income \div Revenues =$$
$$Profit\ Margin$$

The higher the profit margin percentage, the more profitably the company is performing.

Return on Total Assets Ratio

The return on total assets ratio is used to determine if the company's assets are being employed in the best manner. The formula is:

$$Net\ Profit\ (after\ taxes) \div Total\ Assets =$$
$$Return\ on\ Total\ Assets$$

The company is in a favorable position when the percentage return on total assets is high.

Methods of Accounting

An accounting method is a set of rules used to determine when and how income and expenses are reported. There are two basic methods of accounting used to keep track of the company's income and expenses. These are

✓ Cash method

✓ Accrual method

The primary difference between the methods is in when the transactions are recorded to your accounts.

Cash Method

Using the cash method of accounting, you report income in the year you receive it and deduct expenses in the year you paid them. This is the easier of the two accounting methods. Although it is a simpler method, it holds a significant disadvantage. The cash method does not match revenues with the expenses incurred related to that revenue. This gives an inaccurate picture of the company's overall financial situation.

Accrual Method

Using the accrual method, you recognize income when the services occur, not when you collect the money. The same principal is applied to expenses, which are recorded when they are incurred, not when you pay for them. Most construction businesses use the accrual method of accounting.

Changing Your Method of Accounting

Once you have set up your accounting method and file your first tax return, you must get IRS approval before you can change to another method. A change in accounting method not only includes a change in your overall system of accounting, but also a change in the treatment of any material item.

Contract Accounting

Most construction businesses use two tax accounting methods; one for their long-term contracts and one overall method for everything else. A long-term contract is defined as any contract that is not completed in the same year it was started.

The choice of your contract accounting method depends on

✓ the type of contracts you have;

✓ your contracts' completion status at the end of your tax year; and

✓ your average annual gross receipts.

Each method discussed assumes you use a calendar tax year from January 1 to December 31.

Completed Contract Method

Under the completed contract method, income or loss is reported in the year the contract is completed. Direct materials, labor costs, and all indirect costs associated with the contract must be allocated or capitalized to the same account as the income or loss. If the completed contract method is used for long-term contracts (contracts spanning over two calendar years), you may not allocate costs properly and you might overstate deductions.

The advantage of the completed contract method is that it normally achieves maximum deferral of taxes.

The disadvantages of the completed contract method are

✓ the books and records do not show clear information on operations;

✓ income can be bunched into a year when a lot of jobs are completed; and

✓ losses on contracts are not deductible until the contracts are completed.

The completed contract method may be used only by small contractors whose average annual gross receipts do not exceed $10 million for the three tax years preceding the tax year of the contract.

Percentage of Completion Method

The percentage of completion method recognizes income as it is earned during the construction project.

The biggest advantage of using this method for long-term contracts is that it does a better job of matching revenue to the expenses incurred related to that revenue. Accurate matching of revenue to expenses gives you a better picture of your financial position.

The disadvantage of the percentage of completion method is that it relies on estimates. You are estimating the degree of completion on the project and the income and expenses. The true numbers are not realized until the project is complete.

Percentage of completion is calculated individually by project. To determine the percentage of completion, use the following formula:

Project Costs Incurred ÷ Total Estimated Costs = Percentage of Completion

Once the percentage of completion is calculated, the cumulative earnings can be figured by using the following formula:

Percentage of Completion x Contract Amount = Cumulative Earnings

Adjustments must be made on the balance sheet for billings that are over or under the cumulative earnings. To figure the amount over or under cumulative earnings, use the following formula:

Cumulative Earnings – Amount Billed to Date = Billing Overage/Deficiency

Billings in excess of the cumulative earnings are considered a current liability. Billings less than cumulative earnings are considered a current asset.

Using these formulas, a percentage of completion worksheet example is shown below.

Project Name	Contract Amount	Estimated Cost	Project Cost to Date	Percent Complete	Cumulative Earnings	Amount Billed to Date	Billing Overage/ Deficiency
Project #1	70,000	62,350	35,500	56.94%	39,858	40,150	-292
Project #2	50,000	42,150	12,140	28.80%	14,400	13,500	900
Project #3	30,000	25,110	14,050	55.95%	16,785	15,220	1,565

Cost Comparison Method

The cost comparison method is an approach that combines the completed contract and percentage of completion methods. A 10 percent deferral election is allowed under the cost comparison method. This election allows you to defer recognized revenue on a contract until the total costs incurred equal 10 percent of the estimated contract costs. The initial project costs are capitalized and deferred until costs to date exceed 10 percent of total costs. After exceeding 10 percent, all costs incurred are treated as period costs. Revenue is also fully recognized in that period based on the level of project completion. From that point forward, revenue is calculated using the percentage of completion method until the project is finished.

Cash Management

Cash Flow

As discussed in Chapter 11, it is important to track incoming cash and expenditures during the construction project to ensure you have enough working capital to complete the job. Balancing incoming progress payments and outgoing expenditures is important to managing the project effectively and should be a consideration when preparing your schedule.

Positive cash flow, meaning more cash is coming in than going out to pay expenses, is an important indicator of the health of your business. Without positive cash flow, your business cannot pay bills and employees. The business will eventually be unable to sustain itself and ultimately fail.

Two important aspects of maintaining a positive cash flow are collecting accounts receivable (money that is owed to your business) and billing and collecting for current projects.

Collecting Accounts Receivable: Collecting accounts receivable should be a systematic process:

✓ Correspondence should look professional, with the services rendered and amount due clearly displayed on the invoice.

✓ Follow-up invoices should be sent on a regular schedule. This will convey that you are serious about receiving prompt payment.

✓ If the account falls delinquent for more than three months, a stern letter outlining the consequences for non-payment should accompany your follow-up invoices.

✓ If you find you are having problems collecting on accounts receivable, you may want to hire a professional collection agency.

Prompt pay and lien laws may also provide additional payment and collection tools.

Billing and Collecting for Current Projects: Prompt billing for current projects is important to receiving timely payments. Once you receive the approval for partial or final payment, you should immediately send an invoice requesting payment. The payment should clearly outline payment terms. For example, if your payment terms are "Net 30," this means that full payment of the invoice is due in 30 days. If amounts due for current projects are not collected in a prompt manner, you may run into cash flow problems.

Bad Debts: When you extend credit to your customers, this debt is recorded in your accounts receivable. Bad debts are uncollectible accounts receivable. It is important to monitor accounts receivable regularly. If you notice that the amount of accounts receivable is increasing, you may need to adjust collection procedures. Bad debts affect cash flow and must be kept to a minimum.

According to IRS guidelines, a business deducts its bad debts from gross income when figuring taxable income. Bad debts may be deducted in part or in full. For more information on the specific IRS guidelines on business bad debts, refer to IRS Publication 535, Business Expenses. This publication can be downloaded from the IRS website at www.irs.gov.

Payments

Progress Payments: As discussed in Chapter 10, it is important to address the schedule of progress payments in the contract. Progress payments are partial payments made after specified phases of construction are complete.

To ensure adequate cash flow, it is important to monitor the progress payment schedule closely. You may be required to submit a partial payment estimate to the project architect or engineer prior to the payment due date. The partial payment estimate outlines the work performed and proof of materials and equipment delivery required for the next stage of construction. The architect or engineer certifies each progress payment by confirming the information in the partial payment estimate.

A retainage amount (commonly 10 percent) is usually withheld from progress payments. Retainage is released and paid out to the contractor after all final approvals are obtained at the end of a project.

Calculation of progress payments differs slightly, depending on the type of contract.

Payment for Lump Sum Contracts: Payments for lump sum contracts are calculated by the percentage of work completed. A schedule of estimated costs (sometimes called a schedule of values) is used as a basis to determine the degree of project completion.

Material and subcontractor invoices are compared against the schedule of values to support the degree of project completion.

Payment for Unit Price Contracts: Payments for unit price contracts are based on actual work units completed. The unit price payment request is more detailed and may take longer to complete, but it provides a more accurate picture of the degree of work completion.

Payment for Cost-Plus Contracts: Payments for cost-plus contracts are based on actual costs rather than a percentage of completed work. The schedule of payments should be clearly outlined in the contract. Cost-plus contracts generally include a markup in addition to costs. The payment request should include a markup proportionate to the costs. If payment estimates are required, reconciliation must be done once the actual costs occur to adjust for any amounts that fall over or under the estimate.

Final Payment: Final payment requests should include the final payment amount plus any retainages owed. Final payment is released after final inspection, acceptance by the owner, and submittal of proper documentation.

Prompt Payment Act: The Federal Prompt Payment Act ensures that federal contractors are paid in a timely manner. If late payment is made, interest penalties are charged on the amount due. Prime contractors must receive payment within 14 days after submitting a progress payment invoice. Prime contractors must pay subcontractors within seven days after receiving payment, or they must pay interest penalties. Individual states may have additional prompt payment provisions.

North Carolina Prompt Pay Law: Payment guidelines for public contracts are summarized as follows:

✓ *Prime Contractor Payment:* Payment to the prime contractor must be made within 45 days after completion of the project. Completion is defined as acceptance by the owner, certification by the architect, engineer or designer, or occupancy by the owner for the purpose in which the project was constructed.

✓ *Project Delays:* If the project is delayed by the fault of the contractor, the project may be occupied without payment or interest past the 45-day limit. Payment cannot be withheld because of a delay caused by another prime contractor.

✓ *Interest:* If final payment is delayed past the 45 days, the prime contractor is due 1 percent interest per month on the unpaid balance, unless a lower rate is agreed upon. Interest payments begin on the 46th day.

✓ *Subcontractor Payments:* Payment to subcontractors by the prime contractor must be made within seven days of a periodic or final payment receipt. Beginning on the eighth day, 1 percent interest per month on the unpaid balance is due.

✓ *Subcontractor Retainage:* Retainage for subcontractors cannot exceed the retainage percentage withheld from the prime contractors.

Any retainage held in excess is subject to 1 percent interest per month.

Guidelines for payment of subcontractors on private projects are outlined in North Carolina General Statutes, Chapter 22C. Listed below is a summary of these guidelines.

✓ *Subcontractor Payments:* Payment to subcontractors by the prime contractor must be made within seven days of receiving a periodic or final payment.

✓ *Interest:* Beginning on the eighth day, 1 percent interest per month on the unpaid balance is due.

✓ *Grounds for Withholding Payment:* Payment may be withheld under certain conditions. These conditions include unsatisfactory job progress; defective construction not remedied; disputed work; third-party claims filed or reasonable evidence that a claim will be filed; failure of the subcontractor to make timely payments for labor, equipment, and materials; damage to the contractor or another subcontractor; reasonable evidence that the subcontract cannot be completed for the unpaid balance of the subcontract sum; or a reasonable amount for retainage not to exceed the initial percentage retained by the owner.

Liens: Contractors' and material suppliers' liens "cloud" the title to real property but can be an effective method (and sometimes the only method) for securing payment for labor or materials used in the improvement of real property. The lien stops the owner from selling the property with a clear title. The lien may be foreclosed in a lawsuit. The court can order that property be sold and the proceeds used to pay the contractor, subcontractor, laborer, or material supplier.

State statutes and court opinions establish a strict procedure to perfect and foreclose a lien. It is strongly recommended that a professional be routinely used to record and foreclose on construction liens.

Petty Cash Fund

Small payments may sometimes be made without writing a check. A petty cash fund is used to make these payments. When you use the petty cash fund, it is important to document your expenditure. A voucher or petty cash disbursement slip should be completed and attached to your receipt as proof of payment.

The petty cash fund should be balanced and replenished monthly.

Equipment Records and Accounting

Options for owning, renting, and leasing equipment were discussed in Chapter 9. Equipment rates were then used to construct the equipment portion of the estimate. For accounting purposes, information on equipment must be tracked. Important information to record includes:

✓ use rate,

✓ use time,

✓ maintenance costs,

✓ repair costs, and

✓ operating costs (i.e., gas, oil, etc.).

A separate record should be prepared for each piece of equipment.

This information is also useful when analyzing the need for future equipment purchases or upgrades.

Depreciation Methods

Depreciation is the process of devaluing a fixed asset as a result of aging, wear and tear, or obsolescence. The asset is depreciated over the course of its "useful life." Depreciation is considered a non-cash expense. You can depreciate vehicles, office equipment, buildings, and machinery. Land cannot be depreciated, because it does not "wear out" like depreciable items.

To determine the annual depreciation for an item, you must know the initial cost, how many years it will provide value for your business, and the salvage cost of the item when it is fully depreciated. There are two methods to depreciate fixed assets:

✓ Straight line depreciation

✓ Accelerated depreciation

Using **straight line depreciation**, you simply take the initial cost of the item and subtract the salvage cost. Then you take that total and divide it by the number of "useful life" years.

The calculation is as follows:

$$Initial\ Asset\ Cost - Salvage\ Cost = Depreciation\ Cost$$

$$Depreciation\ Cost \div Useful\ Life\ Years = Yearly\ Depreciation\ Amount$$

Using the **accelerated depreciation** method, the asset is depreciated at a higher rate during the early part of its useful life permitting larger tax deductions. This method is typically used for an asset that will probably be replaced before the end of its useful life. Depreciation percentages are based on the type of asset.

The **modified accelerated cost recovery system (MACRS)** is a depreciation method approved by the IRS. It allows for faster depreciation over longer periods. MACRS divides property into several different classes and takes into account the date the equipment was put in service, cost of equipment, cost recovery period, convention, and depreciation method that applies to your property. Given all these factors, a percentage rate is applied.

For further information, you may refer to the IRS website (www.irs.gov) on how to depreciate property, using MACRS and MACRS's percentage tables.

Accounting Process for Materials

As discussed in Chapter 11, purchase orders are an important project management tool. Purchase orders keep your expenses organized and document exactly what you ordered. They also facilitate the receiving process and the timing of deliveries. Purchase orders help track material inventories and related expenses in the accounting system. Invoices should be matched with purchase orders to ensure that the billing is accurate.

Shipping and Delivery Expenses: In addition to the actual material costs, shipping and delivery expenses are factored into the final cost. Shipping and delivery expenses are charged in a few different ways. Two common shipping terms are:

✓ **FOB Freight Prepaid** requires the seller to pay for shipping charges.

✓ **FOB Freight Allowed** requires the buyer to pay shipping charges. A credit for the shipping amount is often given by the seller on the invoice.

It is important to understand the shipping terms ahead of time and note them on the purchase order.

Payment Terms: Payment terms depend on the payment agreement between the buyer and seller. They are generally listed on the seller's invoice. Terms can vary by seller. Listed below are some common terms you may see on your invoices.

✓ Net 10: Payment is due 10 days after receiving the invoice.

✓ Net 30: Payment is due 30 days after receiving the invoice.

✓ Net 60: Payment is due 60 days after receiving the invoice.

✓ COD: Cash payment is due on delivery.

✓ 1/10 Net 30: A 1 percent discount is given to payments received within 10 days; otherwise, payment is due 30 days after receiving the invoice.

✓ EOM: Payment is due at the end of the month.

✓ 1/10 EOM: A 1 percent discount is given to payments received by the 10th of the month following the shipment; otherwise, payment is due at the end of the month following the shipment.

Early payment discounts are a good way to cut costs. Depending on the contract arrangements, project cost savings may be given to the contractor or credited to the overall project budget.

Payroll Accounting

If you have employees, payroll distribution is done on a regular basis. Thorough payroll records are important for several reasons, such as calculating tax liabilities and tracking labor costs. The process for preparing payroll is as follows:

✓ calculate gross pay for each employee;

✓ calculate and deduct applicable taxes and other deductions;

✓ calculate net pay and issue checks; and

✓ update payroll journal.

Calculate Gross Pay

Gross pay is determined either by a salary that you set for the employee or based on an hourly wage multiplied by the number of hours worked. Salaried employees are generally paid the same amount each pay period, no matter how many hours they work. Hourly employees generally complete timecards that track the number of hours worked.

Time cards are important documentation if an unemployment benefit dispute arises. Many states require employers to keep timecards. If projects are tracked on the timecard, this information can be used for job costing purposes. The following is a sample time card.

Project Name or Number	Hours Worked								Work Completed	Supervisor Approval
	M	Tu	W	Th	F	Sa	Su	Total		

Calculate and Deduct Applicable Taxes and Deductions

Several types of taxes must be deducted from an employee's pay.

Federal income tax is based on information the employee provided on the W-4 form. Using IRS Publication: Circular E (sample below), you can determine the appropriate deduction.

MARRIED Persons—**WEEKLY** Payroll Period

(For Wages Paid through December 31, 2015)

And the wages are–		And the number of withholding allowances claimed is—										
At least	But less than	0	1	2	3	4	5	6	7	8	9	10
		The amount of income tax to be withheld is—										
$800	$810	$78	$67	$55	$44	$33	$26	$18	$10	$2	$0	$0
810	820	80	68	57	45	34	27	19	11	3	0	0
820	830	81	70	58	47	35	28	20	12	4	0	0
830	840	83	71	60	48	37	29	21	13	5	0	0
840	850	84	73	61	50	38	30	22	14	6	0	0
850	860	86	74	63	51	40	31	23	15	7	0	0
860	870	87	76	64	53	41	32	24	16	8	1	0
870	880	89	77	66	54	43	33	25	17	9	2	0
880	890	90	79	67	56	44	34	26	18	10	3	0
890	900	92	80	69	57	46	35	27	19	11	4	0
900	910	93	82	70	59	47	36	28	20	12	5	0
910	920	95	83	72	60	49	37	29	21	13	6	0
920	930	96	85	73	62	50	39	30	22	14	7	0
930	940	98	86	75	63	52	40	31	23	15	8	0
940	950	99	88	76	65	53	42	32	24	16	9	1
950	960	101	89	78	66	55	43	33	25	17	10	2
960	970	102	91	79	68	56	45	34	26	18	11	3
970	980	104	92	81	69	58	46	35	27	19	12	4
980	990	105	94	82	71	59	48	36	28	20	13	5
990	1,000	107	95	84	72	61	49	37	29	21	14	6
1,000	1,010	108	97	85	74	62	51	39	30	22	15	7
1,010	1,020	110	98	87	75	64	52	40	31	23	16	8
1,020	1,030	111	100	88	77	65	54	42	32	24	17	9
1,030	1,040	113	101	90	78	67	55	43	33	25	18	10
1,040	1,050	114	103	91	80	68	57	45	34	26	19	11
1,050	1,060	116	104	93	81	70	58	46	35	27	20	12
1,060	1,070	117	106	94	83	71	60	48	36	28	21	13
1,070	1,080	119	107	96	84	73	61	49	38	29	22	14
1,080	1,090	120	109	97	86	74	63	51	39	30	23	15
1,090	1,100	122	110	99	87	76	64	52	41	31	24	16
1,100	1,110	123	112	100	89	77	66	54	42	32	25	17
1,110	1,120	125	113	102	90	79	67	55	44	33	26	18
1,120	1,130	126	115	103	92	80	69	57	45	34	27	19
1,130	1,140	128	116	105	93	82	70	58	47	35	28	20
1,140	1,150	129	118	106	95	83	72	60	48	37	29	21
1,150	1,160	131	119	108	96	85	73	61	50	38	30	22
1,160	1,170	132	121	109	98	86	75	63	51	40	31	23
1,170	1,180	134	122	111	99	88	76	64	53	41	32	24
1,180	1,190	135	124	112	101	89	78	66	54	43	33	25
1,190	1,200	137	125	114	102	91	79	67	56	44	34	26
1,200	1,210	138	127	115	104	92	81	69	57	46	35	27
1,210	1,220	140	128	117	105	94	82	70	59	47	36	28
1,220	1,230	141	130	118	107	95	84	72	60	49	37	29
1,230	1,240	143	131	120	108	97	85	73	62	50	39	30
1,240	1,250	144	133	121	110	98	87	75	63	52	40	31
1,250	1,260	146	134	123	111	100	88	76	65	53	42	32
1,260	1,270	147	136	124	113	101	90	78	66	55	43	33
1,270	1,280	149	137	126	114	103	91	79	68	56	45	34
1,280	1,290	150	139	127	116	104	93	81	69	58	46	35
1,290	1,300	152	140	129	117	106	94	82	71	59	48	36
1,300	1,310	153	142	130	119	107	96	84	72	61	49	38
1,310	1,320	155	143	132	120	109	97	85	74	62	51	39
1,320	1,330	156	145	133	122	110	99	87	75	64	52	41
1,330	1,340	158	146	135	123	112	100	88	77	65	54	42
1,340	1,350	159	148	136	125	113	102	90	78	67	55	44
1,350	1,360	161	149	138	126	115	103	91	80	68	57	45
1,360	1,370	162	151	139	128	116	105	93	81	70	58	47
1,370	1,380	164	152	141	129	118	106	94	83	71	60	48
1,380	1,390	165	154	142	131	119	108	96	84	73	61	50
1,390	1,400	167	155	144	132	121	109	97	86	74	63	51
1,400	1,410	168	157	145	134	122	111	99	87	76	64	53
1,410	1,420	170	158	147	135	124	112	100	89	77	66	54
1,420	1,430	171	160	148	137	125	114	102	90	79	67	56
1,430	1,440	173	161	150	138	127	115	103	92	80	69	57
1,440	1,450	174	163	151	140	128	117	105	93	82	70	59
1,450	1,460	176	164	153	141	130	118	106	95	83	72	60
1,460	1,470	177	166	154	143	131	120	108	96	85	73	62
1,470	1,480	179	167	156	144	133	121	109	98	86	75	63
1,480	1,490	180	169	157	146	134	123	111	99	88	76	65

$1,490 and over — Use Table 1(b) for a **MARRIED person** on page 45. Also see the instructions on page 43.

✓ Social Security tax is calculated at the current prevailing rate. The current tax rate is available online at www.ssa.gov. Employers must pay in an equal amount of Social Security tax but cannot deduct that amount from the employee's payroll.

✓ Medicare tax is calculated at the rate of 1.45 percent of gross pay. Employers must pay in an equal amount of Medicare tax but cannot deduct that amount from the employee's payroll.

✓ Advance earned income credit needs to be taken, based on information the employee provided on IRS Form W-5.

✓ State income tax should be calculated as it applies to each individual state.

✓ Other deductions might include an employee's contribution for medical insurance, 401K, life insurance, etc.

Reporting of payroll taxes is covered in Chapter 16, Tax Basics.

Calculate Net Pay and Issue Checks

Net pay is the payroll amount the employee receives after deductions are taken. Net pay is calculated as:

Gross Pay – Taxes & Deductions = Net Pay

Employees should receive a statement of earnings with their paycheck. The statement of earnings shows how the net pay was calculated. The following is a sample statement of earnings.

				Current	Year to Date
Earnings					
Description	Rate	Hours	Overtime		
			Total Earnings		
			Taxes		
Employee Name:			Federal Withholding		
			Social Security		
Employee ID:					
			Medicare		
Pay Period:					
			State Withholding		
Check Date:			Insurance Deductions		
			Total Deductions		
			Net Pay		

Update Payroll Journal

Once checks are issued, the payroll journal must be updated to reflect the new account balance. The payroll journal should contain the same information as the employee statement of earnings. This topic is discussed in the previous section. This information is important to calculating your employer tax liabilities. Instructions on how to pay in employer taxes are covered in Chapter 16, Tax Basics.

Technology Solutions for Accounting

There are many accounting software programs on the market that can help make the accounting process easier.

As with all software, you still need to know the fundamentals, but it will help streamline the process and improve accuracy.

Accounting software can automate the process of posting transactions, creating financial statements, invoicing customers, creating purchase orders, and much more. Think of accounting software as an investment to make you more analytical and help you think strategically about your business.

When choosing the right software, consider what your needs are and how the technology can grow with your company. There are many options. You may want to look at programs that integrate job cost analysis with accounting that have been developed specifically for the construction industry.

- -

Final Inspection...

Bookkeeping: The first step of the accounting process is bookkeeping. Bookkeeping is the accurate recording of all financial transactions that occur in the business.

The Accounting Cycle: The accounting cycle is a process that happens each reporting period, which starts with recording financial transactions and goes through analyzing financial statements.

Methods of Accounting: Cash and accrual are the two main methods of accounting. The primary difference between the two methods is the timing of when you record the transactions to your accounts.

Contract Accounting: The methods for contract accounting include completed contract, percentage of completion, and cost comparison.

Cash Management: Positive cash flow is an important indicator of the health of your business. Collecting on accounts receivable and billing and collecting on current accounts are important to the cash management process.

Equipment Records and Accounting: Depreciation is the process of devaluing a fixed asset as a result of aging, wear and tear, or obsolescence. The two primary methods of depreciation are straight line and accelerated.

Accounting Process for Materials: Purchase orders help track material inventories and related expenses in the accounting system. Invoices should be matched with purchase orders to ensure that the billing is accurate.

Payroll Accounting: Thorough payroll records are important for such reasons as calculating tax liabilities and tracking labor costs.

Technology Solutions for Accounting: Accounting software can automate the process of posting transactions, creating financial statements, invoicing customers, creating purchase orders, and much more.

Supplemental Forms

Supplemental forms and links are available at NASCLAforms.org using access code NCL129354.

Balance Sheet	Example featured earlier in the chapter that can be modified in Excel
Income Statement	Example featured earlier in the chapter that can be modified in Excel
Time Card	Sample featured earlier in the chapter to track employee time
Earnings Statement	Sample featured earlier in the chapter as a summary of the employee's earnings

.

Chapter 16
TAX BASICS

Employer Identification Number

Before you become an employer and hire employees, you need a Federal Employer Identification Number (EIN) which is also referred to as a taxpayer identification number.

The only entities that do not need an EIN are:

✓ Sole proprietorships that have no employees and file no excise or pension tax returns; and

✓ LLCs with a single owner (where the owner will file employment tax returns).

In these instances, the owner uses his or her social security number as the taxpayer identification number.

All other types of business entities, including partnerships, are required to obtain an EIN.

The EIN is a 9-digit number that the IRS issues. The digits are arranged as follows: 00-0000000. It is used to identify the tax accounts of employers and certain others who have no employees. Use your EIN on all items you send to the Internal Revenue Service (IRS) and Social Security Administration (SSA).

There are several ways to obtain an EIN through the Internal Revenue Service (IRS).

✓ Call the Business and Specialty Tax Line at (800) 829-4933.

✓ Fax the completed Form SS-4 application to the fax number designated for your state.

✓ Mail the completed Form SS-4 application.

✓ Apply online at www.irs.gov.

Federal Business Taxes

The form of business you operate determines what taxes you must pay and how you pay them. The following are three general types of business taxes that you may be responsible for.

✓ **Income tax**

✓ **Self-employment tax**

✓ **Employment taxes**

The following table lists the tax responsibilities by business entity type and the corresponding forms to file with the IRS.

Summary of Federal Tax Forms

IF you are a...	Then you may be liable for...	Use Form...
Sole proprietor	Income tax	1040 and Schedule C [1] or C–EZ
	Self-employment tax	1040 and Schedule SE
	Estimated tax	1040–ES
	Employment taxes:	
	• Social security and Medicare taxes and income tax withholding	941
	• Federal unemployment (FUTA) tax	940 or 940–EZ
	• Depositing employment taxes	8109 [2]
	Excise taxes	See *Excise Taxes*
Partnership	Annual return of income	1065
	Employment taxes	Same as sole proprietor
	Excise taxes	See *Excise Taxes*
Partner in a partnership (individual)	Income tax	1040 and Schedule E [3]
	Self-employment tax	1040 and Schedule SE
	Estimated tax	1040–ES
Corporation or S corporation	Income tax	1120 or 1120–A (corporation) [3] 1120S (S corporation) [3]
	Estimated tax	1120–W (corporation only) and 8109 [2]
	Employment taxes	Same as sole proprietor
	Excise taxes	See *Excise Taxes*
S corporation shareholder	Income tax	1040 and Schedule E [3]
	Estimated tax	1040–ES

[1] File a separate schedule for each business.

[2] Do not use if you deposit taxes electronically.

[3] Various other schedules may be needed.

Income Tax

All businesses except partnerships must file an annual income tax return. Partnerships file an information return. The form you use depends on how your business is organized.

Estimated Tax

The federal income tax is a "pay-as-you-go" tax. You must pay the tax as you earn or receive income during the year. If you do not pay your tax through withholding, or do not pay enough tax that way, you might owe estimated tax. If you are not required to make estimated tax payments, you pay any tax due when you file your return.

Sole proprietors, partners, and S corporation shareholders generally have to make estimated tax payments if expected owed tax is $1,000 or more when the income tax return is filed. Form 1040–ES, Estimated Tax for Individuals, is available through the IRS to figure and pay estimated tax.

Corporations generally have to make estimated tax payments if expected owed tax is $500 or more when the income tax return is filed. Form 1120–W, Estimated Tax for Corporations, is available through the IRS to figure the estimated tax. You must deposit the payments electronically, through the mail, or delivery with a payment coupon.

Self-Employment Tax

Self-employment tax (SE tax) is a social security and Medicare tax primarily for individuals who work for themselves. Your payments of SE tax contribute to your coverage under the social security system. Social security coverage provides you with retirement benefits, disability benefits, survivor benefits, and hospital insurance (Medicare) benefits.

You must pay SE tax and file Schedule SE (Form 1040) if your net earnings from self-employment were $400 or more.

You must also pay SE tax on your share of certain partnership income and your guaranteed payments.

A Word About Deductible Expenses...

As defined by the IRS, to be deductible, a business expense must be both ordinary and necessary. An ordinary expense is one that is common and accepted in your industry. A necessary expense is one that is helpful and appropriate for your trade or business.

It is important to distinguish a business expense from a personal expense. Personal expenses would include living or family expenses which would not be considered deductible business expenses. A deductible business expense would include:

- ✓ Expenses used to figure cost of goods sold, such as cost of product, storage, direct labor, and project overhead; and

- ✓ Capital expenses, such as business assets and improvements (Although you generally cannot take a current deduction for a capital expense, you may be able to recover the amount you spend through depreciation, amortization, or depletion. These recovery methods allow you to deduct part of your cost each year.)

Federal Employment Taxes

When you have employees, you have certain employment tax responsibilities and forms you must file. Most employers must withhold (except FUTA), deposit, report and pay the following taxes:

- ✓ Social security and Medicare taxes (FICA)
- ✓ Federal income tax withholding
- ✓ Federal unemployment (FUTA) tax

Keep all records of employment taxes for at least four years.

Circular E

The IRS Publication *Circular E: Employer's Tax Guide* is a comprehensive reference providing thorough instructions on calculating, withholding and depositing employee taxes. The Circular E is found on the IRS website at www.irs.gov and at NASCLAforms.org.

Social Security and Medicare Taxes (FICA)

 Social security and Medicare taxes pay for benefits that workers and families receive under the Federal Insurance Contributions Act (FICA). Social security tax pays for benefits under the old-age, survivors, and disability insurance part of FICA. Medicare tax pays for benefits under the hospital insurance part of FICA. Medicare is a part of the Social Security Program that provides hospital and medical insurance coverage to persons age 65 and over and those who have permanent kidney failure, or end stage renal disease, and people with other disabilities.

You withhold part of these taxes from your employee's wages and your company must pay a matching amount. Social Security and Medicare tax is calculated at the current prevailing rate. The current tax rate is available online at www.ssa.gov.

Federal Income Tax Withholding

You generally must withhold federal income tax from your employees' wages. To figure how much to withhold from each wage payment, use the employee's form W-4, Employee's Withholding Allowance Certificate, and the methods described in the previous chapter. The W-4 deductions do not expire unless the employee gives you a new one or if the employee is claiming a tax exemption. A new W-4 form must be completed by February 15 each year from employees claiming a tax withholding exemption.

Form W-2: Form W-2, Wage and Tax Statement summarizes the employee's previous year's wages and withholding amounts. All employees must be furnished copies of the form W-2 by January 31 for the previous year's wages. Employees should receive copies B, C, and 2.

If employment ends before the end of the year, the W-2 form can be given to the employee at any time but no later than January 31. If an employee asks for the W-2 form, you must furnish copies within 30 days of the request or 30 days of the final payment, whichever is later.

Employers must send Copy A of the W-2 form with the entire page of the W-3 form to the Social Security Administration (SSA) by the last day of February (or last day of March if you file electronically). Send the forms to:

Social Security Administration
Data Operations Center
Wilkes-Barre, Pennsylvania 18769-0001

Deposit Schedule

There are three deposit schedules, monthly, semiweekly and daily, for determining when you deposit social security, Medicare and withheld income taxes. Prior to the beginning of the calendar year, you must determine which schedule you are required to use.

You are a monthly schedule depositor if your total payroll tax liability for the previous four quarters (July to June) was $50,000 or less. Payments are due on the fifteenth day of the following month after the payments were made. During your first year of business, you are a monthly schedule depositor.

If your total payroll tax liability from the previous four quarters (July to June) is greater than $50,000, you are a semiweekly schedule depositor. The semiweekly deposit schedule depends on your payroll date.

If your payday is on...	Then your deposit date is...
Wednesday, Thursday and/or Friday	Wednesday
Saturday, Sunday, Monday and/or Tuesday	Friday

If your accumulated tax liability is $100,000 or more on any day during a deposit period, you must deposit it on the next banking day. If you are a monthly schedule depositor and accumulate a $100,000 tax liability on any day, you automatically become a semiweekly depositor.

Form 941: If you report less than $2,500 for the quarter, you can use the IRS Form 941, Quarterly Employer's Tax Return to make payments by the due date of the return. If your tax obligation exceeds $2,500 for the quarter, you are subject to payments according to a deposit schedule.

Federal Unemployment Tax (FUTA)

The federal unemployment tax is part of the federal and state program under the Federal Unemployment Tax Act (FUTA) that pays unemployment compensation to workers who lose their jobs.

You report and pay FUTA tax separately from social security and Medicare taxes and withheld income tax. Employers are responsible for FUTA and cannot withhold this amount from the employees' payroll.

You are generally liable for both state and federal unemployment taxes if

✓ you pay wages to employees totaling $1,500, or more, in any quarter of a calendar year, or

✓ you had at least one employee during any day of a week during 20 weeks in a calendar year, regardless of whether or not the weeks were consecutive.

Calculating FUTA: The FUTA tax base and tax rate is calculated at the current prevailing rate. The current tax information is available online at www.irs.gov. Employers who pay the state unemployment tax, on a timely basis, will receive an offset credit to the federal tax. State tax rates are based on requirements of state law.

Deposit Requirements: For deposit purposes, figure FUTA tax quarterly. If your FUTA tax liability is less than $500, you are not required to deposit the tax. Instead, carry it forward and add it to the liability figured in the next quarter to see if you must make a deposit. Use the following schedule to determine when to deposit FUTA taxes.

Quarter	Ending	Due Date
Jan-Feb-Mar	March 31	April 30
Apr-May-June	June 30	July 31
July-Aug-Sept	Sept. 30	Oct. 31
Oct-Nov-Dec	Dec. 31	Jan. 31

Form 940: Report FUTA taxes on Form 940, Employer's Annual Federal Unemployment (FUTA) Tax Return or if you qualify, you can use the simpler Form 940-EZ instead.

Penalties

Accurate and prompt deposits are required to avoid penalties which can range from 2 percent to 100 percent of your tax liability.

Penalties may apply if

✓ you do not make payroll tax deposits on time;

✓ make deposits for less than the required amount; or

✓ do not use the Electronic Federal Tax Payment System (EFTPS) when required.

These penalties are as follows:

2%	Deposits made 1-5 days late.
5%	Deposits made 6-15 days late.
10%	Deposits made more than 16 days late. Also applies to amounts paid within 10 days of the date of the first notice the IRS sent asking for the tax due.
10%	Deposits made at an unauthorized financial institution, paid directly to the IRS, or paid with your tax return.
10%	Amounts subject to electronic deposit requirements but not deposited using EFTPS.
15%	Amounts still unpaid more than 10 days after the date of the first notice that the IRS sent asking for the tax due or the day on which you received notice and demand for immediate payment, whichever is earlier.
100%	Failure to pay "trust fund" taxes defined as withheld income, social security and Medicare taxes. The amount of the penalty is equal to the unpaid balance of the trust fund tax.

Information Returns – 1099-MISC

You may be required to file information returns to report certain types of payments made during the year to persons not treated as employees. Form 1099-MISC, Miscellaneous Income may be used to report payments of $600 or more to independent contractors. Form 1099-MISC must be filed by January 31 for the prior year's payments. Form 1096, Annual Summary and Transmittal of U.S. Information Returns, is used to transmit 1099 forms to the IRS. Form 1096 is due by February 28 for the previous year's 1099s.

Tax Calendar

Listed below are key employment tax deadlines as outlined in the IRS Publication Circular E. IRS Publication 509-Tax Calendar is also a good resource to keep track of other various tax due dates including income and employment taxes.

By January 31	Furnish W-2 Form, Wage and Tax Statement to All Employees
	Furnish Form 1099 to Each Other Payee (for example, independent contractors with payments of $600 or more)
	File Form 940 or 940-EZ, Employer's Annual Federal Unemployment Tax (FUTA) Return
	File Form 945, Annual Return of Withheld Federal Income Tax
By February 15	Request a New W-4 Form from Employees Claiming a Tax Withholding Exemption
On February 16	Exempt W-4 Forms Expire
By February 28	File Copy A of All 1099 Forms with Form 1096, Annual Summary and Transmittal of U.S. Information Returns with the IRS
	File Copy A of W-2 Forms, Wage and Tax Statement with W-3 Form, Transmittal of Wage and Tax Statements with the Social Security Administration
By March 31	File Electronic Forms 1099 and 8027 with IRS
	File Electronic W-2 Forms with the Social Security Administration
By April 30, July 31, October 31, and January 31	Deposit FUTA Taxes
	File Form 941, Employer's Quarterly Federal Tax Return and deposit any undeposited income, social security and Medicare taxes
Before December 1	Remind Employees to Submit New W-4 Forms if withholding allowances have changed
On December 31	W-5 Form, Earned Income Credit Advance Payment Certificate Expires

North Carolina State Tax Specifics

The North Carolina Department of Revenue is responsible for the administration of tax programs in the state. Activities include issuing sales tax licenses, assigning payroll and sales tax account numbers, and collecting various taxes. The department can be reached at the following address:

> State of North Carolina
> Department of Revenue
> P.O. Box 25000
> Raleigh, North Carolina 27640-0640
>
> General Information: (877) 252-3052
> Forms: (877) 252-3052
>
> Website: www.dor.state.nc.us

The website contains many of the forms needed to conduct business with the department. Most of the forms include instructions to assist you.

Corporate Income Tax

Corporate Income Tax: The corporate income tax rate in North Carolina is 6.9 percent. Corporations with a taxable base in North Carolina and at least one other state are allowed to apportion their income. Apportionment is based on several factors, including a sales formula and property and payroll ratios.

Tax Credits: North Carolina provides several credits for new and expanding businesses that may be taken against corporate income tax. It is best to consult a tax professional when determining which credits apply to your business.

Estimated Tax: A declaration of estimated tax must be filed by a corporation for each taxable year in which it can reasonably expect a state income tax liability of $500 or more.

LLCs: An LLC is subject to taxation as a partnership or corporation depending on how it is classified for federal income tax purposes.

Franchise Tax

The franchise tax rate in North Carolina is $1.50 per $1,000. The minimum franchise tax is $35. Franchise tax is levied on the largest of 3 alternative tax bases. These bases are

✓ the amount of the capital stock, surplus, and undivided profits apportionable to the state;

✓ 55 percent of the appraised value of property in the state subject to local taxation; or

✓ the book value of real and tangible personal property in the state less any debt outstanding which was created to acquire or improve the property.

Sales and Use Tax

Most property, such as construction materials and equipment rental and purchase, is subject to the 4.75 percent state and 2 percent local rate of tax (2.25 percent in Alexander, Buncombe, Cabarrus, Catawba, Cumberland, Duplin, Durham, Halifax, Haywood, Hertford, Lee, Martin, Montgomery, New Hanover, Onslow, Orange, Pitt, Randolph, Robeson, Rowan, Sampson, Surry, and Wilkes counties) for a combined 6.75 percent rate (7 percent in Alexander, Buncombe, Cabarrus, Catawba, Cumberland, Duplin, Durham, Halifax, Haywood, Hertford, Lee, Martin, Montgomery, New Hanover, Onslow, Orange, Pitt, Randolph, Robeson, Rowan, Sampson, Surry, and Wilkes counties). Sales tax is generally not due on services and is not charged to the final construction project.

Withholding Tax

Employers are required to withhold individual state income tax from the wages and salaries of their employees.

Registering to Withhold Tax: You must submit a completed business registration application, Form AS/RP1, to obtain a withholding tax identification number. After your application is processed, the Department of Revenue will mail information concerning your North Carolina withholding tax account number and pre-printed forms on which to report and submit your payment of the tax withheld.

Determining Withholding Amounts: Each employee must furnish you with a signed North Carolina Employee's Withholding Allowance Certificate, Form NC-4. You should use these forms along with the tax tables found in the publication, NC-30, to determine how much income tax should be withheld from each employee's paycheck.

Filing Withholding Tax Returns: Withholding tax returns are filed on a quarterly, monthly, or semi-weekly basis depending on the average amount of tax you withhold each month.

If you withhold an average of less than $250 from employee wages each month, you should file a return and pay the withheld taxes on a quarterly basis. The tax is due the last day of the month following the end of the quarter.

If you withhold an average of at least $250 but less than $2,000 from employee wages each month, you should file a return and pay the withheld taxes on a monthly basis. This tax is due on the fifteenth of the following month. The December report is due by January 31 of the following year.

If you withhold an average of at least $2,000 or more from employee wages each month, you should file a return and pay the withheld taxes at the same time you are required to file the reports and pay the tax withheld on the same wages for federal income tax purposes. If payroll is made on Saturday, Sunday, Monday or Tuesday, it is due the following Friday of the same week. If payroll is made on Wednesday, Thursday, or Friday, it is due the following Wednesday.

Penalties: There is a 10 percent penalty for late payment of the tax due. There is also a penalty of 5 percent per month, with a maximum of 25 percent, for failure to file the report when due.

Income Tax Withholding Tables and Instructions: Publication NC-30 outlines the withholding process in detail and includes the withholding tables needed to withhold the proper amounts for each payroll. Listed on page 16-8 are key due dates included in the NC-30 publication.

At the Time a New Employee is Hired	✓ Obtain Form NC-4, N.C. Employee's Withholding Allowance Certificate from each new employee when hired. ✓ Withhold North Carolina income tax upon each payment of wages to the employee.
On or Before January 31st and At the End of Employment	✓ Give each employee a W-2, Wage and Tax Statement. ✓ Give each nonresident who received non-wage compensation for personal services performed in North Carolina a NC-1099PS, Personal Services Income Paid to a Nonresident, or Federal Form 1099-MISC. ✓ Give each recipient of distributions a completed Form 1099-R.
By February 15th	Ask for a new Form NC-4, Employee's Withholding Allowance Certificate from each employee who claimed total exemption from withholding during the prior year.
On February 16th	Begin withholding for each employee who previously claimed exemption from withholding but has not given you a Form NC-4 for the current year. If the new employee does not give you a new Form NC-4, withhold tax as if the employee is single with zero withholding allowances.
On or Before February 28th (Feb. 29th if a leap year)	File Annual Withholding Reconciliation (Form NC-3 or NC 3M) together with all N.C. Department of Revenue copies (copy 1) of the forms W-2, 1099-MISC, 1099-R or Form 1099PS.
Due Dates for Quarterly Returns	File Form NC-5, Withholding Return, and payment by the last day of the month following the end of the calendar quarter.
Due Dates for Monthly Returns	File Form NC-5, Withholding Return and payment by the 15th day of the month following the month in which the tax was withheld. The return and payment for the month of December are due by January 31.
Due Dates for Semiweekly Tax Payments	Pay tax with Form NC-5P, Withholding Payment Voucher, at the same time as required for federal purposes. Each time you are required to deposit federal employment taxes, you must remit North Carolina withholding. If you withhold $100,000 or more during any deposit period, you are required to deposit federal taxes by the next banking day. North Carolina did not adopt this rule and taxes are only submitted on or before the normal federal semiweekly schedule.
On or Before the Last Day of the Month Following the Quarter	File Form NC-5Q, North Carolina Quarterly Income Tax Withholding Return which reconciles the tax paid for the quarter against the actual tax withheld for the quarter for semiweekly filers.

- -

Final Inspection...

Employer Identification Number: An employer identification number is used to identify the tax accounts of employers and certain others who have no employees.

Federal Business Taxes: The form of business you operate determines what taxes you must pay and how you pay them.

Summary of Federal Tax Forms: You must file the specific federal tax forms that correspond to your business entity type.

Income Tax: All businesses except partnerships must file an annual income tax return. Partnerships file an information return.

Self-Employment Tax: Self-employment tax (SE tax) is a social security and Medicare tax primarily for individuals who work for themselves.

Federal Employment Taxes: Federal employment taxes include social security and Medicare (FICA), federal income tax withholding, and federal unemployment tax (FUTA).

Penalties: Accurate and prompt deposits are required to avoid penalties which can range from 2 percent to 100 percent of your tax liability.

Information Returns-1099 MISC: Form 1099-MISC, Miscellaneous Income may be used to report payments of $600 or more to independent contractors.

Tax Calendar: IRS Publication Circular E and Publication 509 provide tax calendars for various taxes that may apply to your business.

North Carolina State Tax Specifics: Corporate income, franchise, sales and use, and withholding are a few state taxes that may apply to your business.

Supplemental Forms

Supplemental forms and links are available at **NASCLAforms.org** using access code **NCL129354**.

IRS Publication 334	Tax Guide for Small Business
IRS Publication 463	Travel, Entertainment and Gift Expenses
IRS Publication 505	Tax Withholding and Estimated Tax
IRS Publication 509	General Tax Calendar
IRS Publication 533	Self-Employment Tax
IRS Publication 535	Business Expenses
IRS Publication 538	Accounting Periods and Methods
IRS Publication 541	Tax Information on Partnerships
IRS Publication 542	Tax Information on Corporations
IRS Publication 583	Taxpayers Starting a Business
IRS Publication 587	Business Use of Your Home
IRS Publication 946	How to Begin Depreciating Your Property
IRS Publication 1544	Reporting Cash Payments of Over $10,000

IRS Form W-2	Wage and Tax Statement
IRS Form W-3	Tax Reconciliation
IRS Form W-4	Employee Withholding
IRS Form SS-4	Application for Employer Identification Number
IRS Form 940	Employer Annual Federal Unemployment Tax Return
IRS Form 941	Employer's Quarterly Federal Tax Return
IRS Form 1040	U.S. Individual Income Tax Return
IRS Schedule C	Profit or Loss from Business
IRS Schedule-EZ	Net Profit from Business
IRS Schedule SE	Self-Employment Tax
IRS Form 1040-ES	Estimated Tax for Individuals
IRS Form 1065	U.S. Partnership Return of Income Schedule K-1, Partner's Share of Income, Credits, Deductions, etc.
IRS Form 1120	U.S. Corporation Income Tax Return
IRS Form 1120S	U.S. Income Tax Return for an S Corporation Schedule K-1
IRS Form 4562	Depreciation and Amortization
IRS Form 8300	Report of Cash Payments over $10,000 Received in a Trade or Business
Employer's Tax Guide (Circular E)	Publication used to determine federal income tax withholding for employees

Chapter 17
NORTH CAROLINA MECHANICS' LIEN LAW

Chapter Survey...

⇨ *What is a Lien?*

⇨ *Who is Entitled to a Mechanics' Lien?*

⇨ *Notice of Contract*

⇨ *Notice of Subcontract*

⇨ *Filing a Notice of Claim of Lien*

⇨ *Filing a Claim of Lien*

⇨ *Monetary Awards*

⇨ *Time in Which to File a Lien Foreclosure Petition*

⇨ *Sale of Land to Satisfy Lien*

What is a Lien?

Mechanics' and materialmen's liens "cloud" the title to real property but can be an effective method (and sometimes the only method) for securing payment for labor or materials used in the improvement of real property. The lien stops the owner from selling the property with a clear title. The lien may be foreclosed in a lawsuit. The court can order that property be sold and the proceeds used to pay the contractor, subcontractor, laborer, or material supplier. This may be true even if the owner has already paid a general contractor, meaning that the owner may have to pay twice. This is one of the reasons that a lien can be such a powerful collection tool.

The law governing mechanics' liens is found in Chapter 44A of the General Statutes of North Carolina. The state statutes and court opinions establish a strict procedure to perfect and foreclose a lien. It is strongly recommended that a professional be routinely used to record and foreclose on construction liens.

Who is Entitled to a Mechanics' Lien?

Contracts with the Owner: The state statutes specify that "any person who performs or furnishes labor or professional design or surveying services or furnishes materials or furnishes rental equipment" and who contracted directly with the owner has lien rights against the property where the construction project was performed.

Contracts with the General Contractor: First-tier subcontractors are those who contract with the general contractor. First-tier subcontractors have lien rights against the money owed to the contractor by the owner.

Contracts with First-Tier Subcontractors: Second-tier contractors are those who contract with first-tier contractors. Second-tier subcontractors have lien rights against the money owed to the first-tier contractor by the general contractor.

Contracts with Second-Tier Subcontractors: Third-tier contractors are those who contract with second-tier contractors. Third-tier subcontractors have lien rights against the money owed to the second-tier contractor by the first-tier contractor.

Remote Contracts: Contracts more remote than third-tier have lien rights against the funds owed to the party with whom they contracted with to perform the work.

Notice of Contract

Within 30 days of the building permit issuance, the general contractor can file a notice of contract with the office of the clerk of superior court. The notice must be posted on the property in a visible location adjacent to the posted building permit.

The notice of contract must follow a similar format to the following form:

NOTICE OF CONTRACT

(1) Name and address of the Contractor:

(2) Name and address of the owner of the real property at the time this Notice of Contract is recorded:

(3) General description of the real property to be improved (street address, tax map lot and block number, reference to recorded instrument, or any other description that reasonably identifies the real property):

(4) Name and address of the person, firm or corporation filing this Notice of Contract:

Dated: _____

_____

Contractor

Filed this the _____ day of _____, _____.

_____

Clerk of Superior Court

Notice of Subcontract

To preserve lien rights, the second- or third-tier subcontractor must serve upon the contractor who has filed a notice of contract with a completed and signed notice of subcontract form.

The notice of subcontract must follow a similar format to the following form:

NOTICE OF SUBCONTRACT

(1) Name and address of the subcontractor:

(2) General description of the real property where the labor was performed or the material was furnished (street address, tax map lot and block number, reference to recorded instrument, or any description that reasonably identifies the real property):

(3)(i)   General description of the subcontractor's contract, including the names of the parties thereto:

(ii)   General description of the labor and material performed and furnished thereunder:

(4) Request is hereby made by the undersigned subcontractor that he be notified in writing by the contractor of, and within five days following, each subsequent payment by the contractor to the first-tier subcontractor for labor performed or material furnished at the improved real property within the above descriptions of such in paragraph (2) and subparagraph (3)(ii), respectively, the date payment was made and the period for which payment is made.

Dated: _____

_____

Subcontractor

Filing a Notice of Claim of Lien

Prior to filing a claim of lien, first-tier, second-tier, third-tier, and remote contractors must file a notice of claim of lien.

Required Information: This notice must contain the following information:

- ✓ name and address of the person claiming the lien upon funds;

- ✓ general description of the real property improved;

- ✓ name and address of the person with whom the lien claimant contracted to improve real property;

- ✓ name and address of each person against or through whom subrogation rights are claimed;

- ✓ general description of the contract and the person against whose interest the lien upon funds is claimed; and

- ✓ amount of the lien upon funds claimed by the lien claimant under the contract.

First, Second and Third-Tier Notice Format: The notice for first, second and third-tier contractors must follow a similar format to the following form:

NOTICE OF CLAIM OF LIEN UPON FUNDS BY
FIRST, SECOND, OR THIRD-TIER SUBCONTRACTOR

To:

1. _____, owner of property involved.

(Name and address)

2. _____, general contractor.

(Name and address)

3. _____, first-tier subcontractor against or through

(Name and address)   whom subrogation is claimed, if any.

4. _____, second-tier subcontractor against or through

(Name and address)   whom subrogation is claimed, if any.

General description of real property where labor performed or material furnished:

_____

General description of undersigned lien claimant's contract including the names of the parties thereto:

_____

The amount of lien upon funds claimed pursuant to the above described contract:

$ _____

The undersigned lien claimant gives this notice of claim of lien upon funds pursuant to North Carolina law and claims all rights of subrogation to which he is entitled under Part 2 of Article 2 of Chapter 44A of the General Statutes of North Carolina.

Dated _____

_____, Lien Claimant

_____(Address)

Remote Contractors Notice Format: The notice for contractors more remote than third-tier must follow a similar format to the following form:

NOTICE OF CLAIM OF LIEN UPON FUNDS BY SUBCONTRACTOR
MORE REMOTE THAN THE THIRD TIER

To:

_____, person holding funds against which lien

(Name and Address)

upon funds is claimed.

General description of real property where labor performed or material furnished:

_____

_____

General description of undersigned lien claimant's contract including the names of the parties thereto:

_____

_____

The amount of lien upon funds claimed pursuant to the above described contract:

$ _____

The undersigned lien claimant gives this notice of claim of lien upon funds pursuant to North Carolina law and claims all rights to which he or she is entitled under Part 2 of Article 2 of Chapter 44A of the General Statutes of North Carolina.

Dated: _____

_____, Lien Claimant

(Address)

Filing a Claim of Lien

Time in Which to File: A claim of lien must be filed within 120 days of the last date that labor or materials were furnished.

Required Information: The claim of lien must contain the following information:

- ✓ name and address of the person claiming the claim of lien on real property;

- ✓ name and address of the record owner of the real property claimed to be subject to the claim of lien on real property at the time the claim of lien on real property is filed;

- ✓ description of the real property upon which the claim of lien on real property is claimed: (Street address, tax lot and block number, reference to recorded instrument, or any other description of real property is sufficient, whether or not it is specific, if it reasonably identifies what is described.);

- ✓ name and address of the person with whom the claimant contracted for the furnishing of labor or materials;

- ✓ date upon which labor or materials were first furnished upon said property by the claimant;

- ✓ date upon which labor or materials were last furnished upon said property by the claimant;

- ✓ general description of the labor performed or materials furnished and the amount claimed; and

- ✓ signature of the lien claimant.

Where to File: All claims of lien must be filed in the office of the clerk of the superior court in each county where the property subject to the claim of lien is located.

Lien Waiver: A waiver of lien rights as part of a contract's provisions is unenforceable.

Monetary Awards

Prorating Liens: If the amount due to the contractor is not sufficient to pay all the lienors, the owner will prorate the amount due to all of those claiming a lien.

If the amount due to the lower-tier contractor is not sufficient, the party claiming the lien will prorate the amount due to all of those claiming a lien.

Time in Which to File a Lien Foreclosure Petition

A lawsuit to foreclose on the lien must be filed within 180 days after the lienor last provided materials or labor for the construction project.

Sale of Land to Satisfy Lien

A judge can order the sale of the land to pay the lien or can remove the lien if it is not valid. An owner can also bond around the lien. This allows the sale of the land with a clear title but also makes the bond available to pay the lien-holder and any of the lower-tier contractors if the lawsuit is successful.

Summary of Lien Process

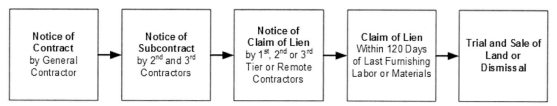

| Notice of Contract by General Contractor | Notice of Subcontract by 2nd and 3rd Contractors | Notice of Claim of Lien by 1st, 2nd or 3rd Tier or Remote Contractors | Claim of Lien Within 120 Days of Last Furnishing Labor or Materials | Trial and Sale of Land or Dismissal |

- -

Final Inspection...

What is a Lien? A lien can be a useful tool in securing payment for labor or materials for improvement on real property.

Who is Entitled to a Mechanics' Lien? State statutes give those who contract with the owner and first-tier, second-tier, third-tier, and remote contractors lien rights.

Notice of Contract: The general contractor can file a notice of contract within 30 days of receiving a building permit.

Notice of Subcontract: If the general contractor filed a notice of contract, the second- and third-tier contractors must file a notice of subcontract.

Filing a Notice of Claim of Lien: Before filing a claim of lien, the notice of claim of lien must be filed.

Filing a Claim of Lien: A claim of lien must contain all the required information and be filed within 120 days of last furnishing labor or materials.

Monetary Awards: Monetary awards are prorated if the amount due is not sufficient to pay the lienors.

Time in Which to File a Lien Foreclosure Petition: A lawsuit to foreclose on a lien must be filed within 180 days of last furnishing labor or materials.

Sale of Land to Satisfy Lien: A judge can order the sale of land or remove a lien if it is not valid.

Appendix A: Glossary

A

Accelerated Depreciation: A method of depreciation where an asset is depreciated at a higher rate during the early part of its useful life permitting larger tax deductions.

Acceptance (Legal): An agreement to an offer made and generally is done by signing the offer. In some cases, a counteroffer is made. A counteroffer is not considered acceptance. It is only when both parties agree to the contract terms that you obtain acceptance.

Accounting Cycle: A process that happens each financial reporting period which starts with recording financial transactions and goes through analysis of financial statements.

Accounts Receivable: Monies that are owed to a business for products and/or services provided.

Accrual Method of Accounting: A method of accounting where income is recognized when the services occur, not when the money is collected. Expenses are recorded when they are incurred, not when they are paid.

Acid Test Ratio: See Quick Ratio.

Activity Ratio: A formula that measures how effectively a company manages its credit. It is calculated by dividing sales per day into current receivables.

Addenda or Addendum: Changes made to bid documents after they are issued but before they are due. Addenda ultimately become part of the contract after the bid is accepted.

ADA: The abbreviation for the Americans with Disabilities Act. See Americans with Disabilities Act.

AGC: The abbreviation for the Associated General Contractors of America.

Age Discrimination in Employment Act (ADEA): A federal law that prohibits discrimination against individuals who are age 40 or older.

AIA: The abbreviation for the American Institute of Architects.

All-Risk Builders' Risk Insurance: A form of property insurance that covers property owners and builders for buildings under construction typically covering machinery, equipment, materials, supplies, and fixtures that are part of the structure or will become part of the structure. Additional coverage can be added for items, such as temporary structures and scaffolding, used during construction. In general, major construction defects such as poor workmanship and faulty design are not covered.

Allowance: A specified amount designated in an estimate for items that are not specified in the project plans, such as finish materials (carpeting, fixtures, lighting, etc.).

Americans with Disabilities Act (ADA): The Americans with Disabilities Act (ADA) makes it unlawful to discriminate in employment against a qualified individual with a disability.

Arbitration: Arbitration uses a third-party arbitrator or arbitrators to act as a judge or judges to render a decision by which all parties are legally bound. Arbitration is held in a format less formal than a trial.

Asbestos: These naturally occurring, fibrous materials are woven together to create a product with high tensile strength. This material is commonly found in thermal insulation and fireproofing, roofing, and flooring materials.

When these fibers become airborne, they cause a hazard due to their ability to enter the lungs. Diseases associated with asbestos include asbestosis, lung cancer, and mesothelioma.

Asset: Items of value owned by a business.

At-Will Employment: An employment agreement where either the employer or the employee may terminate employment at any time without notice or cause.

Automobile Insurance: A type of insurance providing coverage for liability and physical damage associated with a company vehicle or a fleet of vehicles. All states require vehicle owners to carry some level of liability insurance covering bodily injury and property damage incurred in a vehicle accident.

B

Bad Debt: Uncollectible accounts receivable which is deducted from gross income when figuring taxable income.

Balance Sheet: One of the basic accounting financial statements that shows a company's assets, liabilities, and owners' equity.

Bank Letter of Credit: A cash guarantee that can be converted to a payment to the owner by a bank or lending institution.

Bid: A formal offer to complete a project according to the terms and conditions of the contract for a specified price.

Bid Bond: A type of bond that guarantees the contractor, if awarded the job, will do work at the submitted bid price, enter into a contract with the owner, and furnish the required performance and payment bonds.

Bid Documents: A bid package put together in a competitive bid situation. It may include an invitation to bid, bid instructions, bid sheet, bid schedule, bidder's questionnaire on experience, financial responsibility and capability, copy of the contract, and supplements.

Bid Peddling: An unethical situation where the subcontractor approaches the general contractor after the project is awarded with the intent of lowering the original price submitted on bid day.

Bid Rigging: A form of collusion where contractors coordinate their bids to fix the award outcome of a project.

Bid Shopping: An unethical situation where the general contractor approaches subcontractors other than those who have submitted bids to seek a lower offer than what was quoted in the original bids.

Boilerplate Provisions: Standard language or clauses used in a legal contract that generally appear at the end of the contract. Their purpose is to protect the business in the event of a lawsuit.

Bond: A risk transfer mechanism between a surety bonding company, the contractor, and the project owner. The agreement binds the contractor to comply with the terms and conditions of a contract. If the contractor cannot perform the contract, the surety bonding company assumes the contractor's responsibilities and ensures that the project is completed.

Breach of Contract: When one of the parties involved fails to perform in accordance with any of the terms and conditions of a contract.

Burglary and Theft Insurance: A type of insurance covering loss or damage caused by burglary, theft, larceny, robbery, forgery, fraud, and vandalism.

Business Owner's Policies (BOPs): A type of insurance that bundles property and liability coverage together to eliminate policy gaps or overlaps.

Business Plan: A planning document that outlines business strategies and goals. It is particularly useful for newly-formed or early-stage businesses and companies making major strategic changes. Typical contents are an executive and company summary, products and services description, market analysis, marketing plan, and financial plan.

C

Capital Assets: See Fixed Assets.

Cash Method of Accounting: A method of accounting where income is reported in the year it is received and expenses are deducted in the year they are paid.

Certificate of Occupancy: A certificate issued by a building inspector that deems a structure meets all applicable codes and is safe for occupancy.

Certificate of Substantial Completion: A certificate issued by the architect that deems a structure can be used for its intended purpose.

CFR: The abbreviation for Code of Federal Regulations.

Change Order: A written agreement between the owner and contractor to change the contract. Change orders add to, delete from, or otherwise alter the work set forth in the construction documents.

Circular E: An IRS Publication that provides instructions on calculating, withholding and depositing employee taxes and tax tables.

Clean Air Act: A federal law that allows the EPA to set limits on how much of a pollutant is allowed in the air anywhere in the United States.

Clean Water Act: A federal law that establishes the basic structure for regulating discharges of pollutants into the waters of the United States. This act gives the EPA authority to implement pollution control programs, such as setting wastewater standards for the industry and water quality standards for all contaminants in surface waters.

Collaborative Law: A facilitative process wherein all parties agree at the onset to work to identify a solution that is beneficial to all parties involved. In collaborative law, the parties use their advocates, most often their lawyers, to facilitate a mutually beneficial result through the process of negotiation.

Commercial General Liability Insurance (CGL): A basic liability insurance covering bodily injury that results in actual physical damage or loss for individuals who are not employees, damage or loss to property not belonging to the business, personal injury, including slander or damage to reputation, and advertising injury, including charges of negligence that result from promotion of goods or services.

Company Overhead: The expenses that are necessary to keep business operations running but not directly associated with a project (e.g. taxes, legal fees, etc.).

Completed Contract Method: A method of contract accounting where income or loss is reported in the year the contract is completed.

Completed Operations Liability Insurance: A type of liability insurance that provides coverage for loss arising out of completed projects.

Completion Bond: A type of bond that provides assurance to the financial backers of a construction project that it will be completed on time.

Conceptual Estimate: An estimate prepared by the architect using cost models from previous projects.

Consideration (Legal): When both parties give up something of value, typically, services and products in exchange for monetary compensation.

Consolidated Omnibus Budget Act of 1985 (COBRA): A federal law that gives "qualified beneficiaries" (a covered employee's spouse and dependent children) the right to maintain, at their own expense, coverage under their health plan that would be lost due to a "qualifying event," such as termination of employment, at a cost comparable to what it would be if they were still members of the employer's group.

Construction Management (Contracting): A type of contracting where the project owner contracts with a professional construction manager to coordinate and manage a construction project.

Construction Safety Act: See Contract Work Hours and Safety Standards Act.

Construction Wrap-Up Liability Insurance: A type of insurance that bundles liability and workers' compensation insurance for general contractors and subcontractors on large construction projects to eliminate gaps in coverage. To qualify for this type of insurance, certain contract cost requirements must be met. These requirements vary by state.

Contingency: A specified amount added to an estimate to protect the contractor if an unanticipated problem or condition arises during the course of the project.

Contract: Legally binding agreement between two or more parties with the main purpose of preventing disputes between parties entering into the agreement. A legally binding contract must have offer and acceptance, consideration, competent parties, and legal purpose.

Contract Work Hours and Safety Standards Act: A federal law that sets overtime standards for service and construction contracts on federal projects. Commonly referred to as the Construction Safety Act.

Contractor's Protective Public and Property Damage Liability Insurance: A type of liability insurance that protects contractors who supervise and subsequently are held liable for actions of subcontractors from claims for personal injury and property damage.

Contractual Liability Insurance: A type of liability insurance that provides contractors with protection for damages that result from their negligence while under written contract.

Corporation (sometimes referred to as C Corporation): A legal business entity that has independent ownership of assets and liabilities from its shareholders. Its existence continues even if one or more shareholders leave.

Cost Comparison Method: A method of contract accounting that combines the completed contract and percentage of completion methods.

Cost-Plus Contract: A type of contract where the contractor is reimbursed for the actual cost of labor and materials and is paid a markup fee for overhead and profit.

Critical Path: The sequence of tasks that determines the duration of the project. Subsequent project tasks cannot begin until a critical path item is complete.

Current Assets: Cash and other assets that can be converted into cash in less than one year.

Current Liabilities: Liabilities that will mature and must be paid within one year.

Current Ratio: See Liquidity Ratio.

D

Davis-Bacon Act: The federal law that requires payment of prevailing wage rates and fringe benefits on federally-financed or assisted construction.

Debt Ratio: A formula that measures the percent of total funds provided by creditors. It is calculated by dividing total assets into total debt.

De Minimis Violation: A violation of standards which have no direct or immediate relationship to safety or health.

Depreciation: The process of devaluing a fixed asset as a result of aging, wear and tear, or obsolescence.

Design/Build: A type of contracting where the owner contracts with one company to complete a construction project from start to finish. The company awarded the design/build contract puts together a team of construction professionals, which may include designers, architects, engineers, and contractors.

Direct Costs: Costs directly linked with a particular project.

E

EEOC: Abbreviation for the Equal Employment Opportunity Commission.

Employee Polygraph Protection Act: A federal law that prohibits most private employers from using any type of lie detector test, either for pre-employment screening of job applicants or for testing current employees during the course of employment.

Endangered Species Act (ESA): A federal law that protects threatened or endangered species from further harm.

Entrepreneur: A person engaged in strategic activities that involve the initiation and development of a new business, created to build long-term value and steady cash flow streams.

Equal Pay Act of 1963: A federal law that prohibits employers from paying different wages to men and women who perform essentially the same work under similar working conditions.

Equipment Floater Policy: A type of inland marine insurance covering direct physical loss to equipment and mobile equipment while it is stored on premises, in transit, or at temporary locations or jobsites.

Errors and Omissions Insurance: See Professional Liability Insurance.

Expenses: Monies paid out or owed for goods or services.

F

Failure to Abate Prior Violation: A safety violation given when a previous violation has not been corrected.

Fair Labor Standards Act (FLSA): The federal law which prescribes standards for the basic minimum wage and overtime pay and affects most private and public employment. It applies to employers who have one or more employees. FLSA is administered by the Employment Standards Administration's Wage and Hour Division within the U.S. Department of Labor.

Family and Medical Leave Act (FMLA): A federal law that entitles eligible employees of covered employers to take up to 12 weeks of unpaid job-protected leave each year, with the maintenance of group health insurance, for the birth and care of a child, for the placement of a child for adoption or foster care, for the care of a child, spouse, or parent with a serious health condition, or for the employee's serious health condition.

Fast Track Construction: A phased approach where the construction process begins before completion of the contract documents. Generally, the cost is not fixed until after construction documents are complete and some construction commitments have already been made.

Federal Employer Identification Number (EIN): A 9-digit number issued by the IRS, which is used to identify the tax accounts of employers and certain others who have no employees (also referred to as a taxpayer identification number).

Federal Unemployment Tax Act (FUTA): The federal unemployment tax that is part of the federal and state program under which unemployment compensation is paid to workers who lose their jobs.

Fidelity Bond: A type of bond that covers business owners for losses due to dishonest acts by their employees.

Fixed Assets: Assets needed to carry on the business of a company, which are not normally consumed in the operation of the business (sometimes referred to as capital assets).

Foreign Entity: A business originally established in another state or another country.

Foreman: An individual who assists the superintendent with daily project operations and usually supervises specific areas by trade.

For Profit Corporation: A corporation in existence to make a profit for its owners or shareholders. Corporate tax status is determined by the Internal Revenue Service.

FUTA: An abbreviation for Federal Unemployment Tax Act.

H

Health Insurance Portability and Accountability Act of 1996 (HIPAA): A federal law that provides for improved portability and continuity of health insurance coverage connected with employment.

I

I-9 Form: The form required for employers to complete to verify employment eligibility under the Immigration and Nationality Act. I-9 forms must be kept on file for at least three years after the date of hire or for one year after the date employment ends, whichever is later.

Immaterial Breach (Partial Breach): A less serious violation of a contract that usually does not result in termination of the contract. The injured party may only sue for the value of the damages.

Immigration and Nationality Act (INA): A federal law that outlines the conditions for the temporary and permanent employment of aliens in the United States. It includes provisions for all employers that address employment eligibility and employment verification.

Income Statement: A financial statement that provides a summary of the company's revenues and expenses over a given period of time (sometimes called the profit-and-loss statement).

Indemnification: A way to transfer risk and exemption from loss that absolves the indemnified party from any payment for losses and damages incurred by a third party.

Indemnity: A way to transfer risk and exemption from loss incurred by any course of action. Sometimes an insurance payout is called an indemnity.

Indirect Expenses: See Operating Expenses.

Inland Marine Insurance (Equipment Theft Insurance): A type of property insurance for your tools and equipment that provides coverage for goods in transit and projects under construction.

Insurance: A protective measure in which coverage is obtained for a specific risk (or set of risks) through a contract. In this contract or policy, one party indemnifies another against specified loss in return for premiums paid.

K

Key Man Insurance: A type of insurance coverage for a specific individual necessary for the continuing success of a business. Key man insurance is available as life insurance, disability insurance, or both.

L

Lead-Based Paint Renovation, Repair and Painting Program: This federal regulation involves those who perform renovations for compensation in residential housing that may contain lead paint. It requires for additional provisions to the Lead PRE regulations. Under the Lead-Based Paint Renovation, Repair and Painting Program, contractors must be certified to perform renovation work that disturbs lead-based paint in homes, child care facilities, and schools built before 1978.

Lead PRE: This federal regulation involves those who perform renovations for compensation in residential housing built before 1978 that may contain lead paint. It requires mandatory notification for owners and occupants of the building being renovated.

Liabilities: All debt and obligations owed by a business.

Liability Insurance: A type of insurance designed to protect against third-party claims that arise from alleged negligence resulting in bodily injury or property damage.

Lien Bond: A type of bond that guarantees liens cannot be placed against the owner's property by contractors for payment of services.

Liquid Assets: Assets that are easily converted to cash.

Limited Liability Company (LLC): A legal business entity that has characteristics of both sole proprietorships and corporations. Federal income taxes are paid only on income distributed to members as ordinary income. Members have protection from liability for actions taken by the company or by other members of your company but are not protected from liability for personal actions.

Liquidity Ratio: A calculation used to determine if a company can pay its current debts. Calculated by dividing current liabilities into the current assets (sometimes called current ratio).

Little Miller Acts: Laws enacted by individual states and local governments regarding required bonds to bid and perform public works projects.

Long-Term Liabilities: Debt obligations that extend beyond one year.

Lump Sum Contract: A contract where the contractor agrees to complete the project for a predetermined, specified price. The contractor essentially assumes all of the risk under this contract agreement because the contractor is responsible for additional costs associated with unforeseen circumstances.

M

Maintenance Bond: A type of bond that guarantees for a stated period, typically for one year, no defective workmanship or material will appear in the completed project.

Marketing: Strategies and techniques used to bring in new customers and retain current customers to ensure a steady flow of leads and customers. This process includes advertising and promotion, pricing strategies, timely distribution, and product design and attributes to meet customer needs.

Marketing Plan: A formal document focusing on a company's marketing strategy by outlining the company's vision, customer base, methods of promotion (e.g. advertising, public relations, online marketing, direct sales, etc.), marketing budget, individual responsible for executing the plan, and industry opportunities and challenges.

MasterFormat: A classification system published by the Construction Specifications Institute that includes numbers and job tasks grouped by major construction activities.

Material Breach: A serious violation of a contract that may void the contract and will most likely end up in litigation.

Material Safety Data Sheet (MSDS): A form that accompanies chemicals and is important to workplace safety. The MSDS contains information such as first aid when contact occurs, disposal, storage, protective equipment required, and spill handling procedures.

Materials Expediter: An individual who supervises the materials procurement process to ensure accurate and timely delivery of materials.

Mechanics' Lien: A legal action that "clouds" the title to real property and serves as an effective method (and sometimes the only method) for securing payment for labor or materials used in the improvement of real property. The lien stops the owner from selling the property with a clear title.

Medicare: Social Security and Medicare taxes pay for benefits that workers and families receive under the Federal Insurance Contributions Act (FICA). Medicare tax pays for benefits under the hospital insurance part of FICA.

Miller Act: The Miller Act requires performance and payment bonds on all federal construction projects valued at greater than $100,000.

Minimum Wage: The minimum amount an employer can pay employees. FLSA and individual state laws designate the minimum pay rate.

Minor: An individual under 18 years of age.

Modified Accelerated Cost Recovery System (MACRS): A depreciation method approved by the IRS that allows for faster depreciation over longer periods.

Motor Truck Cargo Insurance: A type of inland marine insurance protecting the transporter in the event of damaged or lost freight.

N

Named Peril Builders' Risk Insurance: An insurance policy with narrower coverage than all-risk insurance that specifies which perils are covered.

National Environmental Policy Act (NEPA): A federal law that ensures that federal agencies consider environmental impacts in federal planning and decision making and covers construction and post-construction activities.

National Historic Preservation Act (NHPA): A federal law that protects property that is eligible for or included on the National Register of Historic Places (NRHP).

Negotiation (Alternative Dispute Resolution): A dialogue entered into for the purpose of resolving disputes or producing an agreed upon course or courses of action.

Negotiation (Contract): The process where the owner and contractor come to an agreement on the price and terms of the contract.

Net Pay: The payroll amount an employee receives after taxes and deductions are taken out.

Net Profit: The difference between revenues and expenses. Net profit directly contributes to the net worth of the company.

NPDES: The abbreviation for the National Pollutant Discharge Elimination System.

O

Occupational Safety and Health Act (OSHA): Federal law governing safe and healthy working conditions by developing standards, providing assistance, information and training, and conducting research.

Offer: An offer specifically outlines the obligations of the contract, including the work to be done and compensation for this work (e.g. estimate or bid).

Operating Expenses: General items that contribute to the cost of operating the business. These expenses can be put into two categories, selling expenses and fixed overhead (sometimes called indirect expenses).

OSHA: An abbreviation for Occupational Safety and Health Administration; Occupational Safety and Health Act.

OSHA Form 300: An OSHA form that serves as an injury/illness log, with a separate line entry for each recordable injury or illness.

OSHA Form 300A: An OSHA form that includes a summary of the previous year's work-related injuries and illnesses.

OSHA Form 301: An OSHA form that serves as an individual incident report providing details about each specific recordable injury or illness.

Other Than Serious Violation: A safety violation that has a direct relationship to workplace safety and health, but probably would not cause death or serious physical harm.

Overhead: See company overhead; project overhead.

Overtime: The hours an employee works when it exceeds more than 40 hours in a workweek. FLSA designates that eligible employees are paid one-and-one-half-times the regular rate for overtime hours.

Owners' Equity: Consists of the initial investment in a business, plus accumulated net profits not paid out to the owners.

Owner's Representative (Owner's Agent): An appointed representative designated to oversee a project and serve as a liaison to the owner. The owner's representative (agent) may have legal authority to make certain legal decisions on behalf of the owner.

P

Partnership: A business relationship between two or more persons who join to carry on a trade or business. Each person contributes money, property, labor, or skill, and each partner expects to share in the profits and losses of the business.

Payment Bond: A type of bond that guarantees subcontractors and suppliers will be paid for work if they perform properly under the contract.

Percentage of Completion Method: A method of contract accounting that recognizes income as it is earned during the construction project.

Performance Bond: A type of bond that guarantees the contractor will complete a contract within its time frame and conditions.

Petty Cash Fund: A cash fund used to make small payments instead of writing a check.

Positive Cash Flow: A term used to describe when more cash is received than is going out to pay expenses.

Professional Liability Insurance (sometimes called Errors and Omissions Insurance): A type of liability insurance that protects contractors from negligence resulting from errors or omissions of designers and architects.

Profitability Ratio: A formula used to calculate the profit margin of a company. It is calculated by dividing revenues into net income.

Profit-and-Loss Statement: See Income Statement.

Progressive Discipline: A method of corrective action where the consequences of the improper behavior become more significant if it continues.

Progress Payments: Partial payments made after completion of specified phases of construction. Payments are generally calculated by taking the difference between the completed work and materials delivered and a predetermined schedule of unit costs.

Project Manager: An individual who plans and coordinates a construction project to meet the overall goals of the project and serves as the main contact with the owner.

Project Overhead: Items necessary to complete the project but not directly associated with labor and materials (e.g. temporary storage, dumpsters, etc.).

Property Insurance: An insurance policy covering property when damage, theft, or loss occurs. Specific risk provisions are often available for occurrences such as fire or theft. Broad-based policies cover a variety of risks (including fire, theft, vandalism, and "acts of God" such as lightning strikes).

Q

Quick Ratio: Similar to the liquidity ratio, it is calculated by dividing the current liabilities into the current assets minus inventory (sometimes called the acid test ratio).

R

Recitals (Legal): Language at the beginning of a contract that provides background to the contract.

Repeated Violation: A safety violation of any standard, regulation, rule, or order where, upon reinspection, a substantially similar violation is found.

Retainage: A specified amount withheld from each progress payment as protection for the owner to ensure completion of the construction project and provide protection against liens, claims, and defaults.

Return on Total Assets Ratio: A formula used to determine if the company's assets are being employed in the best manner. It is calculated by dividing total assets into net profit (after taxes).

Revenues: The income received from the daily operations of the business.

Right-to-Work Laws: Laws passed at the state-level that secure the right of employees to decide for themselves whether or not to join or financially support a union.

Risk Management: An assessment of all areas of a business from operations to administrative functions for the risk of financial loss, lower profit margins, and unnecessary liabilities.

S

S Corporation: A legal business entity formed under the rules of Subchapter S of the Internal Revenue Code. It is taxed like a partnership by passing items of income, loss, deduction, and credits through to its shareholders to be included on their separate returns.

Self-Employment Tax: A social security and Medicare tax primarily for individuals who work for themselves.

Serious Violation: A violation where there is substantial probability that death or serious physical harm could result and that the employer knew, or should have known, of the hazard.

Service Contract Act: The federal act that requires payment of prevailing wage rates and fringe benefits on contracts to provide services to the federal government.

Single Prime Contracting: Traditional form of contracting where the project owner typically hires an architectural firm to design the project and the contractor then performs the work according to the specifications of the project and is responsible for the costs of all materials and labor to obtain project completion.

Social Security Tax: Social Security and Medicare taxes pay for benefits that workers and families receive under the Federal Insurance Contributions Act (FICA). Social Security tax pays for benefits under the old-age, survivors, and disability insurance part of FICA.

Sole Proprietorship: A business that has one individual as the owner (proprietor) who is responsible for 100 percent of the decisions made on behalf of the business and owns all of the business assets. It can employ others but may just be the owner who works for the business.

Square-Foot Method Estimate: An estimate based on a calculation of the square footage of the project multiplied by a unit cost.

Statement of Cash Flows: A financial statement that summarizes current cash position, cash sources, and use of these funds over a given period of time.

Statute of Limitations: Laws that set a maximum period of time within which a lawsuit or claim may be filed.

Straight Line Depreciation: A method of depreciation where the salvage cost is subtracted from the initial cost of the item.

Subcontractor: An individual or business that contracts with the general contractor or other subcontractors to complete a portion of a larger project.

Subcontractor's Bond: A type of bond that protects the general contractor in the event that the subcontractor does not fully perform the contract and/or pay for labor and materials.

Superintendent: An onsite supervisor responsible for the daily operations.

SUTA Dumping: The transfer of employees between businesses for the purpose of obtaining a lower unemployment compensation tax rate. SUTA dumping is illegal and subject to criminal and/or civil penalties.

T

Taxpayer Identification Number: See Federal Employer Identification Number.

Tax Provision Expenses: Tax liabilities owed for federal, state, and local taxes.

Title III of the Consumer Credit Protection Act (CCPA): A federal law that protects employees from being discharged by their employers because their wages have been garnished for any one debt and limits the amount of employees' earnings that may be garnished in any one week.

Title VII of the Civil Rights Act of 1964: A federal law that prohibits discrimination on the basis of race, color, religion, national origin, and sex.

Transportation Floater Insurance: A type of inland marine insurance protecting the transporter against damage that occurs to freight during transport.

Turnkey Construction: Similar to the design/build model, the contractor puts together and manages the construction and design team but also obtains financing and land.

U

Unemployment Insurance: A type of insurance that provides unemployment benefits to eligible workers who become unemployed through no fault of their own and meet certain other eligibility requirements. This program is jointly financed through federal and state employer payroll taxes.

Uniformed Services Employment and Reemployment Rights Act (USERRA): A federal law that protects service members' reemployment rights when returning from a period of service in the uniformed services, including those called up from the reserves or National Guard, and prohibits employer discrimination based on military service or obligation.

Unit-Price Contract: A type of contract where a price per unit is calculated for each item and the contractor is paid according to the actual quantities used.

Unit Price Estimating Method: A method of estimating that bundles all of the cost factors such as labor, materials, equipment, and subcontractors to come up with a unit price for the entire task.

V

Value Engineering: A project management approach with the primary objective of understanding the owner's cost, quality, and time priorities to deliver a product of the highest value.

W

Wage Garnishment Law: A federal law that limits the amount an individual's income may be legally garnished and prohibits firing an employee whose pay is garnished for payment of a single debt.

Walsh-Healey Public Contracts Act: A federal law that requires payment of minimum wage rates and overtime pay on contracts that provide goods to the federal government.

Willful Violation: A safety violation that the employer knowingly commits or commits with plain indifference to the law.

Work Hours: As defined under FLSA, hours that ordinarily include all time during which an employee is required to be on the employer's premises, on duty, or at a prescribed work place.

Worker Adjustment and Retraining Notification Act (WARN): A federal law that offers protection to workers, their families, and communities by requiring employers to provide notice 60 days in advance of covered plant closings and covered mass layoffs.

Workers' Compensation Insurance: A type of insurance providing monetary compensation to employees who are injured or disabled on the job and benefits for dependents of those workers who are killed because of work-related accidents or illnesses. The insurance is purchased by the employer; no part of it should be paid for by employees or deducted from their pay.

Working Capital: The amount of cash available after liabilities or debts are paid. Working capital measures the liquidity of the company's assets.

Workweek: As defined under FLSA, it is a period of 168 hours during seven consecutive 24-hour periods. It may begin on any day of the week and at any hour of the day established by the employer.

Appendix B: Business Plan Template

The following business plan template can be customized for your company. These forms are also located at www.NASCLAforms.org using access code NCL129354 in case you need to modify them on your computer. You may want to work through this plan as you review each chapter, as some of the business plan section topics are covered in more depth.

Business Plan Outline	
Section 1: Cover Sheet	**Section 5: Market Analysis**
1a. Name of Business	5a. Target Market Definition
1b. Contact Information	5b. Market Needs
	5c. Market Trends
Section 2: Executive Summary	5d. Market Growth
2a. Plan Highlights	5e. Competitive Comparison
2b. Keys to Success	
	Section 6: Marketing Strategy
Section 3: Company Summary	6a. Value Proposition
3a. Vision	6b. Competitive Edge
3b. Mission	6c. Pricing Strategy
3c. Legal Structure	6d. Promotion Strategy
3d. Management and Personnel Plan	6e. Marketing Programs
3e. Proposed Location	
3f. Facilities Requirements	**Section 7: Financial Plan**
3g. Operational Hours	7a. Sales Forecast and Assumptions
	7b. Profit and Loss Pro Forma
Section 4: Products and/or Service	7c. Source of Financing
4a. Product and/or Service Description	
4b. Vendors	
4c. Technology	
4d. Expansion Opportunities	

Note: You may also refer to the Financial Management chapter for additional financial documentation such as a balance sheet, income statement, and statement of cash flows. The profit and loss pro forma is a good tool for newly-established businesses to determine how much revenue is needed to break even.

Section 1: Cover Sheet

The cover sheet should contain the name of the business, address, phone number, fax number, e-mail address, and contact name. Some cover sheets also contain a confidentiality statement.

Section 2: Executive Summary

A business plan normally starts with an executive summary, which should be concise and interesting. This summary includes the highlights of your plan and serves as an introduction to the rest of your plan. Topics in your executive summary should include, but not be limited to, the following:

- ✓ Business name
- ✓ Business location
- ✓ Product or service offered
- ✓ Purpose of the plan
- ✓ Projected sales
- ✓ Profitability
- ✓ Keys to success

The executive summary should only be a page or two long. Although the executive summary appears first in the printed document, most business plan developers do not write it until after the plan is complete.

Section 3: Company Summary

1. **Vision and Mission:** Include a vision and mission statement for your company. The vision should be a short statement about the company's aspirations for the future. The mission describes the company's primary business purpose or goal. These statements outline the business concept and provide a concise definition of where your company fits in the market.

2. **Legal Structure:** Define the legal structure of your company (i.e., sole proprietorship, partnership, corporation, or limited liability company). Explain why you chose this structure and the benefits it will provide to you and your company. Legal structure is covered in Chapter 2.

3. **Management:** Outline the key management personnel needed to run your business. Can you run the business yourself or do you need to hire managers to help run the operations? What are the job responsibilities of these managers?

4. **Employees:** How many employees do you require? What are the job responsibilities of the employees?

5. **Location:** Describe the location of your business. You do not need to provide a specific address if you do not have one, but describe the area (e.g., downtown location, at home, in a rural area). Explain why this location will provide you with the best opportunity for success.

6. **Facility Requirements:** Identify your facility requirements. Do you need office space, a production area, storage space, or mobile storage? You may want to draw a diagram of the space.

7. **Hours of Operation:** What are your hours of operation? Explain how these hours will provide the maximum benefit to your customer. How will you handle emergency situations that arise outside of normal working hours?

Section 4: Product or Service Description

Defining your product or service (or both) may seem simple. You must describe not only your product or service but how you will provide it to your customers. For example, you may be a general contractor, but without reliable subcontractors and suppliers, you may not be able to complete your projects in the time frame promised to the customer.

1. **Product or Service Description:** Write a summary explaining your specialty. For example, are you a general contractor, plumbing contractor, etc.?

2. **Legal Requirements:** Do you have any licensing or registration requirements? Are there any legal requirements for practicing your trade or running your business?

3. **Subcontractors and Suppliers:** Who will be your primary subcontractors and suppliers? What process will you use to evaluate subcontractors and suppliers?

4. **Technology Trends:** Summarize how technology will affect your business. Are there efficiencies that can be gained through technology? For example, can you integrate scheduling or estimating into your business processes?

5. **Growth Opportunities:** What expansion opportunities exist in the future after your company is established? Can you offer additional products or services, or expand your customer base to other locations?

Section 5: Market Analysis

A market analysis is often performed as one of the first tasks in researching and formulating a business plan. Understanding your customers, the demand for your work, and your competition is important to the future success of your business.

1. **Target Market:** Define the target market for your product or service. Describe the key characteristics of your customers. For example, do your primary customers include families, retired adults, or businesses?

2. **Product or Service Description:** Describe the need your product or service will be filling for your customers. If you will provide both products and services, describe how these will benefit your customers.

3. **Trends:** Describe how your product or service aligns with the consumer trends of your customers. What are the construction trends for your trade and how do these fit your customer's needs?

4. **Growth Opportunities:** Outline growth opportunities that exist within your target market. For example, if you are a pool builder and your target market is young families, you may want to concentrate on single-family homes rather than commercial projects.

5. **Competition:** List your major competitors. Are they local, regional, or national?

Section 6: Marketing Strategy

A marketing strategy is easily formulated by using the "4 P's:" Product, Price, Promotion, and Place. Product is not just your product or service, but how it will benefit your customer. Price refers to your pricing strategy, which can vary based on the market, your goals, and your competition. Promotion deals with marketing in a traditional sense. Your customers will find out about your business through your promotional efforts. Place defines your distribution strategy. In the construction industry, distribution defines the type of customers you want to target. For example, you may decide to differentiate yourself by specializing in certain types of construction.

1. **Value Proposition:** Describe the value that your company will provide your customers. What benefits of using your company will you promote to your customers? For example, you may promote your level of quality or service.

2. **Competitive Edge:** Describe what makes your product or service unique and how you have differentiated yourself from your competitors.

3. **Pricing Strategy:** What pricing strategy will you use? Some options include:
   - ✓ Cost-plus pricing, where you determine a markup percentage and add it to the cost of the job.
   - ✓ Consistency with competition, where your pricing reflects what the competition is charging.
   - ✓ Value pricing, where you try to undercut your competition with lower prices.

4. **Promotion:** How will you familiarize potential customers with your business? Will you promote your product in special venues (i.e., trade shows or special events)? Are there any businesses you can build a co-op relationship with so you can cross-promote each other? For example, you might partner with another trade or supplier to promote each other.

5. **Advertising:** How will you advertise? Will you use media such as radio, TV, newspapers, and the Internet? How often will you advertise?

6. **Sales:** Will you hire sales representatives to promote your company? If so, how many? How will the sales force be divided up? By area or region?

Section 7: Financial Plan

A financial plan can include several aspects of the potential financial health of the company. At a minimum, it should include projected profits over a specific period. This template, for example, shows the first three years of operation. The financial plan should also explain projected cash flow and identify any additional capital required from outside investors or loans.

The profit-and-loss statement is a tabulation of the gross sales income for the company from which all attributed costs must be deducted. A *pro forma* is a "best guess" at these sales numbers and the associated costs. From this *pro forma*, you can see your profit or loss based on the numbers you projected and adjust your budget accordingly. A blank profit-and-loss form is located at the end of this section, if you are unable to use the form on the NASCLAforms.org website. If you use the spreadsheet located on the website, it will automatically calculate gross profit and net income. These calculations were derived from the following formulas:

Income – Cost of Goods Sold = Gross Profit

Gross Profit – Expenses = Net Income

You will learn more about financial calculations in the financial management chapter.

Sales/Income

Use the following points to help you make your sales and expense projections.

You need to determine the average price of the jobs you perform and the number of customers you are projecting for the year. This is your "best guess," but if you have any historical sales data, you may want to use this information in your calculations to determine how your business sales will grow over time.

However you determine your sales, you must list your assumptions so the person reviewing your business plan will understand the numbers presented in your plan.

Projected sales numbers

	Sales (in dollars)
Year 1	
Year 2	
Year 3	

Transfer sales numbers into the profit-and-loss worksheet.

Cost of Goods Sold (COGS)

Cost of goods sold shows the cost of materials and production of the goods a business sells. For each year, enter your inventory cost and the cost to produce the final product for the customer and add together to show the totals. This total represents the cost of goods sold.

	Year 1	Year 2	Year 3
Inventory			
Production Payroll			
Total			

Transfer COGS numbers into the profit-and-loss worksheet.

Management Salaries

Determine how many managers or supervisors you will need to operate your business. A published salary survey will help you estimate what they make in your type of business and in your region. Determine if you will need to add managers or supervisors in years two and three if you have an increase in business.

	Number of Managers	Manager Annual Salary	Total Management Salaries
Year 1			
Year 2			
Year 3			

Enter the total management salaries in the respective boxes on your spreadsheet.

Payroll Taxes

Payroll taxes are calculated at approximately 13 percent of the salaries listed on your spreadsheet. A formula has been entered to calculate that amount automatically.

Payroll taxes include the following items:

✓ Social Security, also known as FICA (a set percentage deducted from an employee's check and EMPLOYER MATCHED)

✓ Medicare, also called FICA Medicare (a set percentage deducted from an employee's check and EMPLOYER MATCHED)

✓ FUTA - Federal Unemployment Tax Act, authorizes the IRS to use monies for job service and training funded through the federal employment agency; EMPLOYER PAID ONLY

✓ SUTA - State Unemployment Tax Act, authorizes the state to use monies for job service/training and retraining of displaced workers; EMPLOYER-PAID ONLY

✓ FUI - Federal Unemployment Insurance; EMPLOYER-PAID ONLY

✓ SUI - State Unemployment Insurance; EMPLOYER-PAID ONLY

More details on payroll taxes are provided in Chapter 16.

Outside Services

These services apply to people or businesses who provide services to your company not directly related to the sales or income of the company. They would not appear on your payroll. Estimate your annual expenses for the following outside services. Keep in mind that the cost may be higher in the first year due to start-up needs. The cost may drop in the second year and then level off in the third year.

	Year 1	Year 2	Year 3
Lawyer			
Accountant			
Technology Consultant			
Total			

Enter the year totals into the spreadsheet.

Advertising and Promotion

Consider the type of marketing you will need. If you are creating a radio, newspaper or TV ad, get an estimate on what that would cost. Don't forget to calculate the frequency of advertising you will do. For example, let's say a magazine ad costs $1,000 for a quarter-page ad and the magazine comes out monthly. Your advertising cost would be $12,000 a year. You may want to advertise by printing flyers and mailing them out. Calculate the printing costs as well as the postage to send out the flyers.

	Year 1	Year 2	Year 3
Radio			
TV			
Newspaper			
Magazine			
Flyers			
Direct Mail			
Special Events			
Online Ads			
Other *Please Specify:*			
Total			

Enter the year totals into the spreadsheet.

Rent

If you rent a facility, determine the rental costs per year. If you have not decided on a location, you may want to look at a few locations and calculate an average rent cost to determine a figure for this category. Keep in mind the square footage requirements that you have set out.

	Annual Rent
Location #1	
Location #2	
Location #3	
Average of all three locations	

If you are going to stay in one location, your rent should remain fixed over three years. If you plan on expanding in years two and three, you may want to increase rent accordingly.

Enter the average of all three locations in the rent column on your spreadsheet.

Office Supplies

Office supplies include items such as paper, pens, printer cartridges, tape, and other materials as well as cleaning supplies. As your business increases, the consumption of these supplies may increase accordingly.

	Year 1	Year 2	Year 3
Office Supplies			
Cleaning Supplies			
Total			

Enter the year totals into the spreadsheet.

Dues, Subscriptions, and Licenses

You may want to join a Chamber of Commerce or trade group or subscribe to trade publications. Your business may also need a license to operate. For example, if you are starting a plumbing company, you may be required to get a contractor's license.

	Year 1	Year 2	Year 3
Chamber of Commerce Membership			
Business Organization Membership (i.e., National Homebuilders Association)			
Magazine/Newspaper Subscriptions			
Business License Fees			
Total			

Enter the year totals into the spreadsheet.

Travel

Does your business require you to travel to meet with customers? Will you travel locally, regionally, or nationally? What are the air travel, rental car, and hotel costs for this travel requirement? Note that the spreadsheet has a separate section for automobile expenses, where you enter costs such as gasoline or repairs. Use the automobile expense section for trips that will be taken in a company or personal vehicle.

	Year 1	Year 2	Year 3
Air Travel			
Rental Cars			
Hotel			
Other *Please Specify*:			
Total			

Enter the year totals into the spreadsheet.

Meals and Entertainment

Determine if you will be providing meals or taking your clients and vendors out for entertainment.

Keep in mind that the IRS allows you to take only a 50 percent deduction on meals and entertainment. It is not considered a 100 percent business expense. Although you enter the full amount on your profit-and-loss statement, your tax accountant will make the proper adjustments on your tax return at the end of the year.

	Year 1	Year 2	Year 3
Meals			
Entertainment			
Total			

Enter the year totals into the spreadsheet.

Automobile Expense

Determine if you will need one or more automobiles or trucks to operate your business. The cost to purchase each vehicle appears under "Assets" on your balance sheet, and the cost to operate the vehicles appears under automobile expense on the profit-and-loss statement.

	Year 1	Year 2	Year 3
Gasoline			
Oil Changes			
Car Washes			

Other (Repairs) *Please Specify:*			
Total			

Enter the annual totals into the spreadsheet.

Utilities and Telephone

Determine what your utilities and telephone costs will be for the first three years your business is operational. To arrive at this estimate, you will need to determine how many telephone lines and cell phones you need. You should also itemize Internet service and record these totals under this line item.

	Year 1	Year 2	Year 3
Electric			
Water			
Garbage			
Telephone			
Internet Service			
Other *Please Specify:*			
Total			

Enter the annual totals into the spreadsheet.

Auto Insurance

If you have business vehicles, you will need to carry insurance on them. If you increase the number of vehicles in years two and three, insurance expenses will increase as well. Certain vehicles may also cost more to insure than others. For example, if you have delivery trucks, the insurance will probably be more expensive than a mid-size car.

	Year 1	Year 2	Year 3
Vehicle #1			
Vehicle #2			
Vehicle #3			
Total			

Enter the annual totals into the spreadsheet.

Group Medical Insurance

You may want to carry medical, dental, or life insurance for your employees as a benefit and to increase employee retention.

	Year 1	Year 2	Year 3
Medical			
Dental			
Life			
Total			

Enter the annual totals into the spreadsheet.

Business Insurance

By law, businesses are required to carry workers' compensation insurance. Business liability insurance protects your business against accidents such as fire, flooding, burglary, etc. Business liability insurance is not required by law but by contract. For example, most landlords require you to carry business liability insurance, as do banks and governmental agencies with which you have a contract. Insurance and risk management are covered in more detail in the managing risk chapter.

	Year 1	Year 2	Year 3
Workers' Compensation			
Business Liability			
Total			

Enter the annual totals into the spreadsheet.

Worksheet

This is a scratch sheet for entering estimates and data that can then be entered in the spreadsheet.

	Year 1	Year 2	Year 3
Income			
Sales			
Total Income	0.00	0.00	0.00
Cost of Goods Sold			
Inventory Cost			
Production Payroll Cost			
Total COGS	0.00	0.00	0.00
Gross Profit	0.00	0.00	0.00
Expense			
Management Salaries			
Payroll Taxes	0.00	0.00	0.00
Outside Services			
Advertising and Promotion			
Rent			
Office Supplies			
Dues, Subscriptions, and Licenses			
Travel			
Meals and Entertainment			
Automobile Expense			
Utilities/Telephone			
Insurance Auto			
Insurance Group Medical			
Business Insurance			
Total Expense	0.00	0.00	0.00
Net Income	0.00	0.00	0.00

Appendix C: Useful Links

Listed below are website links that relate to each of the chapters. These websites are provided for your reference for more in-depth searches of the topic areas contained in this book. Internet links to these websites are provided at www.NASCLAforms.org using access code NCL129354.

Chapter 1 – The Plan

American Express Small Business	American Express offers business planning links and an area where you can post questions for a small business advisor.	www.americanexpress.com/us/small-business/openforum
Business Plan Pro	This site offers tools on how to write a business plan including samples and tips to starting a business.	www.bplans.com
Sample Business Plans	These sites provide sample business plans and other valuable business management materials.	www.allbusiness.com www.inc.com www.bizmove.com/small-business/business-plan.htm
SBA Business Planning	The SBA has several different links on writing and using your business plan.	www.sba.gov

Chapter 2 – Choosing Your Business Structure

IRS Business Structures	The IRS provides a summary of tax considerations by business structure.	www.irs.gov/businesses/small/article/0,,id=98359,00.html
SBA Legal Aspects	The SBA has several different links on forms of ownership and licenses.	www.sba.gov/starting_business/legal/buslaws.html

Chapter 3 – Becoming a Licensed Landscape Contractor

The North Carolina Board of Landscape Architects	Established by legislation in 1969 to register professional landscape architects. Their purpose is the protection of public health, safety and welfare within the realm of large scale landscape planning.	www.ncbola.org
North Carolina Department of Agriculture & Consumer Services	The State of North Carolina's official office of all things agriculture. Coordinates the certification and licensing of pesticide application.	www.ncagr.gov/SPCAP/pesticides/license.htm
North Carolina Irrigation Contractors' Licensing Board	The Board oversees the licensing of Irrigation Contractors in North Carolina.	www.nciclb.org

| **North Carolina Landscape Contractors' Licensing Board** | The NCLCLB is the state licensing board created by the North Carolina General Assembly by statute on August 1, 2014. The board's defined duties include giving examinations, issuing license certificates, maintaining records of licensees and monitoring for violations to ensure the health and safety of consumers. | www.nclclb.com |
| **North Carolina Nursery & Landscape Association** | NCNLA is a membership organization of firms interested in the welfare of North Carolina's green industry, with emphasis on the nursery and landscape industries. Members include wholesale growers, retailers, suppliers, landscapers, horticulture students and educators. Hosts the Plant ID Exam. | www.ncnla.com |

Chapter 4 – Managing Risk

Entrepreneur.com	Entrepreneur.com has links to insurance resources.	www.entrepreneur.com
North Carolina Industrial Commission	This site has information on the rules, practice and procedures involved with workers' compensation.	www.ic.nc.gov
Surety Information Office	This site has resources related to bonding, bank letters of credit and publishes the "Construction Project Owners Guide to Surety Bond Claims."	www.sio.org

Chapter 5 – Your Business Toolbox

North Carolina Business	The North Carolina Department of Commerce Business website has information on starting and operating your business in North Carolina and a new business checklist.	www.nccommerce.com/business
North Carolina Community College, Economic and Workforce Development Division	The community college site has information on the Small Business Center Network that provides business counseling, training and resource centers.	www.ncsbc.net
North Carolina Institute for Minority Economic Development (NCIMED)	The NCIMED site has information on financial and technical assistance available to minority businesses.	www.ncimed.com
SBA Special Interests	The SBA has several different links for women and minority entrepreneurs.	www.sba.gov/content/minority-owned-businesses
Service Corps of Retired Executives (SCORE)	The SCORE website has useful links for small business and a listing of local SCORE centers.	www.score.org

Small Business Administration (SBA)	The SBA website has resources for small businesses.	www.sba.gov
Small Business Administration (SBA) North Carolina	The SBA website has resources for small businesses and a link to the North Carolina District Office website.	www.sba.gov/nc
U.S. Department of Commerce, Economic Development Administration (EDA)	The U.S. Department of Commerce, EDA division, has information on funding opportunities and additional resources.	www.eda.gov
U.S. Minority Business Development Agency (MBDA)	The U.S. MBDA website has links on starting, managing, and financing your business.	www.mbda.gov

Chapter 6 - Marketing and Sales

Entrepreneur.com Marketing	Entrepreneur.com has several articles on small business marketing.	www.entrepreneur.com/topic/marketing
KnowThis.com Sample Marketing Plans	KnowThis.com has information on writing marketing plans and sample plans.	www.knowthis.com/general/marketplan.htm
SBA Marketing Basics	The SBA has several different links on marketing research and writing your marketing plan.	www.sba.gov

Chapter 7 - Legal Requirements

Nolo.com	Nolo.com has articles about contract law.	www.nolo.com
North Carolina Department of Labor (DOL)	The North Carolina DOL site gives information on employment laws and resources for employers.	www.nclabor.com
Surety Information Office	This site has resources related to bonding, bank letters of credit and publishes the "Construction Project Owners Guide to Surety Bond Claims."	www.sio.org
U.S. Department of Labor, Bureau of Labor Statistics	The Bureau of Labor Statistics site has helpful information on wages, earnings, and business costs.	www.bls.gov

Chapter 8 - Bidding and Estimating

Bidshop.com Estimating Software	This site gives a list of software by type of estimating program.	www.bidshop.org
DMOZ.com Estimating Software	This site gives a comprehensive list of estimating software.	www.dmoz.org/Computers/Software/Industry-Specific/ Construction/Project_Management/Estimating
U.S. Department of Labor, Bureau of Labor Statistics	The Bureau of Labor Statistics site has helpful information on wages, earnings, and business costs.	www.bls.gov

Chapter 9 – Contract Management

B4UBuild.com	B4UBuild.com has articles on contract law for residential builders.	www.b4ubuild.com
FreeAdvice.com	FreeAdvice.com has links to different contract topics.	www.law.freeadvice.com/general_practice/contract_law
Nolo.com	Nolo.com has articles about contract law.	www.nolo.com

Chapter 10 – Scheduling and Project Management

Constructionplace.com	Constructionplace.com has an informative glossary of terms focused on construction management.	www.constructionplace.com
FreeDownloadCenter.com	FreeDownloadCenter.com has project management software downloads.	www.freedownloadscenter.com/Business/Project_Management

Chapter 11 – Customer Relations

Microsoft Small Business Center	The Microsoft site offers helpful customer relations links.	www.microsoft.com
Quicken Small Business Center	The Quicken site offers articles on building excellent customer relations.	www.quicken.com

Chapter 12 – Employee Management

Construction Employee Interview Sample Questions	These sites provide sample employee interview questions for the construction industry.	www.interviewquestionsandanswers.biz/construction-interview-questions-and-answers www.constructionarticle.com/common-job-interview-questions
IRS Forms	This site contains IRS forms, such as the W-4 and W-5, that you can download.	www.irs.gov/Forms-&-Pubs
North Carolina Department of Labor (DOL)	The North Carolina DOL site gives information on employment laws and resources for employers.	www.nclabor.com
North Carolina Employment Security Commission	The North Carolina Employment Security Commission website gives information on the state unemployment program.	www.ncesc.com/business/default.asp
North Carolina Industrial Commission	The North Carolina Industrial Commission website provides information on the state workers' compensation program.	www.ic.nc.gov
North Carolina New Hire Reporting	The North Carolina new hire link has information on reporting requirements for new hires.	www.ncnewhires.com
SBA Employment Law	The SBA has several different links on employment law.	www.sba.gov

U.S. Citizenship and Immigration Services	The I-9 form can be downloaded from this site.	www.uscis.gov
U.S. Department of Labor Employment Compliance Guide	The U.S. Department of Labor has several links on employment law compliance, a compliance guide, and a compliance advisor.	www.dol.gov/compliance/guide/index.htm www.dol.gov/elaws
U.S. Department of Labor Employment Guide	The U.S. Department of Labor Employment Guide has information on wage, benefit, safety and health, and nondiscrimination policies.	www.dol.gov/compliance/guide/index.htm
U.S. Equal Employment Opportunity Commission (EEOC)	The EEOC website has information about the Americans with Disabilities Act (ADA).	www.eeoc.gov

Chapter 13 – Jobsite Safety and Environmental Factors

Common Ground Alliance (CGA)	The Common Ground Alliance is available by calling 811. CGA can connect contractors to One Call Centers to locate underground utilities.	www.call811.com/state-specific.aspx
Construction Industry Compliance Center	The Construction Industry Compliance Center website has information available on environmental regulations including hazardous and non-hazardous waste.	www.cicacenter.org
Energy Star	The Energy Star website has eco-friendly resources for home improvement and residential and commercial construction.	www.energystar.gov
Environmental Protection Agency	The Environmental Protection Agency provides a publication called *Managing Your Environmental Responsibilities*.	www.epa.gov/Compliance/resources/publications/ assistance/sectors/constructmyer/myerguide.pdf
Environmental Protection Agency-Asbestos-Containing Materials List	The Environmental Protection Agency website provides a list of asbestos-containing materials.	www.epa.gov/asbestos
Environmental Protection Agency-Green Building	The Environmental Protection Agency website provides information on components of green building, national, state and local funding opportunities, and publications on various environmental topics.	www.epa.gov/greenbuilding
Environmental Protection Agency-Lead in Paint, Dust, and Soil	The Environmental Protection Agency website provides information on lead hazards.	www.epa.gov/lead
North Carolina Department of Environment and Natural Resources (NCDENR)	The NCDENR website has information on environmental regulations and permits.	www.ncdenr.gov
North Carolina Industrial Commission-Health Hazards Control Unit	The Health Hazards Control Unit website has information on asbestos regulations and permits.	epi.publichealth.nc.gov/asbestos/ahmp.html

North Carolina Department of Labor, Occupational Health and Safety Division	The Occupational Health and Safety Division is responsible for assisting employers in complying with federal OSHA requirements.	www.nclabor.com/osha/osh.htm
North Carolina 811	The North Carolina direct hotline for safe digging process requirements.	http://www.nc811.org/safe-digging-process.html
OSHA	The OSHA website has links regarding safety on the job and safety laws and programs.	www.osha.gov
OSHA Compliance Assistance for Construction	The OSHA website has a page with numerous construction compliance assistance links.	www.osha.gov/doc
OSHA Construction Resource Manual	OSHA publishes a construction resource manual online with safety rules and regulations.	www.osha.gov/Publications/Const_Res_Man

Chapter 14 – Working with Subcontractors

IRS Publication 1779	This IRS publication provides criteria to determine employee versus independent contractor status.	www.irs.gov/pub/irs-pdf/p1779.pdf

Chapter 15 – Financial Management

IRS Publication 15: Circular E	Circular E, used for federal income tax withholding, is available on the IRS website.	www.irs.gov/publications/p15/index.html
SBA Balance Sheet Template	The SBA has a balance sheet template that you can customize.	www.sba.gov/library/balsheet.xls
SBA Income Statement Template	The SBA has an income statement template that you can customize.	www.sba.gov/library/incstmt.xls
SBA Financing Basics	The SBA has several different links on financing and financial statements.	www.sba.gov/starting_business/financing/basics.html
Social Security Administration	The Social Security Administration website has information on the current social security tax rate.	www.ssa.gov

Chapter 16 – Tax Basics

How to Apply for an EIN	There are several ways to apply for an EIN. The IRS outlines the procedure on their website.	www.irs.gov/Businesses/Small-Businesses-&-Self-Employed/How-to-Apply-for-an-EIN
IRS Service	The IRS site has tax forms, publications, and useful information for small businesses.	www.irs.gov
North Carolina Department of Revenue	The North Carolina Department of Revenue site provides helpful information on state taxes.	www.dor.state.nc.us
Tax Basics	The SBA has several different links on federal, state, and local taxes.	www.sba.gov

Chapter 17 – North Carolina Mechanics' Lien Law

FindLaw.com	FindLaw.com has useful articles on lien law.	www.findlaw.com
North Carolina General Assembly	You can search for legislation including mechanics' lien law on the North Carolina General Assembly site.	www.ncga.state.nc.us

Trade Links

American Institute of Architects (AIA)	This site has information about the organization and contract documents for purchase.	www.aia.org
American National Standards Institute (ANSI)	The ANSI website has information on membership, accreditation services, and educational resources.	www.ansi.org
American Society of Plumbing Engineers (ASPE)	The ASPE website has information on membership, certifications, and useful resources.	www.aspe.org
American Society of Civil Engineers (ASCE)	The ASCE website has information on membership, conferences, publications, and continuing education.	www.asce.org
American Subcontractors Association (ASA)	This site has information for subcontractors and suppliers in the construction industry.	www.asaonline.com
American Water Works Association (AWWA)	The AWWA website has information on membership, accreditation services, and educational resources.	www.awwa.org
Associated Builders and Contractors (ABC)	The ABC website has information on membership, training, a list of contractors, and links to business development, safety, insurance, and legal resources.	www.abc.org
Associated General Contractors (AGC)	This site has information for construction contractors and industry related companies.	www.agc.org
International Association of Plumbing and Mechanical Officials (IAPMO)	The IAPMO website has information on membership, certification, and educational resources.	www.iapmo.org
National Association of Home Builders (NAHB)	This site is for people interested in homebuilding and the industry.	www.nahb.org
National Association of the Remodeling Industry (NARI)	This site is for people interested in the remodeling industry.	www.nari.org
National Association of State Contractor Licensing Agencies (NASCLA)	This site contains useful information about state licensing agencies and information about the organization.	www.nascla.org
National Association of Women in Construction (NAWIC)	This site has information for women in the construction industry.	www.nawic.org

National Electrical Contractors Association (NECA)	The NECA website has information on membership, codes and standards, industry news, and educational resources.	www.necanet.org
Plumbing, Heating and Cooling Contractors Association (PHCC)	The PHCC website has information on membership, educational resources, and a list of contractors.	www.phccweb.org
Water Quality Association (WQA)	The WQA website has information on membership, certifications, educational resources, and a list of contractors.	www.wqa.org

Appendix D: New Business Checklist

The following is a checklist of steps to starting your business. These steps provide a general overview, but you should check with a professional to determine the legal, financial, and tax obligations specific to your business.

Complete Your Business Plan (covered in Chapter 1 and Appendix B)
✓ Establish your business vision and mission.
✓ Determine your management structure.
✓ Identify your facility requirements and location.
✓ Research your market and identify your competitors.
✓ Establish a marketing plan and expansion goals.
✓ Determine your break-even point and your financial goals.

Choose Your Form of Organization (covered in Chapter 2)
✓ Hire a lawyer to prepare organization documents and give legal advice on business issues.
✓ Choose a form of organization (i.e., sole proprietorship, partnership, or corporation).
✓ Prepare and file business organization documents (i.e., Partnership Agreement, Articles of Organization, Articles of Incorporation, etc.).
✓ Register any fictitious names with the proper state and local municipalities.
✓ Obtain the required business licenses from state and local municipalities.

Set Up Business Finances
✓ Select an accountant to prepare financial documents and give business financial advice.
✓ Select a banker and open a business checking account.
✓ Apply for business loans (if applicable).
✓ Apply for business credit cards and establish a line of credit.

Obtain the Proper Contractor's Licensure (covered in Chapter 3)
✓ Obtain the proper application materials and review the process for obtaining licensure.
✓ Complete application materials with required documentation.
✓ Understand the requirements for maintaining proper licensure.

Assess Your Areas of Risk and Obtain the Proper Insurance Coverage (covered in Chapter 4)
✓ Select an insurance company and agent to help assess your risk and coverage requirements.
✓ Obtain business insurance (liability, workers' compensation, automobile, etc.).
✓ Obtain required bonds.
✓ Obtain unemployment insurance registration materials from the proper state agency.

Obtain the Proper Tax Documentation (covered in Chapter 16)
✓ Apply for a federal employer identification number (if applicable).
✓ Obtain a state employer identification number (if applicable).
✓ Obtain the proper federal and state tax forms (i.e., sales and use tax, withholding tax, etc.).

Appendix E: Landscape Contractor Licensing Law

GENERAL ASSEMBLY OF NORTH CAROLINA, SESSION 2013

SESSION LAW 2014-103, HOUSE BILL 366

REWRITE THE LANDSCAPE CONTRACTOR LICENSING STATUTES

SECTION 3.(a) G.S. 89D-1 through G.S. 89D-10 are repealed.

SECTION 3.(b) Chapter 89D of the General Statutes is amended by adding the following new sections to read:

"**§ 89D-11. Definitions.** The following definitions apply in this Chapter:

(1)   Board.—The North Carolina Landscape Contractors' Licensing Board.

(2)   Landscape construction or contracting.—The act of providing services as a landscape contractor, as defined in this section, for compensation or other consideration.

(3)   Landscape contractor.—Any person who, for compensation or other consideration, does any of the following:

    a.   Engages in the business requiring the art, experience, ability, knowledge, science, and skill to prepare contracts and bid for the performance of landscape services, including installing, planting, repairing, and managing gardens, lawns, shrubs, vines, trees, or other decorative vegetation, including the finish grading and preparation of plots and areas of land for decorative utilitarian treatment and arrangement.

    b.   Practices the act of horticulture consultation or planting design for employment purposes.

    c.   Constructs, installs, or maintains landscape drainage systems and cisterns; provided the landscaping contractor makes no connection to pipes, fixtures, apparatus, or appurtenances installed upon the premises, or in a building, to supply water thereto or convey sewage or other waste therefrom as defined in G.S. 87-21.

    d.   Designs, installs, or maintains low-voltage landscape lighting systems, provided (i) the work does not exceed the scope of the exception set forth in G.S. 87-43.1(7) and (ii) the low-voltage lighting systems do not exceed 50 volts and constitute a Class II or Class III cord and plug connected power system.

    e.   Engages in the construction of garden pools, retaining walls, walks, patios, or other decorative landscape features.

(4)   Person.—An individual, firm, partnership, association, corporation, or other legal entity.

"**§ 89D-12. License required; use of seal; posting license.**

(a)   Except as otherwise provided in this Chapter, no person shall engage in the practice of landscape construction or contracting, use the designation "landscape contractor," or advertise using any title or description that implies licensure as a landscape contractor unless the person is licensed as a landscape contractor as provided by this Chapter. All landscape construction or contracting performed by a partnership, association, corporation, firm, or other group shall be performed under an individual who is readily available to exercise supervision over the landscape construction and contracting work and who is licensed by the Board under this Chapter.

(b)   Nothing in this Chapter shall be construed to authorize a landscape contractor to engage in any of the following:

   (1)   The practice of landscape architecture, as defined in G.S. 89A-1.

   (2)   The practice of engineering, as defined in G.S. 89C-3.

   (3)   Practice as a well contractor certified under Article 7A of Chapter 87 of the General Statutes.

   (4)   The practice of irrigation contracting, as defined in G.S. 89G-1.

   (5)   The practice of architecture, as defined in G.S. 83A-1.

   (6)   The practice of plumbing, heating group number one, heating group number two, heating group number three, fire sprinkler, or fuel piping contracting, as defined in G.S. 87-21, provided the landscaping contractor may install piping, fittings, valves, and associated components for the purpose of landscape contracting that is downstream of a potable water source, groundwater source, or grey water source, and downstream of a backflow prevention assembly.

   (7)   The practice of electrical contracting, as defined in G.S. 87-43.

(c)   A landscape contractor licensed under this Chapter is not required to be licensed as a general contractor under Article 1 of Chapter 87 of the General Statutes if the licensed landscape contractor is performing landscape construction or contracting work valued at an amount greater than thirty thousand dollars ($30,000).

(d)   Upon licensure by the Board, each landscape contractor shall obtain a seal of the design authorized by the Board and bearing the name of the licensee, the number of the license, and the legend "N.C. Licensed Landscape Contractor." A landscape contractor may use the seal only while the license is valid.

(e)   Every landscape contractor issued a license under this Chapter shall display the license conspicuously in the landscape contractor's place of business. Every landscape contractor shall display the license number issued to the contractor by the Board on all business cards, contracts, and vehicles used by the contractor in the landscape contracting business.

"§ 89D-13. Exemptions. The provisions of this Chapter shall not apply to the following:

(1)   Any federal, State, or local governmental agency performing landscaping on public property.

(2)   The North Carolina Department of Transportation (NCDOT). However, for landscape installations or establishment periods for any project that exceeds the current contract amount requiring performance and payment bonds according to State law, NCDOT shall require a licensed landscape contractor to perform the work. NCDOT, at its discretion, may require a licensed landscape contractor for landscape projects of any cost.

(3)   Any property owner performing landscape work on his or her own property.

(4)   Any person or business owning or operating a golf course.

(5)   Any landscaping work where the price of all contracts for labor, material, and other items for a given job site during any consecutive 12-month period is less than thirty thousand dollars ($30,000). A local governmental unit shall not enact a local ordinance or regulation requiring licensure for landscaping work performed pursuant to this subdivision.

(6)   A general contractor licensed under Article 1 of Chapter 87 of the General Statutes who possesses a classification under G.S. 87-10(b) as a building contractor, a residential contractor, or a public utilities contractor.

(7)   Any person or business licensed as an electrical contractor under Article 4 of Chapter 87 of the General Statutes who is designing, installing, or maintaining any electric work, wiring, devices, appliances, or equipment.

(8)   Any person or business licensed as a plumbing contractor under Article 2 of Chapter 87 of the General Statutes who is installing pipes, fixtures, apparatus, or appurtenances to supply water thereto or convey sewage or other waste therefrom, including the installation, repair, or maintenance of water mains, water taps, services lines, water meters, or backflow prevention assemblies supplying water for irrigation systems or repairs to an irrigation system.

(9)   A professional engineer licensed pursuant to Chapter 89C of the General Statutes.

(10)   A professional landscape architect licensed under Chapter 89A of the General Statutes.

(11)   An individual or a business engaged in any of the following activities while performing that activity:

   a.   Clearing and grading plots and areas of land.

   b.   Erosion control.

   c.   Arboriculture, including consultations on pruning and removal of trees.

   d.   The installation of sod, seed, or plugs by sod producers certified by the Plant Industry Division of the North Carolina Department of Agriculture and Consumer Services.

   e.   Landscape construction performed by utilities contractors for the purpose of grading and erosion control.

   f.   Lawn mowing, turf edging, and debris removal services.

   g.   Turf management or lawn care services only, including fertilization, aeration, weed control, or other turf management or lawn care practices other than mowing or edging.

   h.   Design, installation, and maintenance of on-site wastewater disposal or reuse systems within the on-site wastewater permit specifications.

(12)   Any person performing landscaping work on a farm for use in agriculture production, farming, or ranching.

"§ 89D-14. The North Carolina Landscape Contractors' Licensing Board.

(a)   There is created the North Carolina Landscape Contractors' Licensing Board. The Board shall consist of nine members appointed as follows:

   (1)   One member appointed by the Governor who is a member of the general public.

   (2)   One member appointed by the Commissioner of Agriculture pursuant to recommendations from The North Carolina Green Industry Council.

   (3)   One member appointed by the Board of Directors of the North Carolina Nursery and Landscape Association, Inc., who is a practicing nurseryman operating a nursery certified by the North Carolina Department of Agriculture and Consumer Services Plant Industry Division.

   (4)   Four members who are licensed landscape contractors in the business of landscape construction or contracting. One of the four members shall be appointed by the General Assembly upon the recommendation of the Speaker of the House of Representatives

pursuant to recommendations from The North Carolina Green Industry Council; one shall be appointed by the General Assembly upon the recommendation of the President Pro Tempore of the Senate pursuant to recommendations from the Carolinas Irrigation Association, who is also a licensed irrigation contractor; and two shall be appointed by the Board of Directors of the North Carolina Nursery and Landscape Association, Inc.

(5) One member appointed by the Board of Directors of the North Carolina Chapter of the American Society of Landscape Architects who is a registered landscape architect.

(6) One member appointed by the President of The University of North Carolina from within the land grant university community who is knowledgeable in landscaping methods and practices.

(b) All appointments shall be for three-year terms. No member shall serve more than two complete consecutive terms.

(c) A vacancy on the Board created by death, resignation, or otherwise shall be filled in the same manner as the original appointment, except that all unexpired terms of Board members appointed by the General Assembly shall be filled in accordance with G.S. 120-122. Appointees to fill vacancies shall serve the remainder of the unexpired term and until their successors are appointed and qualified.

(d) The Board shall elect annually a chair and other officers as it deems necessary to carry out the purposes of this Chapter and shall hold meetings at least twice a year. A majority of the Board shall constitute a quorum.

(e) Each member of the Board may receive per diem and reimbursement for travel and subsistence as set forth in G.S. 93B-5.

(f) The Board shall be entitled to the services of the Attorney General in connection with the affairs of the Board or may, in its discretion, employ an attorney to assist or represent it in the enforcement of this Chapter.

"§ 89D-15. Powers and duties. The Board shall have the following powers and duties:

(1) Administer and enforce the provisions of this Chapter.

(2) Adopt, amend, or repeal rules to carry out the provisions of this Chapter.

(3) Examine and determine the qualifications and fitness of applicants for licensure and licensure renewal.

(4) Issue, renew, deny, restrict, suspend, or revoke licenses.

(5) Reprimand or otherwise discipline licensees under this Chapter.

(6) Receive and investigate complaints from members of the public.

(7) Conduct investigations to determine whether violations of this Chapter exist or constitute grounds for disciplinary action against licensees under this Chapter.

(8) Conduct administrative hearings in accordance with Article 3A of Chapter 150B of the General Statutes.

(9) Seek injunctive relief through any court of competent jurisdiction for violations of this Chapter.

(10) Collect fees required by G.S. 89D-21 and any other moneys permitted by law to be paid to the Board.

(11) Require licensees to file and maintain an adequate surety bond.

(12)   Establish and approve continuing education requirements for persons licensed under this Chapter.

(13)   Employ a secretary-treasurer and any other clerical personnel the Board deems necessary to carry out the provisions of this Chapter and to fix compensation for employees.

(14)   Maintain a record of all proceedings conducted by the Board and make available to licensees and other concerned parties an annual report of all Board action.

(15)   Adopt and publish a code of professional conduct for all persons licensed under this Chapter.

(16)   Adopt and publish a code of minimum practice standards for landscape construction and contracting.

(17)   Adopt a seal containing the name of the Board for use on licenses and official reports issued by the Board.

"§ 89D-16. Application for license; qualifications; examination; issuance.

(a)   Upon application to the Board and payment of the required fees, an applicant for licensure as a landscape contractor may sit for the examination if the applicant submits evidence demonstrating the applicant's qualifications for licensure under this Chapter as prescribed in rules adopted by the Board and meets all of the following qualifications:

   (1)   Is at least 18 years of age.

   (2)   Is of good moral character as determined by the Board.

   (3)   Provides evidence of business identification as required by the Board.

   (4)   Files with the Board and maintains a corporate surety bond executed by a company authorized to do business in this State or an irrevocable letter of credit issued by an insured institution. The surety bond or the letter of credit shall be in the amount of ten thousand dollars ($10,000). The surety bond or letter of credit shall be approved by the Board as to form and shall be conditioned upon the obligor faithfully conforming to and abiding by the provisions of this Chapter. Any person claiming to be injured by an act of a licensed landscape contractor that constitutes a violation of this Chapter may institute an action to recover against the licensee and the surety.

(b)   If the applicant meets all the qualifications in subsection (a) of this section, the applicant shall be required to pass an examination administered by the Board before the Board may issue the license. The Board shall establish the scope and subject matter of the examination to be administered. The Board shall administer examinations at least twice a year at a time and place to be determined by the Board.

(c)   When the Board determines that an applicant has met all the qualifications for licensure, submitted the required fee, and passed the examination, the Board shall issue a license to the applicant.

"§ 89D-17. Corporations; partnerships; persons doing business under trade name.

(a)   The Board may issue a license in the name of a corporation if the corporation complies with the following:

   (1)   One or more officers or full-time employees, or both, empowered to act for the corporation are individuals licensed under this Chapter.

   (2)   Only the officers or employees described in subdivision (1) of this subsection execute contracts for landscape construction or contracting in the name of a corporation and are readily available to exercise supervision over the work performed pursuant to the contract.

(b)   The Board may issue a license in the name of a limited liability company if the company complies with the following:

    (1)   One or more managers, as defined in G.S. 57D-1-03, executives, or full-time employees, or a combination thereof, are individuals licensed under this Chapter.

    (2)   Only the managers, executives, or employees described in subdivision (1) of this subsection execute contracts for landscape construction or contracting in the name of the limited liability company and are readily available to exercise supervision over the work performed pursuant to the contract.

(c)   The Board may issue a license in the name of a partnership if the partnership complies with the following:

    (1)   One or more general partners or full-time employees empowered to act for the partnership are individuals licensed under this Chapter.

    (2)   Only the partners or employees described in subdivision (1) of this subsection execute contracts for landscape construction or contracting in the name of the partnership and are readily available to exercise supervision over the work performed pursuant to the contract.

(d)   The Board may issue a license in an assumed or designated trade name if the owner of the business complies with the following:

    (1)   The owner or one or more full-time employees empowered to act for the owner is an individual licensed under this Chapter.

    (2)   Only the persons described in subdivision (1) of this subsection execute contracts for landscape construction or contracting in the assumed or designated trade name of the business and are readily available to exercise supervision over the work performed pursuant to the contract.

(e)   When the Board issues a license under this section, the Board shall indicate on the license the name and license number of the individual licensee connected to the corporation, partnership, or business conducted under an assumed or designated trade name.

(f)   A person licensed pursuant to this section shall be readily available to exercise supervision over a contract for landscape construction or contracting until the contract is completed.

(g)   When a licensee executes a contract for landscape construction or contracting in any capacity other than as a sole proprietor contracting on the licensee's own behalf, the person on whose behalf the licensee is executing the contract shall be licensed under this section.

(h)   A corporation, partnership, or person doing business under an assumed or designated trade name shall notify the Board in accordance with rules adopted by the Board if an individual licensee who is indicated in the license issued under this section ceases to be an officer, partner, owner, or employee of the corporation, partnership, or person doing business under the assumed or designated trade name. If the corporation, partnership, or person no longer has an officer, general partner, owner, or employee described in subdivision (1) of subsection (a), subdivision (1) of subsection (b), or subdivision (1) of subsection (c) of this section, the corporation, partnership, or person shall have 120 days from the date the officer, general partner, owner, or employee ceases the relationship with the corporation, partnership, or person to satisfy the requirements described in subdivision (1) of subsection (a), subdivision (1) of subsection (b), or subdivision (1) of subsection (c) of this section. The Board may, in its discretion, grant the corporation, partnership, or person a period greater than 120 days to satisfy the requirements described in subdivision (1) of subsection (a), subdivision (1) of subsection (b), or subdivision (1) of subsection (c) of this section as it deems appropriate. After 120 days, or a time period greater than 120 days as approved by the Board, if the corporation, partnership, or person does not have an officer, general partner, owner, or employee as described in subdivision (1) of subsection (a), subdivision (1) of subsection (b), or subdivision (1) of subsection (c) of this section, the license issued under this section is automatically suspended and the corporation, partnership, or person shall cease practicing landscape construction or contracting.

"§ 89D-18. Licensing of nonresidents.

(a)   Definitions.—The following definitions apply in this section:

    (1)   Delinquent income tax debt.—The amount of income tax due as stated in a final notice of assessment issued to a taxpayer by the Secretary of Revenue when the taxpayer no longer has the right to contest the amount.

    (2)   Foreign corporation.—A corporation as defined in G.S. 55-1-40.

    (3)   Foreign entity.—A foreign corporation, a foreign limited liability company, or a foreign partnership.

    (4)   Foreign limited liability company.—A company as defined in G.S. 57D-1-03.

    (5)   Foreign partnership.—One of the following that does not have a permanent place of business in this State:

        a.   A foreign limited partnership as defined in G.S. 59-102.

        b.   A general partnership formed under the laws of a jurisdiction other than this State.

(b)   Licensing.—Except as provided in this section, the Board may issue a license to a nonresident individual or a foreign entity that meets the requirements for licensure under this Chapter.

(c)   Certificate of Authority Required.—The Board shall not issue a license for a foreign corporation unless the corporation has obtained a certificate of authority from the Secretary of State pursuant to Article 15 of Chapter 55 of the General Statutes. The Board shall not issue a license for a foreign limited liability company unless the company has obtained a certificate of authority from the Secretary of State pursuant to Article 7 of Chapter 57D of the General Statutes.

(d)   Information.—The Board, upon request, shall provide the Secretary of Revenue the name, address, and tax identification number of every nonresident individual and foreign entity licensed by the Board. The information to be provided under this section shall be in a form required by the Secretary of Revenue.

(e)   Delinquents.—If the Secretary of Revenue determines that any nonresident individual or foreign entity licensed by the Board owes a delinquent income tax debt, the Secretary of Revenue may notify the Board of the nonresident individual or foreign entity and instruct the Board not to renew the nonresident individual or foreign entity's license. The Board shall not renew the license of a nonresident individual or foreign entity identified by the Secretary of Revenue unless the Board receives a written statement from the Secretary that (i) the debt has been paid or (ii) the debt is being paid pursuant to an installment agreement.

"§ 89D-19. Reciprocity. The Board may issue a license, without examination, to any person who is a landscape contractor licensed, certified, or registered in another state or country if the requirements for licensure, certification, or registration in the other state or country are substantially equivalent to the requirements for licensure in this State.

"§ 89D-20. License renewal and continuing education.

(a)   Every license issued under this Chapter shall be renewed on or before the first day of August of each year. Any person who desires to continue to practice shall apply for a license renewal and shall submit the required fee. Licenses that are not renewed shall be automatically revoked. A license may be renewed at any time within one year after its expiration if (i) the applicant pays the required renewal fee and late renewal fee, (ii) the Board finds that the applicant has not used the license in a manner inconsistent with the provisions of this Chapter or engaged in the practice of landscape construction or contracting after notice of revocation, and (iii) the applicant is otherwise eligible for licensure under the provisions of this Chapter. When necessary, the Board may require licensees to demonstrate continued competence as a condition of license renewal.

(b)   As a condition of license renewal, a licensee shall meet the continuing education requirements set by the Board. Each licensee shall complete seven continuing education units per year. The Board may suspend a licensee's license for 30 days for failure to obtain continuing education units required by this subsection. Upon payment of a reinstatement fee, submission to the Board of proof of the continuing education units required by this subsection, and payment of the license renewal fee and late renewal fee, the licensee's license shall be reinstated. Failure to request a reinstatement of the license and failure to pay the reinstatement fee, renewal fee, and late renewal fee shall result in the forfeiture of a license. Upon forfeiture, a person shall be required to submit a new application and retake the examination as provided in this Chapter.

"§ 89D-21. Expenses and fees.

(a)   The Board may impose the following fees not to exceed the amounts listed below:

(1)   Application fee $100.00

(2)   Examination fee   250.00

(3)   Individual license fee and individual license renewal   100.00

(4)   Initial corporate, limited liability company, partnership, or trade name license   100.00

(5)   Corporate, limited liability company, partnership, or trade name license renewal   100.00

(6)   Late renewal fee   50.00

(7)   Reinstatement fee   250.00

(8)   License by reciprocity   250.00

(9)   Duplicate license   25.00

(b)   When the Board uses a testing service for the preparation, administration, or grading of examinations, the Board may charge the applicant the actual cost of the examination services and a prorated portion of the examination fee.

"§ 89D-22. Disciplinary action.

(a)   The Board may deny, restrict, suspend, or revoke a license or refuse to issue or renew a license if a licensee or applicant does any of the following:

(1)   Employs the use of fraud, deceit, or misrepresentation in obtaining or attempting to obtain a license or the renewal of a license.

(2)   Practices or attempts to practice landscape construction or contracting by fraudulent misrepresentation.

(3)   Commits an act of gross malpractice or incompetence as determined by the Board.

(4)   Has been convicted of or pled guilty or no contest to a crime that indicates that the person is unfit or incompetent to practice as a landscape contractor or that indicates that the person has deceived or defrauded the public.

(5)   Has been declared incompetent by a court of competent jurisdiction.

(6)   Has willfully violated any provision in this Chapter or any rules adopted by the Board.

(7)   Uses or attempts to use the seal in a fraudulent or unauthorized manner.

(8)   Fails to file the required surety bond or letter of credit or to keep the bond or letter of credit in force.

(b)   The Board may assess costs, including reasonable attorneys' fees and investigatory costs, in a proceeding under this section against an applicant or licensee found to be in violation of this Chapter.

"§ 89D-23. Civil penalties.

(a)   In addition to taking any of the actions permitted under G.S. 89D-22, the Board may assess a civil penalty not in excess of two thousand dollars ($2,000) for each violation of any section of this Chapter or the violation of any rules adopted by the Board. The clear proceeds of any civil penalty assessed under this section shall be remitted to the Civil Penalty and Forfeiture Fund in accordance with G.S. 115C-457.2.

(b)   Before imposing and assessing a civil penalty and fixing the amount of the penalty, the Board shall, as a part of its deliberations, take into consideration the following factors:

(1)   The nature, gravity, and persistence of the particular violation.

(2)   The appropriateness of the imposition of a civil penalty when considered alone or in combination with other punishment.

(3)   Whether the violation was willful and malicious.

(4)   Any other factors that would tend to mitigate or aggravate the violations found to exist.

"§ 89D-24. Injunction to prevent violation; notification of complaints.

(a)   If the Board finds that a person who does not have a license issued under this Chapter is engaging in the practice of landscape construction or contracting, the Board may appear in its own name in superior court in actions for injunctive relief to prevent any person from violating the provisions of this Chapter or the rules adopted by the Board.

(b)   A licensed landscape contractor shall notify the Board of any written complaints filed against the landscape contractor not resolved within 30 days from the date the complaint was filed by registered mail to the Board."

SECTION 3.(c) Members serving on the North Carolina Landscape Contractors' Registration Board on the effective date of this act shall continue to serve until members of the North Carolina Landscape Contractors' Licensing Board, G.S. 89D-14(a), as enacted by Section 3(b) of this act, are appointed.

SECTION 3.(d) Once the term of one of the current public members appointed by the Governor expires, the General Assembly, upon the recommendation of the Speaker of the House of Representatives, shall appoint a licensed landscape contractor in the business of landscape construction and contracting. Once the term of one of the current members appointed by the Commissioner of Agriculture expires, the General Assembly, upon the recommendation of the President Pro Tempore of the Senate, shall appoint a licensed landscape contractor in the business of landscape construction and contracting. All records, staff, funds, and other items of the North Carolina Landscape Contractors' Registration Board are transferred to and made the property of the North Carolina Landscape Contractors' Licensing Board.

SECTION 3.(e) Any person who, on or before December 31, 2014, meets at least one of the following criteria shall be issued a landscape contractor's license by the North Carolina Landscape Contractors' Licensing Board, without the requirement of examination, upon submission of a completed application and payment of the application fee on or before August 1, 2015:

(1)   Is registered as a landscape contractor.

(2)   Is licensed as an irrigation contractor.

(3)   Is certified as a turf grass professional.

(4)   Has three years of documented experience in the person's own business as a landscape contractor or three years of documented experience as an employee in a landscape contracting business and

meets all other requirements and qualifications for licensure as a landscape contractor. Educational experience can be applied toward the three-year experience requirement as follows:

a.   One year of credit for a two-year degree in related educational training.

b.   Two years of credit for a four-year degree in related educational training.

c.   Up to two years of credit for education or business experience in general business management.

Landscape contractors currently registered under Chapter 89D of the General Statutes shall not be required to renew the registration for the 2015 calendar year to qualify for the landscape contractor's license, as enacted by Section 3(b) of this act.

SECTION 3.(f) This section becomes effective August 1, 2015.

Appendix F: North Carolina E-Verify Law

GENERAL ASSEMBLY OF NORTH CAROLINA, SESSION 2011

SESSION LAW 2011-263, HOUSE BILL 36

AN ACT TO REQUIRE COUNTIES, CITIES, AND EMPLOYERS TO USE THE FEDERAL E-VERIFY PROGRAM TO VERIFY THE WORK AUTHORIZATION OF NEWLY HIRED EMPLOYEES.

The General Assembly of North Carolina enacts:

SECTION 1. Chapter 64 of the General Statutes is amended by adding a new Article to read:

"Article 1. Various Provisions Related to Aliens."

SECTION 2. G.S. 64-1 through G.S. 64-5 are recodified as Article 1 of Chapter 64 of the General Statutes, as created by Section 1 of this act.

SECTION 3. Chapter 64 of the General Statutes is amended by adding a new Article to read:

"Article 2. Verification of Work Authorization."

"§ 64-25. Definitions. The following definitions apply in this Article:

(1)   Commissioner.—The North Carolina Commissioner of Labor.

(2)   Employ.—Hire an employee.

(3)   Employee.—Any individual who provides services or labor for an employer in this State for wages or other remuneration.

(4)   Employer.—Any person, business entity, or other organization that transacts business in this State and that employs 25 or more employees in this State. This term does not include State agencies, counties, municipalities, or other governmental bodies.

(5)   E-Verify.—The federal E-Verify program operated by the United States Department of Homeland Security and other federal agencies, or any successor or equivalent program used to verify the work authorization of newly hired employees pursuant to federal law.

(6)   Unauthorized alien.—As defined in 8 U.S.C. § 1324a(h)(3).

"§ 64-26. Verification of employee work authorization.

(a)   Employers Must Use E-Verify.—Each employer, after hiring an employee to work in the United States, shall verify the work authorization of the employee through E-Verify.

(b)   Employer Preservation of E-Verify Forms.—Each employer shall retain the record of the verification of work authorization required by this section while the employee is employed and for one year thereafter.

(c)   Exemption.—Subsection (a) of this section shall not apply with respect to a seasonal temporary employee who is employed for 90 or fewer days during a 12-consecutive-month period.

"§ 64-27. Commissioner of Labor to prepare complaint form.

(a)   Preparation of Form.—The Commissioner shall prescribe a complaint form for a person to allege a violation of G.S. 64-26. The form shall clearly state that completed forms may be sent to the Commissioner.

(b)   Certain Information Not Required.—The complainant shall not be required to list the complainant's social security number on the complaint form or to have the complaint notarized.

"§ 64-28. Reporting of complaints.

(a)   Filing of Complaint.—Any person with a good faith belief that an employer is violating or has violated G.S. 64-26 may file a complaint with the Commissioner setting forth the basis for that belief. The complaint may be on a form prescribed by the Commissioner pursuant to G.S. 64-27 or may be made in any other form that gives the Commissioner information that is sufficient to proceed with an investigation pursuant to G.S. 64-29. Nothing in this section shall be construed to prohibit the filing of anonymous complaints that are not submitted on a prescribed complaint form.

(b)   False Statements a Misdemeanor.—A person who knowingly files a false and frivolous complaint under this section is guilty of a Class 2 misdemeanor.

"§ 64-29. Investigation of complaints.

(a)   Investigation.—Upon receipt of a complaint pursuant to G.S. 64-28 that an employer is allegedly violating or has allegedly violated G.S. 64-26, the Commissioner shall investigate whether the employer has in fact violated G.S. 64-26.

(b)   Certain Complaints Shall Not Be Investigated.—The Commissioner shall not investigate complaints that are based solely on race, religion, gender, ethnicity, or national origin.

(c)   Assistance by Law Enforcement.—The Commissioner may request that the State Bureau of Investigation assist in investigating a complaint under this section.

(d)   Subpoena for Production of Documents.—The Commissioner may issue a subpoena for production of employment records that relate to the recruitment, hiring, employment, or termination policies, practices, or acts of employment as part of the investigation of a valid complaint under this section.

"§ 64-30. Actions to be taken; hearing. If, after an investigation, the Commissioner determines that the complaint is not false and frivolous:

(1)   The Commissioner shall hold a hearing to determine if a violation of G.S. 64-26 has occurred and, if appropriate, impose civil penalties in accordance with the provisions of this Article.

(2)   If, during the course of the hearing required by subdivision (1) of this section, the Commissioner concludes that there is a reasonable likelihood that an employee is an unauthorized alien, the Commissioner shall notify the following entities of the possible presence of an unauthorized alien:

    a.   United States Immigration and Customs Enforcement.

    b.   Local law enforcement agencies.

"§ 64-31. Consequences of first violation.

(a)   Affidavit Must Be Filed.—For a first violation of G.S. 64-26, the Commissioner shall order the employer to file a signed sworn affidavit with the Commissioner within three business days after the order issued pursuant to this subsection is issued. The affidavit shall state with specificity that the employer has, after consultation with the employee, requested a verification of work authorization through E-Verify.

(b)   Effect of Failure to File Affidavit.—If an employer fails to timely file an affidavit required by subsection (a) of this section or by G.S. 64-32 or G.S. 64-33, the Commissioner shall order the employer to pay a civil penalty of ten thousand dollars ($10,000).

"§ 64-32. Consequences of second violation. For a violation of G.S. 64-26 that occurs after an order has been issued pursuant to G.S. 64-31, the Commissioner shall order the measures required by G.S. 64-31(a) and shall also order the employer to pay a civil penalty of one thousand dollars ($1,000), regardless of the number of required employee verifications the employer failed to make.

"§ 64-33. Consequences of third or subsequent violation. For a violation of G.S. 64-26 that occurs after an order has been issued pursuant to G.S. 64-32, the Commissioner shall order the measures required by G.S. 64-31(a), and shall also order the employer to pay a civil penalty of two thousand dollars ($2,000) for each required employee verification the employer failed to make.

"§ 64-34. Commissioner to maintain copies of orders. The Commissioner shall maintain copies of orders issued pursuant to G.S. 64-31, 64-32, and 64-33, and shall maintain a database of the employers and business locations that have a violation of G.S. 64-26 and make the orders available on the Commissioner's Web site.

"§ 64-35. Work authorization shall be verified through the federal government. When investigating a complaint under this Article, the Commissioner shall verify the work authorization of the alleged unauthorized alien with the federal government pursuant to 8 U.S.C. § 1373(c). The Commissioner shall not attempt to independently make a final determination of whether an alien is authorized to work in the United States.

"§ 64-36. Appeal of Commissioner's order. A determination by the Commissioner pursuant to this Article shall be final, unless within 15 days after receipt of notice thereof by certified mail with return receipt, by signature confirmation as provided by the U.S. Postal Service, by a designated delivery service authorized pursuant to 26 U.S.C. § 7502(f)(2) with delivery receipt, or via hand delivery, the employer charged with the violation takes exception to the determination, in which event final determination shall be made in an administrative proceeding pursuant to Article 3 of Chapter 150B of the General Statutes and in a judicial proceeding pursuant to Article 4 of Chapter 150B of the General Statutes.

"§ 64-37. Rules. The Commissioner may adopt rules needed to implement this Article.

"§ 64-38. Article does not require action that is contrary to federal or State law. This Article shall not be construed to require an employer to take any action that the employer believes in good faith would violate federal or State law."

SECTION 4. Article 5 of Chapter 153A of the General Statutes is amended by adding a new section to read:

"§ 153A-99.1. County verification of employee work authorization.

(a)   Counties Must Use E-Verify.—Each county shall register and participate in E-Verify to verify the work authorization of new employees hired to work in the United States.

(b)   E-Verify Defined.—As used in this section, the term 'E-Verify' means the federal E-Verify program operated by the United States Department of Homeland Security and other federal agencies, or any successor or equivalent program used to verify the work authorization of newly hired employees pursuant to federal law.

(c)   Nondiscrimination.—This section shall be enforced without regard to race, religion, gender, ethnicity, or national origin."

SECTION 5. Article 7 of Chapter 160A of the General Statutes is amended by adding a new section to read:

"§ 160A-169.1. Municipality verification of employee work authorization.

(a)   Municipalities Must Use E-Verify.—Each municipality shall register and participate in E-Verify to verify the work authorization of new employees hired to work in the United States.

(b)   E-Verify Defined.—As used in this section, the term 'E-Verify' means the federal E-Verify program operated by the United States Department of Homeland Security and other federal agencies, or any successor or equivalent program used to verify the work authorization of newly hired employees pursuant to federal law.

(c)   Nondiscrimination.—This section shall be enforced without regard to race, religion, gender, ethnicity, or national origin."

SECTION 6. Sections 4, 5, and 6 of this act become effective October 1, 2011. The remainder of this act becomes effective in accordance with the following schedule:

(1)   October 1, 2012, for employers that employ 500 or more employees.

(2)   January 1, 2013, for employers that employ 100 or more but less than 500 employees.

(3)   July 1, 2013, for employers that employ 25 or more but less than 100 employees.

In the General Assembly read three times and ratified this the 18th day of June, 2011.

Additionally: N.C.G.S. § 160A-20.1(b) prohibits municipalities from contracting with employers who have not complied with the State's E-Verify law. Under that law, employers are required to use the federal E-Verify program for all new hires if they have 25 or more employees who have terms of employment of nine months or more in a calendar year. As a corollary, employers who do not meet the law's 25 employee threshold are exempt from using E-Verify. Accordingly, for purposes of N.C.G.S. § 160A-20.1(b), these exempt employers are in compliance with the State's E-Verify statutes.

Appendix G: Landscape Architect Law

CHAPTER 89A

§ 89A-1. Definitions.

The following definitions apply in this Chapter:

(1)   Board.—The North Carolina Board of Landscape Architects.

(2)   Landscape architect.—A person who, on the basis of demonstrated knowledge acquired by professional education or practical experience, or both, has been granted, and holds a current certificate entitling him or her to practice "landscape architecture" and to use the title "landscape architect" in North Carolina under the authority of this Chapter.

(3)   Landscape architecture or the practice of landscape architecture.—The performance of services in connection with the development of land areas where, and to the extent that the dominant purpose of the services is the preservation, enhancement or determination of proper land uses, natural land features, ground cover and planting, naturalistic and aesthetic values, the settings, approaches or environment for structures or other improvements, natural drainage and the consideration and determination of inherent problems of the land relating to the erosion, wear and tear, blight or other hazards. This practice shall include the preparation of plans and specifications and supervising the execution of projects involving the arranging of land and the elements set forth in this subsection used in connection with the land for public and private use and enjoyment, embracing the following, all in accordance with the accepted professional standards of public health, safety and welfare:

    a.   The location and orientation of buildings and other similar site elements.

    b.   The location, routing and design of public and private streets, residential and commercial subdivision roads, or roads in and providing access to private or public developments. This does not include the preparation of construction plans for proposed roads classified as major thoroughfares or a higher classification.

    c.   The location, routing and design of private and public pathways and other travelways.

    d.   The preparation of planting plans.

    e.   The design of surface or incidental subsurface drainage systems, soil conservation and erosion control measures necessary to an overall landscape plan and site design. (1969, c. 672, s. 1; 1997-406, s. 1; 2001-496, s. 12.1(a).)

§ 89A-2. Practice of landscape architecture or use of title "landscape architect" without registration prohibited; use of seal.

(a)   No person shall use the designation "landscape architect," "landscape architecture," or "landscape architectural," or advertise any title or description tending to convey the impression that he or she is a landscape architect or shall engage in the practice of landscape architecture unless the person is registered as a landscape architect in the manner hereinafter provided and thereafter complies with the provisions of this Chapter. Every holder of a certificate shall display it in a conspicuous place in his or her principal office, place of business or employment.

(a1)   No firm, partnership, or corporation shall engage in the practice of landscape architecture unless the firm, partnership, or corporation registered with the Board and has paid the fee required by G.S. 89A-6. All landscape architecture performed by a firm, partnership, or corporation shall be under the direct supervision of an individual who is registered under this Chapter.

(b)   Nothing in this Chapter shall be construed (i) to authorize a landscape architect to engage in the practice of architecture, engineering, or land surveying, (ii) to restrict from the practice of landscape architecture or otherwise affect the rights of any person licensed to practice architecture under Chapter 83A, or engineering or land surveying under Chapter 89C of the General Statutes if the person does not use the title landscape architect, landscape architecture, or landscape architectural, (iii) to restrict any person from engaging in the occupation of grading lands whether by hand tools or machinery, (iv) to restrict the planting, maintaining, or marketing of plants or plant materials or the drafting of plans or specifications related to the location of plants on a site, (v) to require a certificate for the preparation, sale, or furnishing of plans, specifications and related data, or for the supervision of construction pursuant thereto, where the project involved is a single family residential site, or a residential, institutional, or commercial site of one acre or less, or the project involved is a site of more than one acre where only planting and mulching is required, or (vi) to prevent any individual from making plans or data for their own building site or for the supervision of construction pursuant thereto.

(c)   Each landscape architect shall, upon registration, obtain a seal of the design authorized by the Board, bearing the name of the registrant, number of certificate and the legend "N.C. Registered Landscape Architect." Such seal may be used only while the registrant's certificate is in full force and effect.

Nothing in this Chapter shall be construed as authorizing the use or acceptance of the seal of a landscape architect instead of or as a substitute for the seal of an architect, engineer, or land surveyor. (1969, c. 672, s.2; 1989, c. 673, s. 3; 1997-406, s. 2.)

§ 89A-3. North Carolina Board of Landscape Architects; appointments.

(a)   There is created the North Carolina Board of Landscape Architects, consisting of seven members appointed by the Governor for four-year staggered terms. Five members of the Board shall have been engaged in the practice of landscape architecture in North Carolina at least five years at the time of their respective appointments. Two members of the Board shall not be landscape architects and shall represent the interest of the public at large. Each member shall hold office until the appointment and qualification of his or her successor. Vacancies occurring prior to the expiration of the term shall be filled by appointment for the unexpired term. No member shall serve more than two complete consecutive terms.

The Board shall be subject to the provisions of Chapter 93B of the General Statutes.

(b)   The Board shall elect annually from its members a chair and a vice-chair and shall hold such meetings during the year as it may determine to be necessary, one of which shall consist of the annual meeting. A quorum of the Board shall consist of not less than three members.

(b1)   The members of the Board shall not be compensated. However, members shall be entitled to be reimbursed from Board funds for all proper traveling and incidental expenses incurred in carrying out the provisions of this Chapter.

(c),(d) Repealed by Session Laws 1997-406, s. 3. (1969, c. 672, s. 3; 1979, c. 872, s. 1; 1997-406, s. 3.)

§ 89A-3.1. Board's powers and duties.

The Board shall have the following powers and duties:

(1)   Administer and enforce the provisions of this Chapter.

(2)   Adopt rules to administer and enforce the provisions of this Chapter.

(3)   Examine and determine the qualifications and fitness of applicants for registration and renewal of registration.

(4)   Determine the qualifications of firms, partnerships, or corporations applying for a certificate of registration.

(5)   Issue, renew, deny, suspend, or revoke certificates of registration and conduct any disciplinary actions authorized by this Chapter.

(6)   Establish and approve continuing education requirements for persons registered under this Chapter.

(7)   Receive and investigate complaints from members of the public.

(8)   Conduct investigations for the purpose of determining whether violations of this Chapter or grounds for disciplining registrants exist.

(9)   Conduct administrative hearings in accordance with Article 3 of Chapter 150B of the General Statutes.

(10)   Maintain a record of all proceedings conducted by the Board and make available to registrants and other concerned parties an annual report of all Board action.

(11)   Employ and fix the compensation of personnel that the Board determines is necessary to carry out the provisions of this Chapter and incur other expenses necessary to perform the duties of the Board.

(12)   Adopt and publish a code of professional conduct for all registrants.

(13)   Adopt a seal containing the name of the Board for use on all certificates of registration and official reports issued by the Board.

(14)   Retain private counsel subject to G.S. 114-2.3. (1997-406, s. 4; 1997-456, s. 27; 2002-168, s. 7.)

§ 89A-4. Application, examination, certificate.

(a)   Any person hereafter desiring to be registered and licensed to use the title "landscape architect" and to practice landscape architecture in the State, shall make a written application for examination to the Board, on a form prescribed by the Board, together with such evidence of his or her qualifications as may be prescribed by rules of the Board. Minimum qualifications under such rules shall require that the applicant:

    (1)   Shall be at least 18 years of age.

    (2)   Shall be of good moral character.

    (3)   Shall be a graduate of a Landscape Architect's Accreditation Board (LAAB) accredited collegiate curriculum in landscape architecture as approved by the Board.

    (4)   Shall have at least four years' experience in landscape architecture.

(a1)   Notwithstanding the requirements of subdivisions (a)(3) and (4) of this section, any person who has had a minimum of 10 years of education and experience in landscape architecture, in any combination deemed suitable by the Board, may make application to the Board for examination.

(b)   If the application is satisfactory to the Board, and is accompanied by the fees required by this Chapter, then the applicant shall be entitled to an examination to determine his or her qualifications. If the result of the examination of any applicant shall be satisfactory to the Board, then the Board shall issue to the applicant a certificate to use the title "landscape architect" and to practice landscape architecture in North Carolina. Examinations shall be held at least once a year at a time and place to be fixed by the Board which shall determine the subjects and scope of the examination. The Board may adopt rules for administering the examination in one or more parts at the same time or at different times.

(c)　　The Board, within its discretion, may issue licenses without examination and licenses by reciprocity or comity to persons holding a license or certificate in landscape architecture from any legally constituted board of examiners in another state or country whose registration requirements are deemed to be equal or equivalent to those of this State.

(d)　　Repealed by Session Laws 1997-406, s. 5.

(e)　　The Board, within its discretion, may grant an honorific title license to persons who have held for a minimum of 20 years a license or certificate in landscape architecture issued by the Board or a legally constituted board of examiners in another state or country whose registration requirements are equal or equivalent to those of this State. The honorific title license shall allow the person to use the title "landscape architect emeritus," but the person shall not practice landscape architecture or provide expert testimony as a landscape architect in this State unless the person complies with the provisions of this Chapter. There shall be no fee charged for an honorific title license. (1969, c. 672, s. 4; 1971, c. 162; 1979, c. 872, ss. 2, 3; 1997-406, s. 5.)

§ 89A-5. Annual renewal of certificate.

Every registrant under this Chapter shall, on or before the first day of July in each year, obtain a renewal of a certificate for the ensuing year, by application, accompanied by the required fee. Upon failure to renew, the certificate shall be automatically revoked. The certificate may be renewed at any time within one year after its expiration if the applicant pays the required renewal fee and late renewal penalty, and the Board finds that the applicant has not used his or her certificate or title or engaged in the practice of landscape architecture after notice of revocation and is otherwise eligible for registration under the provisions of this Chapter. When necessary to protect the public health, safety, or welfare, the Board shall require such evidence as it deems necessary to establish the continuing competency of licensees as a condition of license renewal. (1969, c. 672, s. 5; 1979, c. 872, s. 4; 1997-406, s. 6.)

§ 89A-6. Fees.

Fees are to be determined by the Board, but shall not exceed the amounts specified herein, however; fees must reflect actual expenses of the Board.

Application...$100.00

License by reciprocity or comity..$250.00

Annual license renewal..$100.00

Late renewal penalty...$50.00

Reissue of certificate...$25.00

Corporate certificate...$250.00

In all instances where the Board uses the services of a testing service for preparation, administration, or grading of examinations, the Board may charge the applicant the actual cost of the examination services, in addition to its other fees. Fees shall be paid to the Board at the times specified by the Board. (1969, c. 672, s. 6; 1979, c. 872, s. 5; 1989, c. 673, s. 4; 1997-406, s. 7; 1999-315, s. 1.)

§ 89A-7. Disciplinary actions.

(a)   The Board may deny or refuse to renew a certificate of registration, suspend, or revoke a certificate of registration if the registrant or applicant:

    (1)   Obtains a certificate of registration by fraudulent misrepresentation.

    (2)   Uses or attempts to use another's certificate of registration to practice landscape architecture.

    (3)   Uses or attempts to use another's name for purposes of obtaining a certificate of registration or practicing landscape architecture.

    (4)   Has demonstrated gross malpractice or gross incompetency as determined by the Board.

    (5)   Has been convicted of or pled guilty or no contest to a crime that indicates that the person is unfit or incompetent to practice landscape architecture or that indicates the person has deceived or defrauded the public.

    (6)   Has been declared mentally incompetent by a court of competent jurisdiction.

    (7)   Has willfully violated any of the provisions of this Chapter or the Board's rules.

(b)   The Board may require a registrant to take a written or oral examination if the Board finds evidence that the person is not competent to practice landscape architecture as defined in this Chapter.

(c)   The Board may take any of the actions authorized in subsection (a) of this section against any firm, partnership, or corporation registered with the Board.

(d)   In addition to taking any of the actions authorized in subsection (a) of this section, the Board may assess a civil penalty not in excess of two thousand dollars ($2,000) for the violation of any section of this Chapter or the violation of any rules adopted by the Board. All civil penalties collected by the Board shall be remitted to the school fund of the county in which the violation occurred. Before imposing and assessing a civil penalty and fixing the amount thereof, the Board shall, as a part of its deliberations, take into consideration the following factors:

    (1)   The nature, gravity, and persistence of the particular violation.

    (2)   The appropriateness of the imposition of a civil penalty when considered alone or in combination with other punishment.

    (3)   Whether the violation was willful.

    (4)   Any other factors that would tend to mitigate or aggravate the violations found to exist. (1969, c. 672, s. 7; 1973, c. 1331, s. 3; 1987, c. 827, ss. 1, 71; 1997-406, s. 8.)

§ 89A-8. Violation a misdemeanor; injunction to prevent violation.

(a)   It shall be a Class 2 misdemeanor for any person to use, or to hold himself or herself out as entitled to practice under the title of landscape architect or landscape architecture or to practice landscape architecture unless he or she is duly registered under the provisions of this Chapter.

(b)   The Board may appear in its own name in the courts of the State and apply for injunctions to prevent violations of this Chapter. (1969, c. 672, s. 8; 1973, c. 1331, s. 3; 1987, c. 827, s. 72; 1993, c. 539, s.610; 1994, Ex. Sess., c. 24, s. 14(c); 1997-406, s. 9.)

Appendix H: Irrigation Contractor Law

CHAPTER 89G

§ 89G-1. Definitions.

The following definitions apply in this Chapter:

(1)   Board.—The North Carolina Irrigation Contractors' Licensing Board.

(1a)   Business entity.—A corporation, association, partnership, limited liability company, limited liability partnership, or other legal entity that is not an individual or a foreign entity.

(1b)   Foreign corporation.—Defined in G.S. 55-1-40.

(1c)   Foreign entity.—A foreign corporation, a foreign limited liability company, or a foreign partnership.

(1d)   Foreign limited liability company.—Defined in G.S. 57C-1-03.

(1e)   Foreign partnership.—One of the following that does not have a permanent place of business in this State:

    a.   A foreign limited partnership as defined in G.S. 59-102.

    b.   A general partnership formed under the laws of a jurisdiction other than this State.

(2)   Irrigation construction or irrigation contracting.—The act of providing services as an irrigation contractor for compensation or other consideration.

(3)   Irrigation contractor.—Any person who, for compensation or other consideration, constructs, installs, expands, services, or repairs irrigation systems.

(4)   Irrigation system.—All piping, fittings, sprinklers, drip tubing, valves, control wiring of 30 volts or less, and associated components installed for the delivery and application of water for the purpose of irrigation that are downstream of a well, pond or other surface water, potable water or groundwater source, or grey water source and downstream of a backflow prevention assembly. Surface water, potable water or groundwater sources, water taps, utility piping, water service lines, water meters, backflow prevention assemblies, stormwater systems that service only the interior of a structure, and sanitary drainage systems are not part of an irrigation system.

(4a)   Nonresident individual.—An individual who is not a resident of this State.

(5)   Person.—An individual, firm, partnership, association, corporation, or other legal entity. (2008-177, s. 1; 2013-383, s. 1.)

§ 89G-2. License required.

Except as otherwise provided in this Chapter, no person shall engage in the practice of irrigation construction or irrigation contracting, use the designation "irrigation contractor," or advertise using any title or description that implies licensure as an irrigation contractor unless the person is licensed as an irrigation contractor as provided by this Chapter. All irrigation construction or irrigation contracting performed by an individual, partnership, association, corporation, firm, or other group shall be under the direct supervision of an individual licensed by the Board under this Chapter. (2008-177, s. 1; 2013-383, s. 8.)

§ 89G-3. Exemptions.

The provisions of this Chapter shall not apply to:

(1)   Any federal or State agency or any political subdivision performing irrigation construction or irrigation contracting work on public property and using its own employees.

(2)   Any property owner who performs irrigation construction work on his or her own property.

(3)   A landscape architect registered under Chapter 89A of the General Statutes.

(4)   A professional engineer licensed under Chapter 89C of the General Statutes.

(5)   Any irrigation construction or irrigation contracting work where the price of all contracts for labor, material, and other items for a given jobsite is less than two thousand five hundred dollars ($2,500).

(6)   Any person performing irrigation construction or irrigation contracting work for temporary irrigation to establish vegetative cover for erosion control.

(7)   Any person performing irrigation construction or irrigation contracting work to control dust on commercial construction sites or mining operations.

(8)   Any person performing irrigation construction or irrigation contracting work for use in agricultural production, farming, or ranching, including land application of animal wastewater.

(9)   Any person performing irrigation construction or irrigation contracting work for use in commercial sod production.

(10)   Any person performing irrigation construction or irrigation contracting work for use in the commercial production of horticultural crops, including nursery and greenhouse operators.

(11)   A general contractor licensed under Article 1 of Chapter 87 of the General Statutes who possesses a classification under G.S. 87-10(b) as a building contractor, a residential contractor, or a public utilities contractor.

(12)   A wastewater contractor certified under Article 5 of Chapter 90A of the General Statutes who performs only the construction of or repair to a wastewater dispersal system.

(13)   Repealed by Session Laws 2013-383, s. 2, effective October 1, 2013.

(14)   A plumbing contractor licensed under Article 2 of Chapter 87 of the General Statutes who performs only the following work: installation, repairs, or maintenance of water mains, water taps, service lines, water meters, or backflow prevention assemblies supplying water for irrigation systems; or repairs to an irrigation system.

(15)   Any person performing irrigation construction or irrigation contracting work for a golf course.

(16)   Any full-time employee of a homeowners association maintaining or repairing an irrigation system owned by the homeowners association of a planned community and located within the planned community's common elements as defined in G.S. 47F-1-103.

(17)   Any person who can document 10 years in business as an irrigation contractor as of January 1, 2009, can document competency in the practice of irrigation construction or irrigation contracting, as determined by the North Carolina Irrigation Contractors' Licensing Board, and meets all other requirements and qualifications for licensure may be issued an irrigation contractor's license under Chapter 89G of the General Statutes, without the requirement of examination, provided that the person submits an application for licensure to the Board prior to October 1, 2012.

(18)   Any unlicensed person or entity who enters into a subcontract with a North Carolina licensed irrigation contractor, where the irrigation work is performed entirely by the North Carolina licensed irrigation contractor in accordance with this Chapter. (2008-177, s. 1; 2012-194, s. 65.8(a); 2013-383, s. 2.)

§ 89G-4. The North Carolina Irrigation Contractors' Licensing Board.

(a) Composition and Terms.—The North Carolina Irrigation Contractors' Licensing Board is created. The Board shall consist of nine members who shall serve staggered terms. The initial Board shall be selected on or before October 1, 2008, as follows:

  (1) The Commissioner of Agriculture, upon the recommendation of the Carolinas Irrigation Association, shall appoint two irrigation contractors, one to serve a one-year term and one to serve a three-year term.

  (2) The General Assembly, upon the recommendation of the Speaker of the House of Representatives and pursuant to recommendations from the North Carolina Green Industry Council, shall appoint two members, one who is a registered landscape contractor in good standing with the North Carolina Landscape Contractors Registration Board to serve a one-year term and one who is an irrigation contractor to serve a three-year term.

  (3) The General Assembly, upon the recommendation of the President Pro Tempore of the Senate, shall appoint two irrigation contractors, one to serve a one-year term and one to serve a two-year term.

  (4) The President of The University of North Carolina System shall appoint one member from within the ranks of the land grant university community who is knowledgeable in irrigation methods and practices to serve a three-year term. The position is open to both current employees of The University of North Carolina System and persons who have earned emeritus status with The University of North Carolina System.

  (5) The Board of Directors of the North Carolina Chapter of the American Society of Landscape Architects shall appoint one member who is a registered landscape architect to serve a two-year term.

  (6) The Governor shall appoint one public member to serve a two-year term.

  Upon the expiration of the terms of the initial Board members, each member shall be appointed by the appointing authorities designated in subdivisions (1) through (6) of this subsection for a three-year term and shall serve until a successor is appointed and qualified. No member may serve more than two consecutive full terms.

(b) Qualifications.—Members of the Board shall be residents of this State. The irrigation contractor members shall meet the requirements for licensure under this Chapter and remain in good standing with the Board during their terms. The public member of the Board shall not be: (i) trained or experienced in irrigation construction or irrigation contracting; (ii) an agent or employee of a person engaged in the practice of irrigation construction or irrigation contracting; or (iii) the spouse of an individual who may not serve as a public member of the Board.

(c) Vacancies.—Any vacancy on the Board created by death, resignation, or otherwise shall be filled in the same manner as the original appointment, except that all unexpired terms of Board members appointed by the General Assembly shall be filled in accordance with G.S. 120-122. Appointees to fill vacancies shall serve the remainder of the unexpired term and until their successors are appointed and qualified.

(d) Removal.—The Board may remove any of its members for neglect of duty, incompetence, or unprofessional conduct. A member subject to disciplinary proceedings in the member's capacity as a licensed irrigation contractor shall be disqualified from participating in the official business of the Board until the charges have been resolved.

(e)   Officers and Meetings.—The Board shall elect annually a chair and other officers as it deems necessary to carry out the purposes of this Chapter and shall hold meetings at least twice a year. A majority of the Board shall constitute a quorum.

(f)   Compensation.—Each member of the Board may receive per diem and reimbursement for travel and subsistence as set forth in G.S. 93B-5.

(g)   Assistance.—The Board shall be entitled to the services of the Attorney General in connection with the affairs of the Board or may, in its discretion, employ an attorney to assist or represent it in the enforcement of this Chapter. (2008-177, s. 1; 2013-383, s. 8.)

§ 89G-5. Powers and duties.

The Board shall have the following powers and duties:

(1)   To administer and enforce the provisions of this Chapter.

(2)   To adopt, amend, or repeal rules to carry out the provisions of this Chapter.

(3)   To examine and determine the qualifications and fitness of applicants for licensure and licensure renewal.

(4)   To issue, renew, deny, restrict, suspend, or revoke licenses.

(5)   To reprimand or otherwise discipline licensees under this Chapter.

(6)   To receive and investigate complaints from members of the public.

(7)   To conduct investigations to determine whether violations of this Chapter exist or constitute grounds for disciplinary action against licensees under this Chapter.

(8)   To conduct administrative hearings in accordance with Chapter 150B of the General Statutes.

(9)   To seek injunctive relief through any court of competent jurisdiction for violations of this Chapter.

(10)   To collect fees required by G.S. 89G-10 and other monies permitted by law to be paid to the Board.

(11)   To require licensees to file and maintain an adequate surety bond or letter of credit.

(12)   To establish and approve continuing educational requirements for persons licensed under this Chapter.

(13)   To employ a secretary-treasurer and any other clerical personnel the Board deems necessary to carry out the provisions of this Chapter and to fix compensation for employees.

(14)   To maintain a record of all proceedings conducted by the Board and make available to licensees and other concerned parties an annual report of all Board actions.

(15)   To adopt and publish a code of professional conduct and practice for all persons licensed under this Chapter. The code shall establish minimum standards for water conservation in the practice of irrigation construction and contracting.

(16)   To publish a list of irrigation best management practices to be followed by licensed irrigation contractors.

(17)   To adopt a seal containing the name of the Board for use on licenses and official reports issued by the Board. (2008-177, s. 1; 2013-383, s. 3.)

§ 89G-6. Application; qualifications; examination; issuance.

(a)   Upon application to the Board and the payment of the required fees, an applicant may be licensed under this Chapter as an irrigation contractor if the applicant submits evidence that demonstrates his or her qualifications as prescribed in rules adopted by the Board and meets all of the following qualifications:

(1)   Is at least 18 years of age.

(2) Is of good moral character as determined by the Board.

(3) Has at least three years of experience in irrigation construction or irrigation contracting or the educational equivalent. Two years of educational training in irrigation construction or irrigation contracting shall be the equivalent of one year of experience.

(4) Files with the Board and maintains a corporate surety bond executed by a company authorized to do business in this State or an irrevocable letter of credit issued by an insured institution. The surety bond or the letter of credit shall be in the amount of ten thousand dollars ($10,000). The surety bond or letter of credit shall be approved by the Board as to form and shall be conditioned upon the obligor's faithfully conforming to and abiding by the provisions of this Chapter. Any person claiming to be injured by an act of a licensed irrigation contractor that constitutes a violation of this Chapter may institute an action to recover against the licensee and the surety.

(b) If the application is satisfactory to the Board, the applicant shall be required to pass an examination administered by the Board. The Board shall establish the scope and subject matter of the examination, and an examination shall be held at least twice a year at a time and place to be determined by the Board. The examination, at a minimum, shall test the applicant's understanding of the following:

(1) Efficiency of water use and conservation in the practice of irrigation construction and contracting.

(2) Proper methods of irrigation construction.

(3) Proper methods for irrigation installation.

(4) Basic business skills.

(c) When the Board determines that an applicant has met all the requirements for licensure, the Board shall issue a license to the applicant. (2008-177, s. 1; 2013-383, s. 8.)

§ 89G-6.1. Licensing of business entities, nonresident individuals, and foreign entities.

(a) The Board may issue a license in the name of a business entity if the business entity pays the license fee required by G.S. 89G-10 and one of the following applies:

(1) For a corporation, one or more officers or full-time employees empowered to act for the corporation are individuals licensed under this Chapter, and only the individuals licensed under this Chapter execute contracts for irrigation construction and irrigation contracting.

(2) For a limited liability company, one or more managers or executives as defined in G.S. 57C-1-03 or full-time employees empowered to act for the company are individuals licensed under this Chapter, and only the individuals licensed under this Chapter execute contracts for irrigation construction and irrigation contracting.

(3) For a partnership, one or more general partners or full-time employees empowered to act for the partnership are individuals licensed under this Chapter, and only the individuals licensed under this Chapter execute contracts for irrigation construction and irrigation contracting.

(4) For a business entity using an assumed name or designated trade name, the owner or one or more full-time employees empowered to act for the owner are individuals licensed under this Chapter, and only the individuals licensed under this Chapter execute contracts for irrigation construction and irrigation contracting.

(b) The Board may issue a license to a nonresident individual who meets the requirements for licensure under this Chapter. A nonresident individual licensed under this Chapter may qualify as the licensed individual under subdivisions (1), (2), and (3) of subsection (a) of this section.

(c)   The Board may issue a license in the name of a foreign entity if the following apply:

   (1)   For a foreign corporation, the corporation has obtained a certificate of authority from the Secretary of State pursuant to Article 15 of Chapter 55 of the General Statutes and complies with the requirements of subdivision (1) of subsection (a) of this section.

   (2)   For a foreign limited liability company, the company has obtained a certificate of authority from the Secretary of State pursuant to Article 7 of Chapter 57C of the General Statutes and complies with the requirements of subdivision (2) of subsection (a) of this section.

   (3)   For a foreign partnership, the partnership complies with the requirements of subdivision (3) of subsection (a) of this section.

(d)   When the Board issues a license to a business entity or a foreign entity under this section, the Board shall indicate on the license the name and license number of the individual licensee required under subsection (a) of this section. The individual licensee required under subsection (a) of this section shall exercise direct supervision over a contract by a business entity or a foreign entity for irrigation construction or irrigation contracting until the contract is completed.

(e)   A business entity or foreign entity licensed under this section shall provide written notice to the Board if the individual licensee required under subsection (a) of this section ceases to be an officer, full-time employee, manager, executive, general partner, or owner of the business entity or foreign entity. The business entity or foreign entity must satisfy the requirements of subsection (a) of this section within 90 days of the effective date of the notice required under this subsection. The Board shall suspend the license of a business entity or foreign entity licensed under this section that fails after 90 days to satisfy the requirements of subsection (a) of this section. (2013-383, s. 4.)

§ 89G-7. Use of seal; posting license.

(a)   Upon licensure by the Board, each irrigation contractor shall obtain a seal of the design authorized by the Board and bearing the name of the licensee, the number of the license, and the legend "N.C. Licensed Irrigation Contractor." An irrigation contractor may use the seal only while the license is valid.

(b)   Every irrigation contractor issued a license under this Chapter shall display the license conspicuously in the contractor's place of business. (2008-177, s. 1.)

§ 89G-8. Reciprocity.

The Board may issue a license, without examination, to any person who is an irrigation contractor licensed, certified, or registered in another state or country if the requirements for licensure, certification, or registration in the other state or country are substantially equivalent to the requirements for licensure in this State. (2008-177, s. 1.)

§ 89G-9. License renewal and continuing education.

(a)   Every license issued under this Chapter shall be renewed on or before December 31 of each year. Any person who desires to continue to practice irrigation contracting or irrigation construction shall apply for license renewal and shall submit the required fees. Licenses that are not renewed shall be automatically revoked. A license may be renewed at any time within one year after its expiration, if: (i) the applicant pays the required renewal fee and late renewal fee; (ii) the Board finds that the applicant has not used the license in a manner inconsistent with the provisions of this Chapter or engaged in the practice of irrigation construction or irrigation contracting after notice of revocation; and (iii) the applicant is otherwise eligible for licensure under the provisions of this Chapter. When necessary, the Board may require a licensee to demonstrate continued competence as a condition of license renewal.

(b)   As a condition of license renewal, an individual licensee shall meet continuing education requirements set by the Board. Each individual licensee shall complete 10 continuing education units per year.

(c)   The Board shall suspend an individual licensee's license for 60 days for failure to obtain continuing education units required by subsection (b) of this section. The Board shall suspend a business entity's or a foreign entity's license for 60 days for failure by the individual licensee required under G.S. 89G-6.1(a) to obtain continuing education units required by subsection (b) of this section. Upon completion of the required continuing education and payment of the reinstatement fee, the Board shall reinstate the license. Failure by an individual licensee to meet the education requirements, to request a reinstatement of the license, or to pay the reinstatement fee within the time provided shall result in the revocation of the license. Upon revocation, an individual shall be required to submit a new application and retake the examination as provided in this Chapter. (2008-177, s. 1; 2013-383, ss. 5, 8.)

§ 89G-10. Expenses and fees

(a)   The Board may impose the following fees not to exceed the amounts listed below:

(1)   Application fee $100.00

(2)   Examination fee $200.00

(3)   License renewal $100.00

(3a) Business entity or foreign entity license fee
      and business entity or foreign entity license renewal fee $100.00

(4)   Late renewal fee $50.00

(5)   License by reciprocity $250.00

(6)   Corporate license $100.00

(7)   Duplicate license $25.00

(b)   When the Board uses a testing service for the preparation, administration, or grading of examinations, the Board may charge the applicant the actual cost of the examination services.

(c)   The Board must annually review the fees set out in this section to determine whether these fees reflect the actual cost of administering this act and seek legislative changes to the fees if necessary. (2008-177, ss. 1, 5; 2013-383, s. 6.)

§ 89G-11. Disciplinary action.

(a)   The Board may deny, restrict, suspend, or revoke a license or refuse to issue or renew a license if a licensee or applicant:

(1)   Employs the use of fraud, deceit, or misrepresentation in obtaining or attempting to obtain a license or the renewal of a license.

(2)   Practices or attempts to practice irrigation construction or irrigation contracting by fraudulent misrepresentation.

(3)   Commits an act of gross malpractice or incompetence as determined by the Board.

(4)   Has been convicted of or pled guilty or no contest to a crime that indicates that the person is unfit or incompetent to practice as an irrigation contractor or that indicates that the person has deceived or defrauded the public.

(5)   Has been declared incompetent by a court of competent jurisdiction.

(6)   Has willfully violated any provision in this Chapter or any rules adopted by the Board.

(7)   Uses or attempts to use the seal in a fraudulent or unauthorized manner.

(8)   Fails to file the required surety bond or letter of credit or to keep the bond or letter of credit in force.

(b)   The Board may assess costs, including reasonable attorneys' fees and investigatory costs, in a proceeding under this section against an applicant or licensee found to be in violation of this Chapter. (2008-177, s. 1; 2013-383, ss. 7, 8.)

§ 89G-12. Civil penalties.

(a)   In addition to taking any of the actions permitted under G.S. 89G-11, the Board may assess a civil penalty not in excess of two thousand dollars ($2,000) for each violation of any section of this Chapter or the violation of any rules adopted by the Board. The clear proceeds of any civil penalty assessed under this section shall be remitted to the Civil Penalty and Forfeiture Fund in accordance with G.S. 115C-457.2.

(b)   Before imposing and assessing a civil penalty and fixing the amount of the penalty, the Board shall, as a part of its deliberations, take into consideration the following factors:

(1)   The nature, gravity, and persistence of the particular violation.

(2)   The appropriateness of the imposition of a civil penalty when considered alone or in combination with other punishment.

(3)   Whether the violation was willful and malicious.

(4)   Any other factors that would tend to mitigate or aggravate the violation found to exist.

(c)   Schedule of Civil Penalties.—The Board shall establish a schedule of civil penalties for violations of this Chapter and rules adopted by the Board. (2008-177, s. 1.)

§ 89G-13. Injunction to prevent violation; notification of complaints.

(a)   If the Board finds that a person who does not have a license issued under this Chapter is engaging in the practice of irrigation construction or irrigation contracting, the Board may appear in its own name in superior court in actions for injunctive relief to prevent any person from violating the provisions of this Chapter or rules adopted by the Board.

(b)   A licensed irrigation contractor shall notify the Board by registered mail of any complaints filed against the contractor within 30 days from the date the complaint was filed. (2008-177, s. 1; 2013-383, s. 8.)

Appendix I: Irrigation Contractor Exemptions

The $2500 exemption under NC General Statute 89G-3 (5) refers to all components that must be installed to make an irrigation system operable for the life of the system. It is for a single site, and includes all costs for the life of the irrigation system. This includes maintenance, repair and service. The Board realizes that the irrigation installer may not install all components, but total system cost includes everything required to make the system operational.

The total cost of a landscape irrigation system includes:

a)   all costs to make the irrigation system operational;

b)   all expenses for the life of the system (repairs, maintenance and service).

c)   the water meter where water is supplied by a municipality or community water supplier;

d)   a backflow assembly, with any electrical, sleeving and irrigation system components and installation costs, where required by local laws.

e)   if the water is supplied by a well that is constructed for irrigation, the total system cost including:

- the well cost;
- the backflow assembly, if required;
- pump, electrical, sleeving and irrigation system components and installation.

f)   for a surface water supply, i.e. stream or pond constructed for irrigation, the total system cost includes:

- pond construction costs;
- pump(s);
- electrical;
- sleeving;
- irrigation system components; and
- installation;

g)   for roof runoff or storm water supplied irrigation, the total system cost includes:

- the water collection and storage facility;
- pump;
- filter;
- electrical components;
- sleeving;
- irrigation system components; and
- installation.

And if the irrigation system was installed after January 1, 2009, even if you were not the installer, the cost of the irrigation system would be included in the $2,500 limit.

Appendix J: Payments to Subcontractors

CHAPTER 22C

§ 22C1. Definitions.

Unless the context otherwise requires in this Chapter:

(1) "Contractor" means a person who contracts with an owner to improve real property.

(2) "Improve" means to build, effect, alter, repair, or demolish any improvement upon, connected with, or on or beneath the surface of any real property, or to excavate, clear, grade, fill or landscape any real property, or to construct driveways and private roadways, or to furnish materials, including trees and shrubbery, for any of such purposes, or to perform any labor upon such improvements, and shall also mean and include any design or other professional or skilled services furnished by architects, engineers, land surveyors and landscape architects registered under Chapters 83A, 89C or 89A of the General Statutes.

(3) "Improvement" means all or any part of any building, structure, erection, alteration, demolition, excavation, clearing, grading, filling, or landscaping, including trees and shrubbery, driveways, and private roadways, on real property.

(4) An "owner" is a person who has an interest in the real property improved and for whom an improvement is made and who ordered the improvement to be made. "Owner" includes successors in interest of the owner and agents of the owner acting within their authority.

(5) "Real property" means the real estate that is improved, including lands, leaseholds, tenements and hereditaments, and improvements placed thereon.

(6) "Subcontractor" means any person who has contracted to furnish labor or materials to, or has performed labor for, a contractor or another subcontractor in connection with a contract to improve real property. (1987 (Reg. Sess., 1988), c. 946, s. 1.)

§ 22C2. Performance by subcontractor.

Performance by a subcontractor in accordance with the provisions of its contract shall entitle it to payment from the party with whom it contracts. Payment by the owner to a contractor is not a condition precedent for payment to a subcontractor and payment by a contractor to a subcontractor is not a condition precedent for payment to any other subcontractor, and an agreement to the contrary is unenforceable. (1987 (Reg. Sess., 1988), c. 946; 1991, c. 620.)

§ 22C3. Time of payment to subcontractors after contractor or other subcontractor has been paid.

When a subcontractor has performed in accordance with the provisions of his contract, the contractor shall pay to his subcontractor and each subcontractor shall pay to his subcontractor, within seven days of receipt by the contractor or subcontractor of each periodic or final payment, the full amount received for such subcontractor's work and materials based on work completed or service provided under the subcontract. (1987 (Reg. Sess., 1988), c. 946.)

§ 22C4. Conditions of payment.

Nothing in this Chapter shall prevent the contractor, at the time of application and certification to the owner, from withholding such application and certification to the owner for payment to the subcontractor for: unsatisfactory job progress; defective construction not remedied; disputed work; third party claims filed or reasonable evidence that claim will be filed; failure of subcontractor to make timely payments for labor, equipment, and materials; damage to contractor or another subcontractor; reasonable evidence that subcontract cannot be completed for the unpaid balance of the subcontract sum; or a reasonable amount for retainage not to exceed the initial percentage retained by the owner. (1987 (Reg. Sess., 1988), c. 946.)

§ 22C5. Late payments to bear interest.

Should any periodic or final payment to a subcontractor be delayed by more than seven days after receipt of periodic or final payment by the contractor or subcontractor, the contractor or subcontractor shall pay his subcontractor interest, beginning on the eighth day, at the rate of one percent (1%) per month or a fraction thereof on such unpaid balance as may be due. (1987 (Reg. Sess., 1988), c. 946.)

§ 22C6. Applicability of this Chapter.

The provisions of this Chapter shall not be applicable to residential contractors as defined in G.S. 87 10(1a), or to improvements to real property intended for residential purposes which are exempted from the application of Chapter 83A of the General Statutes pursuant to G.S. 83A13(c)(1), or to improvements to real property intended for residential purposes which consist of 12 or fewer residential units. (1987 (Reg. Sess., 1988), c. 946.)

Appendix K: Statutory Liens on Real Property

CHAPTER 44A, ARTICLE 2

Part 1. Liens of Mechanics, Laborers, and Materialmen Dealing with Owner.

§ 44A7. Definitions.

Unless the context otherwise requires in this Article:

(1) "Improve" means to build, effect, alter, repair, or demolish any improvement upon, connected with, or on or beneath the surface of any real property, or to excavate, clear, grade, fill or landscape any real property, or to construct driveways and private roadways, or to furnish materials, including trees and shrubbery, for any of such purposes, or to perform any labor upon such improvements, and shall also mean and include any design or other professional or skilled services furnished by architects, engineers, land surveyors and landscape architects registered under Chapter 83A, 89A or 89C of the General Statutes, and rental of equipment directly utilized on the real property in making the improvement.

(2) "Improvement" means all or any part of any building, structure, erection, alteration, demolition, excavation, clearing, grading, filling, or landscaping, including trees and shrubbery, driveways, and private roadways, on real property.

(3) An "owner" is a person who has an interest in the real property improved and for whom an improvement is made and who ordered the improvement to be made. "Owner" includes successors in interest of the owner and agents of the owner acting within their authority.

(4) "Real property" means the real estate that is improved, including lands, leaseholds, tenements and hereditaments, and improvements placed thereon. (1969, c. 1112, s. 1; 1975, c. 715, s. 1; 1985, c. 689, s. 13; 1995 (Reg. Sess., 1996), c. 607, s. 1.)

§ 44A8. Mechanics', laborers', and materialmen's lien; persons entitled to claim of lien on real property.

Any person who performs or furnishes labor or professional design or surveying services or furnishes materials or furnishes rental equipment pursuant to a contract, either express or implied, with the owner of real property for the making of an improvement thereon shall, upon complying with the provisions of this Article, have a right to file a claim of lien on real property on the real property to secure payment of all debts owing for labor done or professional design or surveying services or material furnished or equipment rented pursuant to the contract. (1969, c. 1112, s. 1; 1975, c. 715, s. 2; 1995 (Reg. Sess., 1996), c. 607, s. 2; 2005229, s. 1.)

§ 44A9. Extent of claim of lien on real property.

A claim of lien on real property authorized under this Article shall extend to the improvement and to the lot or tract on which the improvement is situated, to the extent of the interest of the owner. When the lot or tract on which a building is erected is not surrounded at the time of making the contract with the owner by an enclosure separating it from adjoining land of the same owner, the lot or tract to which any claim of lien on real property extends shall be the area that is reasonably necessary for the convenient use and occupation of the building, but in no case shall the area include a building, structure, or improvement not normally used or occupied or intended to be used or occupied with the building with respect to which the claim of lien on real property is claimed. (1969, c. 1112, s. 1; 2005229, s. 1.)

§ 44A10. Effective date of claim of lien on real property.

A claim of lien on real property granted by this Article shall relate to and take effect from the time of the first furnishing of labor or materials at the site of the improvement by the person claiming the claim of lien on real property. (1969, c. 1112, s. 1; 2005229, s. 1.)

§ 44A11. Perfecting claim of lien on real property.

A claim of lien on real property granted by this Article shall be perfected as of the time provided in G.S. 44A10 upon the filing of the claim of lien on real property under G.S. 44A12 and may be enforced pursuant to G.S. 44A13. (1969, c. 1112, s. 1; 2005229, s. 1.)

§ 44A12. Filing claim of lien on real property.

(a)   Place of Filing.—All claims of lien on real property must be filed in the office of the clerk of superior court in each county where the real property subject to the claim of lien on real property is located. The clerk of superior court shall note the claim of lien on real property on the judgment docket and index the same under the name of the record owner of the real property at the time the claim of lien on real property is filed. An additional copy of the claim of lien on real property may also be filed with any receiver, referee in bankruptcy or assignee for benefit of creditors who obtains legal authority over the real property.

(b)   Time of Filing.—Claims of lien on real property may be filed at any time after the maturity of the obligation secured thereby but not later than 120 days after the last furnishing of labor or materials at the site of the improvement by the person claiming the lien.

(c)   Contents of Claim of Lien on Real Property to Be Filed.—All claims of lien on real property must be filed using a form substantially as follows:

CLAIM OF LIEN ON REAL PROPERTY

(1) Name and address of the person claiming the claim of lien on real property:

(2) Name and address of the record owner of the real property claimed to be subject to the claim of lien on real property at the time the claim of lien on real property is filed:

(3) Description of the real property upon which the claim of lien on real property is claimed: (Street address, tax lot and block number, reference to recorded instrument, or any other description of real property is sufficient, whether or not it is specific, if it reasonably identifies what is described.)

(4) Name and address of the person with whom the claimant contracted for the furnishing of labor or materials:

(5) Date upon which labor or materials were first furnished upon said property by the claimant:

(5a) Date upon which labor or materials were last furnished upon said property by the claimant:

(6) General description of the labor performed or materials furnished and the amount claimed therefor:

                                                                    _____

                                                                                    Lien Claimant

         Filed this _____ day of _____, _____

         _____

         Clerk of Superior Court

A general description of the labor performed or materials furnished is sufficient. It is not necessary for lien claimant to file an itemized list of materials or a detailed statement of labor performed.

(d) No Amendment of Claim of Lien on Real Property.—A claim of lien on real property may not be amended. A claim of lien on real property may be cancelled by a claimant or the claimant's authorized agent or attorney and a new claim of lien on real property substituted therefor within the time herein provided for original filing.

(e) Notice of Assignment of Claim of Lien on Real Property.—When a claim of lien on real property has been filed, it may be assigned of record by the lien claimant in a writing filed with the clerk of superior court who shall note the assignment in the margin of the judgment docket containing the claim of lien on real property. Thereafter the assignee becomes the lien claimant of record.

(f) Waiver of Right to File, Serve, or Claim Liens as Consideration for Contract Against Public Policy.— An agreement to waive the right to file a claim of lien on real property granted under this Part, or an agreement to waive the right to serve a notice of claim of lien upon funds granted under Part 2 of this Article, which agreement is in anticipation of and in consideration for the awarding of any contract, either expressed or implied, for the making of an improvement upon real property under this Article is against public policy and is unenforceable. This section does not prohibit subordination or release of a lien granted under this Part or Part 2 of this Article. (1969, c. 1112, s. 1; 1977, c. 369; 1983, c. 888; 1999456, s. 59; 2005229, s. 1.)

§ 44A12.1. No docketing of lien unless authorized by statute.

(a) The clerk of superior court shall not index, docket, or record a claim of lien on real property or other document purporting to claim or assert a lien on real property in such a way as to affect the title to any real property unless the document:

    (1) Is offered for filing under this Article or another statute that provides for indexing and docketing of claims of lien on real property; and

    (2) Appears on its face to contain all of the information required by the statute under which it is offered for filing.

(b) The clerk may accept, for filing only, any document that does not meet the criteria established for indexing, docketing, or recording under subsection (a) of this section. If the clerk does accept this document, the clerk shall inform the person offering the document that it will not be indexed, docketed, or recorded in any way as to affect the title to any real property.

(c) Any person who causes or attempts to cause a claim of lien on real property or other document to be filed, knowing that the filing is not authorized by statute, or with the intent that the filing is made for an improper purpose such as to hinder, harass, or otherwise wrongfully interfere with any person, shall be guilty of a Class 1 misdemeanor.

(d) A claim of lien on real property, a claim of lien on real property with a notice of claim of lien upon funds attached thereto, or other document purporting to claim or assert a lien on real property that is filed by an attorney licensed in the State of North Carolina and that otherwise complies with subsection (a) of this section shall not be rejected by the clerk of superior court for indexing, docketing, recording, or filing. (2001495, s. 1; 2005229, s. 1.)

§ 44A13. Action to enforce claim of lien on real property.

(a) Where and When Action Commenced.—An action to enforce a claim of lien on real property may be commenced in any county where venue is otherwise proper. No such action may be commenced later than 180 days after the last furnishing of labor or materials at the site of the improvement by the person claiming the claim of lien on real property. If the title to the real property against which the claim of lien on real property is asserted is by law vested in a receiver or is subject to the control of the bankruptcy court, the claim of lien on real property shall be enforced in accordance with the orders of the court having jurisdiction over said real property. The filing of a proof of claim with a receiver or in bankruptcy and the filing of a notice of lis pendens in each county where the real property subject to the claim of lien on real property is located within the time required by this section satisfies the requirement for the commencement of a civil action.

(b)   Judgment.—A judgment enforcing a lien under this Article may be entered for the principal amount shown to be due, not exceeding the principal amount stated in the claim of lien enforced thereby. The judgment shall direct a sale of the real property subject to the lien thereby enforced.

(c)   Notice of Action.—In order for the sale under G.S. 44A14(a) to pass all title and interest of the owner to the purchaser good against all claims or interests recorded, filed or arising after the first furnishing of labor or materials at the site of the improvement by the person claiming the claim of lien on real property, a notice of lis pendens shall be filed in each county in which the real property subject to the claim of lien on real property is located except the county in which the action is commenced. The notice of lis pendens shall be filed within the time provided in subsection (a) of this section for the commencement of the action by the lien claimant. If neither an action nor a notice of lis pendens is filed in accordance with this section, the judgment entered in the action enforcing the claim of lien on real property shall not direct a sale of the real property subject to the claim of lien on real property enforced thereby nor be entitled to any priority under the provisions of G.S. 44A14(a), but shall be entitled only to those priorities accorded by law to money judgments. (1969, c. 1112, s. 1; 1977, c. 883; 2005229, s. 1.)

§ 44A14. Sale of property in satisfaction of judgment enforcing claim of lien on real property or upon order prior to judgment; distribution of proceeds.

(a)   Execution Sale; Effect of Sale.—Except as provided in subsection (b) of this section, sales under this Article and distribution of proceeds thereof shall be made in accordance with the execution sale provisions set out in G.S. 1339.41 through 1339.76. The sale of real property to satisfy a claim of lien on real property granted by this Article shall pass all title and interest of the owner to the purchaser, good against all claims or interests recorded, filed or arising after the first furnishing of labor or materials at the site of the improvement by the person claiming a lien.

(b)   Sale of Property upon Order Prior to Judgment.—A resident judge of superior court in the district in which the action to enforce the claim of lien on real property is pending, a judge regularly holding the superior courts of the said district, any judge holding a session of superior court, either civil or criminal, in the said district, a special judge of superior court residing in the said district, or the chief judge of the district court in which the action to enforce the claim of lien on real property is pending, may, upon notice to all interested parties and after a hearing thereupon and upon a finding that a sale prior to judgment is necessary to prevent substantial waste, destruction, depreciation or other damage to said real property prior to the final determination of said action, order any real property against which a claim of lien on real property under this Article is asserted, sold in any manner determined by said judge to be commercially reasonable. The rights of all parties shall be transferred to the proceeds of the sale. Application for such order and further proceedings thereon may be heard in or out of session. (1969, c. 1112, s. 1; 2005229, s. 1.)

§ 44A15. Attachment available to lien claimant.

In addition to other grounds for attachment, in all cases where the owner removes or attempts or threatens to remove an improvement from real property subject to a claim of lien on real property under this Article, without the written permission of the lien claimant or with the intent to deprive the lien claimant of his or her claim of lien on real property, the remedy of attachment of the property subject to the claim of lien on real property shall be available to the lien claimant or any other person. (1969, c. 1112, s. 1; 2005229, s. 1.)

§ 44A16. Discharge of record claim of lien on real property.

(a)   Any claim of lien on real property filed under this Article may be discharged by any of the following methods:

(1)   The lien claimant of record, the claimant's agent or attorney, in the presence of the clerk of superior court may acknowledge the satisfaction of the claim of lien on real property indebtedness, whereupon the clerk of superior court shall forthwith make upon the record of such claim of lien on real property an entry of such acknowledgment of satisfaction, which shall be signed by the lien claimant of record, the claimant's agent or attorney, and witnessed by the clerk of superior court.

(2)   The owner may exhibit an instrument of satisfaction signed and acknowledged by the lien claimant of record which instrument states that the claim of lien on real property indebtedness has been paid or satisfied, whereupon the clerk of superior court shall cancel the claim of lien on real property by entry of satisfaction on the record of such claim of lien on real property.

(3)   By failure to enforce the claim of lien on real property within the time prescribed in this Article.

(4)   By filing in the office of the clerk of superior court the original or certified copy of a judgment or decree of a court of competent jurisdiction showing that the action by the claimant to enforce the claim of lien on real property has been dismissed or finally determined adversely to the claimant.

(5)   Whenever a sum equal to the amount of the claim or claims of lien on real property claimed is deposited with the clerk of court, to be applied to the payment finally determined to be due, whereupon the clerk of superior court shall cancel the claim or claims of lien on real property or claims of lien on real property of record.

(6)   Whenever a corporate surety bond, in a sum equal to one and onefourth times the amount of the claim or claims of lien on real property claimed and conditioned upon the payment of the amount finally determined to be due in satisfaction of said claim or claims of lien on real property, is deposited with the clerk of court, whereupon the clerk of superior court shall cancel the claim or claims of lien on real property of record.

(b)   The clerk may release funds held or a corporate surety bond upon receipt of one of the following:

(1)   Written agreement of the parties.

(2)   A final judgment of a court of competent jurisdiction.

(3)   A consent order. (1969, c. 1112, s. 1; 1971, c. 766; 2005229, s. 1; 2011411, s. 3.)

Part 2. Liens of Mechanics, Laborers, and Materialmen Dealing with One Other Than Owner.

§ 44A17. Definitions.

Unless the context otherwise requires in this Article:

(1)   "Contractor" means a person who contracts with an owner to improve real property.

(2)   "First tier subcontractor" means a person who contracts with a contractor to improve real property.

(3)   "Obligor" means an owner, contractor or subcontractor in any tier who owes money to another as a result of the other's partial or total performance of a contract to improve real property.

(4)   "Second tier subcontractor" means a person who contracts with a first tier subcontractor to improve real property.

(5)   "Third tier subcontractor" means a person who contracts with a second tier subcontractor to improve real property. (1971, c. 880, s. 1.)

§ 44A18. Grant of lien upon funds; subrogation; perfection.

Upon compliance with this Article:

(1)   A first tier subcontractor who furnished labor, materials, or rental equipment at the site of the improvement shall be entitled to a lien upon funds that are owed to the contractor with whom the first tier subcontractor dealt and that arise out of the improvement on which the first tier subcontractor worked or furnished materials.

(2)   A second tier subcontractor who furnished labor, materials, or rental equipment at the site of the improvement shall be entitled to a lien upon funds that are owed to the first tier subcontractor with whom the second tier subcontractor dealt and that arise out of the improvement on which the second tier subcontractor worked or furnished materials. A second tier subcontractor, to the extent of the second tier subcontractor's lien provided in this subdivision, shall also be entitled to be subrogated to the lien of the first tier subcontractor with whom the second tier contractor dealt provided for in subdivision (1) of this section and shall be entitled to perfect it by notice of claim of lien upon funds to the extent of the claim.

(3)   A third tier subcontractor who furnished labor, materials, or rental equipment at the site of the improvement shall be entitled to a lien upon funds that are owed to the second tier subcontractor with whom the third tier subcontractor dealt and that arise out of the improvement on which the third tier subcontractor worked or furnished materials. A third tier subcontractor, to the extent of the third tier subcontractor's lien upon funds provided in this subdivision, shall also be entitled to be subrogated to the lien upon funds of the second tier subcontractor with whom the third tier contractor dealt and to the lien upon funds of the first tier subcontractor with whom the second tier subcontractor dealt to the extent that the second tier subcontractor is entitled to be subrogated thereto, and in either case shall be entitled to perfect the same by notice of claim of lien upon funds to the extent of the claim.

(4)   Subcontractors more remote than the third tier who furnished labor, materials, or rental equipment at the site of the improvement shall be entitled to a lien upon funds that are owed to the person with whom they dealt and that arise out of the improvement on which they furnished labor, materials, or rental equipment, but such remote tier subcontractor shall not be entitled to subrogation to the rights of other persons.

(5)   The liens upon funds granted under this section shall secure amounts earned by the lien claimant as a result of having furnished labor, materials, or rental equipment at the site of the improvement under the contract to improve real property, including interest at the legal rate provided in G.S. 245, whether or not such amounts are due and whether or not performance or delivery is complete. In the event insufficient funds are retained to satisfy all lien claimants, subcontractor lien claimants may recover the interest due under this subdivision on a pro rata basis, but in no event shall interest due under this subdivision increase the liability of the obligor under G.S. 44A20.

(6)   A lien upon funds granted under this section is perfected upon the giving of notice of claim of lien upon funds in writing to the obligor as provided in G.S. 44A19 and shall be effective upon the obligor's receipt of the notice. The subrogation rights of a first, second, or third tier subcontractor to the claim of lien on real property of the contractor created by Part 1 of Article 2 of this Chapter are perfected as provided in G.S. 44A23. (1971, c. 880, s. 1; 1985, c. 702, s. 3; 1995 (Reg. Sess., 1996), c. 607, s. 3; 2005229, s. 1.)

§ 44A19. Notice of claim of lien upon funds.

(a)   Notice of a claim of lien upon funds shall set forth all of the following information:

(1)   The name and address of the person claiming the lien upon funds.

(2)   A general description of the real property improved.

(3)   The name and address of the person with whom the lien claimant contracted to improve real property.

(4)   The name and address of each person against or through whom subrogation rights are claimed.

(5)   A general description of the contract and the person against whose interest the lien upon funds is claimed.

(6)   The amount of the lien upon funds claimed by the lien claimant under the contract.

(b)   All notices of claims of liens upon funds by first, second, or third tier subcontractors must be given using a form substantially as follows:

NOTICE OF CLAIM OF LIEN UPON FUNDS BY FIRST, SECOND, OR THIRD TIER SUBCONTRACTOR

To:

1. _____, owner of property involved.

   (Name and address)

2. _____, general contractor.

   (Name and address)

3. _____, first tier subcontractor against or through whom subrogation is claimed, if any.

   (Name and address)

4. _____, second tier subcontractor against or through whom subrogation is claimed, if any.

   (Name and address)

General description of real property where labor performed or material furnished:

_____

_____

General description of undersigned lien claimant's contract including the names of the parties thereto:

_____

_____

The amount of lien upon funds claimed pursuant to the above described contract:

$ _____

The undersigned lien claimant gives this notice of claim of lien upon funds pursuant to North Carolina law and claims all rights of subrogation to which he is entitled under Part 2 of Article 2 of Chapter 44A of the General Statutes of North Carolina.

Dated _____

_____, Lien Claimant

_____

(Address)

(c)   All notices of claims of liens upon funds by subcontractors more remote than the third tier must be given using a form substantially as follows:

NOTICE OF CLAIM OF LIEN UPON FUNDS BY SUBCONTRACTOR MORE REMOTE THAN THE THIRD TIER

To:

_____, person holding funds against which lien upon funds is claimed.

(Name and Address)

General description of real property where labor performed or material furnished:

_____

_____

General description of undersigned lien claimant's contract including the names of the parties thereto:

_____

_____

The amount of lien upon funds claimed pursuant to the above described contract: $ _____

The undersigned lien claimant gives this notice of claim of lien upon funds pursuant to North Carolina law and claims all rights to which he or she is entitled under Part 2 of Article 2 of Chapter 44A of the General Statutes of North Carolina.

Dated: _____

_____, Lien Claimant

_____

(Address)

(d) Notices of claims of lien upon funds under this section shall be served upon the obligor by personal delivery or in any manner authorized by Rule 4 of the North Carolina Rules of Civil Procedure. A copy of the notice of claim of lien upon funds shall be attached to any claim of lien on real property filed pursuant to G.S. 44A20(d) or G.S. 44A23.

(e) Notices of claims of lien upon funds shall not be filed with the clerk of superior court and shall not be indexed, docketed, or recorded in any way as to affect title to any real property, except a notice of a claim of lien upon funds may be filed with the clerk of superior court under either of the following circumstances:

    (1) When the notice of claim of lien upon funds is attached to a claim of lien on real property filed pursuant to G.S. 44A20(d) or G.S. 44A23.

    (2) When the notice of claim of lien upon funds is filed by the obligor for the purpose of discharging the claim of lien upon funds in accordance with G.S. 44A20(e).

(f) Filing a notice of claim of lien upon funds pursuant to subsection (e) of this section is not a violation of G.S. 44A12.1. (1971, c. 880, s. 1; 1985, c. 702, s. 1; 2005229, s. 1.)

§ 44A20. Duties and liability of obligor.

(a) Upon receipt of the notice of claim of lien upon funds provided for in this Article, the obligor shall be under a duty to retain any funds subject to the lien or liens upon funds under this Article up to the total amount of such liens upon funds as to which notices of claims of lien upon funds have been received.

(b) If, after the receipt of the notice of claim of lien upon funds to the obligor, the obligor makes further payments to a contractor or subcontractor against whose interest the lien or liens upon funds are claimed, the lien upon funds shall continue upon the funds in the hands of the contractor or subcontractor who received the payment, and in addition the obligor shall be personally liable to the person or persons entitled to liens upon funds up to the amount of such wrongful payments, not exceeding the total claims with respect to which the notice of claim of lien upon funds was received prior to payment.

(c)   If an obligor makes a payment after receipt of notice of claim of lien on funds and incurs personal liability under subsection (b) of this section, the obligor shall be entitled to reimbursement and indemnification from the party receiving such payment.

(d)   If the obligor is an owner of the property being improved, the lien claimant shall be entitled to a claim of lien upon real property upon the interest of the obligor in the real property to the extent of the owner's personal liability under subsection (b) of this section, which claim of lien on real property shall be enforced only in the manner set forth in G.S. 44A7 through G.S. 44A16 and which claim of lien on real property shall be entitled to the same priorities and subject to the same filing requirements and periods of limitation applicable to the contractor. The claim of lien on real property is perfected as of the time set forth in G.S. 44A10 upon the filing of the claim of lien on real property pursuant to G.S. 44A12. The claim of lien on real property shall be in the form set out in G.S. 44A12(c) and shall contain, in addition, a copy of the notice of claim of lien upon funds given pursuant to G.S. 44A19 as an exhibit together with proof of service thereof by affidavit, and shall state the grounds the lien claimant has to believe that the obligor is personally liable for the debt under subsection (b) of this section.

(e)   A notice of claim of lien upon funds under G.S. 44A19 may be filed by the obligor with the clerk of superior court in each county where the real property upon which the filed notice of claim of lien upon funds is located for the purpose of discharging the notice of claim of lien upon funds by any of the methods described in G.S. 44A16.

(f)   A bond deposited under this section to discharge a filed notice of claim of lien upon funds shall be effective to discharge any claim of lien on real property filed by the same lien claimant pursuant to subsection (d) of this section or G.S. 44A23 and shall further be effective to discharge any notices of claims of lien upon funds served by lower tier subcontractors or any claims of lien on real property filed by lower tier subcontractors pursuant to subsection (d) of this section or G.S. 44A23 claiming through or against the contractor or higher tier subcontractors up to the amount of the bond. (1971, c. 880, s. 1; 1985, c. 702, s. 2; 2005229, s. 1.)

§ 44A21. Pro rata payments.

(a)   Where the obligor is a contractor or subcontractor and the funds in the hands of the obligor and the obligor's personal liability, if any, under G.S. 44A20 are less than the amount of valid liens upon funds that have been received by the obligor under this Article, the parties entitled to liens upon funds shall share the funds on a pro rata basis.

(b)   Where the obligor is an owner and the funds in the hands of the obligor and the obligor's personal liability, if any, under G.S. 44A20 are less than the sum of the amount of valid claims of liens upon funds that have been received by the obligor under this Article and the amount of the valid claims of liens on real property upon the owner's property filed by the subcontractors with the clerk of superior court under G.S. 44A23, the parties entitled to liens upon funds and the parties entitled to subrogation claims of liens on real property upon the owner's property shall share the funds on a pro rata basis. (1971, c. 880, s. 1; 1998217, s. 4(d); 2005229, s. 1.)

§ 44A22. Priority of liens upon funds.

Liens upon funds perfected under this Article have priority over all other interests or claims theretofore or thereafter created or suffered in the funds by the person against whose interest the lien upon funds is asserted, including, but not limited to, liens arising from garnishment, attachment, levy, judgment, assignments, security interests, and any other type of transfer, whether voluntary or involuntary. Any person who receives payment from an obligor in bad faith with knowledge of a lien upon funds shall take such payment subject to the lien upon funds. (1971, c. 880, s. 1; 2005229, s. 1.)

§ 44A23. Contractor's claim of lien on real property; perfection of subrogation rights of subcontractor.

(a)   First tier subcontractor.—A first tier subcontractor, who gives notice of claim of lien upon funds as provided in this Article, may, to the extent of this claim, enforce the claim of lien on real property of the contractor created by Part 1 of this Article. The manner of such enforcement shall be as provided by G.S. 44A7 through 44A16. The claim of lien on real property is perfected as of the time set forth in G.S. 44A10 upon filing of the claim of lien on real property pursuant to G.S. 44A12. Upon the filing of the claim of lien on real property, with the notice of claim of lien upon funds attached, and the commencement of the action, no action of the contractor shall be effective to prejudice the rights of the subcontractor without his written consent.

(b)   Second or third subcontractor.—

   (1)   A second or third tier subcontractor, who gives notice of claim of lien upon funds as provided in this Article, may, to the extent of his claim, enforce the claim of lien on real property of the contractor created by Part 1 of Article 2 of the Chapter except when:

      a.   The contractor, within 30 days following the date the building permit is issued for the improvement of the real property involved, posts on the property in a visible location adjacent to the posted building permit and files in the office of the clerk of superior court in each county wherein the real property to be improved is located, a completed and signed notice of contract form and the second or third tier subcontractor fails to serve upon the contractor a completed and signed notice of subcontract form by the same means of service as described in G.S. 44A19(d); or

      b.   After the posting and filing of a signed notice of contract and the service upon the contractor of a signed notice of subcontract, the contractor serves upon the second or third tier subcontractor, within five days following each subsequent payment, by the same means of service as described in G.S. 44A19(d), the written notice of payment setting forth the date of payment and the period for which payment is made as requested in the notice of subcontract form set forth herein.

   (2)   The form of the notice of contract to be so utilized under this section shall be substantially as follows and the fee for filing the same with the clerk of superior court shall be the same as charged for filing a claim of lien on real property:

NOTICE OF CONTRACT

   (1)   Name and address of the Contractor:

   (2)   Name and address of the owner of the real property at the time this Notice of Contract is recorded:

   (3)   General description of the real property to be improved (street address, tax map lot and block number, reference to recorded instrument, or any other description that reasonably identifies the real property):

   (4)   Name and address of the person, firm or corporation filing this Notice of Contract:

Dated: _____

                                                            _____

                                                                        Contractor

Filed this the _____ day of _____, _____.

_____

Clerk of Superior Court

(3)   The form of the notice of subcontract to be so utilized under this section shall be substantially as follows:

NOTICE OF SUBCONTRACT

(1)   Name and address of the subcontractor:

(2)   General description of the real property where the labor was performed or the material was furnished (street address, tax map lot and block number, reference to recorded instrument, or any description that reasonably identifies the real property):

(3)

    (i)   General description of the subcontractor's contract, including the names of the parties thereto:

    (ii)   General description of the labor and material performed and furnished thereunder:

(4)   Request is hereby made by the undersigned subcontractor that he be notified in writing by the contractor of, and within five days following, each subsequent payment by the contractor to the first tier subcontractor for labor performed or material furnished at the improved real property within the above descriptions of such in paragraph (2) and subparagraph (3)(ii), respectively, the date payment was made and the period for which payment is made.

Dated: _____

_____

Subcontractor

(4)   The manner of such enforcement shall be as provided by G.S. 44A7 through G.S. 44A16. The lien is perfected as of the time set forth in G.S. 44A10 upon the filing of a claim of lien on real property pursuant to G.S. 44A12. Upon the filing of the claim of lien on real property, with the notice of claim of lien upon funds attached, and the commencement of the action, no action of the contractor shall be effective to prejudice the rights of the second or third tier subcontractor without his written consent. (1971, c. 880, s. 1; 1985, c. 702, s. 4; 1991 (Reg. Sess., 1992), c. 1010, s. 1; 1993, c. 553, s. 13; 1997456, s. 27; 1999456, s. 59; 2005229, s. 1.)

Part 3. Criminal Sanctions for Furnishing a False Statement in Connection with Improvement to Real Property.

§ 44A24. **False statement a misdemeanor.**

If any contractor or other person receiving payment from an obligor for an improvement to real property or from a purchaser for a conveyance of real property with improvements shall knowingly furnish to such obligor, purchaser, or to a lender who obtains a security interest in said real property, or to a title insurance company insuring title to such real property, a false written statement of the sums due or claimed to be due for labor or material furnished at the site of improvements to such real property, then such contractor, subcontractor or other person shall be guilty of a Class 1 misdemeanor. Upon conviction and in the event the court shall grant any defendant a suspended sentence, the court may in its discretion include as a condition of such suspension a provision that the defendant shall reimburse the party who suffered loss on such conditions as the court shall determine are proper.

The elements of the offense herein stated are the furnishing of the false written statement with knowledge that it is false and the subsequent or simultaneous receipt of payment from an obligor or purchaser, and in any prosecution hereunder it shall not be necessary for the State to prove that the obligor, purchaser, lender or title insurance company relied upon the false statement or that any person was injured thereby. (1971, c. 880, s. 1.1; 1973, c. 991; 1993, c. 539, s. 406; 1994, Ex. Sess., c. 24, s. 14(c).)

Appendix L: Pesticide Application Law

Article 52. Pesticide Board.

Part 1. Pesticide Control Program: Organization and Functions.

§ 143-434. Short title. This Article may be cited as the North Carolina Pesticide Law of 1971. (1971, c. 832, s. 1.)

§ 143-435. Preamble.

(a) The Legislative Research Commission was directed by House Resolution 1392 of the 1969 General Assembly "to study agricultural and other pesticides," and to report its findings and recommendations to the 1971 General Assembly. Pursuant to said Resolution a report was prepared and adopted by the Legislative Research Commission in 1970 concerning pesticides. In this report the Legislative Research Commission made the following findings concerning the use and effects of pesticides and the need for legislation concerning control of pesticide use, of which the General Assembly hereby takes cognizance:

(1) The use of chemical pesticides has developed since the 1940's into a major, new billion-dollar industry. Pesticides have bettered the lot of mankind in many ways and especially have assisted the farmer by their contribution to a stable and inexpensive supply of high quality food, fiber and forest products. The control of insects, fungi and other pests is essential to the public health and welfare and specifically to the prevention of disease, to the production and preservation of food, fiber, and forests and to the protection of other aspects of modern civilization.

(2) The use of pesticides for these important purposes is currently a matter of serious public concern and their use in some instances presents risks to man and the environment which must be weighed against the benefits of those uses in the overall public interest. Evidence is accumulating that extensive use of persistent pesticides poses hazards to health and the environment. Environmental problems resulting from the use, overuse and misapplication of some chemicals, and the disposal of unused chemicals and containers, have grown to the point where contamination of the environment is approaching significant proportions. There is concern among scientists and public health personnel about the long-term chronic effects of pesticide pollution on human health. Contamination by DDT has been shown to be global in extent. Moreover, recent experience in North Carolina and elsewhere has shown that the more toxic but less persistent pesticides cannot safely be substituted for the persistent "hard" pesticides without stringent safeguards.

(3) More extensive observation, study and monitoring of the effectiveness and the use of pesticides and of undesirable side effects on man and on the environment and of their relative importance for the overall public health and welfare are desirable in the public interest.

(4) Continued and strengthened control of the quality of pesticides and the control of labeling claims, direction for use and warnings are necessary for the protection of the purchasing public, including the household consumer, the farmer and other users.

(5) No existing legislation in North Carolina effectively limits or controls the use of pesticides. Misuse and misapplication of pesticides, while effectively controlled by law with respect to structural pest control operators, is not adequately controlled with respect to some other major groups of pesticide applicators. Careless disposal of unused pesticides and contaminated containers

is not controlled by law, and no North Carolina legislation requires that pesticide dealers, who are the principal source of advice for many pesticide users, be qualified to give advice or be held responsible for their advice. These gaps in legal control of pesticides are important and should be remedied.

(b)   The purpose of this Article is to regulate in the public interest the use, application, sale, disposal and registration of insecticides, fungicides, herbicides, defoliants, desiccants, plant growth regulators, nematicides, rodenticides, and any other pesticides designated by the North Carolina Pesticide Board. New pesticides are continually being discovered or synthesized which are valuable for the control of insects, fungi, weeds, nematodes, rodents, and for use as defoliants, desiccants, plant regulators and related purposes. However, such pesticides may be ineffective or may seriously injure health, property, or wildlife if not properly used. Pesticides may injure man or animals, either by direct poisoning or by gradual accumulation of poisons in the tissues. Crops or other plants may also be injured by their improper use. The drifting or washing of pesticides into streams or lakes can cause appreciable danger to aquatic life. A pesticide applied for the purpose of killing pests in a crop, which is not itself injured by the pesticide, may drift and injure other crops or nontarget organisms with which it comes in contact. In furtherance of the findings and recommendations of the Legislative Research Commission, it is hereby declared to be the policy of the State of North Carolina that for the protection of the health, safety, and welfare of the people of this State, and for the promotion of a more secure, healthy and safe environment for all the people of the State, the future sale, use and application of pesticides shall be regulated, supervised and controlled by the State in the manner herein provided. (1971, c. 832, s. 1.)

§ 143-436. North Carolina Pesticide Board; creation and organization.

(a)   There is hereby established the North Carolina Pesticide Board which, together with the Commissioner of Agriculture, shall be responsible for carrying out the provisions of this Article.

(b)   The Pesticide Board shall consist of seven members, to be appointed by the Governor, as follows:

   (1)   One member each representing the North Carolina Department of Agriculture and Consumer Services, the State Health Director or his designee, and one member from an environmental protection agency in the Department of Environment and Natural Resources. The persons so selected may be either members of a policy board or departmental officials or employees.

   (2)   A representative of the agricultural chemical industry.

   (3)   A person directly engaged in agricultural production.

   (4)   Two at-large members, from fields of endeavor other than those enumerated in subdivisions (2) and (3) of this subsection, one of whom shall be a nongovernmental conservationist.

(c)   The members of the Pesticide Board shall serve staggered four-year terms. Of the persons originally appointed, the members representing State agencies shall serve two-year terms, and the four at-large members shall serve four-year terms. All members shall hold their offices until their successors are appointed and qualified. Any vacancy occurring in the membership of the Board prior to the expiration of the term shall be filled by appointment by the Governor for the remainder of the unexpired term. The Governor may at any time remove any member from the Board for gross inefficiency, neglect of duty, malfeasance, misfeasance, or nonfeasance in office. Each appointment to fill a vacancy in the membership of the Board shall be of a person having the same credentials as his predecessor.

(d)   The Board shall select its chair from its own membership, to serve for a term of two years. The chair shall have a full vote. Any vacancy occurring in the chair's position shall be filled by the Board for the remainder of the term. The Board may select such other officers as it deems necessary.

(e)   Any action of the Board shall require at least four concurring votes.

(f) The members of the Board who are not officers or employees of the State shall receive for their services the per diem and compensation prescribed in G.S. 1385. (1971, c. 832, s. 1; 1973, c. 476, s. 128; 1989, c. 727, s. 170; 1997-261, s. 90; 1997-443, s. 11A.97.)

§ 143-437. Pesticide Board; functions.

The Pesticide Board shall be the governing board for the programs of pesticide management and control set forth in this Article. The Pesticide Board shall have the following powers and duties under this Article:

(1) To adopt rules and regulations and make policies for the programs set forth in this Article.

(2) To carry out a program of planning, environmental and biological monitoring, and of investigation into long-range needs and problems concerning pesticides. In order to encourage the cooperation of private property owners needed to implement the provisions of this subdivision, the Board may enter into agreements with private property owners to conduct sampling, testing, monitoring, and related activities on their property. Information obtained pursuant to these agreements shall not be disclosed in a manner that would permit the identification of an individual property owner unless the property owner has given permission to disclose the information.

(3) To collect, analyze and disseminate information necessary for the effective operation of the programs set forth in this Article.

(4) To provide professional advice to public and private agencies and citizens of the State on matters relating to pesticides, in cooperation with other State agencies, with professional groups, and with North Carolina State University and other educational institutions.

(5) To accept gifts and devises, and with the approval of the Governor to apply for and accept grants from the federal government and its agencies and from any foundation, corporation, association or individual, and may comply with the terms, conditions and limitations of the grant, in order to accomplish any of the purposes of the Board, such grant funds to be expended pursuant to the Executive Budget Act.

(6) To inform and advise the Governor on matters involving pesticides, and to prepare and recommend to the Governor and the General Assembly any legislation which may be deemed proper for the management and control of pesticides in North Carolina.

(7) To make annual reports to the Governor and to make such other investigations and reports as may be requested by the Governor or the General Assembly.

(8) To exempt any federal or State agency from any provision of this Article if it is determined by the Board that emergency conditions exist which require exemption. (1971, c. 832, s. 1; 1977, c. 199; 1979, c. 448, s. 14; 1995, c. 445, s. 1; 2011-284, s. 94.)

§ 143-438. Commissioner of Agriculture to administer and enforce Article.

The Commissioner of Agriculture shall have the following powers and duties under this Article:

(1) To administer and enforce the provisions of this Article.

(2) To attend all meetings of the Pesticide Board, but without power to vote (unless he be designated as the ex officio member of the Board from the Department of Agriculture and Consumer Services).

(3) To keep an accurate and complete record of all Board meetings and hearings, and to have legal custody of all books, papers, documents and other records of the Board.

(4) To assign and reassign the administrative and enforcement duties and functions assigned to him in this Article to one or more of the divisions and other units within the Department of Agriculture and Consumer Services.

(5) To direct the work of the personnel employed by the Board and of the personnel of the Department of Agriculture and Consumer Services who have responsibilities concerning the programs set forth in this Article.

(6)   To delegate to any division head or other officer or employee of the Department of Agriculture and Consumer Services any of the powers and duties given to the Department by statute or by the rules, regulations and procedures established pursuant to this Article.

(7)   To perform such other duties as the Board may from time to time direct. (1971, c. 832, s. 1; 1997-261, s. 91.)

§ 143-439. Pesticide Advisory Committee; creation and functions.

(a)   There is hereby authorized the establishment of the Pesticide Advisory Committee, which shall assist the Board and the Commissioner in an advisory capacity on matters which may be submitted to it by the Board or the Commissioner, including technical questions and the development of rules and regulations.

(b)   The Pesticide Advisory Committee shall consist of: three practicing farmers; one conservationist (at large); one ecologist (at large); one representative of the pesticide industry; one representative of agribusiness (at large); one local health director; three members of the North Carolina State University School of Agriculture and Life Sciences, at least one of which shall be from the area of wildlife or biology; one member representing the North Carolina Department of Agriculture and Consumer Services; one member representing the Department of Environment and Natural Resources; the State Health Director or his designee; one representative of a public utility or railroad company which uses pesticides; one representative of the Board of Transportation; one member of the North Carolina Agricultural Aviation Association; one member of the general public (at large); one member actively engaged in forest pest management; and one member representing the Division of Waste Management of the Department of Environment and Natural Resources. Each State agency represented [representative] on the Committee shall be appointed by the head of the agency. Other members of the Committee shall be appointed by the Board.

(c)   Members of the Pesticide Advisory Committee shall serve at the pleasure of the Board. The members who are not officers or employees of the State shall receive regular State subsistence and travel expenses. (1971, c. 832, s. 1; 1973, c. 476, s. 128; c. 507, s. 5; 1975, c. 824; 1987, c. 559, s. 1; 1989, c. 727, s. 171; 1989 (Reg. Sess., 1990), c. 1004, s. 14; 1995 (Reg. Sess., 1996), c. 743, s. 19; 1997-261, s. 109; 1997-443, s. 11A.119(a).)

Part 2. Regulation of the Use of Pesticides.

§ 143-440. Restricted use pesticides regulated.

(a)   The Board may, by regulation after a public hearing, adopt and from time to time revise a list of restricted use pesticides for the State or for designated areas within the State. The Board may designate any pesticide or device as a "restricted use pesticide" upon the grounds that, in the judgment of the Board (either because of its persistence, its toxicity, or otherwise) it is so hazardous or injurious to persons, pollinating insects, animals, crops, wildlife, lands, or the environment, other than the pests it is intended to prevent, destroy, control, or mitigate that additional restriction on its sale, purpose, use or possession are required.

(b)   The Board may include in any such restricted use regulation the time and conditions of sale, distribution, or use of such restricted use pesticides, may prohibit the use of any restricted use pesticide for designated purposes or at designated times; may require the purchaser or user to certify that restricted use pesticides will be used only as labeled or as further restricted by regulation; may require the certification and recertification of private applicators, and charge a fee of up to ten dollars ($10.00), with the fee set at a level to make the certification/recertification program self-supporting, and, after opportunity for a hearing, may suspend, revoke or modify the certification for violation of any provision of this Article, or any rule or regulation adopted thereunder; may adopt rules to classify private applicators; and may, if it deems it necessary to carry out the provisions of this Part, require that any or all restricted use pesticides shall be purchased, possessed, or used only under permit of the Board and under its direct supervision in certain areas and/or under certain conditions or in certain quantities or concentrations except that any person licensed to sell such pesticides may purchase and possess such pesticides without a permit. The

Board may require all persons issued such permits to maintain records as to the use of the restricted use pesticides. The Board may authorize the use of restricted use pesticides by persons licensed under the North Carolina Structural Pest Control Act without a permit. A nonrefundable fee of ten dollars ($10.00) shall be charged for each examination required by this section. This examination fee is in addition to the certification or recertification fee, and any other fee authorized pursuant to any other provision of Article 4C of Chapter 106 of the General Statutes.

(c)   A fee of fifty dollars ($50.00) shall be charged for examination of individuals seeking to be designated as Worker Protection Designated Trainers, in accordance with provisions of the Federal Worker Protection Standard set forth in 40 C.F.R. Part 170, and subsequent amendments to those regulations. (1971, c. 832, s. 1; 1979, c. 448, s. 1; 1981, c. 592, s. 1; 1987, c. 559, s. 2; c. 846; 2010-31, s. 11.1(a); 2014-100, s. 13.10(a); 2014-103, s. 16.)

§ 143-441. Handling, storage and disposal of pesticides.

(a)   The Board may adopt regulations:

(1)   Concerning the handling, transport, storage (which may include security precautions), display or distribution of pesticides, and concerning the disposal of pesticides and pesticide containers.

(2)   Restricting or prohibiting the use of certain types of containers or packages for specific pesticides. These restrictions may apply to type of construction, strength, and/or size to alleviate danger of spillage, breakage, or misuse.

(b)   No person shall handle, transport, store, display, or distribute pesticides in such a manner as to endanger man and his environment or to endanger food, feed, or any other products that may be transported, stored, displayed, or distributed with pesticides, or in any manner contrary to the regulations of the Board.

(c)   No person shall dispose of, discard, or store any pesticides or pesticide containers in such a manner as may cause injury to humans, vegetation, crops, livestock, wildlife, or to pollute any water supply or waterway, or in any manner contrary to the regulations of the Board. (1971, c. 832, s. 1.)

§ 143-442. Registration.

(a)   Every pesticide prior to being distributed, sold, or offered for sale within this State or delivered for transportation or transported in intrastate commerce or between points within this State through any point outside this State shall be registered in the office of the Board, and such registration shall be renewed annually before January 1 for the ensuing calendar year. Beginning in 1988, the Board may by rule adopt a system of staggered three-year registrations. The applicant for registration shall file with the Board a statement that includes all of the following:

(1)   The name and address of the applicant and the name and address of the person whose name will appear on the label, if other than the applicant.

(2)   The name of the pesticide.

(3)   A complete copy of the labeling accompanying the pesticide and a statement of all claims to be made for it including directions for use.

(4)   If requested by the Board, a full description of the tests made and the results thereof upon which the claims are based.

(5)   In the case of renewal of registration, a statement with respect to information which is different from that furnished when the pesticide was last registered.

(6)   Repealed by Session Laws 2011-239, s. 1, effective June 23, 2011, and applicable to applications for registration or renewals of registration filed on or after that date.

(7)   Any other information needed by the Board to determine the amount of annual assessment payable by the applicant.

(b)   The applicant shall pay an annual registration fee of one hundred fifty dollars ($150.00) plus an additional annual assessment for each brand or grade of pesticide registered. The annual assessment shall be fifty dollars ($50.00) if the applicant's gross sales of the pesticide in this State for the preceding 12 months for the period ending September 30th were more than five thousand dollars ($5,000.00) and twenty-five dollars ($25.00) if gross sales were less than five thousand dollars ($5,000.00). An additional two hundred dollars ($200.00) delinquent registration penalty shall be assessed against the registrant for each brand or grade of pesticide which is marketed in North Carolina prior to registration as required by this Article. In the case of multiyear registration, the annual fee and additional assessment for each year shall be paid at the time of the initial registration. The Board shall give a pro rata refund of the registration fee and additional assessment to the registrant in the event that registration is canceled by the Board or by the United States Environmental Protection Agency.

(c)   The Board, when it deems necessary in the administration of this Article, may require the submission of the complete formula of any pesticide.

(d)   If the pesticide is properly registered with the United States Environmental Protection Agency and is in compliance with the requirements of G.S. 143-443, the Board shall register the pesticide. Provided, however, that if it does not appear to the Board that the article is such as to warrant the proposed claims for it or if the article and its labeling and other material required to be submitted do not comply with the provisions of this Part, it shall not register the article and in turn shall notify the applicant of the manner in which the article, labeling, or other material required to be submitted fail to comply. The Board may suspend or cancel the registration of a pesticide when the pesticide or its labeling does not comply with this Part.

(e)   The Board is authorized and empowered to refuse to register, or to cancel the registration of any brands and grades of pesticides as herein provided, if the registrant fails or refuses to comply with the provisions of this Part, or any rules and regulations promulgated thereunder, or, upon satisfactory proof that the registrant or applicant has been guilty of fraudulent and deceptive practices in the evasions or attempted evasions of the provisions of this Part, or any rules and regulations promulgated thereunder. The Board may require the manufacturer or distributor of any pesticide, for which registration has been refused, cancelled, suspended or voluntarily discontinued or which has been found adulterated or deficient in its active ingredient, to remove such pesticide from the marketplace.

(f)   Notwithstanding any other provisions of this Part, registration is not required in the case of a pesticide shipped from one plant within this State to another plant within this State operated by the same person.

(g)   Any pesticide declared to be discontinued by the registrant must be registered by the registrant for one full year after distribution is discontinued. Any pesticide in channels of distribution after the aforesaid registration period may be confiscated and disposed of by the Board, unless the pesticide is acceptable for registration and is continued to be registered by the manufacturer or the person offering the pesticide for wholesale or retail sale. Provided, however, this subsection shall not apply to any brand or grade of pesticide which the Board determines does not remain in channels of distribution due to method of sale by registrant directly to users thereof.

(h)   A pesticide may be registered by the Board for experimental use, including use to control wild animal or bird populations, even though the Wildlife Resources Commission may not have concurred in the declaration of the animal or bird populations as pests under the terms of Article 22A of Chapter 113 of the General Statutes.

(i)   The Board shall be empowered to set forth criteria for determining when a given product constitutes a different or separate brand or grade of pesticide.

(j)   Each manufacturer, distributor or registrant of a pesticide shall supervise the activities of any employee or agent to prevent the making of deceptive or misleading statements about the pesticide. (1971, c. 832, s. 1; 1973, c. 389, ss. 1, 7; 1975, c. 425, ss. 1, 2; 1979, c. 448, ss. 2, 3; c. 830, s. 10; 1981, c. 592, s. 2; 1987, c. 559, ss. 37; c. 827, s. 39; 1989, c. 544, s. 13; 1993, c. 481, ss. 1.1, 2; 1995, c. 445, s. 2; 2003-284, s. 35.4(e); 2009-451, s. 11.2; 2011-239, s. 1.)

§ 143-443. Miscellaneous prohibited acts.

(a)   It shall be unlawful for any person to distribute, sell, or offer for sale within this State or deliver for transportation or transport in intrastate commerce or between points within this State through any point outside this State any of the following:

(1)   Any pesticide which has not been registered pursuant to the provisions of G.S. 143-442, or any pesticide if any of the claims made for it or any of the directions for its use differ in substance from the representations made in connection with the registration, or if the composition of a pesticide differs from its composition as represented in connection with its registration: Except that, in the discretion of the Board, a change in the labeling or formula of a pesticide may be made within a registration period without requiring reregistration of the product.

(2)   Any pesticide unless it is in the registrant's or the manufacturer's unbroken immediate container, and there is affixed to such container, and to the outside container or wrapper of the retail package, if there be one through which the required information on the immediate container cannot be clearly read, a label bearing:

a.   The name and address of the manufacturer, registrant, or person for whom manufactured;

b.   The name, brand, or trademark under which said article is sold; and

c.   The net weight or measure of the content subject, however, to such reasonable variations as the Board may permit.

(3)   Any pesticide which contains any substance or substances in quantities highly toxic to man, determined as provided in G.S. 143-444, unless the label shall bear, in addition to any other matter required by this Part:

a.   The skull and crossbones;

b.   The word "poison" prominently, in red, on a background of distinctly contrasting color; and

c.   A statement of an antidote for the pesticide.

(4)   The pesticides commonly known as standard lead arsenate, basic lead arsenate, calcium arsenate, magnesium arsenate, zinc arsenate, zinc arsenite, sodium fluoride, sodium fluosilicate, and barium fluosilicate unless they have been distinctly colored or discolored as provided by regulations issued in accordance with this Part, or any other white or lightly colored pesticide which the Board, after investigation of and after public hearing on the necessity for such action for the protection of the public health and the feasibility of such coloration or discoloration, shall, by regulation, require to be distinctly colored or discolored; unless it has been so colored or discolored, provided, that the Board may exempt any pesticide to the extent that it is intended for a particular use or uses from the coloring or discoloring required or authorized by this section if the Board determines that such coloring or discoloring for such use or uses is not necessary for the protection of the public health.

(5)   Any pesticide which is adulterated or misbranded, (or any device which is misbranded).

(6)   Any pesticide in containers violating regulations adopted pursuant to G.S. 143-441. Pesticides found in containers which are unsafe due to damage or defective construction may be seized and impounded.

(b)   It shall be unlawful:

(1)   For any person to detach, alter, deface, or destroy, in whole or in part, any label or labeling provided for in this Part or regulations promulgated hereunder, or to add any substance to, or take any substance from a pesticide in a manner that may defeat the purpose of this Part;

(2)   For any person to use for his own advantage or to reveal, other than to the Board or proper officials or employees of the State or federal government or to the courts of this State in response to a subpoena, or to physicians, or in emergencies to pharmacists and other qualified persons, for use in the preparation of antidotes, any information relative to formulas of products acquired by authority of G.S. 143-442.

(2a)   Repealed by Session Laws 1981, c. 592, s. 3.

(3)   For any person to use any pesticide in a manner inconsistent with its labeling.

(4)   For any person who contracts for the aerial application of a pesticide to permit the application of any pesticide that is designated on its labeling as toxic to bees without first notifying, based on available listings, the owner or operator of any apiary registered under the North Carolina Bee and Honey Act of 1977 that is within a distance designated by the Pesticide Board as necessary and appropriate to prevent damage or injury.

(5)   For any person to distribute, sell or offer for sale any restricted use pesticide to any dealer who does not hold a valid North Carolina Pesticide Dealer License.

(6)   For any person to assault, resist, impede, intimidate, or interfere with any State employee while that employee is engaged in the performance of his or her duties under this Article.

(7)   For any person to apply, for compensation, a pesticide that has not been registered pursuant to G.S. 143-442. (1971, c. 832, s. 1; 1975, c. 425, s. 3; 1979, c. 448, ss. 4, 5; 1981, c. 547; c. 592, ss. 3, 4; 1987, c. 559, s. 8; 1995, c. 445, s. 3.)

§ 143-444. Determinations.

The Board is authorized:

(1)   To declare as a pest any form of plant or animal life or virus which is injurious to plants, man, domestic animals, articles, or substances;

(2)   To determine whether pesticides are highly toxic to man; and

(3)   To determine standards of coloring or discoloring for pesticides, and to subject pesticides to the requirements of G.S. 143-443(a)(4). (1971, c. 832, s. 1.)

§ 143-445. Exemptions.

(a)   The penalties provided for violations of G.S. 143-443(a) shall not apply to:

(1)   Any carrier while lawfully engaged in transporting pesticides within this State, if such carrier shall, upon request, permit the Board or its designated agent to copy all records showing the transactions in and movement of the articles;

(2)   Public officials of this State or local subdivisions thereof and the federal government engaged in the performance of their official duties;

(3)   The manufacturer or shipper of a pesticide for experimental use only,

        a.   By or under the supervision of an agency of this State or of the federal government authorized by law to conduct research in the field of pesticides, or

        b.   By others if the pesticide is not sold and if the container thereof is plainly and conspicuously marked "For experimental use only—Not to be sold," together with the manufacturer's name and address; (except that if a written permit has been obtained from the Board, pesticides may be sold for experimental purposes subject to such restrictions and conditions as may be set forth in the permit).

(b)   No article shall be deemed in violation of this Part when intended solely for export to a foreign country, and when prepared or packed according to the specifications or directions of the purchaser. If not so exported, all the provisions of this Part shall apply. (1971, c. 832, s. 1.)

§ 143-446. Samples; submissions.

(a)   The Board, or its agent, is authorized and directed to sample, test, inspect and make analyses of pesticides sold or offered for sale or distributed within this State, at time and place and to such an extent as it may deem necessary to determine whether such pesticides are in compliance with the provisions of this Article. The Board is authorized to adopt regulations concerning the collection and examination of samples (or devices), and to adopt regulations establishing tolerances providing for reasonable deviations from the guaranteed analysis.

(b)   The official analysis shall be made from the official sample. Official samples shall be collected from material that has been packaged, labeled and released for shipment. A sealed and identified sample, herein called "official check sample" shall be kept until the analysis is completed on the official sample, except that the registrant may obtain upon request a portion of said official sample. If the official analysis conforms with the provisions of this Part, the official check sample may be destroyed. If the official analysis does not conform with the provisions of this Part, then the official check sample shall be retained for a period of 90 days from the date of the certificate of analysis of the official sample.

(c)   The Board, of its own motion or upon complaint, may cause an examination to be made for the purpose of determining whether any pesticide complies with the requirements of this Part. If it shall appear from such examination that a pesticide fails to comply with the provisions of this Part, the Board may cause notice to be given to the offending person in the manner provided in G.S. 143-464, and the proceedings thereupon shall be as provided in such section; provided that pesticides may be seized and confiscated as provided in G.S. 143-447.

(d)   The Board shall, by publication in such manner as it may prescribe, give notice of all judgments entered in actions instituted under the authority of this Article. (1971, c. 832, s. 1; 1987, c. 559, s. 9.)

§ 143-447. Emergency suspensions; seizures.

(a)   The Board may order the summary suspension of the registration of a pesticide if it finds the suspension necessary to prevent an imminent hazard to the public, a nontarget organism, or a segment of the environment. In no event shall registration of a pesticide be construed as a defense to any charge of an offense prohibited under this Article.

(b)   It shall be the duty of the Board to issue and enforce a written or printed "stop sale, stop use, or removal" order to the owner or custodian of any lot of pesticide and for the owner or custodian to hold said lot at a designated place when the Board finds said pesticide is being offered or exposed for sale in violation of any of the provisions of this Article until the law has been complied with and said pesticide is released in writing by the Board or said violation has been otherwise legally disposed of by written authority. The Board shall release the pesticide so withdrawn when the requirements of the provisions of this Article have been complied with and upon payment of all costs and expenses incurred in connection with the withdrawal.

The Board may issue a "stop sale, use or removal order" to prevent or stop the use of a pesticide in a manner inconsistent with its labeling or to prevent or stop the disposal of a pesticide or a pesticide container in violation of this Article or the rules of the Board adopted thereunder.

(c)   Any pesticide (or device) that is distributed, sold, or offered for sale within this State or delivered for transportation or transported in intrastate commerce between points within this State through any point outside this State shall be liable to be proceeded against in superior court in any county of the State where it may be found and seized for confiscation by process or libel for condemnation:

(1)   In the case of a pesticide,

a.   If it is adulterated or misbranded,

b.   If it has not been registered under the provisions of G.S. 143-442, or has had its registration suspended or revoked or is the subject of a stop sale, stop use, or removal order,

    c.   If it fails to bear on its label the information required by this Part,

    d.   If it is a white or lightly colored pesticide and is not colored as required under this Part.

(2)   In the case of a device, if it is misbranded.

(d)   If the article is condemned, it shall, after entry of decree, be disposed of by destruction or sale as the court may direct and the proceeds, if such article is sold, less legal costs, shall be paid to the State Treasurer; provided that the article shall not be sold contrary to the provisions of this Part; and provided further that upon payment of costs and execution and delivery of a good and sufficient bond conditioned that the article shall not be disposed of unlawfully, the court may direct that said article be delivered to the owner thereof for relabeling or reprocessing or disposal, as the case may be.

(e)   When a decree of condemnation is entered against the article, court costs and fees and storage and other proper expenses shall be awarded against the person, if any, intervening as claimant of the article. (1971, c. 832, s. 1; 1979, c. 448, s. 6; 1981, c. 592, s. 5; 1987, c. 559, s. 10, c. 827, s. 41.)

Part 3. Pesticide Dealers.

§ 143-448. Licensing of pesticide dealers; fees.

(a)   No person shall act in the capacity of a pesticide dealer, or shall engage or offer to engage in the business of, advertise as, or assume to act as a pesticide dealer unless he is licensed annually as provided in this Part. A separate license and fee shall be obtained for each location or outlet from which restricted use pesticides are distributed, sold, held for sale, or offered for sale.

(b)   Applications for a pesticide dealer license shall be in the form and shall contain the information prescribed by the Board. Each application shall be accompanied by a nonrefundable fee of seventy-five dollars ($75.00). All licenses issued under this Part shall expire on December 31 of the year for which they are issued.

(c)   The license for a pesticide dealer may be renewed annually upon application to the Board, accompanied by a fee of seventy-five dollars ($75.00) for each license, on or before the first day of January of the calendar year for which the license is issued.

(d)   Repealed by Session Laws 1981, c. 592, s. 6.

(e)   Every licensed pesticide dealer who changes his address or place of business shall immediately notify the Board.

(f)   The Board shall issue to each applicant that satisfies the requirements of this Part a license which entitles the applicant to conduct the business described in the application for the calendar year for which the license is issued, unless the license is sooner revoked or suspended. (1971, c. 832, s. 1; 1981, c. 592, s. 6; 1987, c. 559, ss. 2, 11; 1989, c. 544, s. 11; 1995, c. 445, s. 4; 2003-284, ss. 35.4(b), 35.4(c); 2010-31, s. 11.1(b); 2011-145, s. 31.8(c).)

§ 143-449. Qualifications for pesticide dealer license; examinations.

(a)   An applicant for a license must present evidence satisfactory to the Board concerning his qualifications for such license.

(b)   Each applicant shall satisfy the Board as to his responsibility in carrying on the business of a pesticide dealer. Each applicant for an original license must demonstrate upon written, or written and oral, examination to be prescribed by the Board his knowledge of pesticides, their usefulness and their hazards; his competence as a pesticide dealer; and his knowledge of the laws and regulations governing the use and sale of pesticides. A nonrefundable fee of fifty dollars ($50.00) shall be charged for each examination required by this section. This examination fee is in addition to any fee authorized pursuant to any other provision of Article 4C of Chapter 106 of the General Statutes.

(c)   The Board shall by regulation:

    (1)   Designate what persons or class of persons shall be required to pass the examination in the case of a pesticide dealer operating more than one location, and in the case of an applicant that is a corporation, governmental unit or agency, or other organized group;

    (2)   Provide for renewal license examinations at intervals not more frequent than four years. (1971, c. 832, s. 1; 1975, c. 425, s. 4; 2010-31, s. 11.1(c).)

§ 143-450. Employees of pesticide dealers; dealer's responsibility.

(a)   Every licensed pesticide dealer shall submit to the Board, at such times as the Board or the Commissioner may prescribe, the names of all persons employed by him who sell or recommend "restricted use pesticides."

(b)   Each pesticide dealer shall be responsible for the actions of every person who acts as his employee or agent in the solicitation or sale of pesticides, and in all claims and recommendations for use or application of pesticides. (1971, c. 832, s. 1; 1979, c. 448, s. 7; 1987, c. 559, s. 2.)

§ 143-451. Denial, suspension and revocation of license.

(a)   The Board may deny, suspend, modify, or revoke a license issued under this Part if it finds that the applicant or licensee or his employee has committed any of the following acts, each of which is declared to be a violation of this Part:

    (1)   Made false or fraudulent claims through any media, misrepresenting the effect of materials or methods to be utilized or sold;

    (2)   Made a pesticide recommendation not in accordance with the label registered pursuant to this Article;

    (3)   Violated any provision of this Article or of any rule or regulation adopted by the Board or of any lawful order of the Board;

    (4)   Failed to pay the original or renewal license fee when due, and continued to sell restricted use pesticides without paying the license fee, or sold restricted use pesticides without a license;

    (5)   Was guilty of gross negligence, incompetency or misconduct in acting as a pesticide dealer;

    (6)   Refused or neglected to keep and maintain the records required by this Article, or to make reports when and as required, or refusing to make these records available for audit or inspection;

    (7)   Made false or fraudulent records, invoices, or reports;

    (8)   Used fraud or misrepresentation, or presented false information, in making an application for a license or renewal of a license, or in selling or offering to sell restricted use pesticides;

    (9)   Refused or neglected to comply with any limitations or restrictions on or in a duly issued license or permit;

    (10)   Aided or abetted a licensed or an unlicensed person to evade the provisions of this Article, combined or conspired with such a licensed or unlicensed person to evade the provisions of this Article, or allowed one's license to be used by an unlicensed person;

    (11)   Impersonated any state, county, or city inspector or official;

    (12)   Stored or disposed of containers or pesticides by means other than those prescribed on the label or adopted regulations.

    (13)   Provided or made available any restricted use pesticide to any person other than a certified private applicator, licensed pesticide applicator, certified structural pest control applicator, structural pest control licensee or an employee under the direct supervision of one of the aforementioned certified or licensed applicators.

(b)   Any licensee whose license is revoked under the provisions of this Article shall not be eligible to apply for a new license hereunder until such time has elapsed from the date of the order revoking said license as established by the Board (not to exceed two years), or if an appeal is taken from said order or revocation, not to exceed two years from the date of the order or final judgment sustaining said revocation. (1971, c. 832, s. 1; 1975, c. 425, ss. 6, 7; 1987, c. 559, ss. 2, 13, c. 827, s. 40.)

Part 4. Pesticide Applicators and Consultants.

§ 143-452. Licensing of pesticide applicators; fees.

(a)   No person shall engage in the business of pesticide applicator within this State at any time unless he is licensed annually as a pesticide applicator by the Board.

(b)   Applications for pesticide applicator license shall be in the form and shall contain the information prescribed by the Board. Each application shall be accompanied by a nonrefundable fee of seventy-five dollars ($75.00) for each pesticide applicator's license. In addition, an annual inspection fee of twenty-five dollars ($25.00) shall be submitted for each aircraft to be licensed. Should any aircraft fail to pass inspection, making it necessary for a second inspection to be made, the Board shall require an additional twenty-five-dollar ($25.00) inspection fee. In addition to the required inspection, unannounced inspections may be made without charge to determine if equipment is properly calibrated and maintained in conformance with the laws and regulations. All aircraft licensed to apply pesticides shall be identified by a license plate or decal furnished by the Board at no cost to the licensee, which plate or decal shall be affixed on the aircraft in a location and manner prescribed by the Board. No applicator inspection or license fee, original or renewal, shall be charged to State agencies or local governments or their employees. Inspections of ground pesticide application equipment may be made. Any such equipment determined to be faulty or unsafe shall not be used for the purpose of applying a pesticide(s) until such time as proper repairs and/or alterations are made.

(c)   Repealed by Session Laws 1981, c. 592, s. 6.

(d)   The Board shall classify licenses to be issued under this Part. Separate classifications or subclassifications shall be specified for (i) ground and aerial methods of application, and (ii) State and local government units engaged in the control of rodents and insects of public health significance. The Board may include such further classifications and subclassifications as the Board considers appropriate, including provisions for licensing of apprentice pesticide applicators. For aerial applicators, a license shall be required for both the contractor and the pilot. Each classification and subclassification may be subject to separate testing procedures and requirements.

(e)   Every licensed pesticide applicator who changes his address shall immediately notify the Board.

(f)   If the Board finds the applicant qualified to apply pesticides in the classifications he has applied for and, if the applicant files the bond or insurance required under G.S. 143-467, and if the applicant applying for a license to engage in aerial application of pesticides has met all of the requirements of the Federal Aviation Agency to operate the equipment described in the application, the Board shall issue a pesticide applicator's license limited to the classifications for which he is qualified. Every such license shall expire at the end of the calendar year of issue unless it has been revoked or suspended prior thereto by the Board for cause, or unless such financial security required under G.S. 143-467 is dated to expire at an earlier date, in which case said license shall be dated to expire upon expiration date of said financial security. The license may restrict the applicant to the use of a certain type or types of equipment or pesticides or to certain areas if the Board finds that the applicant is qualified to use only such type or types. If a license is not issued as applied for, the Board shall inform the applicant in writing of the reasons therefor.

(g)   A pesticide applicator's license shall not be transferable. When there is a transfer of ownership, management, or operation of a business of a licensee hereunder, the new owner, manager, or operator (as the case may be) whether it be an individual, firm, partnership, corporation, or other entity, must have available a licensed pesticide applicator to supervise the pesticide application business prior to continuance of such business.

(h)   Repealed by Session Laws 1987, c. 559, s. 15. (1971, c. 832, s. 1; 1973, c. 389, ss. 2, 5; 1977, c. 100; 1981, c. 592, ss. 6, 7; 1987, c. 559, ss. 14, 15; 1989, c. 544, s. 10; 2003-284, s. 35.4(a); 2010-31, s. 11.1(d).)

§ 143-453. Qualifications for pesticide applicator's license; examinations.

(a)   An applicant for a license must present satisfactory evidence to the Board concerning his qualifications for a pesticide applicator license. The contractor and each pilot involved in aerial application of pesticides shall be licensed.

Those qualifications, in the case of a pilot, shall include at least 125 hours and one year's flying experience as a pilot in the field of aerial pesticide application. A pilot lacking 125 hours and one year's experience as a pilot in the field of aerial pesticide application shall be licensed as an apprentice aerial pesticide applicator pilot. All aerial applications of pesticides by a licensed apprentice shall be conducted under the direct supervision of a licensed pesticide applicator pilot. The supervising pilot, while directly supervising an apprentice, shall operate out of the same airstrip as the apprentice and shall be available periodically throughout each day to provide advice and assistance to the apprentice. A nonrefundable fee of fifty dollars ($50.00) shall be charged for the examination required by this subsection. Such examination fee shall be charged in addition to the fees authorized pursuant to subsection (b) of this section or any other provision of Article 4C of Chapter 106 of the General Statutes.

(b)   Each applicant shall satisfy the Board as to his knowledge of the laws and regulations governing the use and application of pesticides in the classifications he has applied for (manually or with various equipment that he may have applied for a license to operate), and as to his responsibility in carrying on the business of a pesticide applicator. Each applicant for an original license must demonstrate upon written, or written and oral, examination to be prescribed by the Board his knowledge of pesticides, their usefulness and their hazards; his competence as a pesticide applicator; and his knowledge of the laws and regulations governing the use and application of pesticides in the classification for which he has applied. A nonrefundable fee of fifty dollars ($50.00) shall be charged for the core examination, and an additional twenty dollars ($20.00) shall be charged for each additional specific classification licensure. Such examination fees shall be charged in addition to the fees authorized pursuant to subsection (a) of this section or any other provision of Article 4C of Chapter 106 of the General Statutes.

(c)   The Board shall by regulation:

(1)   Designate what persons or class of persons shall be required to pass the examination in the case of an applicant that is a corporation or governmental unit or agency;

(2)   Provide for license renewal examinations at intervals not more frequent than four years, or more frequently if found by the Board to be required to be necessary in order to qualify North Carolina's State pesticide control plan for federal approval. (1971, c. 832, s. 1; 1973, c. 389, s. 4; 1975, c. 425, ss. 5, 9; 1977, c. 1125; 1985, c. 163; 2010-31, s. 11.1(e).)

§ 143-454. Solicitors, salesmen and operators; applicator's responsibility.

(a)   Every licensed pesticide applicator shall submit to the Board, at such times as the Board or the Commissioner may prescribe, the names of all solicitors, salesmen, and operators employed by him.

(b)   Each licensed pesticide applicator shall be responsible for solicitors, salesmen, and operators in his employment to assure that pesticides are used in a manner consistent with the intent of this Article. (1971, c. 832, s. 1; 1979, c. 448, s. 8.)

§ 143-455. Pest control consultant license.

(a)   No person shall perform services as a pest control consultant without first procuring from the Board a license. Applications for a consultant license shall be in the form and shall contain the information prescribed by the Board. The application for a license shall be accompanied by a nonrefundable annual fee of seventy-five dollars ($75.00).

(b)   An applicant for a consultant license must present satisfactory evidence to the Board concerning his qualifications for such license. The Board may classify consultant licenses into one or more classifications or subclassifications based upon types of consulting services performed or to be performed. Such classifications and subclassifications may reflect the crops involved in the consulting service, the discipline or training of consultant, the discretion or lack of discretion involved in the consulting service, and the site or location of the service. Each classification and subclassification may be subject to separate testing procedures and requirements, and may be subject to its own minimum standards of training in specialized subject matter from a recognized college or university, or equivalent specialized consulting experience or training. A nonrefundable fee of fifty dollars ($50.00) shall be charged for the consultant examination, and an additional twenty dollars ($20.00) shall be charged for each additional specific classification licensure permitted by this subsection. Such examination fee shall be charged in addition to the fees authorized pursuant to subsection (a) of this section or any other provision of Article 4C of Chapter 106 of the General Statutes. Qualifications for licensing may be less stringent if the licensee is restricted to making recommendations contained in publications recognized by the Board as appropriate for a specific consulting classification or subclassification.

(c)   Each applicant shall satisfy the Board as to his responsibility in carrying on the business of a pesticide consultant. Each applicant for an original license must demonstrate upon written, or written and oral, examination to be prescribed by the Board his knowledge of pesticides, their usefulness and their hazards; his competence as a pesticide consultant; and his knowledge of the laws and regulations governing the use and sale of pesticides.

(d)   Pest control consultants shall be subject to the same provisions as pesticide applicators concerning penalties for late applications for license, changes of address, transferability of licenses, periodic reexamination, and examinations for corporate applicants. (1971, c. 832, s. 1; 1975, c. 425, s. 10; 1987, c. 559, s. 16; 1989, c. 544, s. 12; 2003-284, s. 35.4(d); 2010-31, s. 11.1(f).)

§ 143-456. Denial, suspension and revocation of license.

(a)   The Board may deny, suspend, modify, or revoke a license issued under this Part if it finds that the applicant or licensee or his employee has committed any of the following acts, each of which is declared to be a violation of this Part:

(1)   Made false or fraudulent claims through any media, misrepresenting the effect of materials or methods to be utilized;

(2)   Made a pesticide recommendation or application not in accordance with the label registered pursuant to this Article;

(3)   Operated faulty or unsafe equipment;

(4)   Operated in a faulty, careless, or negligent manner;

(5)   Violated any provision of this Article or of any rule or regulation adopted by the Board or any lawful order of the Board;

(6)   Refused or neglected to keep and maintain the records required by this Article, or to make reports when and as required;

(7)   Made false or fraudulent records, invoices, or reports;

(8)   Operated unlicensed equipment;

(9)   Used fraud or misrepresentation, or presented false information, in making an application for a license or renewal of a license;

(10) Refused or neglected to comply with any limitations or restrictions on or in a duly issued license or permit;

(11) Aided or abetted a licensed or an unlicensed person to evade the provisions of this Article, combined or conspired with such a licensed or unlicensed person to evade the provisions of this Article, or allowed one's license to be used by an unlicensed person;

(12) Made false or misleading statements during or after an inspection concerning any infestation or infection of pests found on land;

(13) Impersonated any state, county, or city inspector or official;

(14) Stored or disposed of containers or pesticides by means other than those prescribed on the labeling or by rule;

(15) Failed to pay the original or renewal license fee when due and continued to operate as an applicator, or applied pesticides without a license.

(16) Failed to pay a civil penalty assessed under this Article within 30 days after the date it is assessed.

(b) Any licensee whose license is revoked under the provisions of this Article shall not be eligible to apply for a new license hereunder until such time has elapsed from the date of the order revoking said license as established by the Board (not to exceed two years), or if an appeal is taken from said order or revocation, not to exceed two years from the date of the order or final judgment sustaining said revocation. (1971, c. 832, s. 1; 1975, c. 425, ss. 6, 8; 1987, c. 559, s. 17; c. 827, s. 42; 1995, c. 445, s. 5.)

§ 143-457: Repealed by Session Laws 1981, c. 592, s. 8.

§ 143-458. Rules and regulations concerning methods of application.

(a) The Board may adopt rules prescribing the method to be used in the application of pesticides and the times and places pesticides may be applied. The Board may adopt rules restricting or prohibiting the sale and use of pesticides in designated areas during specified time periods. In adopting rules under this subsection, the Board shall consider factors required to prevent damage or injury to the following by the drift or misapplication of pesticides:

(1) Plants, including forage plants, on adjacent or nearby land;

(2) Wildlife in the adjoining or nearby areas;

(3) Fish and other aquatic life in waters in reasonable proximity to the area to be treated;

or

(4) Other animals, persons or beneficial insects.

In issuing such regulations, the Board shall give consideration to pertinent research findings and recommendations of other agencies of this State or of the federal government.

(b) The Board may by regulation require that notice of a proposed application of a pesticide be given to landowners adjoining the property to be treated or in the immediate vicinity thereof, if it finds that such notice is necessary to carry out the purpose of this Article.

(c) A pesticide applicator, a pesticide applicator's employee, or an agent of a pesticide applicator shall not apply any substance that:

(1) Has the active ingredients contained in a pesticide that is registered pursuant to G.S. 143-442, and

(2) Is not registered as a pesticide pursuant to G.S. 143-442.

(d) A pesticide applicator, a pesticide applicator's employee, or an agent of a pesticide applicator shall not combine any substance whose application is prohibited under subsection (c) of this section with any other substance to apply as a pesticide or to apply for any other reason, whether the combination occurs before, during, or after the application.

(e)   Any person who violates subsection (c) or (d) of this section shall be guilty of a Class 2 misdemeanor, which shall include a fine of up to one thousand dollars ($1,000) per violation. (1971, c. 832, s. 1; 1987, c. 827, s. 43; 1995, c. 478, s. 1.)

§ 143-459. Reporting of shipments and volumes of pesticides.

Every person selling pesticides directly to the consumer shall file with the Board, in such manner and with such frequency as the Board may prescribe, reports of purchases, sales and shipments of restricted use pesticides and other pesticides designated by the Board. Failure to file any report when due shall be cause for suspension or revocation of any license or registration issued under this Article, or for denial of the issuance or renewal of any such license or registration, and shall be a misdemeanor, punishable as provided by G.S. 143-469. The time for reporting may be extended for an additional 15 days for cause, upon written request to the Board. All reports provided under this Part are provided solely for the purposes of the Board. (1971, c. 832, s. 1; 1987, c. 559, s. 2.)

Part 5. General Provisions.

§ 143-460. Definitions.

As used in this Article, unless the context otherwise requires:

(1)   The term "active ingredient" means

    a.   In the case of a pesticide other than a plant regulator, defoliant, or desiccant, an ingredient which will prevent, destroy, repel, or mitigate insects, nematodes, fungi, rodents, weeds, or other pests;

    b.   In the case of a plant regulator, an ingredient which, through physiological action, will accelerate or retard the rate of growth or rate of maturation or otherwise alter the behavior of ornamental or crop plants or the produce thereof;

    c.   In the case of a defoliant, an ingredient which will cause the leaves or foliage to drop from a plant;

    d.   In the case of a desiccant, an ingredient which will artificially accelerate the drying of a plant tissue.

(2)   The term "adulterated" shall apply to any pesticide if its strength or purity falls below the professed standard or quality as expressed on labeling or under which it is sold, or if any substance has been substituted wholly or in part for the article, or if any valuable constituent of the article has been wholly or in part abstracted.

(2a)   "Antimicrobial pesticide" means any substance or mixture of substances intended for preventing, destroying, repelling, or mitigating any microorganism pest.

(3)   Reserved.

(4)   "Board" means the North Carolina Pesticide Board.

(5)   "Commissioner" means the North Carolina Commissioner of Agriculture.

(6)   "Committee" means the Pesticide Advisory Committee.

(7)   The term "defoliant" means any substance or mixture of substances intended for causing the leaves or foliage to drop from a plant, with or without causing abscission.

(8)   The term "desiccant" means any substance or mixture of substances intended for artificially accelerating the drying of plant tissues.

(9)   The term "device" means any instrument or contrivance intended for trapping, destroying, repelling, or mitigating insects or rodents or destroying, repelling, or mitigating fungi, weeds, nematodes, or such other pests as may be designated by the Board, but not including equipment used for the application of pesticides when sold separately therefrom.

(10)　　Repealed by Session Laws 1995, c. 445, s. 6.

(11)　　"Equipment" means any type of ground, water or aerial equipment, device, or contrivance using motorized, mechanical or pressurized power and used to apply any pesticide on land and anything that may be growing, habitating or stored on or in such land, but shall not include any pressurized hand-sized household device used to apply any pesticide or any equipment, device or contrivance of which the person who is applying the pesticide is the source of power or energy in making such pesticide application.

(12)　　The term "fungus" means any nonchlorophyll-bearing thallophyte (that is any nonchlorophyll-bearing plant of a lower order than mosses and liverworts), as for example, rust, smut, mildew, mold, yeast, and bacteria, except those on or in living man or other animals and those on or in processed food, beverages, or pharmaceuticals.

(13)　　The term "fungicide" means any substance or mixture of substances intended for preventing, destroying, repelling or mitigating any fungi.

(14)　　The term "herbicide" means any substance or mixture of substances intended for preventing, destroying, repelling or mitigating any weed.

(15)　　The term "inert ingredient" means an ingredient which is not an active ingredient.

(16)　　The term "ingredient statement" means

　　　a.　　A statement of the name and percentage of each active ingredient, together with the total percentage of the inert ingredients, in the pesticide; and

　　　b.　　In case the pesticide contains arsenic in any form, a statement of the percentages of total and water-soluble arsenic, each calculated as elemental arsenic.

(17)　　The term "insect" means any of the numerous small invertebrate animals generally having the body more or less obviously segmented, for the most part belonging to the class Insecta, comprising six-legged, usually winged forms, as, for example, beetles, bugs, wasps, flies, and to other allied classes of arthropods whose members are wingless and usually have more than six legs, as, for example, spiders, mites, ticks, centipedes, and wood lice.

(18)　　The term "insecticide" means any substance or mixture of substances intended for preventing, destroying, repelling, or mitigating any insects which may be present in any environment whatsoever.

(19)　　The term "label" means the written, printed, or graphic matter on, or attached to, the pesticide (or device) or the immediate container thereof, and the outside container or wrapper of the retail package, if any there be, of the pesticide (or device).

(20)　　The term "labeling" means all labels and other written, printed, or graphic matter:

　　　a.　　Upon the pesticide (or device) or any of its containers or wrappers;

　　　b.　　Accompanying the pesticide (or device) at any time;

　　　c.　　To which reference is made on the label or in literature accompanying the pesticide (or device) except when accurate, nonmisleading reference is made to current official publications of the United States Department of Agriculture or Interior, the United States Public Health Service, state experiment stations, state agricultural colleges, or other similar federal institutions or official agencies of this State or other states authorized by law to conduct research in the field of pesticides.

(21)　　"Land" means all land and water areas, including airspace, and all plants, animals, structures, buildings, devices and contrivances, appurtenant thereto or situated thereon, fixed or mobile, including any used for transportation.

(22)　　"Manufacturer" includes any person engaged in the business of importing, producing, preparing, formulating, mixing, or processing pesticides.

(22a) "Material Safety Data Sheet" or "MSDS" means a chemical information sheet which would satisfy the requirements of the Hazardous Chemicals Right-to-Know Act, Article 18, Chapter 95 of the General Statutes, or any law enacted in substitution therefor.

(23) The term "misbranded" shall apply:

    a.   To any pesticide or device if its labeling bears any statement, design, or graphic representation relative thereto or to its ingredients which is false or misleading in any particular;

    b.   To any pesticide:

        1.   If it is an imitation of or is offered for sale under the name of another pesticide;

        2.   If its labeling bears any reference to registration under this Article;

        3.   If the labeling accompanying it does not contain instructions for use which are necessary and, if complied with, adequate for the protection of the public;

        4.   If the label does not contain a warning or caution statement which may be necessary and, if complied with, adequate to prevent injury to living man and other vertebrate animals;

        5.   If the label does not bear an ingredient statement on that part of the immediate container and on the outside container or wrapper, if there be one, through which the ingredient statement on the immediate container cannot be clearly read, of the retail package which is presented or displayed under customary conditions of purchase except that the Board may permit the statement to appear prominently on some other part of the container, if the size or form of the container make it impractical to comply with the requirements of this subparagraph;

        6.   If any word, statement, or other information required by or under the authority of this Article to appear on the labeling is not prominently placed thereon with such conspicuousness (as compared with other words, statements, designs, or graphic matter in the labeling) and in such terms as to render it likely to be read and understood by the ordinary individual under customary conditions of purchase and use; or

        7.   If in the case of an insecticide, nematicide, fungicide, or herbicide, when used as directed or in accordance with commonly recognized practice, it shall be injurious to living man or other vertebrate animals or vegetation, except weeds, to which it is applied, or to the person applying such pesticides or

        8.   In the case of a plant regulator, defoliant, or desiccant when used as directed it shall be injurious to living man or other vertebrate animals, or vegetation to which it is applied, or to the person applying such pesticides, except that physical or physiological effects on plants or parts thereof shall not be deemed to be injury, when this is the purpose for which the plant regulator, defoliant, or desiccant was applied, in accordance with the label claims and recommendations.

(24) The term "nematicide" means any substance or mixture of substances intended for preventing, destroying, repelling, or mitigating nematodes.

(25) The term "nematode" means invertebrate animals of the phylum nemathelminthes and class Nematoda, that is, unsegmented round worms with elongated, fusiform, or saclike bodies covered with cuticle, and inhabiting soil, water, plants or plant parts; may also be called nemas or eelworms.

(25a) The phrase "packaged, labeled and released for shipment" means the point in the production and marketing process of a pesticide where the pesticide has been produced, and it is the intent of the producer that such product be introduced into commerce for direct retail sale.

(26) A "person" is any person, including (but not limited to) an individual, firm, partnership, association, company, joint-stock association, public or private institution, municipality or county or local government

unit (as defined in G.S. 143-215.40(b)), state or federal governmental agency, or private or public corporation organized under the laws of this State or the United States or any other state or country.

(26a)   The term "pest" means any insect, rodent, nematode, fungus, weed or any other noxious or undesirable microorganism or macroorganism, except viruses, bacteria, or other microorganisms on or in living persons or other living animals.

(27)   "Pest control consultant" means any person, who, for a fee, offers or supplies technical advice, supervision, or aid, or recommends the use of specific pesticides for the purpose of controlling insects, plant diseases, weeds, and other pests, but does not include any person regulated by the North Carolina Structural Pest Control Act (G.S. Chapter 106, Article 4C).

(28)   The term "pesticide" means:

   a.   Any substance or mixture of substances intended for preventing, destroying, repelling, or mitigating any pest, and

   b.   Any substance or mixture of substances intended for use as a plant regulator, defoliant, or desiccant.

(29)   "Pesticide applicator" means any person who owns or operates a pesticide application business or who provides, for compensation, a service that includes the application of pesticides upon the lands or properties of another; any public operator; any golf course operator; any seed treater; any person engaged in demonstration or research pest control; and any other person who applies pesticides for compensation and is not exempt from this definition. It does not include:

   a.   Any person who uses or supervises the use of a pesticide (i) only for the purpose of producing an agricultural commodity on property owned or rented by him or his employer, or (ii) only (if applied without compensation other than trading of personal services between producers of agricultural commodities) on the property of another person, or (iii) only for the purposes set forth in (i) and (ii) above.

   b.   Any person who applies pesticides for structural pest control, as defined in the North Carolina Structural Pest Control Law (G.S. Chapter 106, Article 4C).

   c.   Any person certified by the Water Treatment Facility Operators Board of Certification under Article 2 of Chapter 90A of the General Statutes or by the Wastewater Treatment Operators Plant Certification Commission under Article 3 of Chapter 90A of the General Statutes who applies pesticides labeled for the treatment of water or wastewater.

   d.   Any person who applies antimicrobial pesticides that are not classified for restricted use and are not being used for agricultural, horticultural, or forestry purposes.

   e.   Any person who applies a general use pesticide to the property of another as a volunteer, without compensation.

   f.   Any person who is employed by a licensed pesticide applicator.

(30)   The term "pesticide dealer" means any person who is engaged in the business of distributing, selling, offering for sale, or holding for sale restricted use pesticides for distribution directly to users. The term pesticide dealer does not include:

   a.   Persons whose sales of pesticides are limited to pesticides in consumersized packages (as defined by the Board) which are labeled and intended for home and garden use only and are not restricted use pesticides, or

   b   Practicing veterinarians and physicians who prescribe, dispense, or use pesticides in the performance of their professional services.

(31)   Repealed by Session Laws 1973, c. 389, s. 3.

(32)   The term "plant regulator" means any substance or mixture of substances, intended through physiological action, for accelerating or retarding the rate of growth or rate of maturation, or for otherwise altering the behavior of ornamental or crop plants or the produce thereof, but shall not include substances to the extent that they are intended as plant nutrients, trace elements, nutritional chemicals, plant inoculants, and soil amendments.

(33)   "Public operator" means any person in charge of any equipment used by public utilities (as defined by General Statutes Chapter 62), State agencies, municipal corporations, or other governmental agencies applying pesticides.

(34)   The term "registrant" means the person registering any pesticide pursuant to the provisions of this Article.

(35)   The term "restricted use pesticide" or "pesticide classified for restricted use" means any pesticide or use classified as restricted by the Administrator of the United States Environmental Protection Agency or other pesticide or use which the Board has designated as such pursuant to G.S. 143-440.

(36)   The term "rodenticide" means any substance or mixture of substances intended for preventing, destroying, repelling, attracting, or mitigating rodents or any other vertebrate animal which the Board shall declare to be a pest.

(36a)   The phrase "to use any pesticide in a manner inconsistent with its labeling" means to use any pesticide in a manner not permitted by the labeling; provided that the phrase shall not include:

   a.   Applying a pesticide at any dosage, concentration, or frequency less than that specified on the labeling,

   b.   Applying a pesticide against any target pest not specified on the labeling if the application is to the crop, animal, or site specified on the labeling, unless the labeling specifically states that the pesticide may be used only for the pests specified on the labeling,

   c.   Employing any method of application not prohibited by the labeling, or

   d.   Mixing pesticides or mixing a pesticide with a fertilizer when such mixture is not prohibited by the labeling.

(37)   The term "weed" means any plant or part thereof which grows where not wanted.

(38)   "Wildlife" means all living things that are neither human, domesticated, nor, as defined in this Article, pests; including but not limited to mammals, birds, and aquatic life. (1971, c. 832, s. 1; 1973, c. 389, s. 3; 1975, c. 425, s. 11; 1979, c. 448, ss. 9, 10; 1981, c. 592, ss. 911; 1987, c. 559, ss. 2, 1820; 1991, c. 87, ss. 1, 2; 1995, c. 445, ss. 6, 7.)

§ 143-461. General powers of Board.

In addition to the specific powers prescribed elsewhere in this Article, and for the purpose of carrying out its duties, the Board shall have the power, at any time and from time to time:

(1)   To adopt from time to time and to modify and revoke official regulations interpreting and applying the provisions of this Article and rules of procedure establishing and amplifying the procedures to be followed in the administration of this Article. Unless the Board deems there are overriding policy considerations involved, any regulation of the Board, which will in the judgment of the Board result in severe curtailment of the usefulness or value of inventories or equipment in the hands of persons licensed under this Article, should be given a future effective date so as to minimize undue potential economic loss to licensees;

(2)   To authorize the Commissioner by proclamation (i) to suspend or implement, in whole or in part, particular regulations of the Board which may be affected by variable conditions, or (ii) to suspend the application of any provision of this Part to any federal or State agency if it is determined by the Commissioner that emergency conditions require such action.

(3)   To conduct such investigations as it may reasonably deem necessary to carry out its duties as prescribed by this Article;

(4)   To conduct public hearings in accordance with the procedures prescribed by this Article;

(5)   To delegate such of the powers of the Board as the Board deems necessary (other than its powers to adopt rules and regulations of any kind) to one or more of its members, to the Commissioner, or to any qualified employee of the Board or of the Commissioner; provided, that the provisions of any such delegation of power shall be set forth in the official regulations of the Board. Any person to whom a delegation of power is made to conduct a hearing shall report the hearing with its evidence and record to the Board for decision;

(6)   To call upon the Attorney General for such legal advice and assistance as is necessary to the functioning of the Board;

(7)   To institute such actions in the superior court in the county in which any defendant resides, or has his or its principal place of business, as the Board may deem necessary for the enforcement of any of the provisions of this Article or of any official actions of the Board, including proceedings to enforce subpoenas or for the punishment of contempt of the Board. Upon violation of any of the provisions of this Article, or of any regulation of the Board adopted under the authority of this Article the Board may, either before or after the institution of any other proceedings (civil or criminal), institute a civil action in the superior court in the name of the State for injunctive relief to restrain the violation and for such other or further relief in the premises as said court shall deem proper. Neither the institution of the action nor any of the proceedings thereon shall relieve any party to such proceedings from any other penalty or remedy prescribed by this Article for any violation of same;

(8)   To agree upon or enter into any settlements or compromises of any actions and to prosecute any appeals or other proceedings. (1971, c. 832, s. 1; 1973, c. 389, s. 6; 1987, c. 827, s. 44.)

§ 143-462. Procedures for revocations and related actions affecting licenses.

In all proceedings, the effect of which would be to revoke, suspend, deny, or withhold renewal of a license issued under Part 3 or Part 4 of this Article, or to deny permission to take an examination for such a license, the provisions of Chapter 150B of the General Statutes shall be applicable. (1971, c. 832, s. 1; 1987, c. 827, s. 1.)

§ 143-463. Adoption and publication of rules.

Chapter 150B of the General Statutes governs the adoption of rules under this Article and the publication of those rules. (1971, c. 832, s. 1; 1975, 2nd Sess., c. 983, s. 84; 1979, c. 448, s. 11; 1987, c. 827, s. 45.)

§ 143-464. Procedures concerning registration of pesticides.

A denial, suspension, or cancellation of a registration of a pesticide shall be made in accordance with the procedures in Chapter 150B of the General Statutes for denying, suspending, or canceling a license. (1971, c. 832, s. 1; 1979, c. 448, s. 12; 1987, c. 827, s. 46.)

§ 143-465. Reciprocity; intergovernmental cooperation.

(a)   The Board may issue any license required by this Article on a reciprocal basis with other states without examination to a nonresident who is licensed in another state substantially in accordance with any of the provisions of the Article, provided that financial security as provided for in G.S. 143-467 is met.

(b)   The Board may cooperate or enter into formal agreements with any other agency of this State or its subdivisions or with any agency of any other state or of the federal government for the purpose of enforcing any of the provisions of this Article.

(c)   In order to avoid confusion resulting from diverse requirements and to avoid increased costs to the people of this State due to the necessity of complying with such diverse requirements in the manufacture and sale of such pesticides, it is desirable that there should be uniformity between the requirements of the several states and the federal government relating to such pesticides. To this end the Board is authorized, after public hearing, to adopt by regulation such regulations, applicable to and in conformity with the primary standards established by this Article, as have been or may be prescribed with respect to pesticides by departments or agencies of the United States government.

(d)   No county, city, or other political subdivision of the State shall adopt or continue in effect any ordinance, rule, regulation, or resolution regulating the use, sale, distribution, storage, transportation, disposal, formulation, labeling, registration, manufacture, or application of pesticides in any area subject to regulation by the Board pursuant to this Article. Nothing in this section shall prohibit a county, city, or other political subdivision of the State from exercising its planning and zoning authority under Article 19 of Chapter 160A of the General Statutes or Article 18 of Chapter 153A of the General Statutes, or from exercising its fire prevention or inspection authority. (1971, c. 832, s. 1; 1995, c. 445, s. 8.)

§ 143-466. Records; information; inspection; enforcement.

(a)   The Board shall require licensees to maintain records with respect to the sale and application of such pesticides as it may from time to time prescribe. Such relevant information as the Board may deem necessary may be specified by rule. The records shall be kept for a period of three years from the date of the application of the pesticide to which the records refer, and shall be available for inspection and copying by the Board or its agents at its request.

(b)   The Board may publish information regarding injury which may result from improper application or use of pesticides and the methods and precautions designed to prevent such injury.

(c)   The Board may provide for inspection of any equipment used for application of pesticides and may require repairs or other changes before its further use for pesticide application. A list of requirements that equipment shall meet may be adopted by the Board by regulation.

(d)   The Board may provide for inspection of any place of business where pesticides are stored or sold and may require changes in methods of handling, displaying and storing of all pesticides. A list of requirements that places of business must meet may be adopted by regulation of the Board.

(e)   For the purpose of carrying out the provisions of this Article, inspectors designated by the Board may enter upon any public or private premises at reasonable times, in order:

   (1)   To have access for the purpose of inspecting the premises and any equipment subject to this Article and such premises on which such equipment is kept or stored;

   (2)   To inspect lands actually or reported to be exposed to pesticides;

   (3)   To inspect storage or disposal areas;

   (4)   To inspect or investigate complaints of injury to humans, land or plants; or

   (5)   To sample pesticides being applied, or to be applied.

   No person shall refuse entry or access to any authorized representative of the Board who requests entry for purposes of inspection, and who presents appropriate credentials, nor shall any person obstruct, hamper or interfere with any such representative while in the process of carrying out his official duties. Should the Board or its designated agent be denied access to any land where such access was sought for the purposes set forth in this Article, the Board may apply to any court of competent jurisdiction for a search warrant authorizing access to such land for said purposes. The court may upon such application issue the search warrant for the purposes requested. (1971, c. 832, s. 1; 1995, c. 445, s. 9.)

§ 143-467. Financial responsibility.

(a)   The Board may require from a licensee or an applicant for a license under this Article evidence of his financial ability to properly indemnify persons suffering damage from the use or application of pesticides, in the form of a surety bond, liability insurance or cash deposit. The amount of this bond, insurance or deposit shall be determined by the Board, in light of the risk of damage. The indemnification requirements may extend to damage to persons and property from equipment used (including aircraft).

(b)   The Board may also require a reasonable performance bond with satisfactory surety to secure the performance of contractual obligations of the licensee, with respect to application of pesticides. Any person injured by the breach of any such obligation or any person damaged by pesticides or by equipment used in their application shall be entitled to sue on the bond in his own name in any court of competent jurisdiction to recover the damages he may have sustained.

(c)   Any regulations adopted by the Board pursuant to G.S. 143-461 to implement this section may provide for such conditions, limitations and requirements concerning the financial responsibility required by this section as the Board deems necessary, including but not limited to notice of reduction or cancellation of coverage, deductible provisions, and acceptability of surety. Such regulations may classify financial responsibility requirements according to the separate license classifications and subclassifications prescribed by the Board pursuant to G.S. 143-452 and the dealer category (Part 3 of this Article). (1971, c. 832, s. 1.)

§ 143-468. Disposition of fees and charges.

(a)   Except as provided in G.S. 143-469 and in subsection (b), all fees and charges received by the Board under this Article shall be credited to the Department of Agriculture and Consumer Services for the purpose of administration and enforcement of this Article.

(b)   The Pesticide Environmental Trust Fund is established as a nonreverting account within the Department of Agriculture and Consumer Services. The Department of Agriculture and Consumer Services shall administer the Fund. The additional assessment imposed by G.S. 143-442(b) on the registration of a brand or grade of pesticide shall be credited to the Fund. The Department shall distribute money in the Fund as follows:

(1)   Two and one-half percent (2.5%) to North Carolina State University Cooperative Extension Service to enhance its agromedicine efforts in cooperation with East Carolina University School of Medicine.

(2)   Two and one-half percent (2.5%) to East Carolina University School of Medicine to enhance its agromedicine efforts in cooperation with North Carolina State University Cooperative Extension Service.

(3)   Twenty percent (20%) to North Carolina State University, Department of Toxicology, to establish and maintain an extension agromedicine specialist position.

(4)   Seventy-five percent (75%) to the Department of Agriculture and Consumer Services for the costs of administering its pesticide disposal program, including the salaries and support of staff for the pesticide disposal program, and for its environmental programs, as directed by the Board, including establishing a pesticide container management program to enhance its pesticide disposal program and its water quality initiatives. (1971, c. 832, s. 1; 1993, c. 481, s. 1; 1997-261, s. 92; 1998-215, s. 26(b); 2005-276, s. 11.1.)

§ 143-469. Penalties.

(a)   Any person who shall be adjudged to have violated any provision of this Article, or any regulation of the Board adopted pursuant to this Article, shall be guilty of a Class 2 misdemeanor. In addition, if any person continues to violate or further violates any provision of this Article after written notice from the Board, the court may determine that each day during which the violation continued or is repeated constitutes a separate violation subject to the foregoing penalties.

(b)   A civil penalty of not more than two thousand dollars ($2,000) may be assessed by the Board against any person who violates or directly causes a violation of any provision of this Article or any rule adopted pursuant to this Article.

(c)   Proceedings for the assessment of civil penalties under this section shall be governed by Chapter 150B of the North Carolina General Statutes. If the person assessed a civil penalty fails to pay the penalty to the North Carolina Department of Agriculture and Consumer Services, the Board may institute an action in the superior court of the county in which the person resides or has his principal place of business to recover the unpaid amount of said penalty. An action to recover a civil penalty under this section shall not relieve any party from any other penalty prescribed by law.

(d)   Notwithstanding any other provision of this Article, the maximum penalty which may be assessed under this section against any person referred to in G.S. 143-460(29)a shall not exceed five hundred dollars ($500.00). Penalties may be assessed under this section against a person referred to in G.S. 143-460(29)a only for willful violations.

(e)   The clear proceeds of civil penalties assessed pursuant to this section shall be remitted to the Civil Penalty and Forfeiture Fund in accordance with G.S. 115C-457.2. (1971, c. 832, s. 1; 1981, c. 592, s. 12; 1987, c. 559, s. 21; c. 827, s. 1; 1993, c. 539, s. 1035; 1994, Ex. Sess., c. 24, s. 14(c); 1995, c. 445, s. 10; 1997-261, s. 109; 1998-215, s. 26(a).)

§ 143-470: Repealed by Session Laws 1981, c. 592, s. 13, effective July 1, 1981.

§ 143-470.1. Report of minor violations in discretion of Board or Commissioner.

Nothing in this Article shall be construed to require the Board or the Commissioner to initiate, or attempt to initiate, any criminal or administrative proceedings under this Article for minor violations of this Article whenever the Board or Commissioner believes that the public interest will be adequately served in the circumstances by a suitable written notice or warning. (1979, c. 448, s. 13.)

Appendix M: Underground Utility Safety and Damage Prevention

Article 8A. Underground Utility Safety and Damage Prevention Act.

§ 87-115. (Effective October 1, 2014) Short title.

This Article may be cited as the "Underground Utility Safety and Damage Prevention Act." (2013-407, s. 2.)

§ 87-116. (Effective October 1, 2014) Declaration of policy and purpose.

The General Assembly of North Carolina hereby declares as a matter of public policy that it is necessary to protect the citizens and workforce of this State from the dangers inherent in excavating or demolishing in areas where underground lines, systems, or infrastructure are buried beneath the surface of the ground, and it is necessary to protect from costly damage underground facilities used for producing, storing, conveying, transmitting, or distributing communication, electricity, gas, petroleum, petroleum products, hazardous liquids, water, steam, or sewage. In order to carry out this public policy and to satisfy these compelling interests, the General Assembly has enacted the provisions of this Article providing for a systematic, orderly, and uniform process to identify existing facilities in advance of any excavation or demolition in this State and to implement safe digging practices. (2013-407, s. 2.)

§ 87-117. (Effective October 1, 2014) Definitions.

The following definitions apply in this Article:

(1)   APWA.—The American Public Works Association or its successors.

(2)   Business continuation plan.—A plan that includes actions to be taken in an effort to provide uninterrupted service during catastrophic events.

(3)   Contract locator.—A person hired by an operator to identify and mark facilities.

(4)   Damage.—The substantial weakening of structural or lateral support of a facility; penetration or destruction of protective coating, housing, or other protective device of a facility; or the partial or complete severance of a facility.

(5)   Demolish or demolition.—Any operation by which a structure or mass of material is wrecked, razed, rendered, moved, or removed by any means, including the use of any tools, equipment, or discharge of explosives.

(6)   Design notice.—A communication to the Notification Center in which a request for identifying existing facilities for advance planning purposes is made. A design notice may not be used for excavation purposes.

(7)   Designer.—Any architect, engineer, or other person who prepares or issues a drawing or blueprint for a construction or other project that requires excavation or demolition work.

(8)   Emergency.—An event involving a clear and imminent danger to life, health, or property, the interruption of essential utility services, or the blockage of transportation facilities, including highways, railways, waterways, or airways that require immediate action.

(9)   Excavate or excavation.—An operation for the purpose of the movement or removal of earth, rock, or other materials in or on the ground by use of manual or mechanized equipment or by discharge of explosives, including, but not limited to, auguring, backfilling, boring, digging, ditching, drilling, directional drilling,

driving, grading, horizontal directional drilling, well drilling, plowing-in, pounding, pulling-in, ripping, scraping, trenching, and tunneling.

(10)   Excavator.—A person engaged in excavation or demolition.

(11)   Extraordinary circumstances.—Circumstances that make it impossible for the operator to comply with the provisions of this Article, including hurricanes, tornadoes, floods, ice, snow, and acts of God.

(12)   Facility.—Any underground line, underground system, or underground infrastructure used for producing, storing, conveying, transmitting, identifying, locating, or distributing communication, electricity, gas, petroleum, petroleum products, hazardous liquids, water, steam, or sewage. Provided there is no encroachment on any operator's right-of-way, easement, or permitted use, for the purposes of this Article, the following shall not be considered an underground facility: (i) swimming pools and irrigation systems; (ii) petroleum storage systems under Part 2A of Article 21A of Chapter 143 of the General Statutes; (iii) septic tanks under Article 11 of Chapter 130A of the General Statutes; and (iv) liquefied petroleum gas systems under Article 5 of Chapter 119 of the General Statutes, unless the system is subject to Title 49 C.F.R. § 192 or § 195.

(13)   Locator.—An individual who identifies and marks facilities for operators who has been trained and whose training has been documented.

(14)   Mechanized equipment.—Equipment operated by means of mechanical power, including, but not limited to, trenchers, bulldozers, power shovels, augers, backhoes, scrapers, drills, horizontal directional drills, cable and pipe plows, and other equipment used for plowing-in or pulling-in cable or pipe.

(15)   Nonmechanized equipment.—Hand tools.

(16)   Notice.—Oral, written, or electronic communication to the Notification Center from any person planning to excavate or demolish in the State that informs an operator of the person's intent to excavate or demolish.

(17)   Notification Center.—A North Carolina member-owned not-for-profit corporation sponsored by operators that will provide a system through which a person can notify operators of proposed excavations and demolitions and submit reports of alleged violations of this Article.

(18)   Operator.—Any person, public utility, communications or cable service provider, municipality, electrical utility, or electric or telephone cooperative that owns or operates a facility in this State.

(19)   Person.—Any individual, owner, corporation, partnership, association, or any other entity organized under the laws of any state, any political subdivision of a state, or any other instrumentality of a state, or any authorized representative thereof.

(20)   Positive response.—An automated information system that allows excavators, locators, operators, and other interested parties to determine the status of a locate request.

(21)   Subaqueous.—A facility that is under a body of water, including rivers, streams, lakes, waterways, swamps, and bogs.

(22)   Tolerance zone.—If the diameter of the facility is known, the distance of one-half of the known diameter plus 24 inches on either side of the designated center line or, if the diameter of the facility is not marked, 24 inches on either side of the outside edge of the mark indicating a facility or, for subaqueous facilities, a clearance of 15 feet on either side of the indicated facility.

(23)   Working day.—Every day, except Saturday, Sunday, or State legal holidays. (2013-407, s. 2.)

§ 87-118. (Effective October 1, 2014) Reserve to the State the power to regulate.

The provisions in this Article supersede and preempt any ordinance adopted by a city or county that purports to do any of the following:

(1)   Require operators to obtain permits from a city or county in order to identify facilities.

(2)   Require premarking or marking of facilities.

(3)   Specify the types of paint or other marking devices that are used to identify facilities.

(4)   Require removal of unexpired marks. The removal of expired marks shall be the responsibility of the city or county. (2013-407, s. 2.)

§ 87-119. (Effective October 1, 2014) Costs associated with compliance; effect of permit.

Any costs or expenses associated with an excavator's compliance with the requirements of this Article shall not be charged to any operator. Any costs or expenses associated with an operator's compliance with the requirements of this Article shall not be charged to any excavator. The Notification Center may not impose any charge on any person giving notice to the Notification Center. This section shall not affect costs related to the operation of the Notification Center apportioned to an operator pursuant to G.S. 87-120(b). This section shall not excuse an operator or excavator from liability for any damage or injury for which the operator or excavator would be responsible under applicable law. (2013-407, s. 2.)

§ 87-120. (Effective October 1, 2014) Notification Center; responsibilities.

(a)   The operators in the State shall maintain a Notification Center for the sole purpose of providing the services required by this Article. The Notification Center shall maintain information concerning receipt of notification of proposed excavation and demolition activities as provided in this Article and shall maintain information received from operators concerning the location of the operators' facilities and the operators' positive responses to marking of the facilities. The Notification Center shall also receive, maintain, and provide general administration of reports of alleged violations of this Article and responses. The Notification Center is not responsible in any way for identifying or marking facilities for operators. The Notification Center is not responsible in any way for resolving reports of alleged violations of this Article. All operators in the State shall join the Notification Center as provided in subsection (b) of this section, and they shall use the services of the Notification Center to perform the acts required by the provisions of this Article. There shall be only one Notification Center for the State of North Carolina. The Notification Center is not an agency of the State or any of the State's political subdivisions and is not subject to the provisions of Chapter 132 or Chapter 133 of the General Statutes.

(b)   Operators who are members of the Notification Center by whatever name that is in existence on October 1, 2013, must remain members. Operators with more than 50,000 customers or 1,000 miles of facilities who are not members on October 1, 2013, must join no later than October 1, 2014. Operators with more than 25,000 customers or 500 miles of facilities who are not members on October 1, 2013, must join no later than October 1, 2015. All operators that do not meet one of the criteria provided in this subsection must join no later than October 1, 2016. Each engineering division of the Department of Transportation established pursuant to G.S. 136-14.1 must join no later than October 1, 2016. The board of directors of the Notification Center shall develop a reasonable method of apportioning the costs of operating the Notification Center among the member operators. Prior to adopting a method of determining such cost allocation, the board of directors shall publish the proposed method of cost allocation to the member operators, and the proposed method of cost allocation shall be approved by the member operators.

(c)   The Notification Center shall have the following duties and responsibilities:

(1)   Maintain a record of the notices received under subsection (d) of this section for at least four years.

(2)   Maintain a record of reports of alleged violations of this Article received under subsection (e) of this section for at least four years, including responses to such reports.

(3)   Receive and transmit notices as provided in subsection (d) of this section.

(4)   Develop and update, as needed, a business continuation plan.

(5)   Notify those persons against whom reports of alleged violations of this Article have been made and receive and maintain information submitted from such persons in defense against the allegations.

(6)   Provide a positive response system.

(7)   Establish and operate a damage prevention training program for members of the Notification Center. No person may recover damages in any manner or form from the Notification Center arising out of or related to the manner in which the Notification Center conducts a damage prevention training program or receives, transmits, or otherwise administers a report of an alleged violation of this Article.

(d)   The Notification Center shall receive notice from any person intending to excavate or demolish in the State and shall, at a minimum, transmit the following information to the appropriate operator:

(1)   The name, address, and telephone number of the person providing the notice and, if different, the person responsible for the proposed excavation or demolition.

(2)   The starting date of the proposed excavation or demolition.

(3)   The anticipated duration of the proposed excavation or demolition.

(4)   The type of proposed excavation or demolition operation to be conducted.

(5)   The location of the proposed excavation or demolition.

(6)   Whether or not explosives are to be used in the proposed excavation or demolition.

(e)   The Notification Center shall receive reports of alleged violations of this Article. The Notification Center shall contact persons against whom reports have been filed to inform them of the alleged violation within 10 days of the filing of the report. The Notification Center shall maintain the following information regarding reports of alleged violations:

(1)   The name, address, and telephone number of the person making the report;

(2)   The nature of the report, including the statute that is alleged to have been violated;

(3)   Information provided by the person making the report, including correspondence, both written and electronic, pictures, and videos; and

(4)   Information provided by the person against whom the report has been filed, including correspondence, both written and electronic, pictures, and videos. (2013-407, s. 2.)

§ 87-121. (Effective October 1, 2014) Facility operator responsibilities.

(a)   An operator shall provide to the excavator the following:

(1)   The horizontal location and description of all of the operator's facilities in the area where the proposed excavation or demolition is to occur. The location shall be marked by stakes, soluble paint, flags, or any combination thereof, as appropriate, depending upon the conditions in the area of the proposed excavation or demolition. The operator shall, when marking as provided under this subdivision, use the APWA Uniform Color Code. If the diameter or width of the facility is greater than four inches, the dimension of the facility shall be indicated at least every 25 feet in the area of the proposed excavation or demolition. An operator who operates multiple facilities in the area of the proposed excavation or demolition shall locate each facility.

(2)   Any other information that would assist the excavator in identifying and thereby avoiding damage to the marked facilities.

(b)   Unless otherwise provided in a written agreement between the operator and the excavator, the operator shall provide to the excavator the information required by subsection (a) of this section within the times provided below:

   (1)   For a facility, within three full working days after the day notice of the proposed excavation or demolition was provided to the Notification Center.

   (2)   For a subaqueous facility, within 10 full working days after the day notice of the proposed excavation or demolition was provided to the Notification Center.

   (3)   If the operator declares an extraordinary circumstance, the times provided in this subsection shall not apply.

(c)   The operator shall provide a positive response to the Notification Center before the expiration of the time provided in subsection (b) of this section. The response shall indicate whether and to what extent the operator is able to provide the information required by subsection (a) of this section to respond to the notice from the excavator.

(d)   If the operator determines that provisions for marking subaqueous facilities are required, the operator will provide a positive response to the Notification Center not more than three full working days after notice has been provided by the excavator.

(e)   If extraordinary circumstances prevent the operator from marking the location of the facilities within the time specified in subsection (b) of this section, the operator shall either notify the excavator directly or notify the excavator through the Notification Center. When providing the notification under this subsection, the operator shall state the date and time when the location will be marked.

(f)   An operator shall prepare or cause to be prepared installation records of all facilities installed on or after the date this Article becomes effective in a public street, alley, or right-of-way dedicated to public use, excluding service drops and services lines. The operator shall maintain these records in the operator's possession while the facility is in service.

(g)   All facilities installed by or on behalf of operators on or after the date this Article becomes effective shall be electronically locatable using a locating method that is generally accepted by operators in the particular industry or trade in which the operator is engaged.

(h)   A locator shall notify the operator if the locator becomes aware of an error or omission in the records or documentation showing the location of the operator's facilities. The operator must update its records to correct any error or omission.

(i)   An operator may reject an excavation or demolition notice due to homeland security considerations based upon federal statutes or federal regulations until the operator can confirm the legitimacy of the notice. The operator shall notify the person making the notice of the denial and may request additional information through the positive response system.

(j)   Gravity fed sanitary sewers installed prior to the date this Article becomes effective and all storm water facilities shall be exempt from the location requirements provided in subsection (a) of this section. Neither the excavator nor the person financially responsible for the excavation will be liable for any damage to an unmarked gravity fed sanitary sewer line or unmarked storm water facility if the person doing the excavation exercises due care to protect existing facilities when there is evidence of the existence of those facilities near the proposed excavation area.

(k)   An operator who does not become a member of the Notification Center as required by G.S. 87-120(b) may not recover for damages to a facility caused by an excavator who has complied with the provisions of this Article and has exercised reasonable care in the performance of the excavation or demolition. (2013-407, s. 2.)

§ 87-122. (Effective October 1, 2014) Excavator responsibilities.

(a)   Before commencing any excavation or demolition operation, the person responsible for the excavation or demolition shall provide or cause to be provided notice to the Notification Center of his or her intent to excavate or demolish. Notice for any excavation or demolition that does not involve a subaqueous facility must be given within three to 12 full working days before the proposed commencement date of the excavation or demolition. Notice for any excavation or demolition in the vicinity of a subaqueous facility must be given within 10 to 20 full working days before the proposed commencement date of the excavation or demolition. Notice given pursuant to this subsection shall expire 15 full working days after the date notice was given. No excavation or demolition may continue after this 15-day period unless the person responsible for the excavation or demolition provides a subsequent notice which shall be provided in the same manner as the original notice required by this subsection. When demolition of a building is proposed, the operator shall be given a reasonable time in which to remove or protect the operator's facilities before the demolition commences.

(b)   The notice required by subsection (a) of this section shall, at a minimum, contain all of the following:

    (1)   The name, address, and telephone number of the person providing the notice.

    (2)   The anticipated starting date of the proposed excavation or demolition.

    (3)   The anticipated duration of the proposed excavation or demolition.

    (4)   The type of proposed excavation or demolition operation to be conducted.

    (5)   The location of the proposed excavation or demolition, not to exceed one-quarter mile in geographical length, or five adjoining addresses, not to exceed one-quarter mile in geographical length.

    (6)   Whether or not explosives are to be used in the proposed excavation or demolition.

(c)   An excavator shall comply with the following:

    (1)   When the excavation area cannot be clearly and adequately identified within the area described in the notice, the excavator shall designate the route, specific area to be excavated, or both by premarking the area before the operator performs a locate. Premarking shall be made with soluble white paint, white flags, or white stakes.

    (2)   Confirm through the Notification Center's positive response system prior to excavation or demolition that all operators have responded and that all facilities that may be affected by the proposed excavation or demolition have been marked.

    (3)   Plan the excavation or demolition to avoid damage to or minimize interference with facilities in or near the construction area.

    (4)   Begin excavation or demolition prior to the specified waiting period only if the excavator has confirmed that all operators have responded with an appropriate positive response.

    (5)   If the operator declares extraordinary circumstances, the excavator shall not excavate or demolish until after the time and date that the operator has provided in the operator's response.

    (6)   If an operator fails to respond to the positive response system, the excavator may proceed if there are no visible indications of a facility at the proposed excavation or demolition area, such as a pole, marker, pedestal, meter, or valve. However, if the excavator is aware of or observes indications of an unmarked facility at the proposed excavation or demolition area, the excavator shall not begin excavation or demolition until an additional call is made to the Notification Center detailing the facility and an arrangement is made for the facility to be marked by the operator within three hours from the time the additional call is received by the Notification Center.

(7)   Beginning on the date provided in the excavator's notice to the Notification Center, the excavator shall preserve the staking, marking, or other designation until they are no longer required. When a mark is no longer visible or is destroyed, but the excavation or demolition continues in the vicinity of the facility, the excavator shall request a remark from the Notification Center to ensure the protection of the facility.

(8)   When demolition of a building is proposed, the excavator shall give the operator a reasonable time in which to remove or protect the operator's facilities before demolition commences.

(9)   An excavator shall not perform any excavation or demolition within the tolerance zone unless the excavator complies with all of the following conditions:

    a.   The excavator shall not use mechanized equipment, except noninvasive equipment specifically designed or intended to protect the integrity of the facility, within the marked tolerance zone of an existing facility until:

        1.   The excavator has visually identified the precise location of the facility or has visually confirmed that no facility is present up to the depth of excavation;

        2.   The excavator has taken reasonable precautions to avoid any substantial weakening of the facility's structural or lateral support, or both, or penetration or destruction of the facilities or their protective coatings; and

        3.   The excavator may use mechanical means, as necessary, for the initial penetration and removal of pavement or other materials requiring use of mechanical means of excavation but only to the depth of the pavement or other materials. For parallel type excavations within the tolerance zone, the existing facility shall be visually identified at intervals not to exceed 50 feet along the line of excavation to avoid damages. The excavator shall exercise due care at all times to protect the facilities when exposing these facilities.

    b.   The excavator shall maintain clearance between a facility and the cutting edge or point of any mechanized equipment, taking into account the known limit of control of the cutting edge or point, as may be reasonably necessary to avoid damage to the facility.

    c.   The excavator shall provide support for facilities in and near the excavation or demolition area, including backfill operations, as may be reasonably required by the operator for the protection of the facilities.

(10)   The excavator shall not use mechanized equipment within 24 inches of a facility that is a gas, oil, petroleum, or electric transmission line unless the facility operator has consented to the use in writing and the operator's representative is on site during the use of the mechanized equipment. For purposes of this subdivision, the term "gas, oil, petroleum transmission line" has the same meaning as the term "transmission line" in Title 49 C.F.R. § 192.3, and the term "electric transmission line" has the same meaning as the term "transmission line" in G.S. 62-100(7). (2013-407, s. 2.)

§ 87-123. (Effective October 1, 2014) Training.

(a)   Every person who is an excavator, locator, or operator under this Article by virtue of engaging in these activities in the course of a business or trade has a duty to provide education and training to employees and to document such education and training. The training shall include sufficient information, guidance, and supervision such that employees can competently and safely operate the equipment used in the course of the business or trade and complete assigned tasks in a competent and safe manner while minimizing the potential for damage.

(b)   When an excavator, locator, or operator under this Article retains an independent contractor to perform activities regulated by this Article, the duty set forth in subsection (a) of this section shall not apply to the excavator, locator, or operator. Independent contractors shall provide training to their employees in accordance with this section.

(c)   Excavation shall be conducted in accordance with OSHA Standard 1926 and under the direction of a competent person, as defined therein.

(d)   Locators shall be properly trained. Locator training shall be documented. (2013-407, s. 2.)

§ 87-124. (Effective October 1, 2014) Exemptions.

The notice requirements in G.S. 87-122(a) and G.S. 87-122(b) do not apply to the following:

(1)   An excavation or demolition performed by the owner of a single-family residential property on his or her own land that does not encroach on any operator's right-of-way, easement, or permitted use.

(2)   An excavation or demolition performed by the owner of a single-family residential property on his or her own land that encroaches on any operator's right-of-way, easement, or permitted use that is performed with nonmechanized equipment.

(3)   An excavation or demolition that involves the tilling of soil for agricultural or gardening purposes.

(4)   An excavation or demolition for agricultural purposes, as defined in G.S. 106-581.1, performed on property that does not encroach on any operator's right-of-way, easement, or permitted use.

(5)   An excavation by an operator or surveyor with nonmechanized equipment for the following purposes:

    a.   Locating for a valid notification request or for the minor repair, connection, or routine maintenance of an existing facility or survey pin.

    b.   Probing underground to determine the extent of gas or water migration.

(6)   An excavation or demolition performed when the Department of Transportation, a local government, special purpose district, or public service district is conducting maintenance activities within its designated right-of-way. Maintenance activities shall include resurfacing, milling, emergency replacement of signs critical for maintaining safety, or the reshaping of shoulders and ditches to the original road profile. Maintenance activities do not include the initial installation of traffic signs, traffic control equipment, or guardrails.

(7)   An excavation or demolition performed by a railroad entirely on land which the railroad owns or operates or, in the event of an emergency, on adjacent land. No provision in this Article shall apply to any railroad which owns, operates, or permits facilities under land which the railroad owns or operates.

(8)   An excavation of a grave space, as defined in G.S. 65-48(10), the installation of a monument or memorial at a grave space, or an excavation related to the placement of a temporary structure or tent by a cemetery regulated under Chapter 65 of the General Statutes that does not encroach on any operator's right-of-way, easement, or permitted use. (2013-407, s. 2.)

§ 87-125. (Effective October 1, 2014) Notice in case of emergency excavation or demolition.

(a)   An excavator performing an emergency excavation or demolition is not required to give notice to the Notification Center as provided in G.S. 87-122. However, the excavator shall, as soon as practicable, give oral notice to the Notification Center which shall include a description of the circumstances justifying the emergency. The excavator may request emergency assistance from each affected operator in locating and providing immediate protection to the facilities in the affected area.

(b)   The declaration of an emergency excavation or demolition shall not relieve any party of liability for causing damage to an operator's facilities even if those facilities are unmarked.

(c)   Any person who falsely claims that an emergency exists requiring an excavation or demolition shall be guilty of a Class 3 misdemeanor. (2013-407, s. 2.)

§ 87-126. (Effective October 1, 2014) Notification required when damage is done.

(a)   The excavator performing an excavation or demolition that results in any damage to a facility shall immediately upon discovery of the damage notify the Notification Center and the facility operator, if known, of the location and nature of the damage. The excavator shall allow the operator reasonable time to accomplish necessary repairs before completing the excavation or demolition in the immediate area of the facility. The excavator shall delay any backfilling in the immediate area of the damaged facility until authorized by the operator. The operator or qualified personnel authorized by the operator shall repair any damage to the facility.

(b)   An excavator who is responsible for an excavation or demolition where any damage to a facility results in the discharge of electricity or escape of any flammable, toxic, or corrosive gas or liquid, or that endangers life, health, or property shall immediately notify emergency responders, including 911 services, the Notification Center, and the facility operator. The excavator shall take reasonable measures to protect himself or herself, other persons in immediate danger, members of the general public, property, and the environment until the operator or emergency responders arrive and complete an assessment of the situation. (2013-407, s. 2.)

§ 87-127. (Effective October 1, 2014) Design notices.

(a)   A designer may submit a design notice to the Notification Center. The design notice shall describe the tract or parcel of land for which the design notice has been submitted with sufficient particularity, as defined by policies and procedures adopted by the Notification Center, to allow the operator to ascertain the precise tract or parcel of land involved.

(b)   Within 10 working days, not including the day the notice was given, after a design notice for a proposed project has been submitted to the Notification Center, the operator shall respond in one of the following manners:

   (1)   By designating the location of all facilities owned by the operator within the area of the proposed excavation as provided in G.S. 87-121(a).

   (2)   By providing to the person submitting the design notice the best available description of all facilities in the area designated by the design notice, which may include drawings marked with a scale, dimensions, and reference points for underground utilities already built in the area or other facility records that are maintained by the operator.

   (3)   Allowing the person submitting the design notice or any other authorized person to inspect the drawings or other records for all facilities within the proposed area of excavation at a location that is acceptable to the operator.

(c)   An operator may reject a design notice based upon homeland security considerations pending the operator obtaining additional information confirming the legitimacy of the notice. The operator shall notify the person making the request through a design notice of the denial and may request additional information through the positive response system. (2013-407, s. 2.)

§ 87-128. (Effective October 1, 2014) Absence of facility location.

If an operator who has been given notice as provided in G.S. 87-120(d) by the Notification Center fails to respond to that notice as provided in G.S. 87-121 or fails to properly locate the facility, the person excavating is free to proceed with the excavation. Neither the excavator nor the person financially responsible for the excavation will be liable to the nonresponding or improperly responding operator for damages to the operator's facilities if the person doing the excavating exercises due care to protect existing facilities when there is evidence of the existence of those facilities near the proposed excavation area. (2013-407, s. 2.)

§ 87-129. (Effective October 1, 2014) Underground Damage Prevention Review Board; enforcement; civil penalties.

(a)   The Notification Center shall establish an Underground Damage Prevention Review Board to review reports of alleged violations of this Article. The members of the Board shall be appointed by the Governor. The Board shall consist of the following members:

  (1)   A representative from the North Carolina Department of Transportation;

  (2)   A representative from a facility contract locator;

  (3)   A representative from the Notification Center;

  (4)   A representative from an electric public utility;

  (5)   A representative from the telecommunications industry;

  (6)   A representative from a natural gas utility;

  (7)   A representative from a hazardous liquid transmission pipeline company;

  (8)   A representative recommended by the League of Municipalities;

  (9)   A highway contractor licensed under G.S. 87-10(b)(2) who does not own or operate facilities;

  (10)   A public utilities contractor licensed under G.S. 87-10(b)(3) who does not own or operate facilities;

  (11)   A surveyor licensed under Chapter 89C of the General Statutes;

  (12)   A representative from a rural water system;

  (13)   A representative from an investor-owned water system;

  (14)   A representative from an electric membership corporation; and

  (15)   A representative from a cable company.

(b)   The Notification Center shall transmit all reports of alleged violations of this Article to the Board, including any information received by the Notification Center regarding the report. The Board shall meet at least quarterly to review all reports filed pursuant to G.S. 87-120(e). The Board shall act as an arbitrator between the parties to the report. If, after reviewing the report and any accompanying information, the Board determines that a violation of this Article has occurred, the Board shall notify the violating party in writing of its determination and the recommended penalty. The violating party may request a hearing before the Board, after which the Board may reverse or uphold its original finding. If the Board recommends a penalty, the Board shall notify the Utilities Commission of the recommended penalty, and the Utilities Commission shall issue an order imposing the penalty.

(c)   A party determined by the Board under subsection (b) of this section to have violated this Article may initiate an arbitration proceeding before the Utilities Commission. If the violating party elects to initiate an arbitration proceeding, the violating party shall pay a filing fee of two hundred fifty dollars ($250.00) to the Utilities Commission, and the Utilities Commission shall open a docket regarding the report. The Utilities Commission shall direct the parties enter into an arbitration process. The parties shall be responsible for selecting and contracting with the arbitrator. Upon completion of the arbitration process, the Utilities Commission shall issue an order encompassing the outcome of the binding arbitration process, including a determination of fault, a penalty, and assessing the costs of arbitration to the nonprevailing party. Any party may appeal an order issued by the Utilities Commission pursuant to this section to the superior court division of the General Court of Justice in the county where the alleged violation of this Article occurred or in Wake County, for trial de novo. The authority granted to the Utilities Commission within this section is limited to this section and does not grant the Utilities Commission any authority that they are not otherwise granted under Chapter 62 of the General Statutes.

(d)   Any person who violates any provision of this Article shall be subject to a penalty as set forth in this subsection. The provisions of this Article do not affect any civil remedies for personal injury or property damage otherwise available to any person, except as otherwise specifically provided for in this Article. The penalty provisions of this Article are cumulative to and not in conflict with provisions of law with respect to civil remedies for personal injury or property damage. The clear proceeds of any civil penalty assessed under this section shall be used as provided in Section 7(a) of Article IX of the North Carolina Constitution. The penalties for a violation of this Article shall be as follows:

(1)   If the violation was the result of negligence, the penalty shall be a requirement of training, a requirement of education, or both.

(2)   If the violation was the result of gross negligence, the penalty shall be a civil penalty of one thousand dollars ($1,000), a requirement of training, a requirement of education, or a combination of the three.

(3)   If the violation was the result of willful or wanton negligence or intentional conduct, the penalty shall be a civil penalty of two thousand five hundred dollars ($2,500), a requirement of training, and a requirement of education. (2013-407, s. 2.)

§ 87-130. (Effective October 1, 2014) Severability.

If any provision of this Article or the application thereof to any person or circumstance is held invalid, such invalidity shall not affect other provisions or applications, and to this end the provisions of this Article are severable. (2013-407, s. 2.)

National Association of State Contractors Licensing Agencies
NASCLA Membership Information

Membership Benefits

- Networking Opportunities with Industry Experts and Representatives

- Complimentary Copies of the Annual Membership Directory, Newsletter, Model Legislation, and *Contractor's State Licensing Information Directory (CSLID)*

- Reduced Registration Fees for NASCLA Annual Conferences & Training Seminars

- Access to the NASCLA Members Only Website *(*for State Members Only)*

  - *Member Reference Library* which includes consumer publications, NASCLA Model Legislation and other information

  - *Track Bills & State Legislation* NASCLA has partnered with a nationwide legislative tracking platform that tracks legislation across all 50 states and congress

  - *Top Regulatory Cases* affecting the construction industry and regulatory agencies

  - **Toolkit for Contractor Regulators* provides a variety of best practices from other states which state members can use to customize your very own programs without reinventing the wheel. Some of the highlighted programs include Elderly Abuse Prevention Program, Disaster Response Program and Understanding the Board's Role in a Legislative Environment to name a few!

  - *Community Forums* are available for *Executive Directors, Attorneys, *Public Information Officers, *Enforcement/Investigators, *IT Personnel, and Contractors. Communicate and engage with your counterparts nationally.

  - *Active Member Directory Search* allows you to search contact information for any NASCLA Member

To Apply for NASCLA Membership, please visit the following link: www.nascla.org

NASCLA's MISSION

"The National Association of State Contractors Licensing Agencies (NASCLA) promotes best practices and license uniformity for agencies that regulate the construction industry."

NASCLA®

NATIONAL ASSOCIATION OF STATE CONTRACTORS LICENSING AGENCIES

23309 N. 17th Drive
Building 1, Unit 110
Phoenix, Arizona 85027

Phone: (623) 587-9354

Fax: (623) 587-9625

www.nascla.org

APPLICANT INFORMATION

To become a member, please return this form with a check made payable to NASCLA at the address listed above or you may visit our website at www.nascla.org to register online for membership.

If you have any questions, please call NASCLA at (866) 948-3363.

MEMBERSHIP CLASSIFICATIONS

Please read the classifications below and check the box that best describes your membership classification.

❑ **Associate Member:** Limited to contractor trade associations, contractor firms, construction material suppliers, individual contractors, and regional (county, city or municipal) contractor licensing agencies.

$125.00 Annual Membership Fee.

❑ **State Member:** Limited to states that have enacted laws to regulate the business of contracting.

$475.00 Annual Membership Fee.

❑ **International Member:** Limited to regulatory agencies from other nations, countries or states other than the 50 United States of America and its territories.

$475.00 Annual Membership Fee.

❑ **Business Member:** Limited to firms whose business is related to the construction industry. These members shall not use the name of the association and its logo or in any manner refer to NASCLA in advertising, selling or soliciting.

$750.00 Annual Membership Fee.

❑ **Affiliate Member:** Limited to former employees and board members of state contractor licensing agencies who are not actively engaged in the contracting business.

$50.00 Annual Membership Fee.

Name: _____

Title: _____

Company: _____

City, State, Zip Code: _____

Phone: _____

Email: _____ Website: _____